Palgrave CIBFR Studies in Islamic Finance

Series Editors
Nafis Alam, Henley Business School,
University of Reading, Selangor, Malaysia
Syed Aun R. Rizvi, Suleman Dawood School of Business,
Lahore University of Management Sciences,
Lahore, Pakistan

The Centre for Islamic Business and Finance Research (CIBFR) is a global center of excellence for developing Islamic business and finance as a scientific academic discipline and for promoting Islamic financial products, monetary and fiscal policies, and business and trade practices. Based at The University of Nottingham campus in Malaysia, CIBFR looks at the multi-dimensional aspects of Islamic business, cutting across the major themes of Islamic economics, Islamic finance and the Halal market. True to the pioneering nature of the research CIBFR undertakes, the Palgrave CIBFR Series in Islamic Finance offers empirical enquiries into key issues and challenges in modern Islamic finance. It explores issues in such varied fields as Islamic accounting, Takaful (Islamic insurance), Islamic financial services marketing, and ethical and socially responsible investing.

Zul Hakim Jumat · Saqib Hafiz Khateeb ·
Syed Nazim Ali
Editors

Islamic Finance, FinTech, and the Road to Sustainability

Reframing the Approach in the Post-Pandemic Era

Editors
Zul Hakim Jumat
Center for Islamic Economics and Finance, College of Islamic Studies
Hamad Bin Khalifa University
Doha, Qatar

Saqib Hafiz Khateeb
Research Division, College of Islamic Studies
Hamad Bin Khalifa University
Doha, Qatar

Syed Nazim Ali
Research Division, College of Islamic Studies
Hamad bin Khalifa University
Doha, Qatar

ISSN 2523-3483 ISSN 2523-3491 (electronic)
Palgrave CIBFR Studies in Islamic Finance
ISBN 978-3-031-13301-5 ISBN 978-3-031-13302-2 (eBook)
https://doi.org/10.1007/978-3-031-13302-2

© The Editor(s) (if applicable) and The Author(s), under exclusive license to Springer Nature Switzerland AG 2023

This work is subject to copyright. All rights are solely and exclusively licensed by the Publisher, whether the whole or part of the material is concerned, specifically the rights of translation, reprinting, reuse of illustrations, recitation, broadcasting, reproduction on microfilms or in any other physical way, and transmission or information storage and retrieval, electronic adaptation, computer software, or by similar or dissimilar methodology now known or hereafter developed.

The use of general descriptive names, registered names, trademarks, service marks, etc. in this publication does not imply, even in the absence of a specific statement, that such names are exempt from the relevant protective laws and regulations and therefore free for general use.

The publisher, the authors, and the editors are safe to assume that the advice and information in this book are believed to be true and accurate at the date of publication. Neither the publisher nor the authors or the editors give a warranty, expressed or implied, with respect to the material contained herein or for any errors or omissions that may have been made. The publisher remains neutral with regard to jurisdictional claims in published maps and institutional affiliations.

This Palgrave Macmillan imprint is published by the registered company Springer Nature Switzerland AG
The registered company address is: Gewerbestrasse 11, 6330 Cham, Switzerland

Preface

The unprecedented economic downturn and global supply chain disruption caused by the recent pandemic have accelerated the urgency of identifying and relying on sustainable financing infrastructures that are agile, adaptable, and transformable. The global health and economic crises have pushed a vast number of populations into extreme poverty. The report of the World Bank soon after the pandemic hit revealed that daily wage workers across the world, including those in Muslim countries, have been impacted severely, and a previous report had highlighted that many people exclude themselves from benefitting from loans due to religious reasons (i.e., interest-based loans). Thus, the Islamic finance institutions come into the picture to play a vital role by structuring interest-free loans, while the essential underlying social good and ethical foundations of Islamic finance promise the sustainability of the individuals and the institutions of the economy irrespective of the good or bad times the economy has been going through.

Islamic social finance, through the institutions of *waqf* (Islamic endowments), *zakat* (compulsory charity), *sadaqah* (voluntary charity), *qard hasan* (interest-free loans), and crowdfunding platforms, has the potential to provide the urgently needed support for poverty alleviation, economic recovery, pandemic response, and sustainable development in the post-pandemic era. The funds and reserves at *awqaf* organizations with the general purpose of serving the people suffering from natural disasters can be a good source for easing the situation and energizing the small and medium sized entities of the economy. Islamic finance can play a huge role in ensuring economic recovery from the current setback and can provide a prospect for a new chapter of human development by utilizing a good blend of both the United Nations Sustainable Development Goals (SDGs) and the higher objectives of Islamic law, otherwise known as the *maqasid al-shariah*. In the past, several initiatives have been undertaken by Islamic multilateral institutions like the Islamic Development Bank (IsDB) to ease the situation of natural calamities and disasters in Pakistan, Afghanistan, Sudan, other member countries. In present times, the prevalence of the internet and omnipresence of technology along with the enhancements in financial products help support the idea of stretching the social finance products and making them pan-global initiatives through the various platforms, which in turn serves both the aims of maqasid al-shariah and SDGs at once in times of emergency and otherwise.

The book, thus, provides critical discussions on the role of Islamic finance in the post-pandemic economic recovery. It highlights how selected Islamic finance tools can help usher in a new era that will not only ensure financial sustainability but also promote socio-economic policies that will aid the much-desired economic recovery. In particular, it focuses on the role of Islamic finance in the post-pandemic economic recovery while focusing its analysis to three key areas: sustainability and socio-economic recovery, social and sustainable impact financing, and the role of FinTech. An effort has been made to bring studies on the current issues related to the tools of Islamic social financing that provide opportunities to usher in much needed resilience in the post-pandemic era. It will help industry leaders, policymakers, and people from all income groups and nations, to navigate financial industry disruptions and transition to a new normal by harnessing converging technologies. Thus, the book aims to discuss the importance of leveraging social finance to mitigate the impacts of the raging pandemic while utilizing the digital world that in turn is creating both vast promises and potential perils. The book compiles current topics related to the adoption of FinTech and its related technologies that have been adopted by Islamic finance institutions, in addition to those promising technologies that may be adopted by them. In brief, it provides fresh discussion in relation to the 4th Industrial Revolution and its relevance to the Islamic Finance industry.

ICIF, the International Conference on Islamic Finance, an annual event at the College of Islamic Studies (CIS), Hamad Bin Khalifa University (HBKU), is the platform for sharing the research results on the burgeoning area of Islamic finance and economy. The Islamic Finance MSc and Ph.D. programs and their faculty members serve as knowledge incubators for the generation of new ideas and concepts. The program under the leadership of its director, Professor Ahmet Faruq Aysan, along with Professor Nasim Shirazi's extensive experience in Islamic social finance continues to provide much leadership for the Center for Islamic Economics and Finance (CIEF). I am grateful to other faculty members; Professor Abdulazeem Abozaid, Dr. Dalal Aassouli, Dr. Mohamed Eskandar Rasid, and Dr Mustafa Disli, who continue to provide support and participate in CIEF-sponsored activities. It's their enthusiasm and interest which motivates CIEF staff to undertake challenging roles and activities. CIS student body deserves to be mentioned especially for their interest in CIEF events and for their keen participation in sharing their research findings.

CIS Dean, Professor Emad El-din Shahin, deserves special endorsement for his vision to make CIS a research-based college as part of HBKU. During the past five years under his stewardship, the college has transformed into creating a vibrant ecosystem by involving stakeholders' engagements in producing impactful research and publications. In this respect, the institution which has joined hands with CIS in this journey is Qatar Financial Centre (QFC) Authority, especially its CEO, Mr. Yousuf Al Jaidah and its Managing Director, Mr. Henk J. Hoogendoorn for their unconditional support and encouragement. QFC's vision and commitment to promote Islamic finance industry in Qatar and globally must be commended.

The chapter contributors and other academics who are behind producing this book are acknowledged for their support. Initially, it was a bit difficult to complete this monograph but their zeal and enthusiasm and availability to respond to our queries has made to produce this volume. Finally, my co-editors, Mr. Zul Hakim Bin Jumat and Mr. Saqib H. Khateeb who took the burden on their shoulders in completing this book. It was not an easy task to undertake especially since both of them are occupied with their roles as researchers at CIS. I would like to congratulate them in completing this volume and I am sure its readership will appreciate and endorse their efforts. We hope that this volume will advance the scholarship and knowledge and create good impact among the scholarly community.

To all those who helped in completing this project including CIEF staff, Ms. Bahnaz Al-Quradaghi, Mr. Umar Farooq Patel and CIEF student researchers, Mr. Mohammed M. Musab and Mr. Munir S. Khamis for their availability for their assistance and cooperation.

Syed Nazim Ali
Director, Research Division, Qatar Foundation
Research Division, College of Islamic Finance
Hamad Bin Khalifa University
Doha, Qatar

Acknowledgments

The editors of the book acknowledge and appreciate Qatar Financial Centre (QFC) Authority's grant to facilitate the 4th International Conference on Islamic Finance (ICIF): Sustainability and the Fourth Industrial Revolution—Implications for Islamic Finance and Economy in the Post-Pandemic Era, held at the virtually at the College of Islamic Studies, Hamad Bin Khalifa University in April 2022, which contributed to the content of this volume.

Contents

Islamic Finance, FinTech and the Road to Sustainability: Reframing the Approach in the Post-Pandemic Era—An Introduction   1
Saqib Hafiz Khateeb, Syed Nazim Ali and Zul Hakim Jumat

Re-Framing Islamic Finance Sustainability and Socio-Economic Development

Islamic Finance and Sustainability: The Need to Reframe Notions of Shariah Compliance, Purpose, and Value   15
Farrukh Habib

Tools and Conditions for Achieving Sustainable Development in Islamic Finance   41
Abdulazeem Abozaid and Saqib Hafiz Khateeb

Maqasid al-Shariah and Sustainable Development Goals Convergence: An Assessment of Global Best Practices   59
Noor Suhaida Kasri, Said Bouheraoua and Silmi Mohamed Radzi

The Resilience of Islamic Finance Against Pandemic-Induced
Future Economic Crisis   107
Umar A. Oseni and Sukaynah O. D. Shuaib

Emergence of Islamic Finance in the Fourth Industrial
Revolution and COVID-19 Post-Pandemic Era   123
Mohammad Sahabuddin, Abu Umar Faruq Ahmad
and Md. Aminul Islam

Innovative Islamic Financial Tools for Sustainable and Socio-Economic Impact

Sukuk Innovation: Powering Sustainable Finance   145
Mustafa Adil, Henk Jan Hoogendoorn and Zul Hakim Jumat

Mobilizing Funds for Industrialization and Development
Through Islamic Value System, Capital Markets, and Social
Finance   159
Salman Ahmed Shaikh

The Role of Green Sukuk in Maqasid Al-Shariah and SDGs:
Evidence from Indonesia   181
Khairunnisa Musari and Sutan Emir Hidayat

Is Islamic Microfinance a Resilient Business Model During
Periods of Crisis? Empirical Evidence from Arab Countries   205
Asma Ben Salem, Ines Ben Abdelkader and Sameh Jouida

FinTech Role in the Road to Sustainability

Digital Finance and Artificial Intelligence: Islamic Finance
Challenges and Prospects   241
Dawood Ashraf

**Open Banking for Financial Inclusion: Challenges and
Opportunities in Muslim-Majority Countries**   259
Nasim Shah Shirazi, Ahmet Faruk Aysan and Zhamal Nanaeva

**Islamic Specialized FinTech for Inclusive and Sustainable
Growth in Sub-Saharan Africa**   283
Jamila Abubakar and Ahmet Faruk Aysan

**The Role of Technology in Effective Distribution
of Zakat to Poor and Needy**   309
M. Kabir Hassan and Aishath Muneeza

**Notion of Value-Added in RegTech Research Work:
What Is There for Islamic Finance?**   333
Muslehuddin Musab Mohammed

Index   351

Notes on Contributors

Abdulazeem Abozaid holds a Ph.D. and a Master's in Islamic financial law. He also holds three BAs in Islamic law, Arabic language, and English literature and two higher studies diplomas in Islamic law and human sciences. He has extensive working experience as a Lecturer at Damascus University since 1998 and then at International Islamic University Malaysia, specializing in Islamic financial law. He has conducted many workshops and training courses at several Islamic banks, financial institutions, and universities. He combines practical Islamic banking experience as a Shariah expert, trainer, and Shariah head at various Islamic banks with academic knowledge of Islamic financial law. His academic works are published in many international journals and newspapers, and he has presented more than 50 papers at international conferences. His expertise in Islamic finance is demonstrated by his release of more than 70 publications in Islamic finance. Currently, he is a Professor at the College of Islamic Studies, Hamad Bin Khalifa University, Qatar Foundation, and Islamic Finance Program.

Ines Ben Abdelkader holds a Ph.D. in Management (Accounting and Finance) from the Higher Institute of Management in Sousse, Tunisia. She is a member of the research laboratory (LaREMFiQ) at the University of Sousse, Tunisia. She teaches accounting and finance at the Faculty of Economics and Management in Sousse. Her main research interest relates to microfinance.

Jamila Abubakar is a Ph.D. Candidate in Islamic Finance at Hamad Bin Khalifa University, researching on FinTech and its contributions to Sustainable Development Goals in Africa. She holds a B.Sc. in International Securities Investment & Banking from the University of Reading (UK) and a Master's in Global Banking and Financial Markets from Barcelona Business School (Spain). She is also a Researcher on the global team at Prospectus (Qatar) with a focus on executive and board roles in the beyond profit sector. Previously, she was the Risk Management Officer (2012–2020) for Asset Management Corporation of Nigeria.

Mustafa Adil is the Head of Islamic Finance, Data & Analytics, for the London Stock Exchange Group. He is responsible for leading the Islamic finance and Islamic markets businesses for the organization, providing knowledge solutions and bespoke services to support the continued growth and increasing depth of the Islamic finance industry. He works in collaboration with government entities, multilateral organizations, and leading financial institutions to support them in fulfilling their aspirations and executing their strategies in the Islamic market space. Previously, he was the Head of Islamic Finance for Refinitiv and for Thomson Reuters. He has also served as a leading consultant in the Islamic Financial Services team at Ernst & Young, providing advisory services to some of the leading Islamic financial institutions in the GCC and globally. He is a qualified Chartered Accountant from the Institute of Chartered Accountants of England and Wales and holds a Bachelor's degree in Mathematics from Imperial College in London.

Abu Umar Faruq Ahmad is currently an Adjunct Professor at United International University, Bangladesh and Guidance College, Texas, USA. An alumnus of Western Sydney University, Australia (with "High Distinction" in Ph.D. and 'distinction' in LLM-Hons.), he is an international figure renowned within the world of Islamic Economics and Finance. His accomplishments are featured in the 2018 and 2019 ISLAMICA500 Global Leaders of the Islamic Economy. His accomplishments include associate professorships at King AbdulAziz University, Jeddah, KSA; INCEIF University in Malaysia; Universiti Brunei Darussalam in Brunei; and Assistant Professorship at Hamdan Bin Mohammed Smart University in the UAE. He has over 100 published peer-reviewed refereed journal articles, books, chapters in edited books, conference proceedings, and other intellectual contributions to his credit on: shariah compliance of Islamic banks' products and structures; the opportunities and challenges of Islamic finance; case studies of Islamic banks and financial institutions; Islamic insurance and reinsurance; Islamic microfinance; sukuk; and dispute resolution in Islamic banking and finance, among others. He is currently the founding editor, senior editor, and editorial advisory board member for a number of internationally renowned refereed journals, including some published by Emerald Group Publishing in the United Kingdom. He is also serving as the Shariah Audit Executive at the Islamic Bank of Australia Group.

Syed Nazim Ali is currently the Director of the Research Division and Director of the Center for Islamic Economics and Finance at the College of Islamic Studies, Hamad Bin Khalifa University (HBKU). Prior to joining HBKU, he was the Executive Director (Acting) of the Islamic Legal Studies Program (2010–2013) at Harvard Law School and the Founding Director of the Islamic Finance Project at Harvard University since its establishment in 1995. During the last thirty years, he has spearheaded many research landmarks in the areas of Islamic finance and faith-based financial initiatives. He has paid special attention to lines of inquiry that seek to examine and interrogate the frontiers, facilitate research, and encourage dialogue among various stakeholders and external discussants. During his nearly two-decade association with Harvard, he has led the organization of several conferences, workshops, and symposia in the field, including the internationally renowned biennial Harvard University Forum on Islamic Finance, the proceedings of which are serially compiled and published under his supervision; and the annual workshop at the London School of Economics, which brings together the sector's leading economists, shariah experts, and practitioners. He is a member of the International Advisory Board of the Centre for Islamic Finance at the University of Bolton. His most recent publications include FinTech, Digital Currency and the Future of Islamic Finance (Springer, 2020), FinTech in Islamic Finance: Theory and Practice (Routledge, 2019), and Shari'a Compliant Microfinance (Routledge, 2012). He received his Ph.D. from the University of Strathclyde, Glasgow, U.K.

Dawood Ashraf is a Senior Research Economist at the Islamic Development Bank (IsDB) in Jeddah, Saudi Arabia. He holds a Ph.D. in Banking and Finance, and he is also a member of the CFA Institute. He has combined banking and academic experience of more than 20 years. Before joining the IsDB, Dr. Ashraf worked with Prince Mohammad Bin Fahad University in Saudi Arabia and TD Bank Financial Group in Canada. His research interests are in sustainable ethical finance, portfolio management, banking, corporate finance, and artificial intelligence applications in finance. He has published in several international journals, and he has presented his research work at various international conferences. He is also a subject editor of Emerging Markets Review and the Journal of International Financial Markets, Institutions, and Money. He has led teams to produce several vital reports on the policy side, including the first two editions of the Global Report on Islamic Finance, the impact of COVID-19 on Islamic finance and the use of artificial intelligence to harness financial inclusion.

Ahmet Faruk Aysan is a Professor and the Director of the Islamic Finance and Economy Ph.D. program at the College of Islamic Studies, Hamad Bin Khalifa University. He has been a board member and monetary policy committee member of the Central Bank of the Republic of Turkey. He served as a consultant for various institutions, such as the World Bank, the Central Bank of the Republic of Turkey, and Oxford Analytica. He has also served as the Deputy Director of the Center for Economics and Econometrics at Bogazici University, a member of the G-20 Financial Safety Net Experts Group, a member of the Advisory Board of the Social Sciences and Humanities Research Group of TUBITAK, a National Expert of the European Union and the Dean of Management and Administrative Sciences at Istanbul Sehir University. He received grants from various international funds, including the ERF, Newton funds, and TUBITAK. He has also served on the advisory board of the Contemporary Turkish Studies at the London School of Economics and Political Sciences (LSE) European Institute.

Said Bouheraoua is currently a Senior Researcher and Director of the Research Affairs Department at the International Shariah Research Academy (ISRA) for Islamic Finance and a lecturer at the Global University of Islamic Finance (INCEIF). He is the editor-in-chief of ISRA International Journal of Islamic Finance, and an Independent Board Member of Affin Islamic Bank. He has published various books, book chapters, and several articles in refereed journals. He has also presented several papers at international conferences, including the International Fiqh Academy of the OIC. He has conducted several trainings in Islamic banking and finance in Malaysia and abroad.

Farrukh Habib is the Co-founder of Alif Technologies (Dubai) and Shariah Experts (London). He is an expert in the areas of Islamic law, finance, and FinTech. He is an advisor, trainer, and product developer by profession, with a strong educational background and vast global experience spanning more than nine years. He is involved in the Islamic FinTech and halal digital economy, focusing on crowdfunding, micro-investments, tokenization, decentralized economy, halal supply chain management, and shariah compliance. He has developed his own proprietary shariah-compliance screening criterion for crypto-assets. Previously, he was a researcher at the International Shariah Research Academy for Islamic Finance (ISRA). He is also the co-editor of the ISRA Journal of Islamic Finance and a reviewer for various reputable academic journals. He holds a Ph.D. degree in Islamic Finance from INCEIF, Kuala Lumpur, Malaysia, and an M.Sc. in Banking and Finance from Queen Mary University of London, UK. Prior to that, he obtained Master's and Bachelor's degrees from the University of Karachi, both in Economics. He also received traditional Islamic (Shariah) education through an extensive eight-year course in Jamia Uloom-E-Islamya Banuri Town, Karachi, acquiring another Bachelor's and Master's degrees in Islamic studies.

M. Kabir Hassan is Professor of Finance in Capital Market Unit at the International Shariah and Finance at the University of New Orleans, Louisiana. He currently holds three endowed chairs—Hibernia Professor of Economics and Finance, Hancock Whitney Chair Professor in Business, and Bank One Professor in Business—at the University of New Orleans. He is the winner of the 2016 Islamic Development Bank (IDB) Prize in Islamic Banking and Finance. He received his BA in Economics and Mathematics from Gustavus Adolphus College, Minnesota, and his MA in Economics and Ph.D. in Finance from the University of Nebraska–Lincoln, Nebraska.

Sutan Emir Hidayat is currently the Director of Islamic Economy Infrastructure Ecosystem at the National Committee for Islamic Economy and Finance (KNEKS), Indonesia. In addition, he has also been involved in regulatory bodies for international Islamic financial institutions, such as Members of the Sustainability Working Group, General Council Islamic Bank and Financial Institutions (CIBAFI), and a member of the FAS1 Working Group, the Accounting and Audit

Organization for Islamic Financial Institutions (AAOFI). He obtained his Ph.D. and MBA degrees in Islamic Banking and Finance from the International Islamic University Malaysia (IIUM). He was the Head of the Business Administration Department at the University College of Bahrain (2015–2019) with the academic rank of Associate Professor (2018–2019). He has published quite a significant number of research papers in reputable international journals. He also serves as an associate editor for the Journal of Economic Cooperation and Development, SESRIC, and as an editor for a number of other journals. He was recognized as one of the top influential 500 personalities on a global scale from 2015 to 2020 by ISFIN, a leading advisory firm for Islamic markets.

Henk Jan Hoogendoorn is the Chief of Financial Sector Office at QFC, where he is responsible for delivering on QFC's mission of attracting financial and regulated businesses to Qatar through the QFC platform. He has extensive experience in international finance, management, and transforming and building businesses in the financial sector. Henk has held senior management roles at **ABN AMRO Bank and Deutsche Bank** in the Netherlands and the Middle East and has a solid track record of implementing businesses in the financial sector. Prior to joining QFC, he served as Mashreq Qatar's Country CEO and Managing Director of Deutsche Bank, Head of Non-Bank Financial Institutions, where he was responsible for insurers, pension funds, FinTech, and implementing strategic and business plans across Europe. He holds a Master's degree in Law from the University of Utrecht in the Netherlands and has participated in executive education at the London Business School and INSEAD.

Md. Aminul Islam is a Professor of Finance at the Faculty of Applied and Human Sciences, Universiti Malaysia Perlis. He received his Bachelor's degree from the International Islamic University Malaysia, and graduated with an MBA and Ph.D. from Universiti Sains Malaysia. He also completed an advanced diploma in teaching in higher education from Nottingham Trent University. He is a Visiting Professor at Ubudiyyah University in Indonesia, Northern University in Bangladesh, Daffodil International University, East Delta University, and Thammasat University in Thailand. He is also an Academic Advisor at Sentral College in Penang. He has bagged a number of accolades, including

"The Best Ph.D. Thesis Award 2011" and Research Excellence Awards in 2020 and 2022 at Universiti Malaysia Perlis. He is a member of the Asian Academy of Management, the Malaysian Institute of Management, and an associate member of the Malaysian Finance Association. His most recent research has focused on FinTech, entrepreneurship, blockchain, the blue economy, Islamic banking, and sukuk.

Sameh Jouida has a Ph.D. in Finance from the Higher Institute of Management in Sousse, Tunisia. She is a member of the research laboratory "Business and Economic Statistics Modeling (BESTMOD)" and a member of the research unit "Management and Risk Management." She has research papers published in international journals like Managerial and Decision Economics, Procedia Economics and Finance, Journal of Multinational Financial Management, and Research in International Business and Finance. Her teaching and research interests are in the areas of corporate finance and accounting.

Zul Hakim Jumat is a Researcher for the Center of Islamic Economics and Finance (CIEF) and a Ph.D. Candidate in Islamic Finance and Economy at the College of Islamic Studies, Hamad Bin Khalifa University (HBKU), Qatar. Before joining CIEF, he was a Research Editor with the Dow Jones Risk & Compliance team that focuses on Sanction Ownership Research. He holds a Bachelor's degree (Hons) in Jurisprudence and Principles of Jurisprudence (minoring in Economics) from Kuwait University (2015) and an M.Sc. (Hons) in Islamic Finance from HBKU.

Noor Suhaida Kasri is a Senior Researcher and Head of the Islamic Capital Market Unit at the International Shariah Research Academy for Islamic Finance (ISRA). Prior to joining ISRA, she had almost twelve years of experience as a Malaysian advocate and solicitor, as well as a shariah lawyer. She sat as one of MUFG Bank (Malaysia) Berhad's Shariah Committee from 2017 to 2020. She received her Ph.D. in Islamic Banking, Finance, and Management from the University of Gloucestershire (in collaboration with Markfield Institute of Higher Education), UK, under the sponsorship of ISRA. After completing her Bachelor of Laws and a Diploma in Shariah Legal Practice from the International Islamic University of Malaysia, she pursued her Master's in Laws from King's College London under the funding of the British Chevening Scholarship Award.

Saqib Hafiz Khateeb is a Research Fellow at the College of Islamic Studies, Hamad Bin Khalifa University (HBKU), Qatar. After graduating from the Islamic University of Madinah (2011) with an LLB in Islamic Law and Jurisprudence, he went on to complete his M.Sc. in Islamic Finance from HBKU (2015). He also holds an MA in Islamic Studies with a major in law from SOAS, University of London (2017). He has worked extensively throughout his academic career as a Research Assistant at the Law Department at SOAS-London and as a graduate research assistant at HBKU-Doha. He had also gained hands-on experience as a research assistant for a year at the Center of Islamic Economics and Finance, Doha. His career includes a stint as a legal assistant at a law firm in London in 2017–18.

Muslehuddin Musab Mohammed is a student pursuing a Ph.D. in Islamic Finance and Economy at the College of Islamic Studies, Hamad Bin Khalifa University, Qatar. His research works have been published by Edinburgh University Press, UK and SESRIC, Turkey. He works as a Senior Shariah Auditor at Bait Al-Mashura Finance Consultations (Doha) and conducts training and workshops in the domain of Islamic finance for working executives. He is also a member of the editorial board of a peer-reviewed international scientific journal called Bait Al-Mashura Journal on Islamic Economics and Finance since its inception in 2014. He has also been an active member of the Scientific Committee of the Doha Islamic Finance Conference since its third edition in 2012.

Aishath Muneeza is an Associate Professor at the International Centre for Education in Islamic Finance (INCEIF), Malaysia. She is the first female Deputy Minister of the Ministry of Islamic Affairs and was the Deputy Minister of the Ministry of Finance and Treasury of the Republic of Maldives. Her contribution to Islamic finance includes structuring of the corporate sukuks and sovereign private sukuk of the country, including the Islamic treasury instruments, designing the first Islamic microfinance scheme, and establishing and heading the Maldives Hajj Corporation, the Tabung Haji of Maldives.

Khairunnisa Musari is currently an Assistant Professor at the Department of Islamic Economics, Postgraduate Program, and the Faculty of Islamic Business Economics (FEBI), KH Ahmad Shiddiq

State Islamic University (UIN KHAS), Indonesia. She is a member of the Indonesian Association of Islamic Economists (IAEI) and a Lead Independent Associate Ambassador of VentureEthica. She worked as a Senior Specialist for Islamic Finance for UNDP Indonesia. She was listed as one of the Top 150 Most Influential Women in Islamic Business & Finance 2020 by Cambridge-IFA. Her areas of research include sukuk, waqf, Ehsan, fiscal and monetary policies, Islamic microfinance, circular economy, and climate change.

Zhamal Nanaeva is a Ph.D. Candidate in Islamic Finance and Economy at Hamad Bin Khalifa University, Doha. She received her BA in Economics from Kyrgyz State National University and her M.Sc. in Finance and Banking from the British University in Dubai, where her thesis focused on comparative analysis of risks in sukuk and conventional bonds. Furthermore, she completed finance and sustainability courses at Harvard Extension School. Her professional experience started at the Kyrgyz Project Promotion Agency, where she facilitated collaboration with multilateral donor agencies. Before moving to Doha, Zhamal worked in multiple startups in the UAE and Estonia, where she performed industry research and wrote about innovation and entrepreneurship.

Umar A. Oseni is the Chief Executive Officer of the International Islamic Liquidity Management Corporation (IILM), a multilateral financial institution headquartered in Kuala Lumpur. Prior to this, he was an Executive Director and Acting Chief Executive Officer of the same multilateral financial organization. At some point in his career, he was an Associate Professor of Law and Regulation of Islamic Finance. He was also a Visiting Fellow at the Islamic Legal Studies Program of the Harvard Law School, Harvard University. Apart from being a Harvard-certified negotiator and dispute resolution expert, he has consulted for numerous bodies in the areas of law and regulation of Islamic finance. With a good blend of both significant academic and industry-wide experience in Islamic finance, he has completed strategic consultancy work for some United Nations agencies, COMCEC of the Organization of Islamic Cooperation (OIC), the Islamic Development Bank (IDB) Group, and other government and government-linked agencies. He is a Solicitor and Advocate of the Supreme Court of Nigeria. With over 100 publications, he has published widely in refereed journals and books on Islamic finance and law. He co-authored the first textbook on Islamic finance titled: *Introduction to Islamic Banking and Finance: Principles and Practice* (United Kingdom: Pearson Education Limited, 2013). He is also a co-author of *IFSA 2013: Commentaries on Islamic Banking and Finance*, and *Alternative Dispute Resolution in Islam* (Kuala Lumpur: IIUM Press, 2013). He co-edited *Islamic Finance and Development* (Cambridge, Massachusetts: ILSP, Harvard Law School, 2014) and *Emerging Issues in Islamic Finance Law and Practice in Malaysia* (United Kingdom: Emerald Publishing, 2019). He is also the lead editor of *FinTech in Islamic Finance: Theory and Practice* (UK: Taylor and Francis, Routledge, 2019), a pioneering, authoritative book on the dynamics of financial technology in Islamic finance. He received his L.L.B. (Hons.) in Common and Islamic Law from the University of Ilorin, Nigeria; a Master of Comparative Laws (with Distinction); a Professional Master's degree in Financial Laws from York University, Canada; and a Ph.D. degree from the International Islamic University Malaysia.

Silmi Mohamed Radzi is a Research Officer at ISRA, where she has gained decent hands-on experience and is involved in various research projects. Among her published works are "Trading of Shares via Salam Contract: An Exploratory Study," "Islamic Banking: A Solution for Unequal Wealth Distribution?", and "Trailblazing Value-Based Intermediation: The Dawn of a New Era in Islamic Banking Experience in Malaysia." She obtained her Bachelor's degree in Shariah (with majors in Islamic Economics & Banking) from Yarmouk University, Jordan and continued her Master's in Islamic Revealed Knowledge and Heritage (Fiqh and Usul Fiqh) at International Islamic University Malaysia (IIUM).

Mohammmad Sahabuddin currently serves as an Assistant Professor at the Faculty of Business Administration, University of Science and Technology Chittagong (USTC), Bangladesh. He is also a Postdoctoral Researcher at the Finance Division of the Faculty of Applied and Human Sciences, Universiti Malaysia Perlis. His areas of interest in research are financial markets and conventional and Islamic finance. His current projects are Islamic FinTech, halal tourism, entrepreneurship, blended learning, internationalization, and a sustainable education system. He has presented papers at national and international conferences and published several articles in international journals. He holds a Ph.D. in Business Economics from Universiti Putra Malaysia (UPM). He graduated with a Master of Business Administration (M.B.A.) and a Bachelor of Business Administration (B.B.A.) majoring in finance from the University of Chittagong, Bangladesh. He is currently an advisor to the Bangladeshi Students' Association in UPM, and is the country representative for Bangladesh in Universiti Putra Malaysia (UPM).

Asma Ben Salem is Assistant Professor at the Higher Institute of Theology, Ez-Zitouna University, Tunisia. She received a Ph.D. in Economics and Finance from Lyon 2 Lumière University in France. She is a member of the research laboratory "Monnaie, Finance et Développement (MOFID)" at the Faculty of Economics and Management of Sousse (Tunisia). She has teaching experience at Umm Al-Qura University (Saudi Arabia), and universities in France and Tunisia. She has published papers in international journals and is a reviewer for the International Journal of Emerging Markets. Her research interests are in the areas of social finance, Islamic microfinance, and philanthropic institutions.

Salman Ahmed Shaikh is an Assistant Professor at Shaheed Zulfikar Ali Bhutto Institute of Science and Technology (SZABIST) University, Pakistan. He holds a Ph.D. in Economics from the National University of Malaysia and has received a Master's in Economics from the Institute of Business Administration, Karachi. He has presented many research papers at international conferences, has published research papers in top international journals, and has contributed book chapters with acclaimed publishers. He is on the editorial advisory board of several research journals. He also won a paper prize at the World Islamic Finance Forum in 2018. His research interests lie in economics, finance, and the role of faith in the post-modern scientific age.

Nasim Shah Shirazi is a Professor at the College of Islamic Studies (CIS), Hamad Bin Khalifa University, Doha. Before joining CIS, he worked as Lead Economist and Acting Manager, Islamic Economics & Finance Research Division, IRTI, Islamic Development Bank. Previously, he worked as Deputy Dean (Suleyman Demirel University, Almaty), Dean, Director of Research, and Director General, International Institute of Islamic Economics (IIIE), International Islamic University

Islamabad (IIUI), Pakistan. He served as a professor at International Islamic University Malaysia as well. He holds a Ph.D. in Economics from the IIIE and IIUI. He has designed, developed, and taught courses at the graduate and post-graduate levels in economics, finance, Islamic economics, and decision sciences at national and international universities. With more than 76 publications, he is well respected for his research in development economics, public finance, and Islamic finance for social development. He has supervised several Ph.D., M.Phil., and Master theses. Besides academic excellence, he has completed several consulting assignments with the World Bank, Asian Development Bank, PPAF, and private organizations.

Sukaynah O. D. Shuaib is currently a Risk Intern at the International Islamic Liquidity Management Corporation. She graduated from the International Islamic University Malaysia (IIUM) majoring in Islamic Finance (B.Sc.). She holds an Associate Islamic Finance Professional (AIFP) certificate from the Institute of Islamic Finance Professionals (IIFP), Nigeria, and is a Certified Islamic Specialist in Risk Management (CISRIM) from the General Council for Islamic Banks and Financial Institutions (CIBAFI). She completed her Diploma in Business Administration from the International University of Malaya-Wales (IUMW), Malaysia, and a Diploma in Arabic for Non-Native Speakers from the Open University of Sudan. She is currently enrolled in the Data Analyst Fellowship at Quantum Analytics, Nigeria, and previously worked as an intern trainee at Masryef Advisory, Malaysia, and EtiqaFinans Limited, Nigeria.

List of Figures

Islamic Finance and Sustainability: The Need to Reframe Notions of Shariah Compliance, Purpose, and Value

Fig. 1	Alignment of Maqasid Al-Shariah with the SDGs (*Source* Adopted from Deloitte-ISRA [2018])	24
Fig. 2	Adopting global standards through a sustainable shariah-based framework. *Source* Adopted from Deloitte-ISRA (2018)	30
Fig. 3	Multi-Stakeholder Collaboration for Social Priority Sectors (*Source* Adopted from Deloitte-ISRA [2018])	36

Maqasid al-Shariah and Sustainable Development Goals Convergence: An Assessment of Global Best Practices

Fig. 1	Structure of IsDB Sustainable Sukuk. *Source* IsDB (2020c)	85
Fig. 2	Sukuk PRIHATIN Transaction Flow. *Source* Adapted from Terms and conditions of Sukuk Prihatin (Malaysia Ministry of Finance, 2020b)	90
Fig. 3	Cash Waqf Linked Sukuk Transaction Flow. *Source* Adapted from Indonesia Ministry of Finance (2020c)	95

Sukuk Innovation: Powering Sustainable Finance

Fig. 1 Global ESG sukuk issuance by year and number of sukuk issues (*Source* Refinitiv) 149

Mobilizing Funds for Industrialization and Development Through Islamic Value System, Capital Markets, and Social Finance

Fig. 1 *Ijārah* Sukuk structure 169
Fig. 2 *Mudhārabah* Sukuk structure 170
Fig. 3 Mushārakah Sukuk structure 171

The Role of Green Sukuk in Maqasid Al-Shariah and SDGs: Evidence from Indonesia

Fig. 1 Green Sukuk in tackling climate change (*Source* Adapted from Musari [2020c] and Musari and Zaroni [2021]) 189

Is Islamic Microfinance a Resilient Business Model During Periods of Crisis? Empirical Evidence from Arab Countries

Fig. 1 Average Z-score developments over time, 1999–2018 (*Source* Authors' calculations based on Mix Market sample) 213
Fig. 2 Average PAR 30 developments over time, 1999–2018 (*Source* Authors' calculations based on Mix Market sample) 214
Fig. 3 Average NONI developments over time, 1999–2018 (*Source* Authors' calculations based on Mix Market sample) 215
Fig. 4 Average interest income developments over time, 1999–2018 (*Source* Authors' calculations based on Mix Market sample) 216
Fig. 5 Average GDIV developments over time, 1999–2018 (*Source* Authors' calculations based on Mix Market sample) 217

Digital Finance and Artificial Intelligence: Islamic Finance Challenges and Prospects

Fig. 1	Artificial intelligence application in finance: A global perspective (*Source* The United Nations Secretary Task Force of Digital Financing of the Sustainable Development Goals [2020])	243
Fig. 2	Evolution of credit scoring models (*Source* Ashraf et al. [2021])	246
Fig. 3	Islamic finance framework for socio-economic development (*Source* Ashraf et al. [2021])	250
Fig. 4	Islamic finance framework for financial inclusion (*Source* Ashraf et al. [2021])	251
Fig. 5	Application of AI for the financial assessment of microentrepreneurs (*Source* Ashraf et al. [2021])	255

Open Banking for Financial Inclusion: Challenges and Opportunities in Muslim-Majority Countries

Fig. 1	Percentage of adults with an account worldwide (*Source* Global Findex database)	263
Fig. 2	Financial inclusion in Muslim-majority countries (*Source* Created by the author using Findex [2018] data)	264
Fig. 3	Open Banking as a platform (*Source* Deloitte [2017])	266

Islamic Specialized FinTech for Inclusive and Sustainable Growth in Sub-Saharan Africa

Fig. 1	Registered mobile money account 2006–2017 (*Note* The figure compares the number of registered mobile money accounts per year for Sub-Saharan Africa and the rest of the world, excluding Sub-Saharan Africa. *Source* Authors' creation based on data from World Bank [2017])	289
Fig. 2	Africa FinTech Segments. *Note* The chart shows the percentage of the FinTech space occupied by each FinTech segment in Africa (*Source* Authors' representation based on information from Tellimer [2020])	289
Fig. 3	The 3 pillar of specialized Islamic FinTech Solutions (*Source* Authors' exposition)	294

The Role of Technology in Effective Distribution of Zakat to Poor and Needy

Fig. 1	Modus Operandi of Crypto *Zakat* (*Source* Authors' own)	317
Fig. 2	Modus Operandi of Rice ATMs (*Source* Muneeza and Nadwi [2020])	323
Fig. 3	Modus Operandi of Iris ATM (*Source* Sainis and Saini [2015])	324
Fig. 4	How smart charity operates (*Source* Developed from Alshammari et al. [2017])	326
Fig. 5	Application of IoT to enhance *Zakat* distribution for poor and needy (*Source* Author's own)	328

Notion of Value-Added in RegTech Research Work: What Is There for Islamic Finance?

Fig. 1	Three main coverages of RegTech (*Source* Author's own)	334
Fig. 2	Comparison between Web 1.0, 2.0 and 3.0 (*Source* Author's Own)	336
Fig. 3	Evolution RegTech (*Source* Author's own based on the references in below text)	340

List of Tables

Islamic Finance and Sustainability: The Need to Reframe Notions of Shariah Compliance, Purpose, and Value

Table 1	Practical discrepancies between SDG's approaches and Islamic finance	29

Maqasid al-Shariah and Sustainable Development Goals Convergence: An Assessment of Global Best Practices

Table 1	Alinma Endowment Funds launched since November 2018 till November 2020	75
Table 2	Eligibility criteria for projects funded by IsDB Sustainable Sukuk	86
Table 3	GoM Economic Stimulus Packages announced from February till October 2020	88
Table 4	Snapshot of SW001 and SWR001	94
Table 5	Type of social projects proposed for SWR001	96

Emergence of Islamic Finance in the Fourth Industrial Revolution and COVID-19 Post-Pandemic Era

Table 1	Evaluation of fourth industrial revolution	127

Sukuk Innovation: Powering Sustainable Finance

Table 1	Similarities and differences between Islamic and ethical finance	148
Table 2	Top 5 ESG sukuk issuances by value	150
Table 3	HSBC Amanah SDG sukuk profile	151
Table 4	IsDB's Debut sustainability sukuk profile	151
Table 5	Timeline of ESG sukuk and funds—key market developments	152
Table 6	Etihad Airways' transition sukuk profile	154

Mobilizing Funds for Industrialization and Development Through Islamic Value System, Capital Markets, and Social Finance

Table 1	Poverty Head Count Ratio (PHCR) in selected OIC countries	161
Table 2	Overall and relative ranking of selected OIC countries on HDI	163
Table 3	Official Development Assistance (ODA) received in selected OIC countries	164
Table 4	Total debt service (% of exports and GNI) for selected OIC countries	165
Table 5	Debt service (% of GNI) and net ODA (% of GNI) for selected OIC countries	166

The Role of Green Sukuk in Maqasid Al-Shariah and SDGs: Evidence from Indonesia

Table 1	Indonesia's Green Bond & Green Sukuk framework	184
Table 2	The projects of eligible green sectors	186
Table 3	Indonesia's Sovereign Global Green Sukuk (2018–2021)	187
Table 4	Relevance of Green Sukuk in *maqasid Al-Shariah*	191
Table 5	Projects of Global Green Sukuk 2018, its results and impacts to SDGs	193
Table 6	Projects of Global Green Sukuk 2019, its results, and impacts to SDGs	196

Is Islamic Microfinance a Resilient Business Model During Periods of Crisis? Empirical Evidence from Arab Countries

Table 1	Descriptive statistics	212
Table 2	Solvency Risk	225
Table 3	Credit risk	227
Table 4	Credit Risk	229
Table 5	Crisis effect on solvency risk in microfinance: conventional vs Islamic MFIs	230

Digital Finance and Artificial Intelligence: Islamic Finance Challenges and Prospects

Table 1	Benefits and limitations of traditional credit scoring versus AI based scoring	247
Table 2	AI and access to finance—products, data, and models	248

Open Banking for Financial Inclusion: Challenges and Opportunities in Muslim-Majority Countries

Table 1	SDGs in which financial inclusion is included as one of the targets	260
Table 2	Comparison of financial inclusion	265
Table 3	Open Banking development in some Muslim-majority countries	269
Table 4	Scopus results on "Open Banking" and "financial inclusion"	275
Table 5	Scopus results on "Open Banking"	275
Table 6	Scopus results on "financial inclusion"	277
Table 7	Financial inclusion in Muslim-majority countries	279

Islamic Specialized FinTech for Inclusive and Sustainable Growth in Sub-Saharan Africa

Table 1	Analysis of implemented specialized FinTech solutions in Sub-Saharan Africa, their social impact, and contribution to the SDGs	300

The Role of Technology in Effective Distribution of Zakat to Poor and Needy

Table 1	Possible Shariah obstacles in *Zakat* distribution	320

Notion of Value-Added in RegTech Research Work: What Is There for Islamic Finance?

Table 1	Salient features of Web 3.0	337
Table 2	Consistent terminologies used in FinTech and RegTech related papers	338
Table 3	Functions of two broad types of regulatory structures in practice	343

Islamic Finance, FinTech and the Road to Sustainability: Reframing the Approach in the Post-Pandemic Era—An Introduction

Saqib Hafiz Khateeb, Syed Nazim Ali and Zul Hakim Jumat

1 INTRODUCTION

The unprecedented economic downturn and global supply chain disruption of 2020 by the recent COVID-19 pandemic have accelerated the urgency for sustainable financing infrastructure that is agile, adaptable,

---

S. H. Khateeb · S. N. Ali
Research Division, College of Islamic Studies, Hamad Bin Khalifa University, Doha, Qatar
e-mail: skhateeb@hbku.edu.qa

S. N. Ali
e-mail: snali@hbku.edu.qa

Z. H. Jumat (✉)
Center for Islamic Economics and Finance, College of Islamic Studies, Hamad Bin Khalifa University, Doha, Qatar
e-mail: zhakim@hbku.edu.qa

© The Author(s), under exclusive license to Springer Nature Switzerland AG 2023
Z. H. Jumat et al. (eds.), *Islamic Finance, FinTech, and the Road to Sustainability*, Palgrave CIBFR Studies in Islamic Finance,
https://doi.org/10.1007/978-3-031-13302-2_1

and transformable. The Economist Intelligence Unit (EIU), the research and analysis division of the Economist Group, warned that the long-term effects on the global economy will be more deadly and much worse than the Global Financial Crisis and the 1919–1946 recessions. The global health and economic crisis have pushed a vast number of population into extreme poverty. Social finance has the potential to provide the urgently needed support for poverty alleviation, economic recovery, pandemic response, and sustainable development in the post-pandemic era. Islamic finance can play a huge role in ensuring economic recovery from the current setback and can provide a prospect for a new chapter of human development with a good blend of both the United Nations Sustainable Development Goals (SDGs) and the higher objectives of Islamic law, otherwise known as the *maqasid al-shariah*.

While the global health, economic, and political institutions are working hard to face the crisis and are hopeful that the pandemic will be over soon, there is a need to prepare for the post-pandemic era or even for future pandemics. Needless to say, critical discussions on the role of Islamic finance in the post-pandemic economic recovery and the proper understanding of FinTech's valuable place in Islamic financial practices can pave the way for a sustainable approach to face any similar unwelcoming economic and financial situations. Banking on the notions of *maqasid al-shariah*, Islamic finance tools can help usher in a new era that will not only ensure financial sustainability but also promote socio-economic policies that will aid the much-desired economic recovery.

Considering public welfare in all areas of life, *maqasid al-shariah* promotes the concept of safeguarding the interests of the people, which includes business transactions and financial relationships. The Islamic legal judgments and rules regulating public contractual relationships, including financial and commercial transactions, are based on the philosophy of *maqasid al-shariah*, which is further centred on the sources of Islamic law (the Qur'an and Sunnah). The objectives of Islamic law promote notions (preservation of religion, life, intellect, progeny, and wealth) that are integral to the practicality of almost all of the United Nations SDGs.

It is an untold responsibility of industry leaders, policymakers, and people from all income groups and nations to navigate financial industry disruptions and transition to a new normal by harnessing converging technologies. The pandemic has accelerated the adoption of technologies of all sorts that could keep the world running while nature takes its time healing (to some extent) from mankind's mistreatment of it. Time and again, the importance of leveraging social financing to mitigate the impacts of the raging pandemic and utilizing the digital world has proved to be the aiding hand towards resilience that in turn is creating both vast promises and potential perils.

The fourth edition of the International Conference on Islamic Finance (ICIF), held in April 2021 in the College of Islamic Studies, Hamad Bin Khalifa University, Doha, Qatar, brought together a substantial body of literature on various aspects of its central theme: Implications for Islamic Finance and the Economy in the Post-Pandemic Era. After a double-blind peer review, 32 papers were selected for presentation. Then, under the theme of reframing the approach of Islamic finance in the post-pandemic era, 14 papers were invited and peer-reviewed before becoming part of this book, apart from the introductory chapter. The chapters are divided into three major sections. Section I is on reframing Islamic financial sustainability and socio-economic developments. Section II deals with innovative Islamic financial tools for sustainable and socio-economic impact. The final Section III covers discussions on the role of FinTech in the road to sustainability.

2 Reframing Islamic Finance Sustainability and Socio-Economic Developments

In this section, five papers deal with the theme of reframing Islamic finance sustainability from a socio-economic and legal objectives approach while assessing global practices. The section starts with Farrukh demonstrating that the ethical and social values and principles of Islamic finance are aligned with environmental, social, and governance (ESG) related issues, although the convergence of ESG with Islamic finance is minimal. This gap can be overcome by interpreting shariah compliance more broadly than mere agreements with shariah rules. Shariah compliance should include the *maqasid al-shariah* perspective and integrate ethical, social, and environmental issues into its definition. The paper calls for a renewed shariah governance role in various shariah topics of Islamic banking and finance by underpinning its foundations from a *maqasid al-shariah* perspective rather than following suit with corporate governance. This requires the creation of a comprehensive *shariah* framework that integrates *maqasid al-shariah* and the SDGs into its guidelines for shariah compliance certification. Islamic financial institutions (IFIs) must recognize and comprehend both the challenges and opportunities in redefining shariah compliance and its purpose. Islamic finance, upholding the religious commitment to social good, should be at the forefront and heart of this long-term economic paradigm brought by the SDGs.

While recognizing the *maqasid al-shariah* necessity of reshaping the practice of shariah compliance, Abdulazeem and Saqib assess the criticisms faced by IFIs in their failure to play the expected social and developmental role. The chapter illustrates that the contribution of IFIs to achieving the desired sustainable socio-economic development is accompanied by a commitment to several tools and conditions. Much of the IFIs' failure to play a positive developmental role in Muslim societies stems from some regulatory and governance issues. The shariah governance framework must make sure the institution is keen to direct their finances and investments in the most feasible and socially beneficial directions. IFIs should not exaggerate credit risk considerations when financing or investing in economically and socially viable projects in order to encourage and support these projects. The authors claim that financing that is compatible with the spirit and purposes of shariah is inherently developmental and socially beneficial, regardless of whether it bears an Islamic label or not. In order to dispose of the conventional products that have leaked into these Islamic institutions, it is recommended to prepare a higher legal advisory board consisting of professional and trustworthy independent scholars that are assisted by trusted economists, to revisit and classify financial products in terms of their contents, effects, and outcomes.

In an attempt to assess whether the religious-based maqasid al-shariah clashes with the secular-based SDGs or converges, Noor, Said, and Silmi, in the next chapter, undertake six case studies of *waqf* investments and sukuk from Singapore, Malaysia, Indonesia, and Saudi Arabia. Using case studies analysis of the establishments' economic activities and practices, they explain that the convergence between SDG and *maqasid al-shariah* has contributed towards the development of a more human-centred and sustainable future. The propositions of maqasid al-shariah and SDGs are found to be almost symmetrical, and the study showcases feasible solutions to finance sustainable development while minimizing the adverse impact of the COVID-19 pandemic.

Umar and Sukaynah studied the impact of Islamic finance in the post-pandemic world and examined policies to be put in place to ensure the resilience of the Islamic finance industry in managing against pandemic-induced future economic crisis. Although government intervention and digitalization provided major assistance in keeping the national and global economies on track during the crisis, the Islamic finance industry (like the conventional finance industry) well-utilized the technological advancements in managing unprecedented pandemic impacts. The level of resilience of the Islamic finance industry in the face of economic distress aided in the exploration and identification of products and practices that may be introduced in the near future to save the industry from unexpected pandemics. The analytical study presumes that Islamic social finance remains an evergreen project that could be utilized to weather the storm of future pandemics. While FinTech remains an important tool for accelerating economic recovery, policymakers must ensure proper governance policies, and supervisory authorities must monitor the ethical use of FinTech in transforming the economy.

The final chapter of the section tries to fill the gap between conceptual and empirical studies on the Fourth Industrial Revolution (4IR) and the COVID-19 pandemic from an Islamic finance perspective. Mohammad, Abu Umar, and Amin explore the impact of the Fourth Industrial Revolution and the pandemic on technological advancement in the Islamic finance industry. Given the vast potential for the application of technology in Islamic finance, Muslim countries and IFIs should pay attention to amending the prevailing rules and regulations in shariah compliance frameworks. With a few specific laws that require vigorous attention, the potential of technological applications in any financial institution, including IFIs, is plentiful. Specific technology-related regulations should be part of shariah compliance. For instance, cyber regulations need to be made more robust for dealing with unethical trespasses into the privacy of customers and other banks' clients. A reassessment of existing usage of technology in IFIs is essential for the expansion of the Islamic financial industry as a development-oriented financial intermediation model in line with the underlying principles of shariah.

3 Innovative Islamic Financial Tools for Sustainable and Socio-Economic Impact

In Section II, Mustafa, Henk, and Zul Hakim study the growing convergence between ESG considerations, Islamic finance, and the United Nations' SDGs. Based on its analysis of the convergence, the chapter further looks at various aspects such as demand for ESG sukuk and the role of Islamic capital markets in fulfilling the SDGs. Shariah-based finance, ESG concerns, and the sustainable development goals share a variety of underlying principles that make them head together towards sustainable finance at the global level. The financial innovation of sukuk has geared the Islamic markets towards sustainable finance at unprecedented levels, courtesy of the key developments in governance aspects that include issuances, regulations, and strategic announcements in IFIs. Sukuk is driving next-generation innovation in Islamic capital markets in three significant aspects, namely green sukuk, sustainability-linked sukuk, and the blue sukuk that has recently emerged.

While some countries have the capacity to source development finance by issuing sovereign sukuk, Salman highlights how other countries with low per capita incomes and national savings require more focus on social finance institutions. Islamic finance has both market-based and non-market-based solutions for mobilizing development funds for effective use in socio-economic development needs. Economic growth cannot necessarily lead to economic development because the growth that increases income inequalities eventually becomes unsustainable and can undermine the democracy and overall well-being of a society. Islamic injunctions of pure altruism insist and reinforce the need for sharing and giving to poor people and social causes, while Islamic institutions can help in contributing towards effective mobilization, institutionalization, and utilization of social savings and philanthropic and humanitarian assistance. The chapter discusses the solutions offered by Islamic finance through its value system and worldview and through its set of commercial and social finance institutions to participate effectively in development assistance through and beyond markets.

Khairunnisa and Sutan undertake Indonesia's Sovereign Green Sukuk as a case study, which is the world's first sovereign green sukuk, to address key topics of green sukuk as an innovative Islamic green financial instrument. Indonesia has prioritized environmental development, disaster resilience, and climate change as its national priorities. The government ensures that policy transformation, an enabling environment, and financial investment go hand in hand to support the national agenda. This sukuk plays an important role in supporting the achievement of various sustainable development goals of the UN, like SDG 7 (Affordable and Clean Energy), SDG 8 (Decent Work and Economic Growth), SDG 9 (Industry, Innovation, and Infrastructure), SDG 11 (Sustainable Cities and Communities), and SDG 13 (Climate Action). Following the success of Sovereign Sukuk and as part of the government's commitment to the Paris Agreement, several other sukuk schemes, like the cash *waqf* linked sukuk and esham alternative, are suggested to the authorities to tackle natural disasters like climate change and pandemic. While Indonesia should increase the number and size of green projects, the chapter recommends preparing guidelines specific to issuing green sukuk as it still takes a longer time compared to issuing a regular sukuk. Furthermore, marketing green sukuk to potential global investors, particularly European investors, needs to be intensified to tap the available global resources.

Asma, Ines, and Sameh investigate the impact of the microfinance business model on the risk of institutions, with a focus on the benefits of diversifying to Islamic microfinance. The study is based on a sample of 68 conventional microfinance institutions (MFI) and 13 Islamic institutions in the Middle East and North Africa (MENA) region between 1999 and 2018, and tries to study if Islamic microfinance is a resilient business model during a crisis by testing whether the microfinance business model has a different effect on the solvency risk of conventional MFIs compared to the stability of Islamic MFIs. The study's results show that with regard to the Islamic MFIs' resilience during the global financial crisis, they have lower financial stability. Similarly, they show a higher credit risk, which confirms the negative effect of crises on their risk. However, these institutions increase their financial stability and, hence, reduce their solvency risk with greater geographic diversification. The study may help different stakeholders of MFIs in the decision-making process about whether expanding to shariah-compliant activities would reduce credit risk and increase their resilience during crises. It is essential for microfinance regulators to judiciously monitor the credit risk in microfinance given the ongoing policy effort for greater financial sector diversification in the MENA region.

4 Role of FinTech in the Road to Sustainability

Section III has five chapters from nine authors. In the first chapter, Dawood highlights the importance of artificial intelligence (AI) as a critical infrastructure to facilitate financial inclusion using the Islamic finance framework. He purports that the use of artificial intelligence and big data has helped fast track the process of accessing finance more than ever before. Access to financial services helps families and businesses save for long-term goals. Achieving financial inclusion is a critical component of poverty reduction and plays a vital role in the expansion of economic opportunities. To ensure financial inclusion, it is crucial that various sectors of society have their needs addressed, supportive policies are well implemented, and appropriate technologies are used. A major obstacle to financial inclusion is the lack of access to services for saving, investing, and accessing credit. AI models often use low-value digital features that apply more complex methods for credit risk assessment. This application is often not directly relevant to the assessment of creditworthiness of micro, small, and medium enterprises (MSMEs), and hence hinders financial inclusion. Furthermore, application of AI cannot resolve systemic issues of financialization and overindebtedness, and hence a policy framework is proposed within the realms of Islamic finance principles. The framework includes developing a sustainable and inclusive policy that keeps a check on the macroeconomic requirements of MSMEs at different stages of development that aligns with the shariah requirements and then including grants, interest-free financing, participatory finance, and equity-financing. A conducive institutional arrangement to implement the policy framework can help solve the issue of access to credit. At the same time, AI can help improve efficiency and reduce operating costs while providing better access to financing for entrepreneurs and improving socio-economic development in society.

The emerging concept of Open Banking is an effective tool to increase access to finance and hence facilitate financial inclusion, which is a means to achieve sustainable development. Nasim, Ahmet, and Zhamal attempt to study the opportunities of open banking and its challenges in Muslim-majority countries. The rapid advancement of FinTech has led to more affordable financial products and services. Open Banking simplifies the process of market entry for FinTechs and their integration into an existing system, by offering further innovation, diversification, and personalization of banking and other financial products. The chapter shows that financial inclusion in Muslim-majority countries is significantly lower than the global average, which implies that the population in OIC member countries may not be able to build sufficient resilience to escape the poverty cycle or face any future crises. While enabling shariah-compliant financial services through Islamic FinTechs, Open Banking platforms in Muslim-majority countries can consider including zakat and *waqf* FinTechs, along with the applications of government assistance funds, to facilitate the distribution of social benefits among lower-income populations. When adopting Open Banking, the chapter suggests that regulators ensure complete transparency in using the customers' financial data by enforcing the standards of digital ethics. It also suggests ensuring that the service providers pay special attention to the inclusion of low-income populations, senior citizens, and people with disabilities, while further considering subsidies for the poorest segments of the population.

The developments in digital economy were proving greater national and global connectivity and easier access to financial services. Jamila and Ahmet investigate the extent to which specialized FinTech solutions have addressed SDGs by solving multi-dimensional problems faced by Africa's most vulnerable people. Although initial experiences of using advanced technology in finance were showing positive results, it was the pandemic that halted the progress and brought health and economic crises that worsened the rising inequalities in sub-Saharan Africa. Even before the pandemic, the diffusion of technology in Africa, specifically FinTech-induced growth, was not equitably distributed across socio-economic divides, excluding some groups from enjoying the dividends of digital transformation. However, studies show that the sub-Saharan African digital economy quickly responded to the crisis with innovative solutions to enhance healthcare response and monitor the pandemic's spread. Apart from the healthcare industry, Africa's digital success is most prominent in the financial sector, with FinTech solutions and other tech solutions in niche segments embedded with financial services. Using specialized FinTech models is an effective way of innovating Islamic finance products and increasing financial inclusion for the predominantly unbanked Muslims in sub-Saharan Africa. Since digitalisation is at the forefront of the African Union's (AU) strategy to achieve its AU2063 vision, a proper and equitable distribution of digital technologies and skills will increase financial inclusion, improve access to global markets, increase transparency and accountability, and create more inclusive, resilient, and efficient economies. Given a suitable and enabling policy environment, adopting the specialized FinTech models will allow Islamic finance to reach a broader group in the sub-Saharan African region. With a 339 million Muslim population in sub-Saharan Africa, which constitutes almost 30% of the overall population, Islamic finance has the potential to accelerate the drive towards financial inclusion and sustainable development using specialized FinTech models.

Kabir and Aishath discuss the role of technology in the effective distribution of zakat to the poor and needy. The scope of technological advancements can include blockchain technology, artificial intelligence, and machine learning. The challenges in proper zakat distribution are either the inability to identify and validate the zakat recipients in a transparent and convenient manner by zakat administrators, and/ or the physical absence of zakat recipients in the administrator's office. Using the Internet of Things (IoT), zakat distribution can be enhanced by ensuring the eligibility of the recipient to receive zakat or not. Furthermore, since the location of the recipient can be traced in real time either by physical delivery of zakat or using QR code, the zakat administrator can distribute these charity funds in an effective and timely manner. Zakat administrators should utilize technology to complement their operations and to formulate legal and regulatory frameworks to manage technology in relation to zakat. Implementation of an effective zakat distribution system is important to achieve the maqasid al-shariah behind the obligation of zakat, i.e., the elimination of poverty, which is one of the goals of the UN-SDGs too.

The final chapter by Muslehuddin explores the value-added elements of Regulatory Technology (RegTech) in the financial literature. Under the impact of the Fourth Industrial Revolution, RegTech has recently gained traction and is being considered across the globe by all the stakeholders; governments, regulators, corporates, researchers, and academicians. The evolution of RegTech has proved to emerge as an impactful trend with a great focus on developing technological solutions to achieve efficient regulatory requirements and result in compliance implementation effectively. The literature review of papers on RegTech published in high impact journals like Wiley Journal Publications and Scopus reveals that elements of cost-efficiency, trust-building, and real-time monitoring and reporting were among the most value-added aspects of RegTech. Speaking of Islamic finance, RegTech could also resolve the issue of dealing with the conflict of opinions among the shariah scholars at various shariah supervisory boards. It can help improve the challenging situation of addressing the diverse regulators' approaches towards Islamic finance across different jurisdictions. In addition to blockchain technology, the recent advancements of Web 3.0 can enhance the domain of Islamic finance by infusing shariah compliance through the appropriate model of RegTech. The literature review found that the value-added elements of RegTech are focused on the topic of commercial sustainability, and has missed to discuss the areas of environmental sustainability and social welfare.

In an attempt to study the necessitated reframing of the financial approach in Islamic finance and its practicality, this book looks beyond technological aspects and finds ways to provide the greatest number of people the ability to positively impact their families, organizations, and communities, and open pathways to stimulate economic activity and promote social welfare, financial inclusion, and shared prosperity. The book focuses on the role of Islamic finance in the post-pandemic economic recovery while limiting its analysis to three key areas of sustainability: socio-economic recovery; social impact financing; and the role of FinTech.

Re-Framing Islamic Finance Sustainability and Socio-Economic Development

Islamic Finance and Sustainability: The Need to Reframe Notions of Shariah Compliance, Purpose, and Value

Farrukh Habib

1 Introduction

The deficiencies in the environmental, social, and governance aspects have recently prompted the United Nations (UN) to endorse many programs and introduce the Sustainable Development Goals (SDGs). The United Nations Development Program (UNDP) defines the SDGs as a worldwide plan that works as a context for holistic development aims. Its purpose is to devise a fairer and more sustainable future and resolve international concerns threatening people and the world. Among the objectives are poverty eradication, climatic and environmental degradation mitigation, human health and education improvement, and a range of other ecological and socio-economic expansion targets. Efforts, such as Sustainable and Responsible Investments (SRI) and Environmental, Social, and Governance (ESG), and Socially Responsible Investment

F. Habib (✉)
ALIF Technologies, Dubai, United Arab Emirates
e-mail: farrukh@shariahexperts.com; farrukh@aliftechs.com

(SRI), are focused on enhancing and encouraging sustainability in Islamic financing institutions. These projects, when considered together, seek to make a significant contribution to ecological preservation and tackling numerous socio-economic development concerns listed in the SDGs.

Among many significant obstacles to attaining the SDGs by 2030 is the shortage of monetary supplies. The Islamic finance industry is competent for assembling money to meet a slice of the USD 5–7 trillion annual financing disparity, which is mandatory to accomplish the aim by 2030. Despite the Islamic Development Bank (IsDB) serving as a model for all multilateral organizations in terms of dispatching financial disbursement to support SDG targets, it seems that the international Islamic finance sector appears to be comparatively inactive in terms of involvement with the SDGs, except for a few rare examples. The issue of their compliance with Islamic ethical principles and *maqasid al-shariah* has arisen in contemporary Islamic financial discussions and processes. The incorporation of *maqasid al-shariah* into modern Islamic financial practices falls short of what is actually needed of the Islamic financial industry to accomplish economic growth and social development. It is unsurprising that the relevance of implementing these measures at the IFI's level is becoming apparent. This is demonstrated by the methods in which IFIs have conducted businesses, with reporting being detailed and clear about ESG and SDG concerns.

The aim of this chapter, therefore, is to discuss in detail the main issue of how to ensure that the principles and practices of Islamic finance can be aligned not only with *maqasid al-shariah* but also with the UN's SDGs. The United Nations' SDGs, SRI, and ESG have now become catchphrases, as opposed to just being common terms for international regulatory bodies and policymakers in reconfiguring their current financial sector toward a more accountable, sustainable, and inclusive financial ecosystem. Accordingly, the chapter suggests a pragmatic approach to solving this issue along with several conceptual changes. The need to reframe the conceptual basis and practical implementation of Islamic finance's shariah compliance, value, and purpose is real and urgent. Sooner than later, Islamic finance industry experts, shariah scholars, policymakers, and other stakeholders need to realize the importance and reframe the concepts.

To achieve this objective, the chapter starts with the introduction of the UN's SDGs and other different approaches and their financing needs. Then it analyses these approaches from the theory of Islamic law and *maqasid al-shariah's* perspective. This discussion is followed by a critical analysis of the issue of why there is an insufficient alignment of Islamic finance with the SDGs. It opines that this minimal orientation is the result of a narrow definition of shariah compliance, which is mentioned in detail later. As a solution, it later discusses how to enhance the scope and develop a comprehensive framework of shariah compliance that also incorporates *maqasid al-shariah* aligned with the SDGs and other approaches. However, this recommendation may not bear fruit if it does not come with a change of mindset that promotes a holistic stakeholder approach as opposed to the shareholder approach. In the end, the chapter concludes the whole discussion by reinforcing the ideas discussed.

2 Understanding Different Approaches Toward Sustainability

The Brundtland Report, also known as "Our Common Future," published by the United Nations World Commission on Environment and Development (WCED) in 1987, was the first to express the concept of sustainable development. According to the report, sustainable development is defined as "development that meets the needs of the present without compromising the ability of future generations to meet their own needs" (U.N., 1987).

The United Nation Sustainable Development Goals

The United Nations published a set of 17 Sustainable Development Goals (SDGs) in 2015 for the member countries to achieve as part of a new global improvement structure for 2015–2030. The SDGs, according to the United Nations Development Program, serve as a global blueprint for advancement. The goal is to prepare for a more equitable and sustainable tomorrow as well as to address worldwide concerns that people and the planet are facing. Among the goals are poverty eradication, climate and ecological devastation prevention, human medical and educational advancement, and a variety of other ecological and social performance targets.

The historically unconstrained desire to maximize profits and short-sightedness in the private sector is increasingly being questioned. Purposeful profit is a new catchphrase, and the SDGs provide an ideal foundation for establishing that "purpose." Institutional investors, fund managers, capital market institutions, banks, and insurers in the financial industry are working to accomplish the SDGs via programs including the Principles for Responsible Investment (PRI), Principles for Responsible Banking (PRB), and Principles for Sustainable Insurance (PSI). To meet the goals of the 2030 Agenda for Sustainable Development, there is a significant need to mobilize funds of between USD 3.3 trillion and USD 4.5 trillion every year. In light of the current level of public and corporate investment in SDG-related industries, developing countries face an annual financing shortfall of around USD 2.5 trillion, on average. Despite the fact that Official Development Assistance (ODA) continues to be a significant funding mechanism, particularly in the least developed countries, only USD 146.6 billion in ODA was secured in 2017, which is far short of the amount necessary to attain the optimistic goals set out in the 2030 Agenda for Sustainable Development (UNSDG-Dag Hammarskjöld Foundation, 2018).

This does not rule out the possibility of ODA becoming obsolete. Instead, it must be utilized more tactically as a tool to obtain other financing options, both public and private, domestic and worldwide in scope. In the transition from "funding" to "funding and financing," international development partners, such as big organizations, non-governmental organizations (NGOs), and the United Nations, are faced with new obligations and expectations. Governments, the United Nations, public and private sector organizations, and civil society organizations must use context-sensitive methods of creative funding to expedite the achievement of the Sustainable Development Goals and guarantee there are no shortfalls and weaknesses (UNSDG-Dag Hammarskjöld Foundation, 2018).

Socially Responsible Investment (SRI)

Socially responsible investing (SRI), sometimes known as a social investment, is another option. It is the sort of investment that takes into account the social implications and the characteristics of a company's operations. Direct capital investments in socially responsible companies are possible, as well as via a socially conscious managed fund or exchange-traded fund (ETF). The main goals of SRI are to generate profits while creating a positive social impact, and they do not need to be mutually exclusive. The prospect of a positive profit is far from saying that the nature of the firm involved is socially conscious. Just because an investment claims to be socially responsible does not mean that it will deliver investors a larger positive profit. Therefore, while attempting to establish an investment's social value, an investor must also consider the investment's financial possibilities (Chen, 2022).

Some of the most common themes in SRI are impact investing and community investing, which have a tendency to reflect the political and social atmosphere of the era in which they are made. Consequently, it is not a perfect method of problem-solving. For investors to comprehend, there is also a significant risk aspect to consider when making an investment decision based on social value, as there is a possibility that the investment will suffer if that social value becomes unpopular in society (Chen, 2022). Even though there is evidence that focusing on this method can increase profits, there is, however, no evidence that proves investing only based on social principles would yield positive returns (Hale, 2022).

As a result, investment professionals frequently examine socially responsible investing from the perspective of environmental, social, and governance (ESG) concerns when evaluating potential investments. This method focuses on the management practices of the organization and determines if they are geared toward the sustainability of the community and its betterment (U.S. Securities and Exchange Commission, 2021).

Environmental, Social, and Governance (ESG)

Environmental, Social, and Governance (ESG) investing is the practice of investing in companies that adhere to ESG principles. More precisely, investors in this field evaluate how factors like the environment, social responsibility, and corporate governance affect the performance of an investment in the market. This method of investing evaluates how these three elements influence the success of an investment and, consequently, the return on investment. Although there are some significant variations between SRI and ESG styles of investment, they are fundamentally similar (Cautero, 2019). According to the Forum for Sustainable and Responsible Investment, *"sustainable, responsible, and impact investing (SRI) is an investment discipline that considers environmental, social,* and corporate governance (ESG) criteria to generate long-term competitive financial returns and positive societal impact" (US-SIF, n.d.).

According to Moody's Investors Service, the year 2020 will be remembered as a watershed year for environmental, social, and governance (ESG) investment, with unprecedented investments into ESG products increasing by 140%. According to statistics from Investopedia and Treehugger, many investors have begun applying environmental, social, and governance factors to make investment decisions for the first time (Greenberg, 2021). In a survey of Investopedia and Treehugger, the majority (58%) stated that their concern for environmental, social, and governance (ESG) issues increased in 2020, and 19% stated that they started implementing ESG standards into their investments during that time. According to the survey, only since 2017 have 62% of the ESG investors polled begun engaging in ESG-related goods. At the same time, 21% have more than a decade of involvement in ESG investing, which means that most of the interest has grown within the last five years (Greenberg, 2021).

ESG investments are also expected to rise in the future, with slightly more than two-thirds of respondents (67%) stating that they want to increase their holdings in firms with strong ESG activities in the coming five years (Greenberg, 2021).

Even though all the categories of investors who answered the poll expressed a desire to invest in ways that are consistent with their beliefs, younger investors were slightly more likely than older investors to claim they apply ESG principles to their investment decisions. Millennials and younger investors, in particular, feel that these concepts will become mainstream in the future, with around 64% believing this. On the other hand, fewer than half, or 42%, of the Baby Boomer and older generations had the same sentiments (Greenberg, 2021).

3 SDGs and ESG from Shariah Perspective

Shariah is defined as divine laws governing the beliefs, worship, ethics, transactions, and way of life of Allah's creations in all their ramifications that control their relationship with their Creator, fellow being, and the universe (Al-Qattan, 2001). It is also defined as the collection of commandments and divine laws governing belief and behavior that have been declared obligatory in Islam to achieve the aim of the welfare of the community (Al-Zarqa, 1998).

From the preceding definitions, shariah refers to a collection of divine laws governing human religion, morality, and behavior, as determined by the Quran and the Sunnah. Furthermore, shariah is more than a collection of regulations in the modern sense, and it is a collection of welfare aims embodied in ethical and moral ideals. Ethical and moral values are in existence to promote human welfare (UKIFC—ISRA, 2021).

Thus, the shariah's higher objectives (*maqasid al-shariah*) necessarily imply a comprehensive perspective aimed at elevating humanity to the highest rank by constructing uprightness, spreading morality, forming public interest, combating damage and destruction of the society, and guaranteeing equitable livelihood relationships between the self, the community, and the universe (UKIFC—ISRA, 2021).

Maintaining the continuity of life on the earth, safeguarding the ecological condition, and addressing a range of socio-economic progress difficulties are among shariah's key concerns. These considerations are in line with shariah's goals of benefitting humanity and preventing harm, as well as the broad ethical standards it promotes. In other words, 1,400 years ago, Islam, as a peaceful religion with the aim of blessing civilization, persuaded communities to incorporate SDGs such as nature conservation, publicizing equity, formation of equality in all forms, society and human resource improvement, consumer rights protection, and effective governance structures establishment. To clarify, ecological conservation in Islam entails maintaining the ecosystem's components through correct utilization and upkeep and banning their inappropriate usage, degradation, or exhaustion in the absence of a pressing need. Shariah experts classify ecological protection as a supplemental goal to the main goal of wealth preservation. They underline, however, that it goes beyond all of the shariah's core aims in a certain way. For example, religion is built on the concept of the world's stewardship and preservation, and the first level of this responsibility is to secure the world's physiological health by preserving the climate in which individuals perform their duties (UKIFC—ISRA, 2021).

In other words, as proposed by UKIFC—ISRA (2021), Islam has developed a distinct worldview about the environment. It provides a holistic and harmonious view of the environment and connects it to the concept of harnessing this universe. According to the Quran, the environment encompasses everything in the heavens and on the earth. Allah says:

He [also] subjected for you whatever is in the heavens and whatever is on the earth—all by His grace. Surely in this are signs for people who reflect. (Quran, 45:13)[1]

This indicates that all-natural forces are harnessed and channeled to support human beings on their path to the Creator. Additionally, Allah created the environment to benefit humankind and to allow them to fulfill their stewardship responsibilities, and this is what deployment and harnessing imply. Allah says:

Have you not seen that Allah has subjected for you whatever is in the heavens and whatever is on the earth and has lavished His favors upon you, both seen and unseen? [Still] there are some who dispute about Allah without knowledge, or guidance, or an enlightening scripture. (Quran, 31:20)[2]

Therefore, human beings' primary obligation toward the environment, as a vicegerent of Allah, is to do good and avoid harm. This is clearly stated in the explanation of the objectives of shariah:

The overall objective of Islamic Law is to populate and civilize the earth and preserve the order of peaceful coexistence therein; to ensure the earth's ongoing well-being and usefulness through the piety of those who have been placed there as God's vicegerents. (Al-Raysuni, 2005)

Moreover, the Quran contains multiple explicit instructions that are against all acts damaging the earth and the natural environment. It says:

Do not spread corruption in the land after it has been set in order." (Quran, 7:56).[3] "Do not seek to spread corruption in the land, for Allah certainly does not like the corruptors." (Quran, 28:77).[4] "Eat and drink of

---

[1] "وَسَخَّرَ لَكُم مَّا فِى ٱلسَّمَٰوَٰتِ وَمَا فِى ٱلْأَرْضِ جَمِيعًا مِّنْهُ إِنَّ فِى ذَٰلِكَ لَءَايَٰتٍ لِّقَوْمٍ يَتَفَكَّرُونَ".

[2] "أَلَمْ تَرَوْا أَنَّ ٱللَّهَ سَخَّرَ لَكُم مَّا فِى ٱلسَّمَٰوَٰتِ وَمَا فِى ٱلْأَرْضِ وَأَسْبَغَ عَلَيْكُمْ نِعَمَهُ ظَٰهِرَةً وَبَاطِنَةً وَمِنَ ٱلنَّاسِ مَن يُجَٰدِلُ فِى ٱللَّهِ بِغَيْرِ عِلْمٍ وَلَا هُدًى وَلَا كِتَٰبٍ مُّنِيرٍ".

[3] "وَلَا تُفْسِدُوا۟ فِى ٱلْأَرْضِ بَعْدَ إِصْلَٰحِهَا".

[4] "وَلَا تَبْغِ ٱلْفَسَادَ فِى ٱلْأَرْضِ ۖ إِنَّ ٱللَّهَ لَا يُحِبُّ ٱلْمُفْسِدِينَ".

Allah's provisions, and do not go about spreading corruption in the land. (Quran, 2:60).[5]

Additionally, shariah expressly prohibits excessive pollution of the air. This prohibition is backed by a fundamental Islamic legal maxim:

> "" لَا ضَرَرَ وَلَا ضِرَارَ ""

> There is no injury nor return of injury. (Muwatta Malik, Book 36, Hadith 1435).

This maxim is a verbatim phrase from the Prophet (PBUH) that has been directly incorporated into law. Likewise, the International Islamic Fiqh Academy issued its Resolution No. 185 (11/19) on "The Environment and Its Protection from the Islamic Perspective," condemning any harm inflicted on the environment and further stating:

> All acts and behavior that entail any harm to the environment or abuse thereof are prohibited; for example, acts and behavior that lead to the disruption of environmental balance, or that target or use resources unfairly without regard to the interests of future generations. [This judgment is] in accordance with the shariah maxims on the necessity of eliminating harm.

Also, shariah has enacted a variety of norms and ethical codes aimed at promoting social inclusion, human capital development, consumer protection, high-quality education, and poverty eradication. There is a plethora of evidence that the shariah places a premium on communal development. For example, the Quran states in Surah *al-Mā'idah*:

> Cooperate with one another in goodness and righteousness, and do not cooperate in sin and transgression. And be mindful of Allah. Surely Allah is severe in punishment. (Quran, 5:2)[6]

Furthermore, *maqasid al-shariah* promotes the concept of defending the interests of the people, which pertains to taking public welfare into

---

[5] "كُلُوا۟ وَٱشْرَبُوا۟ مِن رِّزْقِ ٱللَّهِ وَلَا تَعْثَوْا۟ فِى ٱلْأَرْضِ مُفْسِدِينَ".

[6] "وَتَعَاوَنُوا۟ عَلَى ٱلْبِرِّ وَٱلتَّقْوَىٰ وَلَا تَعَاوَنُوا۟ عَلَى ٱلْإِثْمِ وَٱلْعُدْوَٰنِ وَٱتَّقُوا۟ ٱللَّهَ إِنَّ ٱللَّهَ شَدِيدُ ٱلْعِقَابِ".

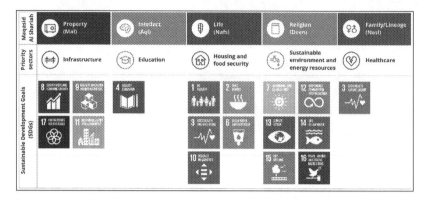

Fig. 1 Alignment of Maqasid Al-Shariah with the SDGs (*Source* Adopted from Deloitte-ISRA [2018])

account in all areas of living, including business transactions and financial relationships. All Islamic legal judgments and rules regulating public contractual relationships, including financial and commercial transactions, are based on this concept. In this context, *maqasid al-shariah* attempts to raise mankind to the greatest degree by promoting straightforwardness, disseminating morality, promoting general welfare, resisting the propagation of evil, injustice, and guaranteeing harmonious connections with oneself, society, and the world in which people exist. (UKIFC—ISRA, 2021). Figure 1. shows the alignment of *maqasid al-shariah* with the SDGs.

4 SDGs and Islamic Finance

The Islamic finance sector was anticipated to be worth USD 3.6 trillion in 2021 and is expected to expand to USD 4.9 trillion by 2025. It is estimated that there are 1,553 Islamic financial institutions worldwide, with Islamic funds valued at USD 174 billion and outstanding sukuk valued at USD 630 billion. Prior to the outbreak of the COVID-19, the industry saw double-digit growth, with a rate of 17.4% in 201, but did not exhibit any growth in 2020. However, based on many major investments and funding of OIC startups, Islamic finance is gradually recuperating from the impacts of COVID-19, with Islamic banks' profitability returning following the 2020 growth stagnant. Since then, it has started to continue its upward trajectory in 2021, with a compound annual growth rate (CAGR) of 7.9%. If this growth rate continues, the assets under control in Islamic finance are estimated to reach USD 4.9 trillion by 2025 (DinarStandard, 2022).

Due to the inherent connection between the SDGs and Islamic principles and the industry's scale, it is ideally positioned to develop instruments that significantly direct money toward the SDGs. Consistent with the SDGs' aims, shariah's higher objectives seek to promote humanity, prevent harm, and secure the sustainability of life on earth. SDG alignment provides an unparalleled opportunity for Islamic financial institutions to demonstrate to their customers the underlying social good and ethical foundations of Islamic finance.

Despite the fact that Islamic finance has begun to show some interest and activity toward sustainability, it is not at the pace or size necessary to achieve the Sustainable Development Goals (SDGs). Given the congruence of its fundamental principles, the financial architecture that is implemented, the emphasis on the utilization of revenues, and the unique governance measures adopted by Islamic finance, the possibility of interacting with the SDGs is plain and unmistakable (UKIFC—ISRA, 2020).

According to the report "Islamic Finance and the SDGs" by ISRA-UKIFC (2020), the SDGs are divided into three phases that Islamic financial institutions must follow in order to achieve the SDGs successfully:

1. Realize and Appreciate: the importance of an Islamic financial institution interacting efficiently with the SDGs.
2. Movement: building a commercial case and putting in place a plan to integrate the SDGs into the institution while also identifying the business possibilities that may arise as a result.
3. Constant Monitoring: perform an evaluation of the institution's performance and encourage continual development.

Hence, the Sustainable Development Goals (SDGs) provide several possibilities for Islamic finance, including:

1. Growing approachability to conventional global liquidity pools interested in "ethical finance."
2. Orientation with development bank funders in terms of strategy.
3. Enhancing the social significance of maqasid al-shariah in relation to the SDGs and further strengthening the relationship.
4. Aligning the Islamic financial institutions with the global regulations and market trends.

The report further states that several instances of the Sustainable Development Goals (SDGs) are already surfacing on the Islamic finance agenda. The Islamic Development Bank (IsDB) is completely dedicated to the Sustainable Development Goals (SDGs) and is exhibiting leadership in this area. In 2019, the IsDB developed a new business strategy to meet the Sustainable Development Goals (SDGs). The International Development Association (IDA) Member Countries will require a yearly investment of between USD 700 billion and USD 1 trillion to meet the Sustainable Development Goals (SDGs), which represents about 40% of the entire global SDG finance gap. In order to effectively incorporate and embed the SDGs into their funding and reporting procedures throughout their investments in member countries, the Islamic Development Bank (IsDB) and the Islamic Corporation for the Development of the Private Sector (ICD) may take practical steps to do so. ICD has also recognized *sukuk* that are associated with the Sustainable Development Goals as a viable funding alternative. There have also been several recent examples of the UN Sustainable Development Goals appearing on the Islamic finance agenda, such as the UAE Guiding Principles on Sustainable Finance, the Securities Commission of Malaysia's Sustainable and Responsible Investment Sukuk Framework, and Bank Negara's Value-based Intermediation (VBI) Financing and Investment Impact Assessment Framework (UKIFC—ISRA, 2020).

Regardless of these efforts, several studies show that Islamic finance is still short on not only the SDGs but also on *maqasid al-shariah*. The Islamic financial institutions still have a long way to adopt best practices for *maqasid al-shariah* criteria (Mergaliyev et al., 2021). One of the most important factors behind this situation is the narrow definition and understanding of shariah governance and compliance. The following section discusses this issue in detail.

5   Narrow Meaning of Shariah Governance and Compliance

Islamic financial institutions (IFIs) were established in the mid-1970s as institutions that serve individual Muslims' religious and financial requirements. They are regarded as value-oriented financial entities formed by Islamic values, morals, and ethics. While shariah rulings define the operational nature of IFIs in the form of compliance, the principles of *maqasid al-shariah* govern the ethical characteristics of their operations. As a result, IFIs are supposed to meet the maqasid al-shariah requirements expressed by various studies (Asutay & Yilmaz, 2018).

This was expected to be achieved by the IFIs through shariah governance because, theoretically, for Islamic finance, a Shariah Governance Framework is essential. To ensure that their operations and products are entirely compliant with shariah rulings and principles, IFIs require a special governance system. Furthermore, shariah governance incorporates a few features found in Islamic values, such as honesty, openness, responsibility, and stewardship, with the goal of safeguarding the interests of all stakeholders (Ahmad & Ishak, 2020).

However, many experts have interestingly elucidated that the term "Shariah Governance" is interpreted narrowly in the academic world. For example, some experts emphasize the key distinction between shariah governance and conventional corporate governance, stating that the former attempts to ensure that all operations, transactions, and procedures in IFIs adhere to shariah principles (Ahmad & Ishak, 2020). This definition and its likes confine the role of shariah governance into products and contractual terms only, where much of the focus is given to the literal meanings of Islamic law. Subsequently, it is seen that the majority of the products and services in Islamic finance are tweaked to achieve the same economic outcome as their counterparts while circumventing the words of the law only. Therefore, many sale-based transactions are being used in the Islamic finance industry for financing purposes, while partnership contracts are utilized for sales transactions.

On the contrary, some Islamic finance experts promote a comprehensive approach to shariah governance. For example, according to Noreen et al. (2016), the Shariah Governance Framework's basic notion is strongly founded in the Quran and Hadith, and hence its role is significantly different from that of the corporate governance model in conventional finance.

Beside their efforts, however, in practice, the shariah governance structure in IFIs is restricted to forbidding interest, excessive ambiguity, and gambling. Only the legal relationship and contractual terms and conditions are covered by the shariah governance, for example. However, shariah governance requires the concepts of trust, openness, and accountability to be embedded in the framework. According to Noordin et al. (2015), existing shariah reporting in IFIs is insufficient to achieve this criterion as a best practice. As a result, it has to be enhanced.

The inception of IFIs was supposed to spur Muslim countries' socio-economic growth as entities supporting *maqasid al-shariah* by meeting Muslim people's financial requirements in accordance with shariah principles and rulings. While IFIs have been effective in gathering monetary backing, they have come under fire for failing to meet the "substance" or *maqasid al-shariah* or "human and societal well-being" (Mergaliyev et al., 2021). Despite the Islamic finance industry's rapid expansion in terms of assets (USD 3.6 trillion) and the number of IFIs (1,553) present, IFI procedures have been harshly criticized for not being genuinely "Islamic." (Asutay, 2012).

Even though there are various alternative interpretations of *maqasid al-shariah*, it is commonly defined as the "fulfillment of the well-being of all stakeholders." Imam al-Ghazali gives the most prevalent reference to *maqasid*, which is defined as "safeguarding their faith (dīn), their self (nafs), their intellect ('aqal), their posterity (nasal), and their wealth (māl)" (Chapra, 2008). Hence, a universally accepted fundamental framework based on *maqasid al-shariah* is possible.

According to Deloitte-ISRA (2018), although Islamic finance theory is conceptually quite similar to the approaches to sustainable finance, it departs significantly from them in many important ways in practice. It has been determined that there are three important differences between these approaches:

1. A great emphasis is given to the harmonization of financial and social well-being.
2. Boosting the role of the finance industry in the real economy.
3. Encourage the development of a safer financial system that is devoid of systemic risk.

Table 1 highlights those differences in a summarized way.

6 Shariah Governance and Maqasid Aligned with ESG and SDGs

According to Deloitte-ISRA (2018), there is a crucial need to enhance shariah governance on the basis of *maqasid al-shariah* to incorporate SDGs and ESG. This would definitely achieve uniformity in the global trends, markets, and practices. However, the drive toward uniform global procedures in Islamic financial institutions presents the industry with two categories of challenges:

Table 1 Practical discrepancies between SDG's approaches and Islamic finance

	Responsible investments	*Islamic finance*
General investment approach	Holistic approach that aims to include any Environmental, Social, and Governance (ESG) information that could be material to investment performance	Value-based approach that has mainly focused on exclusionary screens on specific social and economic grounds
Active ownership	Strong emphasis on being active owners and to engage with companies on ESG issues (including proxy voting)	No widespread practice of engagement or active ownership
Avoiding investments in highly leveraged companies	Not widely considered	Sophisticated approach to analyzing financial structures of corporate entities to understand cash flows and avoid investments in companies with excessive leverage
Impact	Not widely considered, but there is a growing focus on environmental and social impacts of investments (including contributions to the SDGs)	Shariah scholars have typically assessed the compliance of financial

Source Adopted from Deloitte-ISRA (2018)

- Strategic governance framework: Creation of innovative Shariah-based methodology targeted at enhancing governance practices that are grounded in shariah fundamentals and consistent with global sustainable and investment standards. Figure 2 illustrates how these principles can be streamlined to meet shariah's aims while developing Islamic banking goods and services.
- Considerations for compliance and operations: Inconsistent regulation and reporting standards across markets and jurisdictions present investors and issuers with hurdles and operational hazards.

This will ultimately benefit Islamic finance because adopting a sustainable shariah-based framework for Islamic finance products and services can strengthen the Islamic finance industry as a whole. It will also raise its alignment with global SDG approaches. In essence, this will contribute

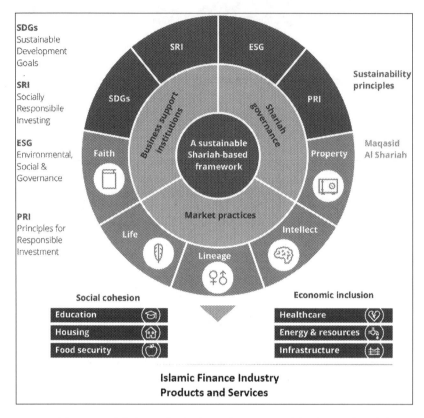

Fig. 2 Adopting global standards through a sustainable shariah-based framework. *Source* Adopted from Deloitte-ISRA (2018)

to the acceleration of the drive toward global common practice, hence, streamlining the Islamic finance industry at a global level.

7 Changing Perspective from Shareholder to Stakeholder

Shariah compliance may be seen as an Islamic corporate governance framework for Islamic financial institutions. Starting with traditional corporate governance, Shleifer and Vishny's (1997) study focuses on the perspective of corporate governance that is limited to the manner in which capital providers ensure that they will earn a return on their investment. The "shareholder approach" to corporate governance is a framework that focuses on investor-manager contracts and relationships. It may be described as a paradigm in which (1) shareholders should have control; (2) management should have a fiduciary obligation to serve only the interests of shareholders; and (3) the firm's goal should be to maximize shareholders' value.

The conventional concept of corporate governance, which is based on the investor-manager agency agreement, is only responsible for taking care of shareholders' or investors' interests. This outcome has been widely regarded as unethical by corporate moral philosophers because it unreasonably disregards the interests of non-shareholder organizations. Opponents of the shareholder-value notion argue that this profit-maximizing approach to the corporation is excessively limited due to disadvantages inflicted on other stakeholders by profit-maximizing decisions. These involve constraints on the social well-being of management and workers who have invested their human capital as well as non-work related-capital (residences, marriage, employment, education institutions, and social connections) in the employer-employee relationship, as well as suppliers and customers who have provided investments in the interaction and deferred alternative prospects, and societies who feel the consequences of business failure (Blair, 1995; Tirole, 1999; Turnbull, 1997). The separation of the objectives of those participating in the company confirms a division that may be detrimental in the long run (Sen, 1993).

According to (Baums et al., 1994), the business's claims extend beyond companies and investors to encompass anybody with whom the firm has any direct or indirect commercial connection. Each business stakeholder, including workers, consumers, vendors, and financiers, provides some value in exchange for some benefit, according to this "nexus-of-contracts" approach. Contracts are the outcome of these groups' negotiating on the terms and conditions of their reward as well as the organizational mechanisms that safeguard that remuneration against appropriation after the contract has been signed (Boatright, 2002). According to this perspective, corporate governance is nothing more than a more complicated variant of normal contractual governance (Zingales, 1997). All stakeholders are treated as employees of the company, and their entitlements are defined via negotiations.

Stakeholder theorists argue that (1) all stakeholders have a right to engage in business choices that influence them; (2) decision-makers have a trustee responsibility to serve the objectives of all stakeholders groups; and (3) the firm's goal should be to promote all preferences, not just those of shareholders. Clients, vendors, producers of supplementary goods and services, marketers, and workers are all considered stakeholders under the "stakeholders" model of corporate governance. As a result, according to this view, organizations should be governed in the interests of all parties (Boatright, 2002; Donaldson & Preston, 1995; Freeman, 1984).

Two essential ideas relating to rights over resources and contracts control the economic and social conduct of people, society, and the state, according to an Islamic perspective on stakeholders. These two principles also govern the main goals of different stakeholders, such as legal business entities. A company can be thought of as a "nexus-of-contracts," with the goal of minimizing contractual costs in order to increase revenues to financiers, based on the condition that these goals do not infringe on the rights over resources of any party that interacts with the company directly or indirectly. In order to achieve these objectives, the corporation fulfills its contractual responsibilities, both explicit and implicit, without jeopardizing the social order. This definition recognizes and protects stakeholders' rights while taking into account their position in the company.

Property Rights and Management

The principles controlling people, community, and government rights and the rules concerning ownership of global resources and contractual framework may be used to improve the understanding of the Islamic governance system architecture. The acknowledgment and preservation of rights in shariah is not confined to people but extends to all areas of existence, including the planet and its environment. Allah has granted specific rights to every one of His creations, and each is bound to recognize and appreciate the rights of others. These rights are linked to the obligations for which people are responsible. As a result, the concept of socially responsible activities (or investments) is already there. According to the Prophet (PBUH), *"give to everyone who has a right his right"* (Sahih at-Tirmidhi, Book 36, Hadith 111). The word right (haq) refers to anything that may be legitimately asserted, as well as the benefits and entitlements that Islam may have given to individuals.

While a portion of these resources is set aside for the exclusive use of the whole community, the remainder is made universally accessible to individuals without the community losing its original right of ownership (Mirakhor, 1989). This proposal establishes the legal foundation for mandating the protection of society's long-term viability, well-being, and objectives.

Along with rights to resources, the shariah imposes duties, including the duty—imposed firmly on a person—not to trash, ruin, squander, or utilize resources for purposes prohibited by the shariah (Quran, 2;188; 25:67). If someone does it, then it would constitute a violation of one's rights as well as an infringement on the rights of others (Quran, 11:87; Ahmad, 1995).

The world's resources are included in the prohibition of discarding and squandering in all sectors. A person may not make a change to their land that may hurt even their neighbor. If the property owner can show that he is unable to utilize the property lawfully (within shariah's bounds), he loses his entitlement to ownership. Under such circumstances, the lawful authority is completely justified in rescinding the usage rights of the resource in order to safeguard it from the owner's abuses (Bashir, 1999). This viewpoint is consistent with the Islamic conceptions of fairness (*al-adl*) and benevolence (*al-ihsān*), as well as individual and communal rights and duties.

From the previous discussion, many inferences may be drawn. First, Islam's notion of property rights differs in that the person has an assigned right to the resource ownership, which must be acquired, used, and disposed of according to shariah's regulations, which include the idea of sharing. Second, although Islam firmly respects a person's right to exclusive resources, these rights are limited by norms meant to preserve society and the government's rights. Third, under the first and second axioms of property rights, every person, organization, society, civilization, and government becomes a stakeholder whose rights are provided and protected by shariah in order to achieve social order, sustainability, and economic progress.

The shariah's contractual basis assesses man's virtue of justice not only on the basis of his material performance but also on the vital quality of his straightforward purpose (*niyyah*) with which he enters into each contract. This purpose consists of honesty, integrity, and a will to carry out what he or she has agreed to do in a strict and faithful manner (or not to do). The Quran says in a short, straightforward, and strong sentence, "*O you who believe, fulfill contracts*" (Quran 5:1). The concept of contracts is so fundamental in shariah that every public position is seen as a contract or agreement that establishes the parties' rights and duties (Mirakhor, 1989).

A person, as well as public and commercial organizations, is obligated to follow Islam's contractual structure, which lays equal weight on duties originating from both direct and indirect contracts. As a result, just as all stakeholders must fulfill explicit contracts, they must also defend the integrity of implicit agreements by acknowledging and preserving the property rights of other stakeholders, the group, the community, and the government. Unlike conventional stakeholders' theory, which looks for strong justifications to include tacit agreements in company theory, Islamic law takes stakeholders' rights and responsibilities for granted.

The framework of property rights and relationships established by Islam also establishes standards for who qualifies as a stakeholder and whether or not that stakeholder has the power to affect a firm's choices and administration. Even if the business has an official agreement with them via mutual understanding, any organization or person with whom the firm has any express or implied contractual responsibilities counts as a stakeholder in a wide sense. In Islam, a stakeholder is someone whose property rights are jeopardized or endangered as a result of the firm's conscious or unconscious acts. When a person's rights are infringed upon or challenged as a result of a company's operations, that person, group, community, or society is considered a stakeholder (Clarkson, 1994).

Although the firm's obligation to various stakeholder groups has been established, the issue of whether stakeholders have the right to be involved in decision-making remains unanswered. Is it feasible and practically efficient if they are granted the right to be involved? The next section delves into these concerns in further depth.

Structure of Shariah Governance Framework

In Islam, the required conduct of a company is not different from the expected behavior of any other member of society. Because the firm lacks conscience, the conduct of its directors is considered the firm's behavior, and their decisions are held to the same high moral and ethical principles as those expected of an individual. In other words, directors acting as the shareholders' representatives determine the business's economic and moral conduct, and it becomes their fiduciary obligation to administer the organization as a trust for all stakeholders, not just the owners. As a result, directors will be responsible for ensuring that the firm's activities adhere to shariah principles and norms. If there is any departure, the institutional structure discourages it. In an ideal situation, where everyone is a believer, those among Muslims whose behavior fully complies with the shariah's requirements, such as truthfulness and responsibility to respect others' property rights, will eliminate difficulties posed by informational asymmetries, moral hazards, and adverse selection, thus, providing improved governance. In a less ideal situation, where individual objectives may be swayed at the expense of societal interests to encourage departure from contract conditions, the construction of a governance model will be necessary to guarantee people's contractual commitments are honored and everyone's rights are protected.

The use of a reward structure in a shariah governance framework guarantees that adherence to the rules provides an effective governance system that preserves social justice and order among all members of society (Iqbal & Mirakhor, 2001).

Similarly, shariah boards are a highly unique notion in the Islamic financial system. The functioning of IFIs has been overseen by a shariah board comprised of Islamic experts to guarantee that its activities and code of conduct adhere to shariah standards. A shariah board for each IFI is inefficient, but all IFIs need just one set of regulations for a proper shariah governance framework based on the shariah. The same shariah board concept may be used in a system-level board made up of academics from several disciplines such as shariah, economics, finance, and commercial law, to guarantee that regulations are created and enforced so that IFIs completely comply with contractual responsibilities to all stakeholders.

For an improved and effective shariah governance framework that is all-inclusive of maqasid al-shariah aspects and sustainable approaches, it is pertinent to have a paradigm shift from the narrow shareholder model to the wider stakeholder approach. This is one of the most important factors to expand the scope of Islamic finance in general. According to Deloitte-ISRA (2018), there are three important considerations about the rise and wider acceptance of the Islamic finance industry that will necessitate multi-stakeholder interaction to be successfully tackled:

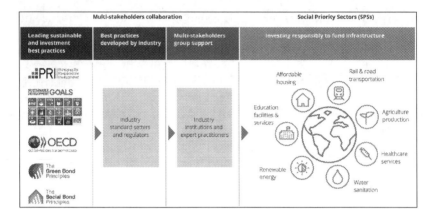

Fig. 3 Multi-Stakeholder Collaboration for Social Priority Sectors (*Source* Adopted from Deloitte-ISRA [2018])

1. New product architectures pose significant regulatory and shariah compliance issues, and leading experts must accept them.
2. Languishing in applying global standards and principles like the GBPs, PRIs, SDGs, ESG, and green financing.
3. FinTech innovations and offerings may heighten the market competitiveness and cost of raising capital in mid and long-term notes.

Figure 3 below depicts a number of organizations, approaches, and programs that lead to the global advancement of responsible and sustainable financing activities, as well as how their outcomes may greatly help directly or indirectly to the development of the Islamic finance industry and sustainable and responsible investments that are environmentally conscious and/or have public welfare and a favorable outcome for the public and the economy.

Islamic finance is a nexus of different dimensions and an effort for multi-players. Bringing the industry closer to maqasid al-shariah and the SDGs require an all-stakeholders strategy. For example, because of the industry's unique characteristics, governments' involvement will lead to a significant convergence of leading maqasid and SDGs practices across the board, enhancing Islamic finance's validity as a credible alternative financial system. The policymakers can also help in various policy implications that can be recognized by the conventional global community.

These steps will support Islamic finance in other various ways, including the following:

- Legislative support that is streamlined: Emerging world efforts and technologies can open up new options for improving legislative coherence across key Islamic financial markets (Asia, Middle East, and Europe). Registering for these initiatives will help to improve legislative convergence.
- Specialty solutions: New innovative product structures will allow for the growth of niche offerings and services, attempting to attract new potential stakeholders.
- Supporting focus areas: Combining product structure innovations with maqasid al-shariah to fund SDGs will help Islamic finance achieve its social and financial inclusion goals.

Further down the road, the pursuit of universal best practices for Islamic finance will form the base for the development of an effective and acceptable Islamic financial system that can better incorporate the global financial system.

During the execution phase, relevant industry stakeholders should follow and examine the tactical issues expressed by the demand for worldwide standard processes for the Islamic finance business. Politicians and market players should be encouraged to open such discussions internally, focusing on the comprehensive shariah governance concept and operational implications of creating universally approved Islamic finance practices.

8 Conclusion

Shariah governance, as a major component in the Islamic finance industry, enjoys a unique focus in this regard. In reality, only those with a firm base in shariah and a thorough understanding of current financial practices are eligible for this role. This is related to shariah governance's role in shariah topics such as structuring, examining, authorizing, auditing, and providing an annual shariah compliance certification. Recognizing its importance, shariah governance must reinforce its foundations from a *maqasid al-shariah* perspective rather than copying conventional corporate governance. To this end, maqasid al-shariah appears to be the best option for integrating the SDGs.

In other words, IFIs are required to take a more proactive approach to meet maqasid al-Shariah standards, which includes associating and integrating SDGs objectives into their business model and policy formulation. Further, the contemporary understanding of maqasid al-shariah necessitates the creation of a comprehensive shariah framework that integrates maqasid al-shariah and the SDGs and establishes guidelines for how financial transactions should be conducted in an Islamic financial system.

The challenge, and a major success element, is thus to educate, inform, and catalyze the global Islamic finance industry around the Sustainable Development Goals, ensuring that Islamic financial institutions (IFIs) recognize and comprehend both the potential and the challenges that exist. Islamic finance, with its deep-seated commitment to social good, should be at the forefront and heart of this new, long-term economic paradigm. In light of the SDGs, which are emerging as a shared blueprint to bring lasting peace and prosperity for people on earth now and in the future, it is imperative for the global Islamic finance sector to demonstrate its credentials as a driving force in the global finance sector to effect positive change in the world.

References

Ahmad, A. A., & Ishak, M. S. (2020). Realizing Maqasid Al-Shari'ah in Shari'ah governance: A case study of Islamic banking institutions malaysia. *International Journal of Islamic Economics and Finance Research, 3*(2), 39–52.

Al-Qattan, M. (2001). *Tarikh Al Tashri Al-Islami*. Maktabah Wahbah.

Al-Raysuni, A. (2005). Imam Al-Shatibi's theory of the higher objectives and intents of Islamic law. International Institute of Islamic Thought.

Al-Zarqa, M. (1998). Al-Madkhal al-Fiqhi al-Aamm. Dar al-Qalam.

Asutay, M. (2012). Conceptualising and locating the social failure of Islamic finance: Aspirations of Islamic Moral economy versus the realities of islamic finance. *Journal of Asian and African Area Studies, 11*(2), 93–113.

Asutay, M., & Yilmaz, I. (2018). Re-embedding Maqasid al-Shariah in the essential methodology of Islamic economics. In M. Mesawi, Maqasid Al-Shari'ah: Explorations and implications. Islamic Book Trust.

Bashir, A.-H. M. (1999). Property rights in Islam. Conference Proceedings of the Third Harvard University Forum on Islamic Finance (pp. 71–82). Harvard University.

Baums, T., Buxbaum, R. M., & Hopt, K. J. (1994). *Institutional Investors and Corporate Governance*. Walter de Gruyter.

Blair, M. M. (1995). Corporate "Ownership." *The Brookings Review, 15*(2), 16–19.

Boatright, J. R. (2002). Contractors as Stakeholders: Reconciling Stakeholder Theory with the Nexus-of-Contracts Firm. *Journal of Banking and Finance, 26*(9), 1837–1852.

Cautero, R. (2019, December 21). SRI vs. ESG: What's the difference? Retrieved from Yahoo finance: https://finance.yahoo.com/news/sri-vs-esg-difference-151633076.html

Chapra, U. (2008). *The Islamic vision of development in light of Maqasid al-Shari'ah*. The International Institute of Islamic Thoughts.

Chen, J. (2022, April 12). What is a socially responsible investment (SRI)? Retrieved from Investopedia: https://www.investopedia.com/terms/s/sri.asp#toc-what-is-a-socially-responsible-investment-sri

Clarkson, M. B. (1994). *A Risk-Based Model of Stakeholder Theory*. The Center for Corporate Social Performance and Ethics.

Clarkson, M. B. (1995). A stakeholder framework for analyzing and evaluating corporate social performance. *Academy of Management Review, 20*(1), 92–117.

Deloitte-ISRA. (2018). Sukuk in focus: The necessity for global common practices. ISRA.

DinarStandard. (2022). State of the global Islamic economy report. DinarStandard.

Donaldson, T. (1989). *The Ethics of International Business*. Oxford University Press.

Donaldson, T., & Preston, L. E. (1995). The Stakeholder Theory of the Corporation: Concepts, Evidence, and Implications. *Academy of Management Review, 20*(1), 65–91.

Freeman, R. E. (1984). *Strategic Management: A Stakeholder Approach*. Pitman.

Greenberg, K. (2021, July 21). Demand for ESG investments soars emerging from COVID-19 pandemic. Retrieved from Investopedia: https://www.investopedia.com/demand-for-esg-investments-soars-emerging-from-covid-19-pandemic-5193532

Hale, J. (2022, January 14). Sustainable index funds produce strong gains in 2021. Retrieved from Morning Star: https://www.morningstar.com/articles/1074881/sustainable-index-funds-produce-strong-gains-in-2021

ICD - Refinitiv. (2019, October 23). Islamic finance development report 2019: Shifting dynamics. Retrieved from Zawya: https://www.zawya.com/mena/en/ifg-publications/231019121250Z/

Iqbal, Z., & Mirakhor, A. (2001). Role of stakeholders in corporate governance of Islamic financial institutions. Conference Proceedings on governance, Transparency and Risk Management of Islamic Financial Institutions.

Mergaliyev, A., Asutay, M., Avdukic, A., & Karbhari, Y. (2021). Higher ethical objective (Maqasid al Shari'ah) augmented framework for Islamic banks: Assessing ethical performance and exploring Its determinants. *Journal of Business Ethics, 170*(4), 797–834.
Mirakhor, A. (1989). General characteristics of an Islamic economic system. In Hasani, Baqir & Mirakhor, Abbas (Eds). *Essays on Iqtisad: The Islamic Approach to Economic Problems* (pp. 45–80). Global Scholarly Publications.
Noordin, N. H., Kassim, S., Prabangasta, D., & Hayeeyahya, N. (2015). Does composition of Shariah committee influence Shariah governance disclosure ? Evidence from Islamic banks in Malaysia. IIUM Institute of Islamic Banking and Finance.
Noreen, S., Majeed, M. T., & Zainab, A. (2016). Corporate Governance at Islamic Financial Institution in Pakistan. *International Journal of Economics and Empirical Research, 4*(411), 582–589.
Sen, A. (1993). Money and Value: On the Ethics and Economics of Finance. *Economics and Philosophy, 2,* 203–227.
Shleifer, A., & Vishny, R. W. (1997). A Survey of Corporate Governance. *Journal of Finance, LI, I*(2), 737–783.
Tirole, J. (1999). *Corporate Governance.* Center for Economic Policy Research.
Turnbull, S. (1997). *Stakeholder Cooperation. Journal of Co-Operative Studies, 29*(3), 18–52.
U. N. (1987). Report of the world commission on environment and development: Our common future. Retrieved from. https://www.are.admin.ch/are/en/home/media/publications/sustainable-development/brundtland-report.html (last accessed on 20 May 2022).
U.S. Securities and Exchange Commission. (2021, February 26). Environmental, Social and Governance (ESG) funds—Investor bulletin. Retrieved from Investor.gov: https://www.investor.gov/introduction-investing/general-resources/news-alerts/alerts-bulletins/investor-bulletins-1
US SIF (Sustainable Investment Forum). (n.d.). Sustainable investing basics. Available on https://www.ussif.org/sribasics (last accessed on 20 May 2022).
UKIFC—ISRA. (2020). *Islamic Finance and the SDGs: Framing the Opportunities.* Islamic Finance Council UK.
UKIFC—ISRA. (2021). *Islamic Finance: Shariah and the SDGs.* Islamic Finance Council UK.
UNSDG—Dag Hammarskjöld Foundation. (2018). *Unlocking SDG Financing: Findings from Early Adopters.* United Nations Sustainable Development Group.
Zingales, L. (1997). Corporate governance. National Bureau of Economic Research (NBER).

Tools and Conditions for Achieving Sustainable Development in Islamic Finance

Abdulazeem Abozaid and Saqib Hafiz Khateeb

1 Introduction

Islamic banks were meant to be institutions that play a developmental and social role in the Islamic societies, unlike traditional financial institutions, whose primary goal is to make profits. However, it has been observed recently that most Islamic financial institutions (IFI) have ignored 'sustainability' as an essential asset in their development projects. They fell short in assuming their developmental and social responsibility, hence seeming indifferent in their purposes from traditional financial institutions.

It is fair to claim that IFIs are profit-making institutions established to make profits for their owners and investors, not as charitable organizations or social institutions. What distinguishes IFIs from traditional financial

A. Abozaid
College of Islamic Studies, Hamad Bin Khalifa University, Doha, Qatar
e-mail: aabozaid@hbku.edu.qa

S. H. Khateeb (✉)
Research Division, College of Islamic Studies, Hamad Bin Khalifa Univeristy, Doha, Qatar
e-mail: skhateeb@hbku.edu.qa

© The Author(s), under exclusive license to Springer Nature Switzerland AG 2023
Z. H. Jumat et al. (eds.), *Islamic Finance, FinTech, and the Road to Sustainability*, Palgrave CIBFR Studies in Islamic Finance,
https://doi.org/10.1007/978-3-031-13302-2_3

institutions is their declaration of compliance with shariah in their profit-making mechanisms and modes of earning. It is the objective of profit generation in accordance with shariah that governs and endorses its *modus operandi*, and not any secondary achievements that may or may not be part of their direction of work. However, it is justified to argue that if achieving the same legitimate profit is possible in ways that can complement serving the community while bearing no loss to these institutions, then it is obligatory for them, in this case, to adhere to those ways. There is no excuse for IFIs in such a case to ignore or neglect these social development measures because building a developed Islamic society is obligatory on its individuals and institutions. There is no excuse for a Muslim or an Islamic institution to refuse to participate in contributing to the upliftment and development of society in ways that do not harm himself.

It is conspicuous in this aspect that the IFIs have not duly contributed with their possible and harmless role, as this social dimension is absent from their operations despite the severe deteriorating economic conditions of Muslims in most Islamic countries. Society hence does not hesitate to allege that IFIs fail to play their possible role where they could have contributed socially and served the Muslim community in a way that does not burden or harm them. The IFIs are not keen to invest in sustainable development projects, environmental projects, and sectors of social benefit such as education, health, support for youth sectors, and to support projects that lead to Neither are these institutions keen on financing small and medium enterprises (SMEs), but rather prefer to support large-scale companies regardless of their developmental role due to magnified and unjustified risk considerations in many cases.

It is also duly noted that IFIs have sought to finance expensive non-essential goods, which has helped the wealthy direct their money toward acquiring these luxuries at the expense of establishing development projects that employ the labor force and helps build a productive economy. It is further alleged that IFIs did not enter into real investment contracts that are developmental in nature, like *Musharaka* or *Mudharaba* contracts. Instead, the IFIs mechanized these investment contracts to adapt to serve their financing models, which resulted in investment contracts becoming pure financing contracts.

The IFIs have burdened their clients with fees and imposed profit rates on finances that were sometimes more than the interest rates charged by conventional institutions, with the excuse of compensation for the additional expenses incurred by IFIs, unlike the conventional financial institutions. Additionally, IFIs offer financing products that carry shariah risks in their transactions, such as *Tawarruq*[1] *Inah*,[2] and organized *salam*[3] products. As a result, the adverse effects of dealing with *riba* are felt while dealing with such obscure products.

These are the claims and criticisms, in brief, that are raised against IFIs as they are not in tandem with any positive developmental or social role that these institutions can play. Before delving into this aspect, it is necessary, in principle, to conceptualize the legal conditions and regulations for IFIs to assume their development and social responsibility because shariah is a law of justice that ensures the rights and interests of all the stakeholders while recognizing the nature and special circumstances of each entity that is charged some responsibility toward others.[4]

---

[1] Tawarruq is when the bank agrees with the customer requesting financing to sell him a commodity at a deferred price and then sell it in the market on behalf of him at a lower face value and deposits that money in the customer's account. So the customer gets the amount he wanted as financing, but in return, he must pay the bank the excess of what he borrowed, i.e., the amount for which he had purchased that commodity from the bank. The International Islamic Fiqh Academy session no. 19 held in Sharjah—April 2009, issued a decision (Resolution no. 179 -5/19) prohibiting this type of organized Tawarruq because it involves indirect riba.

[2] Inah is when the bank sells a commodity to the customer at a deferred price to be paid in installments, and then the bank buys it back from him. A detailed picture of this sale is as such: the bank prepares a list of the goods it currently owns and allocates them for cash financing operations. It asks the financing applicant to sign a contract to buy one of those goods from the bank at an installment price that adjusts the total amount of financing and its profit. The bank then asks him to sign a contract in which he sells the same commodity to the same bank with a price equal to the financing amount, and the amount is placed in his account. Some banks are less regulated, so they do not have a list of owned goods. They rather sell a share of the bank's real estate assets that it uses, and then repurchase it from the client. Such a sale is forbidden in all schools of thought, although some sects state that such a contract is valid due to its clauses yet is not allowed (Al-Kasani 1982, Ibn Qudamah 1983, Al-Dasuqi n.d.). It is wrongly attributed to the Shafi'is that Inah sale is allowed (Abozaid, 2004).

[3] Salam originally is the sale of a described guaranteed item with a future date in exchange of an advanced price. As for what is known as organized salam, it is a financing process in which the procedure is slightly different from Tawarruq and Inah, and is similar to reverse Tawarruq where instead of bank selling the commodity to the client and then selling it further on his behalf, it rather buys a commodity from him, which it later buys from the market for his account. The result of reverse Tawarruq and its effect is the same as Tawarruq, but with modification in form and method.

[4] For instance, shariah does not obligate zakat on a rich who is in debt, or on a person whose wealth is enough only to serve his basic necessities.

2 Legal Conditions to Include IFIs in Socio-Developmental Responsibilities

There are a few legal restrictions that the IFIs should adhere to contribute to social and developmental sectors. Their socio-developmental activities should not be at the expense of harming the shareholders or depositors because they are the owners of the money, and they invested it in the institution with the aim of growing their wealth. The institutions' behavior of this wealth management in a way that harms this goal violates their contract's requirements. If the shareholders or depositors are harmed as a result of the management's actions without their consent, then the management is legally bound for its guarantee to the owners of that money because that act was an infringement. The agent or *mudhārib* is legally bound to guarantee the capital if he transgresses or is negligent, or did not comply with the terms and conditions of the contract (OIC Resolution No. 30, 1988; Zuhayli, 2005).

IFIs contribution should not be in the form of a donation that is not authorized by the institution's shareholders or by the depositors because only the owners of the money have the sole authority to donate it unless with their authorization. If an unauthorized donation takes place from such an agent, then it becomes binding on the agent himself and should be paid from his (agent's) money (Zuhayli, 2005).

Another condition is that the contribution should be in accordance with a business plan with which it is likely to achieve the desired benefits. The social and development contribution from the IFIs should not have an adverse effect due to improper planning or a mistake in implementation. Further, the socio-development contributions should be from legitimate tools and channels and not mixed with invalid tools. It is not permissible by shariah to adopt illegal mechanisms to achieve social or other benefits. According to Islamic legal maxims, the end does not justify the means, and warding off evil takes precedence over achieving benefits. Achieving a legitimate provision requires that it should not conflict with the shariah and its principles (Al-Ghazali, 1992; Al-Buti, 1982; Ibn 'Ashur, 1946).

3 Methods and Tools Perceived for IFIs to Address Their Social Development Responsibilities

After explaining the basic legal conditions that the IFIs must observe to make an effective developmental contribution, we mention below some of the tools and channels envisaged to achieve this contribution according to the means available to the IFIs. This discussion can be formulated in three points:

Selection of the Financed Sector

In this regard, IFIs should facilitate the conditions for granting finance to start-ups and small and medium-sized enterprises (SMEs), with sound financial tools like investment contracts, without giving preference to giant corporations, given the prevalence of credit risk considerations in them over others. It should also be keen on selecting real development projects when deciding on investment and financing, especially those with sustainable development contributions, and differentiate between them by considering the optimum development and production impact. IFIs should also be keen on investing in the economies of poor Muslim countries rather than the economically powerful countries or be keen on investing in a way that serves the interests of these countries. Furthermore, they should cease or limit the financing of luxury goods and services, such as extravagant weddings and luxury cars. They should instead focus on commodity finance that is productive and, at the same time, work and spend on educating customers and developing consumer awareness about abstaining from financing goods that are deemed as luxury and extravagant. On the same line, IFIs should minimize the use of financial products that tend to harm individuals and put them in debt, such as credit cards and personal finance, especially consumer personal finance.

Adopting the Appropriate Internal Policies

In this regard, it is envisaged that the following four policies should be adopted:

1. Fairness in imposing fees, compensations, and fines on clients. In many cases, these fees, exorbitant compensations, and fines burden the customers. This would result in them preferring and supporting those conventional institutions that may not consider any developmental or social aspects in their work.
2. The real risks in financing contracts by selling, leasing, or diminishing *mushārakah* should be borne by IFIs, because assigning these risks to the client instead of the institution is an injustice that will overtax him leading him to possible losses.
3. The IFIs should refrain from attempting to find means to guarantee their capital and the expected return from the financiers through *mushārakah, mudhārabah,* and *wakālah* contracts. Among these fraudulent methods, for instance, is to take a pledge from those financiers to purchase investment assets with amounts that guarantee the IFIs of their desired returns, or when the sukuk manager or issuer issues an undertaking to purchase the *sukuk* assets at their nominal value, which involves the prohibited guarantee of the capital (Abozaid, 2010). Such behavior harms the financiers and results in similar adverse effects of usury because the financing of these institutions will not differ in substance and form from the traditional usurious financing in this case.
4. Employing the IFIs' zakat fund to support disadvantaged needy groups of the society. Additionally, if the IFIs have impure returns[5] to be cleansed, they should use them appropriately to support the needy.

Type of Products

IFIs must be genuinely distinguished from the products and practices of traditional financial institutions in their substance and not just in forms. Islam's prohibition of *riba, gharar,* and similar contracts was due to its catastrophic adverse economic and social effects, not merely due to the formalities of contracts that lead to *riba* and *gharar*. Hence, the real prevention from *riba* and *gharar* contracts lie at the core of the commitment of IFIs to the social mission.

Islamic economists, scholars, and shariah auditors have raised questions about the practices of a few such IFIs where they have found procedures that are fundamentally indifferent to usury, gambling, and gharar

---

[5] Impure returns are the profits that the shariah Board of an institution requires it to set aside due to the occurrence of some shariah violations in its transactions.

contracts. If this claim is found true, it implies that the IFIs' developmental and social message is in jeopardy because they would bear the same economic and social harms as usury and gambling. The type of products that call for caution is as follows.

Contracts That Involve Riba

Among the financing contracts that are in practice by some IFIs that call for scrutiny due to their resemblance to usury, are the following contracts:

Cash Financing Contracts for Individuals and Institutions, Like Tawarruq, 'Inah and Organized Salam

It is well-known that financing through the *'Inah* contract is commonly practiced in South-East Asia, and financing through *the Tawarruq* contract is popular in Arab countries.[6]

As for the organized *salam* financing that has recently appeared, its procedure is that the bank employee asks the customer requesting cash financing to sign a sale contract with the bank, which says that the customer sells the bank a commodity with specific specifications mentioned in the contract by using *salam*. In other words, the dealer (i.e., the bank) is not required to deliver the commodity immediately. Rather its delivery is delayed to a specific date mentioned in the contract. In return, the dealer receives its price immediately, which is lower than the market price for that commodity. Once this contract is signed, the bank deposits the price of the commodity in the customer's account, which

---

[6] As mentioned earlier, 'Inah is to sell something on credit and then buy it with cash, for the purpose of justifying offering a loan with an excess. Tawarruq differs from it in that the bank sells what it bought on credit to a third party but usually through the first seller. None of the scholar of Fiqh said that Inah is allowed, although some jurists such as Imam Al-Shafi'i have spoken about the validity of such a contract considering that the Inah contract fulfills the obvious conditions of sale. According to Imam Shafi'i, he would regard a contract to be valid considering their appearance, but he does not say that it is permissible. He says, "Judgments are based on that which is apparent, and Allah is the Guardian of the unseen. He who judges people by means of intuition, has committed an act that is prohibited from Allah and His messenger (peace be upon him). It is only God who takes account of reward and punishment for the unseen, because only He knows it. Unlike Him, the humans should judge from what is evident. If anyone were to take the inwardly as evidence, that would had been for His messenger (peace be upon him)" (Al-Shafi'i 1973). This is also seconded by Ghazali who was a Shafi'i scholar, as he said that to regard something as valid does not imply that it is permitted (Al-Ghazali 1992).

was his actual financing requirement. To complete the process, the customer will authorize the bank to purchase that commodity they had just sold to the bank at the market price. Then an agreement is placed that the supplier will deliver this commodity directly to the bank based on the first *salam* contract between the customer and the bank. The bank, on behalf of the customer, pays the price of that commodity—which is more than the first price—in the *salam* contract, so the customer owes the bank more than the amount he had deposited in his account earlier. Then, after the bank receives the commodity, in its capacity as the buyer in the previous *salam* contract on behalf of the customer, it immediately sells it at the market price for its own account, profiting from a difference between the purchase price and the selling price. Such a finance product, using the *salam* contract, ends with the same result as financing using '*Inah* and *Tawarruq*. These cash financing contracts do not really differ from interest-based financing contracts except in the formalities, terms, and techniques used. The International Islamic Fiqh Academy (2009) has issued a resolution (No. 179- 5/19) prohibiting *Tawarruq*, whereas the prohibition of '*Inah* is well-established among all the Islamic jurists (Abozaid, 2008).

Considering the economic effects on society, these contracts create a financial obligation (debt) on the customer toward the IFI for a transaction in which the bank provided cash lesser than the amount that the customer is obligated to pay to the bank. This economic effect of the process is identical to the effect of the usurious loan, which is the obligation of the customer to pay an amount that is more than the amount he obtained from the bank. Studies have proven that these usurious loans negatively affect societies. The proponents of the interest-based capitalist economy have also recognized the adverse economic impact on societies, and this is further attested by the global financial crisis. Dr. Mabid al-Jarhi, a pioneer contemporary scholar of Islamic economics, said:

> If tawarruq becomes commonly practiced, and the exchange of cash-in-hand for deferred cash also becomes prevalent, the economy would return to a cash market where the cash at present will have an additional value in exchange for future cash. This is 'interest' even if it is labeled otherwise. Thus, cash will have a price that will drive people to economize on its usage and replace the real productive resources with money that does not generate any wealth. This weakens economic efficiency, and the society will lose what real resources can produce. (Al-Jarhi, 2007)

Just as usurious loans are used to refinance or reschedule previous usurious debts with an increase in them when the customer fails to pay those debts, the same cash financing contracts are also used in some IFIs to pay off bad debts that may have arisen from previous cash financing contracts. Undoubtedly, refinancing or rescheduling the debt using the traditional usurious method or cash financing through *Tawarruq*, *'Inah*, or organized *salam* will result in an increased amount of the previous debt that the dealer had to pay. This is precisely the form of *riba al-jāhiliyyah* (the pre-Islamic method of usury) that shariah prohibits.

In this regard, according to Dr. Anas al-Zarqa, the most important wisdom behind the prohibition of real non-commodity financing (i.e., financing in which the commodity is not actually intended by the buyer or the seller, as is the case in cash financing from *'Inah*, *Tawarruq*, or organized *salam*), is to prevent the means to annulling an existing debt for a new (rescheduled) debt. In the Islamic legal context, jurists term this as *faskh al-dayn bil-dayn*, meaning annulling a debt with a debt, and this is *riba al-jāhiliyya*. He said:

> Linking financing to only genuinely needed commodities prevents from using the fictitious sale to pay off previous debt, which used to happen in the pre-Islamic riba. Unlike institutional murābahah or all other forms of financing, tawarruq and 'inah facilitate borrowing to pay off previous debts. (Zarqa, n.d.)

In contrast to cash financing, which depends on sale contracts for its own justification, real commodity financing (through real *murābahah*, e.g.) is completely different. Real commodity financing is an actual economic activity that revives the economy because of the fact that there is an actual exchange of goods occurring in reality, and not merely on forms between suppliers or manufacturers and consumers. This economic activity motivates producers and factories to increase production by actual sale of their goods, and the Islamic bank is then a mediator between the producer and the real consumer.

Financing Using Questionable Forms of Ijarah Muntahia Bittamleek Product

Its process is that the IFI enters into an agreement with the customer to buy a property from him or a common share of a property and then leases back that property or that portion of it to the same customer as a lease ending with ownership without that institution actually bearing the consequences of owning the leased property during the rental period. So the same asset returns to the customer for an amount higher than the first price for which he had sold to the financial institution. This, in other words, is called '*Inah*.

Such a form of *Ijārah Muntahiya Bittamleek* carries characteristics of *Inah*, and hence characteristics of usurious debt in it, in various aspects:

First: The financing institution does not actually bear the consequences of the leased property. The institution that had previously purchased the leased property from the customer, levies all the expenses of the leased property on the customer itself, such as the insurance cost and basic maintenance expenses. This is done by dividing the rent into three sections:

1. A fixed fee: The total of this fee represents the cost of purchasing the leased asset from the customer.
2. A variable rent: This represents the profit of the lessor institution in addition to the cost of purchasing the leased asset from the customer. Practically, this is the prevailing interest rate in the market when the rent is due.
3. An additional fee: This represents emergency expenses, such as basic maintenance expenses. The lessor institution imposes these expenses on the customer (lessee) by adding these expenses to the rent amount for the rental period following the period in which those expenses were incurred.

The lessee hence must bear the additional expenses which should actually be borne by the lessor himself because the property is in his ownership, and this proves that the lease is unreal and superficial. Even if the leased asset is damaged or destroyed, the insurance company is the one who pays the value of that leased asset. However, the insurance premiums are paid by the lessee, as if the guarantor of the damage and destruction of the leased asset is the lessee himself.

Second: Sometimes, in such a lease-ending-with-ownership financing method, the owner does not actually sell to the customer, as is the case in the issuance of lease-to-own-ownership *sukuk* that occurs on the purchase of government property whose ownership is not transferred by the government to private companies or individuals, such as seaports, airports, and all basic public utilities. It is legally required for the lessor to own what he is renting. However, the fact that such a lease is on assets that the Islamic bank or financial institution cannot actually own indicates that the process is not an actual sale and lease. Instead, it is interest-bearing financing that is disguised as a legitimate contract (Abozaid, 2010).

Third: The asset's purchase price agreed to be leased to the owner is usually linked to the amount required to be financed and not to the asset's market value. If this were to be a real sale contract, the price would have been equivalent to the market value of that asset. However, since it was linked to the financing amount, it clearly indicated the fictitious process and the will to replace the usurious loan in the form of selling and then leasing.

The three aforementioned matters demonstrate that this form of the lease ending with ownership is not different from the '*Inah* sale, which is interest-based.

It is argued that the ownership of the leased asset is returned to the first seller through a gift at the end of the process or through selling it to him at a symbolic price that is much less than the first price, and hence it differs from *Inah*. This argument is, however, rebuffed because a contract is judged regarding its permissibility or prohibition based on the essence of the contract and not merely on the literal meaning of its clauses or the formalities. Furthermore, if this were acceptable, then the pronunciation of embracing Islam would be accepted by a hypocrite, and the consent on adultery by fulfilling the formalities of a marriage contract would have made it acceptable. Hence, the form of the contract here is that the seller received money by his sale of a commodity that he owned in reality and then later paid more than what he received to the same person based on a prior agreement. This, in essence, is '*Inah* whereby the sale asset remains with the seller in reality with the obligation to charge profit from the other party for the amount he paid.

Though *Ijarah Muntahia Bittamleek* is permitted legally as the Islamic Fiqh Academy has also pronounced (Resolution no.110), its application, in a way, leads to '*Inah*—where the lessee is the first owner without levying any responsibility on the owner for the consequences of the leased asset—should be deemed illegal due to its similarity to characteristics of a usurious loan.

Contracts That Involve Gambling
As for the contracts that are practiced by some IFIs and differ from gambling neither in its form nor in their effects on individuals and societies are as follows:

Uncontrolled Trading of Stocks in the Stock Markets and Securities Exchange
Recently, many people have met with misfortunes due to their dealings in the securities and stock markets or investing in encrypted digital currencies. This has resulted in a terrible disturbance in the economic and social conditions of a large segment of society and has left people destitute and indebted after being rich and prosperous. Some of this took place in financial markets that were characterized as Islamic, but the real shariah legal controls for the activities of those markets were absent. The legal violations in these markets can be summarized as follows:

1. Listing the shares of companies that deal in usury and prohibitions based on weak and distorted legal derivations. For example, it is regarded permissible to include the shares of companies that have usurious activities or other prohibited activities if the percentage of those activities is below a certain percentage of the total activities of the institution (20—30%). They bring evidence from juristic reports and phrases indicating that the transaction is not prohibited if it is mixed with forbidden activity in case the permissible portion is predominant. In fact, however, these transmitted reports are actually limited to cases where the permissible is mixed with the forbidden unintentionally, in addition to cases where it is not possible to specify and distinguish what is forbidden according to the jurists cite examples of such applications (Al-Kasani, 1982; Al-Suyuti, 1982). These reports cite specific cases where, for instance, the meat of an animal that is not slaughtered according to the shariah method, is mixed with many other portions of meat that have been slaughtered as per the shariah method, and the mixing of the unclean with the pure in a way that cannot be separated. However, in our discussion here, the company's forbidden activity is known, distinct, and the mixing of forbidden activities and portions is intended. Moreover, the company can and has the option to shun it whenever they want.

2. Adopting weak jurisprudential justifications and *Talfīq*[7] to justify the trading of some of these shares, such as short selling and margin trading, which are in fact, gambling sales that lead to similar consequences as that of gambling.
3. The absence of supervision and necessary restrictions that necessitate the imposition of shariah principles and texts on the movement of trading in these shares, considering the consequences of this exchange from the occurrence of destructive speculations, where a small group of traders is controlling the movements of the market (upward and downward fluctuations)—resulting in the market dealers losing or going bankrupt due to these behaviors.

Dealing in International Commodity Markets and Forex Using Future Contracts

Some IFIs have violated the prohibition of forward dealings in foreign exchange and the prohibition of dealing in international commodity markets via future contracts. They justified their actions by restructuring the contracts in a different format. Either by mutual promises and bilateral binding agreements between the two parties on the execution of exchange or sale on a specified future date and at a price that is agreed in advance or by using fictitious sale contracts (like *Tawarruq*) that achieve their goal of creating a commitment between them to exchange currencies or to buy and sell specific commodities on a specific future date and at a specific price. This act of mutually promising on a contract to avoid shariah prohibitions is regarded as impermissible by International Islamic Fiqh Academy (OIC Fiqh Academy resolution no. 157 (6/17). In addition, some IFIs used swap operations of non-fixed returns for fixed returns via the same methods, such as the *wa'ad* structure product by Deutsche bank, which was issued as an Islamic product and approved by a group of shariah advisors (Delorenzo, 2008).

Most of these dealings are actually undertaken for speculative purposes and not for the genuine purpose of hedging against the sharp price fluctuation risks in the future. The effects of those practices are similar to

---

[7] 'Talfiq' is a legal term describing the merging of the opinions of several schools of thought into one conclusive issue which is often dissimilar to all. It is a mere patchwork rather than a proper integration of juristic opinions.

gambling, such as enriching some at the expense of others, instability in currency rates, and the loss of economic functions of money.

These are examples of some suspicious contracts practiced by some IFIs that, as shown, are not really different from usury and gambling. Hence, the IFIs should abstain from such contracts that resemble them in their practices and products. This is because IFIs, if they practice such contracts, would be drifted away from their shariah principles and objectives and become impotent to any positive development or social role. Regardless of the impermissibility, these conventional institutions might make some positive social contributions. Yet, their impact, no matter how great, will not conceal the adverse impact of those contracts that are contaminated with usury and gambling. Accordingly, in order to rise and carry out some of the desired development and social mission, IFIs must abstain from these products.

4 Basic Administrative Requirements for Islamic Financial Institutions to Carry Out Their Development and Social Responsibility

It is impractical to expect IFIs to carry out some of their social responsibility that were mentioned above as perceived methods and tools unless these institutions fulfill the following conditions at the administrative level:

1. The owners of these institutions have a determination and desire for effective social contribution. IFIs cannot assume any developmental and social responsibility if this approach is opposed and rejected by the owners and shareholders of these institutions.
2. The executive management of the institution also believes in the development and social mission of IFIs, respects shariah, and is keen to implement and adhere to it.
3. The higher management of the institution is keen on improving the selection of the institution's fatwa committee mechanism and process. The selection should be based on the criteria of efficiency, integrity, and piety, not based on leniency and convenience. This is because the fatwa committee is the one who decides the practices for the institution that may either violate or achieve the social responsibility of IFIs. If the fatwa committee believes only in the

interests specific to its employer (the institution) and is known for its leniency, then it will most probably fail to observe any social consideration in its work. In fact, ensuring the integrity of fatwa and their real contribution to achieving commitment to social responsibility requires a more drastic approach in a manner that would sever the direct material link between the institution and its appointed fatwa board so that the issued fatwas are not polluted with personal and material interests of their issuers.
4. Proper selection of internal shariah auditors because they are the ones entrusted with the task of monitoring the correct implementation of the decisions of the fatwa board that are supposed to help achieve this social responsibility. In fact, their choice is dependent on the institution's fatwa board, as it is only a good and honest fatwa board that will be keen on selecting competent and trusted internal legal auditors.
5. Lifting restrictions that are placed by the supervisory and regulatory authorities on some of the perceived social contributions of IFIs. Such as restrictions that may be imposed on the participation of these institutions in real investment projects, in which there is no guarantee of capital or returns, or restrictions that may be imposed by some governments on the charitable and philanthropic activities of these institutions.

5 Conclusion and Recommendations

The contribution of Islamic financial institutions to achieving economic and sustainable development (with an environmental and social dimension) is accompanied by committing to several conditions and adopting a set of methods and tools dictated by the current conditions of the Islamic financial institutions and banking industry. This research records that the management of Islamic financial institutions (IFIs) must consider the best interests of the owners of these institutions and their shareholders. The social contribution of IFIs should not be at the expense of any unlawful harm to the interests of the owners.

IFIs should be willing to direct their finances and investments in the most feasible and socially beneficial options and avoid financing or investments that have a negative impact on the economy and society. IFIs should not exaggerate credit risk considerations when financing or investing in economically and socially viable projects in order to encourage and support these projects.

The study recommends that the IFIs should follow equitable internal policies that do not contradict the desired social message of these institutions, including their commitment to justice in imposing fees, profits, and fines on clients. They should also actually bear and share the consequences of financing and investment activities, its risks, and guarantees.

IFIs should adhere to the proper management and employment of zakat funds by directing it to its true beneficiaries and spending it on social concerns that are beneficial and most rewarding while also working to maintain and increase the resources of these funds. It is necessary that the IFIs purify themselves from suspicious and illegitimate products and replace these products with legitimate ones with real productive impacts on the economy. This is because financing products that are in line with shariah, in essence, is inherently developmental and socially beneficial, and financing products that contradict the spirit and purposes of shariah is economically and socially harmful—even if it takes an Islamic form. Any social contribution by institutions that practice suspicious products will not be effective until these products are revoked and abolished.

In order to protect Islamic financial institutions from suspicious products that have an economic and social impact, the chapter recommends the need to work on preparing a higher legal advisory board consisting of trustworthy, professional, and independent scholars that are assisted by trusted economists, to classify Islamic financial products in terms of their contents, effects, and outcomes, in order to dispose of conventional products that have leaked into these institutions under Islamic labels.

Furthermore, the chapter proposes forming a supervisory body that will set a governance framework for the activities of fatwa boards in financial institutions. The formation of such a body can be undertaken by the central bank. This will help disband the link of personal interests between the fatwa board and the institutions in which it issues fatwas, by supervising the appointment of the shariah board and should be independent in terminating their service. This supervisory body shall pay the salaries of the members of the fatwa committee from the amounts deposited by the institutions.

It should be legally required for the IFIs not to diverge from the decisions and fatwas of *Fiqh* councils. On the other hand, the restrictions imposed by the higher supervisory authorities on Islamic financial institutions should be lifted, which may prevent or restrict the effective development and social contribution of these institutions.

The chapter concludes that if Islamic financial institutions benefit in attracting clients and making profits from branding with the label of Islam, then fairness requires that they serve Islam in return by contributing something to the development of its economy and addressing its social causes.

REFERENCES

Abozaid, A. (2004). *Fiqh al-Riba*. Al-Risala Publishers.
Abozaid, A. (2008). Inah sale and its contemporary practices in Islamic banks. *Journal of Al-Tamaddun*, 3(1), 238–268.
Abozaid, A. (2010). Towards genuine Islamic sukuk. *Contemporary Islamic Thought Journal*, 16(62), 109–142.
Al-Buti, M. S. (1982). *Dhawabit al-Maslaha fi al-Sharia al-Islamiya* (4th ed.). Mu'assasat al-Risala.
Al-Dasuqi, M. (n.d). Hashiyat Al-Dasuqi. Dar Ihya al-Kutub al-Arabiyah.
Al-Ghazali, M. (1992). *Al-Mustasfa* (1st ed.). Dar al-Kutub al-Ilmiyah.
Al-Jarhi, M. (2007). Organized Tawarruq. MPRA Paper 67810. Retrieved from https://mpra.ub.uni-muenchen.de/67810/1/MPRA_paper_67810.pdf (accessed 12 May 2022).
Al-Kasani, A. (1982). *Badaa' Al-Sana'i* (2nd ed.). Dar Al-Kitab Al-Arabi.
Al-Shafi'i, M. (1973). *Al-Umm* (2nd ed.). Dar al-Maarifah.
Al-Suyuti, J. (1982). *Al-ashbah wa al-Nazair* (1st ed.). Dar al-Kutub al-Ilmiyah.
Delorenzo, Y. T. (2008). The total returns swap and the "Shari'ah conversion technology" stratagem. In C. Beard (Ed.) conventional? The relationship between Islamic finance and the financial mainstream. (pp. 11–26). Arab Financial Forum. Retrieved from https://docslib.org/doc/8959149/the-relationship-between-islamic-finance-and-the-financial-mainstream-edited-by-charles-beard (accessed 12 May 2022).
Ibn Ashur, M. (1946). *Maqasid al-Sharia* (1st ed.). Maktaba al-Istiqamah.
Qudamah, I. (1983). *Al-Mughni* (1st ed.). Dar al-Fikr.
International Islamic Fiqh Academy Resolution No. 30, session during the 4th conference of Organization of Islamic Cooperation held at Jeddah, pp. 6–11. February 1988.
International Islamic Fiqh Academy Resolution no. 110, session no. 12 held in Riyadh, pp. 23–28. September 2000.
International Islamic Fiqh Academy Resolution No. 157 (6/17), session no. 17 convened in Amman, pp. 24–28. June 2006.

International Islamic Fiqh Academy Resolution No. 179 (5/19) session no. 19 held in Sharjah, pp. 26–30. April 2009.

Zuhayli, W. (2005). Al-Fiqh al-Islami wa Adillatuhu, Damascus: Dar al-Fikr al-Muasir.

Zarqa, A. (undated). Tawarruq, (unpublished research in Arabic).

Maqasid al-Shariah and Sustainable Development Goals Convergence: An Assessment of Global Best Practices

Noor Suhaida Kasri, Said Bouheraoua and Silmi Mohamed Radzi

1 Introduction

The gravity of COVID-19 on the global economy has shifted global leaders' conversation toward a more sustainable economy and social-impact-based financing and investment. Since then, meeting the United Nation's Sustainable Development Goals (SDG) is becoming the favorite mantra of today's governments. Therefore, a global call for the financial

N. S. Kasri (✉) · S. Bouheraoua
ISRA Research Management Centre, INCEIF University, Kuala Lumpur, Malaysia
e-mail: noor-isra@inceif.org

S. Mohamed Radzi
International Shariah Research Academy (ISRA), Kuala Lumpur, Malaysia

© The Author(s), under exclusive license to Springer Nature Switzerland AG 2023
Z. H. Jumat et al. (eds.), *Islamic Finance, FinTech, and the Road to Sustainability*, Palgrave CIBFR Studies in Islamic Finance, https://doi.org/10.1007/978-3-031-13302-2_4

sector to revisit the existing debt-based financial landscape and consider real-economy-based financing and investment as an alternative is becoming more pressing.

This global plea does not perturb Islamic finance. The real economy, equity, fairness, inclusion, and sustainability are concepts and notions intrinsically aligned with the nature of Shariah (Islamic law) and *maqasid al-shariah* (the higher objectives of Shariah). Moreover, they underline the preservation of the public interest and the prevention of harm, such as exhorting financial and economic dealings to be implemented without transgressing the notion of preservation of religion, life, intellect, progeny, and wealth. However, there is still a need for the Islamic finance industry to further reinforce or internalize the implementation of these fundamental principles into their existing activities.

The introduction of the United Nation's SDG and the adoption of the SDG constituents by Western countries and conventional finance sparked considerable deliberations and debates among the Islamic finance industry players and Shariah scholars. The industry debates revolved around the motions on the need for the SDG in Islamic finance *vis-à-vis maqasid al-shariah* and its impact on the industry's direction when departing from *maqasid al-shariah* considerations to SDG implementation.

This chapter argues that SDG and *maqasid al-shariah* uphold similar notions. They essentially embed humanity, responsibility, accountability, and sustainability into daily human activities that cascade to a better life, community, and planet. To sustain this proposition, this study adopts a qualitative research approach. Using six case studies as analysis, it attempts to expound that convergence between SDG and *maqasid al-shariah* has contributed to formulating and developing a more human-centered and sustainable future through the establishments' economic activities and practices.

The selection of these case studies is due to the diverse *Waqf* (Islamic endowment) integrated business and investment models that they showcase. Importantly, these institutions' contemporary viable business investment models have proven to generate commendable economic growth and positive impacts on their respective nations. In this respect, three of the six case studies describe the best practices of institutions like Singapore-based Warees Investment Pte Ltd, Saudi-based Alinma Investment Company, and Indonesia-based PT Ethis Indo Asia. The last three case studies showcase the latest Sukuk issuances that enable the sovereign issuers to finance their COVID-19 economic measures, namely the Islamic Development Bank's Sustainable Sukuk, Malaysia's Sukuk Prihatin, and Indonesia's Cash Waqf-link Sukuk.

The examination of these case studies is timely as the global economy is searching for exemplary business and investment strategies, approaches, best practices, and social-impact models to address the COVID-19 pandemic adversity. There is no one-size-fits-all solution because each economy has its own set of preferences, needs, and ecosystem. However, these case studies exhibit practical lessons and perhaps could be the genesis of their search for the appropriate real-economy-based financing and investment models for their nation.

This chapter is divided into six sections. Section 1 introduces the scope and perspective of the study. While Sect. 2 elaborates on the fundamental basis and implementation context of *maqasid al-shariah*, Sect. 3 establishes the convergence of *maqasid al-shariah* with SDG. Section 4 is the backbone of this study, in which six case studies are deliberated from the angles of their establishments, best practices, business and investment strategies, and social impact. This section is further divided into Part 1 and Part 2. Part 1 caters to case studies that describe the institutions' best practices, and Part 2 reflects the case studies of the recent COVID-19 Sukuk issuances. Section 5 recommends key takeaways based on the analysis and lessons learned from these case studies. Finally, Sect. 6 concludes the chapter.

2 *Maqasid al-Shariah*—Fundamental Basis and Implementation

Maqasid al-shariah is founded on promoting human well-being and interests and safeguarding them from harm. Al-Ghazali (1937, pp. 139–140), in illustrating this principle, said:

> The very objective of Shariah is to promote the well-being of the people, which lies in safeguarding their faith (dīn), their lives (nafs), their intellect ('aql), their posterity/lineage (nasl), and their wealth (māl). Whatever ensures the safeguarding of these five serves the public interest and is desirable, and whatever hurts them is against the public interest and its removal is desirable.

Contemporary Shariah scholars expanded on this principle by emphasizing that *maqasid al-shariah* entails a comprehensive approach to elevating humanity to the highest rank. It implores them to be upright, spreading virtue, establishing public interest, fighting the promotion of harm, and ensuring a balanced relationship between the self, the community, and the universe in which they live. Allal al-Fassi (d. 1974) presented this modern approach in an elegant and well-structured statement when he defined *maqasid al-shariah* by saying:

> The overall objective of Islamic Law is to populate and civilize the earth and preserve the order of peaceful coexistence therein; to ensure the earth's ongoing well-being and usefulness through the piety of those who have been placed there as God's vicegerents; to ensure that people conduct themselves justly, with moral probity and with integrity in thought and action; and that they reform that which needs reform on earth; and that they derive its resources and plan for the good of all. (al-Fassi, 1993, pp. 45–46)

The *maqasid al-shariah* holistic approach encompasses four main characteristics. First, *maqasid al-shariah* is the basis of legislation, and as legislation, it has to serve the interests of all human beings (*jalb al-maṣaliḥ*) and save them from harm (*daf' al-mafasid*). Second, *maqasid al-shariah* is universal and aims to serve the interests of mankind regardless of their religious affiliation. A verse in surah *al-Anbia* where Allah Almighty says, "Now [as for you, O Muḥammad,] We have not sent you except to mankind at large" (34:28) clearly illustrates such characteristic. Third, *maqasid al-shariah* is inclusive (absolute) and it encompasses all human acts, whether they are related to *'ibadah* (responsibilities to God) or *mu'amalah* (responsibilities toward other human beings). Imam al-Shafi'i (d. 820) stated in his al-Risalah that:

> No misfortune will ever descend upon any of the followers of God's religion for which there is no guidance in the book of God to indicate the right way, for God, Blessed and Most High, said: "And we sent down to you the Book as a clarification for everything" [16:89] (al-Shafi'i, 2003, p. 66).

Fourth, *maqasid al-shariah* is definitive, and it has not been derived from one text or evidence but from a multiplicity of texts and different aspects of evidence. Similar characteristics can be found in usūlī maxims such as: "acts are judged by intentions," which is an example of a legal maxim that is derived from several verses of the Quran and records of hadith.

With regard to the categories of *maqasid al-shariah*, Shariah scholars divided the general objectives into three sub-categories: the necessities (*darūriyyah*), the complementary (*hājiyyah*), and the embellishments (*tahsīniyyah*). The necessities are the core focus of the scholars' discussions and are deemed by Shariah as absolute requirements for the survival and spiritual well-being of individuals, to the extent that their destruction or collapse would create chaos and affect the normal order in society. The essentials comprise of five elements:

1. The protection of religion (*dīn*), which refers to Islamic embodiments of teachings, ritual acts (*'ibādāt*), ethics (*akhlāq*), and dealings (mu'amalāt).
2. The protection of life (nafs), which safeguards human beings regardless of their religion, race, or social status.
3. The protection of intellect ('aql), which refers to establishing legislation, rules, and guidelines to help the human intellect to function in a proper way and protecting it from any harmful consumption or deviated beliefs.
4. The protection of lineage (*nasl*), which refers to the continuity of human life through the process of healthy reproduction.
5. Finally, the protection of wealth (*māl*), which refers to the establishment of rules for economic activities that enable sustainable economic development and prevent harmful wealth utilization such as environmental and social destruction.

Two main points can be further highlighted in the discussion of the five necessities of *maqasid al-shariah*. Firstly, Shariah scholars emphasized that the objectives of Shariah, including the five necessities, can be applied interchangeably in many cases. This means that one Shariah objective can be simultaneously related to other objectives. For example, life preservation emphasizes that the preservation of the environment has been legislated to preserve life, and the preservation of human beings requires that their intellects and bodies be preserved, since there is no meaning to the preservation of life if the intellect is not preserved. Secondly, the means (*al-wasā'il*) to *maqasid al-shariah* are given the same ruling as the objectives, which is based on two important Islamic legal maxims. The first legal maxim is the well-known Islamic legal maxim "*al-wasā'il lahā aḥkām al-maqāṣid*," which translates as "means take the ruling of their objectives." Therefore, the means to lawful ends are lawful, and the means to unlawful ends are unlawful. Similarly, the means to protect religion, life, intellect, lineage, and wealth have the same rulings of protecting these necessities. The second Islamic legal maxim that supports this principle is the maxim that says: "*mā lā yatim al-wāǧib ilā bihi fahūwa wāǧib*," which means "without which an obligatory command cannot be accomplished, it also becomes obligatory." These two legal maxims give the same legal consideration and importance to the means that are crucial for the achievement of their objectives.

The above brief introduction on the fundamentals and implementation of *maqasid al-shariah* sets the stage for the deliberation on the key question of its convergence with the SDG. On that account, the following section examines SDG constitutes in general and addresses pertinent contemporary questions pertaining to the convergence between maqasid al-shariah and SDG.

3 The SDG and Maqasid al-Shariah: A Clash or Convergence?

There is an ongoing discussion among Shariah scholars on the fundamentals of SDG. Questions arose on its basis in Islamic law and *maqasid al-shariah* and on the need to promote SDG. Though SDG, in general, is deemed not to contradict *maqasid al-shariah*, it lacks the epistemological framework that goes beyond the worldly manifestation of acts that transcend *maqasid al-shariah*. To address these questions, this section briefly examines the 17 SDG constituents in light of Islamic law and *maqasid al-shariah*.

In the assessment of the 17 goals, it is found that Goal 1 (No Poverty), Goal 2 (Zero Hunger), and Goal 3 (Good Health and Well-being) fall under the preservation of life, which is the second of the five necessities of *maqasid al-shariah*. This is because poverty, hunger, and disease are direct causes of death, and the same is documented by credible studies from the United Nations. According to the United Nations' 2008 report, 25,000 people, including more than 10,000 children, die of hunger every day (UN, 2018); and according to their 2018 report, 821 million people worldwide suffer from hunger (Holmes, 2008).

Goal 4 (Quality Education) is directly related to the third maqasid al-shariah, which is the preservation of the intellect ('aql). The preservation of intellect is concerned with the rules that help the human intellect function in a proper way. While quality education is fundamental to sound reasoning and critical thinking, intellect is the first requisite for undertaking any activity in Islam. The first verse revealed to Prophet Muhammad (peace be upon him), which says: "*Read, O Prophet, in the Name of your Lord Who created; [He] created humans from a clot (of congealed blood),*" (Quran, 96:1—2) reflects the importance of a sound intellect.

Goal 6 (Clean Water and Sanitation), Goal 7 (Affordable and Clean Energy), Goal 13 (Climate Action), Goal 14 (Life Below Water), Goal 15 (Life on Land) and Goal 12 (Responsible Consumption and Production) represent the core means (*wasā'il*) to preserve life, intellect and lineage. This is because these goals are fundamental to the human physical body, mental health, and the continuation of the human species. The World Health Organisation (WHO), for instance, stated in its 2016 report that air pollution kills an estimated seven million people worldwide every year and that nine out of 10 people breathe air containing high levels of pollutants (World Health Organisation, 2016). The adverse impact of air pollution on mental health is also mentioned in the said report. With regard to water resources, it is reported that nearly 1 million people die every year from water-related diseases and more than 785 million people lack even basic drinking water service (Water.org, 2020). These goals are also closely related to the preservation of intellect, as air and water pollution are among the causes of mental health problems that can lead to depression. The preservation of wealth is also manifested in the abovementioned goals, as air, water, life on earth and underwater, and balanced consumption and production are related to the preservation of wealth.

The same approach applies to Goal 8 (Decent Work and Economic Growth), Goal 9 (Industry, Innovation, and Infrastructure), and Goal 11 (Sustainable Cities and Communities), as they represent means to the preservation of wealth. Preservation of wealth is the fifth necessity of *maqasid al-shariah*, and therefore, affects positively the quality of life and human intellect.

While Goal 16 (Peace, Justice, and Strong Institutions) is the *raison d'être* for Muslims, as Islam is derived from the word *"salām,"* which means peace. As for justice, the word is mentioned 29 times in the Quran. The importance of the concept of justice propelled some scholars such as Ibn Taymiyyah (d. 1328) and Ibn Ashour (d. 1973) to propose it as an additional necessity under *maqasid al-shariah* so as to make it the sixth necessity. Nonetheless, this proposition is rejected by some scholars who argue that justice is a religious value and constitutes part of the fundamentals of Islamic belief (*'aqīdah*), and hence, higher than the five necessities.

Goal 10 (Reduced Inequality) confirms that it is impossible to eliminate inequality as humans differ in ambition and performance due to external factors. However, from the Shariah perspective, human beings are created by Allah in the best stature, as the Quran states: "*We have certainly created man in the best of stature*" (Quran, 95:4). Nonetheless, governments should strive to reduce inequality by incorporating value-based intermediation initiatives to drive and facilitate financial inclusion in society.

Goal 5 (Gender Equality) is considered acceptable by Shariah in its general terms, despite this particular goal being controversial among Shariah scholars. It is worth noting that this goal cannot be applied in its absolute sense, even in the Western liberal environment. There is a need to establish parameters to avoid any abuse of its application in the Islamic sphere. In some recent discussions, some scholars have viewed this goal as contravening Shariah principles, given that the Quran and the prophetic traditions differentiate men and women in their certain rights, duties, and responsibilities. For instance, some notable figures have advocated for equality between men and women in inheritance under the pretext of justice and equality, which may not conform to Shariah rulings in their absolute terms. It is well established that Islam ordained men and women to be equal in all rights and responsibilities, except when the apparent literal equality prevents both from performing the duty of vicegerency (*istikhlāf*). This view is supported by the verse of the Quran that says: "*Verily the most honored of you in the sight of Allah is (he who is) the most righteous of you*" (Quran, 49:13) and the hadith of the Prophet (peace be upon him) that says: "*Yes, for women are the twin halves of men*" (Jami' at-Tirmidhi, 1:113). As for the example on inheritance distribution in Islam, the portion differences are not based on gender consideration, nor does it negate the concept of equality. The difference in the inheritance portion distribution, which is wrongly perceived as discrimination even though in many instances where women receive equal or more quantum than men, is ordained to achieve the higher Shariah objective of maintaining a strong family tie and relationship. The same objective is echoed when the man, in a few instances, is given a greater portion than the woman as a significant responsibility for men to support his mother, wife, daughter, and sister, considering that a strong family is the backbone of a united society.

Goal 17 (Partnerships to achieve the Goal) responds to the natural human need for collaboration, solidarity, and togetherness, which is crucial to the success of any of the above 17 Goals. In short, the brief analysis of the 17 SDG constituents shows that they are generally in line with *maqasid al-shariah* and generally serve the same purpose. However, it has essential religious-based motivation elements which are absent in the SDG. These elements are activated by an inner natural consciousness, which reduces the need for external monitoring and control. The importance of religious motivation in achieving *maqasid al-shariah* is succinctly explained by Al-Shatibi (d. 1388) where he said:

> The primary goal of the Shariah is to free man from the grip of his own whims, so that he may be the servant ('abd) of Allah by choice, just as he is His servant ('abd) in matters about which he has no choice. (al-Shatibi, 1975, p. 768)

4 Convergence Between *Maqasid al-Shariah* and Sustainable Development Goals

The above deliberation on *maqasid al-shariah* and SDG clearly demonstrates that, in general, there is a convergence between *maqasid al-shariah* and SDG. This proposition sets the basis for this section to continue elucidating that the convergence between the SDG and the *maqasid al-shariah* has contributed to formulating and developing a more human-centered and sustainable future through the following six case studies. These case studies are further divided into two parts. Part 1 showcases three institutions' best practices, including their investment and business strategies and the resulting social impact. The selected institutions are Singapore-based Warees Investment Pte Ltd, Saudi-based

Alinma Investment Company, and Indonesia-based PT Ethis Indo Asia. Part 2 depicts Sukuk issued by the Islamic Development Bank, the Government of Malaysia, and the Government of Indonesia, which issuances have financed their respective COVID-19 economic measures.

Institutional Best Practices

The COVID-19 pandemic has triggered the interest of advanced and emerging economies globally in searching for the appropriate formula for sustainable economic development. In this regard, these economies can tap on the existing best practices as demonstrated by the following case studies, which utilize Islamic social finance tools, particularly *Waqf*, in their business and investment models.

Singapore's Warees Investments Pte Ltd

Supervision and Establishment
Singapore-based Warees Investments Pte Ltd (Warees)[1] was incorporated in 2001 and became fully operational in 2002. It was incorporated as a Baitulmal company and a wholly owned subsidiary of the Islamic Religious Council of Singapore[2] (MUIS). Prior to its 'privatization,' Warees was a property development department under MUIS. Being MUIS's property arm, Warees expertise lies in real estate property development, especially in endowment[3] investment management (Osman, 2018).

The establishment of Warees by MUIS is part of the public and private institutions' strategy to accelerate the development of Waqf (Islamic endowment) in Singapore (Osman, 2018). Under the Singapore Administration of Muslim Law Act (AMLA), all *Waqf* are vested and registered with MUIS. MUIS administers all *Waqf*, whether *Waqf*

---

[1] Warees is an acronym for 'WAkafREalEState.' In the Malay language, 'waris' means 'heritage' and 'beneficiary' where both terms have a close connection with the management of trust properties. This naturally matches with the mandate shouldered by Warees to develop prime commercial and residential properties and conserve the culture and heritage, especially endowments and institutional real estate portfolio and several subsidiaries (Warees, 2020a, 2020b).

[2] MUIS is under the Ministry of Culture, Community, and Youth which focuses on socio-religious functions, governance, and policymaking.

[3] The term 'endowment', which connotes Islamic endowment or *Waqf* is used interchangeably with the term 'waqf/wakaf/wakf' throughout this study.

'am (general endowment) or *Waqf Khas* (special endowment), and is empowered to appoint and remove *mutawalli* (Islamic Religious Council of Singapore, 2020). Through Warees, MUIS is set to meet the following *Waqf* objectives (Islamic Religious Council of Singapore, 2020):

1. creating new *Waqf* for new financing needs of the Muslim community;
2. continue developing all *Waqf* properties in its portfolio;
3. ensuring the growth and diversification of Waqf assets;
4. maximizing the potential of *Waqf* assets;
5. efficiently and effectively managing *waqf* fund;
6. establishing *Waqf* as model formula for charitable spending; and
7. channeling proceeds toward community development.

Since its privatization, Warees has transformed many unproductive Awqaf lands and properties into productive and tenable commercial and residential areas. In fact, the boom in Singapore's real estate market in the past decade has helped boost the value of its real estate based-Waqf assets, especially when they are strategically located in prime districts like the Central Business District. The soaring property prices offer higher rental returns and higher opportunity costs if the *Waqf* assets are left undeveloped (Osman, 2018).

Investment and Business Operation
The game changer in the revitalization effort of the *Waqf* assets in Singapore is the pronouncement of the ground-breaking fatwa (Shariah resolution) by MUIS's Fatwa Committee in 1988. The fatwa authorized the implementation of *istibdāl* (asset migration). This fatwa allows the selling of low-performing *Waqf* assets or assets that are prone to an acquisition or located at a non-strategic location in return for purchasing higher-value assets (Osman, 2018).

Following the issuance of the said fatwa, Warees undertook several *Waqf* development initiatives. Nonetheless, this case study focuses on the initiatives undertaken from 2012 onward. The reason for choosing 2012 onward is because, in 2012, MUIS developed and issued Waqf Revitalisation Scheme (WRS), a rolling three-year blueprint. This blueprint guides MUIS in identifying high potential endowment assets that need enhancement and redevelopment, in tandem with the local real estate market and urban development standard, to generate better economic returns to the community beneficiaries (Islamic Religious Council of Singapore, 2020).

Steered by this blueprint, Warees entered joint development with the trustees and/or guardians of *Waqf* assets as an investor and/or developer. Being the premier and reputable specialist in endowment investment management, Warees provides professional expertise in planning the *Waqf* investment to optimize the potential of the *Waqf* assets fully. The service it offers includes managing the project's development, from creative planning for feasibility studies, conceptualization, real estate investment analysis, strategic engagement with stakeholders, and marketing communications (Islamic Religious Council of Singapore, 2020).

The following are the three milestone projects worthy of mentioning in this case study:

- **The Red House**
  The Red House development is the first project under WRS. Six properties (five shophouses and an iconic Red House bequeathed to Wakaf Sheriffa Zain Alsharoff Alsagoff) along the East Coast Road were redeveloped into an integrated heritage development. The massive redevelopment saw the assets enhanced into 42 residential units, five retail shophouses, a bakery, and an open gallery. The residential units comprise four lofts, ten suites, and 28 residences ranging from 441 sq ft to 1206 sq ft. The cost per sq ft is about SGD 1,500 (USD 1129)[4] of which the cost of the smallest unit is around SGD 661,500 (USD 498,117) (Lin, 2015). The enhancement of these *Waqf* assets has generated better returns for the *Waqf* beneficiary, which is to establish, maintain and upkeep a dispensary (Islamic Religious Council of Singapura, 2020).
- **Alias Villas**
  The Alias Villas development also went through a similar rigor of redevelopment, which transformed two dilapidated village houses on a portion of the land belonging to Wakaf Al-Huda into a prestigious semi-detached strata cluster housing development. The six semi-detached strata landed units, located along Jalan Haji Alias off Sixth Avenue, range from 3000 to 3670 sq ft. at SGD 1500 (USD 1129) per sq ft. (Jo, 2015). The enhancement of

---

[4] The exchange rate is based on Singapore's Monetary Authority of Singapore's rate on 29 December 2020, namely USD1 = SGD1.328 (Monetary Authority of Singapore, 2020).

this *Waqf* property helped maximize the income, which returns are channeled to the *Waqf's* sole beneficiary, Masjid Al-Huda (Islamic Religious Council of Singapore, 2020).

- **Institutional Investments Initiative (3I)**
  As part of the WRS initiatives, Warees initiated the Institutional Investments Initiative (3I). 3I is an innovative Waqf development financing scheme that allows benefits to flow to community institutions while unlocking the potential of *Waqf*. The added value of 3I is that capital is guaranteed throughout the 2-year investment tenure. Unsurprisingly, 3I garnered the support of five mosques in Singapore. These mosques injected their reserves totaling SGD 5 million (USD 3,765,060), of which each mosque contributed SGD 1 million (USD 753,012) into the Red House development project. 3I allows funds to be channeled into two options. Either financing the Red House development (instead of using external sources such as banks) or ownership of residential units, where funds are used to hold several units for a 99-year lease. Six months after signing and disbursing their funds, each of these mosques received their first *hibah* (gift) payout of SGD 5250 (USD 3804), equivalent to 1.05% of their investment value. Another 1.05%, making it up to 2.1%, annually is projected to be paid in the following six months (Warees, 2014).[5]

As part of its best practices and in accordance with AMLA, Warees reports its activities and finances to MUIS on an annual basis within the stipulated time. However, it is observed that Warees annual report is not on its website, and it is assumed that its annual report is integrated with MUIS's Annual Report. The assumption is based on the statement in the MUIS Annual Report that stipulates the financial statement reported by MUIS includes *Waqf* funds that are not directly managed by MUIS (Islamic Religious Council of Singapore, 2019). Besides complying with the legal requirement for reporting, Warees regularly updates the public on its latest news, asset development launches, and other relevant key market trends on its website (Warees, 2020a, 2020b).

---

[5] The said return is higher than the fixed deposit returns of around 1% per annum for a deposit period of 24 months during that period, in 2014.

Social Impact

The income generated from the *Waqf* assets' revitalization has increased the amount distributed to the *Waqf* beneficiaries. It was reported that out of the total *Waqf* assets in Singapore valued at SGD 750 million (USD 564,759,036), Warees manages SGD 370 million (USD 278,614,458) worth of Waqf assets, equivalent to 64 *Waqf* properties and 60 *Waqf* accounts. Under its management, these assets generated a gross income of SGD 7.8 million (USD 5,873,493) at a gross yield of 2.1% (Osman, 2018).

The high income made from the assets of *Waqf* allowed MUIS to distribute more to the community beneficiaries. For example, in 2019, MUIS distributed more than SGD 4 million (USD 3,012.048) to various beneficiaries, locally and abroad. Out of that total amount distributed, about SGD 1.8 million (USD 1,355,421) was channeled to 32 mosques in Singapore to fund their upgrading projects and community programs. In addition to that, six full-time madrasahs and part-time mosque madrasahs received more than SGD 400,000 (USD 301,204). It is important to note that madrasahs in Singapore play an essential role in nurturing future religious leaders of the community. These funds assisted the madrasahs in developing programs and upgrading their facilities to a more conducive learning environment (Masood, 2019).

Apart from the mosques and madrasahs, MUIS disbursed more than SGD 380,000 (USD 286,144) to 30 Muslim and Voluntary Welfare Organizations to help support social initiatives and religious programs for the community. These include welfare homes that shelter individuals facing adverse family or personal circumstances, food banks that provide food supplies and rations to the poor and needy, and youth-focused and welfare organizations that provide services to those who struggle with mental illness, women facing injustice, and cancer patients (Masood, 2019).

In short, Warees demonstrates an exemplary model of convergence between SDG and *maqasid al-shariah*, where protection of life and wealth is fostered through the effective and strategic collaboration between public and private institutions. Warees's expertise in property development and specialization in endowment investment management have unlocked the value of *Waqf* assets, accelerating the growth of real estate Waqf assets and resulting in better returns to the community. Likewise, MUIS's effective supervision ensures that values for the community and its social beneficiaries are sustained and safeguarded, thereby rooting out the trust deficit in the community.

Saudi's Alinma Investment Company

Supervision and Establishment

Alinma Investment Company (Alinma) was established in 2009 in Saudi Arabia as a joint-stock company. It is wholly owned by Alinma Bank and is deemed as the Bank's investment arm. Alinma is regulated and supervised by Saudi's Capital Market Authority (CMA) and Public Authority for Endowment. Alinma took the spotlight in 2018 when it launched an open-ended public Alinma Wareef Endowment Fund, the first endowment investment fund in the Kingdom of Saudi (Arab News, 2018).

The establishment of Alinma's endowment fund is a result of the developments that occurred on the *Waqf* authoritative body in Saudi Arabia. In 2015, Saudi Arabia set up the General Authority for Awqaf with the following responsibilities (General Authority of Awqaf, 2020):

1. to organize, maintain and develop endowments in a manner that achieves the requirements of the *Waqf*, and
2. to enhance the role of *Waqf* in economic, social development, and social solidarity in accordance with the purposes of Shariah and regulations.

In line with the above national development mandate and agenda, Alinma's parent bank, Alinma Bank, spearheaded the re-activation of the endowment sector. In fact, Alinma Bank has been at the forefront of supporting and facilitating endowment developments in Saudi Arabia. For example, in 2017, Alinma Bank launched a new unit dedicated specifically to the needs of endowments within Saudi Arabia. Staffed by top experts in the field, the unit aims to understand and respond to the unique service requirements of endowment, a key critical sector in the economy of Saudi Arabia (Alinma Bank, 2020).

Investment, Business Operation, and Social Impact

To support Saudi's Vision 2030, Alinma developed private endowment funds that are open for individuals' and corporations' participation. Vision 2030 promotes endowments as a sustainable source of financing. It encourages leading companies to play a leading role in fostering social responsibility and to help expand the scope of the non-profit sector. The launch of Alinma's organized and regulated endowment mutual funds has assisted the non-profit sector in contributing more effectively to key economic sectors, for example, health, education, housing, research, social programs, and cultural activities (Abraham, 2020).

Since the inauguration of the Alinma Wareef Endowment Fund in 2018, Alinma has launched four other open-ended public endowment funds, namely Alinma Orphan Care Endowment Fund, Alinma Enayah Endowment Fund, Alinma Endowment Fund for Mosque, and Bir Al-Riyadh Endowment Fund. To grow and sustain these funds and meet their goals, Alinma invests the funds in the money market, real estate, and securities (Alinma Investment, 2020). This includes investing in REITs, Sukuk, murābahah contracts, and traditional investments. A portion of the return on these investments is distributed annually on a continuous basis through specific *Waqf* channels (Al-Naggar, 2019). Alinma's Shariah council of scholars ensures that all these investment activities are in adherence to the Shariah principles and rules.

The endowment funds mentioned earlier are illustrated in more detail in Table 1 which describes the funds' establishment, aim, purpose, social impact, and beneficiaries of the respective endowment funds.

Based on the Quarterly Disclosure published by Alinma on its website, these funds seem to perform well, particularly in the third and fourth quarters of 2019, prior to the spread of the COVID-19 pandemic. Though the global economy was affected by COVID-19 in 2020, these funds still displayed some re-bounced in the third quarter of 2020, particularly for Alinma Wareef, Alinma Orphans, and Alinma Enayah Funds. Despite the efforts to develop and grow *Waqf* assets, some have criticized the small scale of the investments made by these funds, considering Saudi Arabia is a high-income country, and charity and *Waqf* are deemed common activities in that jurisdiction (Al-Naggar, 2019).

As part of its best practice and in line with the CMA requirement, Alinma regularly discloses material information and the progress of these funds by reporting them on its websites and disclosing information pertaining to the fund's performance, asset class distribution, and equity sector allocation. The documents uploaded on its website also include information about the *Waqf* beneficiaries, quarterly disclosure, interim and annual reports, and interim and annual financial reports. This information and the listing of Alinma Wareef Fund on Saudi's stock exchange (Tadawul) help in creating awareness among the public, especially potential local investors who are inclined toward social-impact investment.

In short, Alinma is yet another outstanding case study of convergence between *maqasid al-shariah* and SDG, where preservation of life and wealth are created through the deployment of professionally managed endowment-based investment funds with robust governance and

Table 1 Alinma Endowment Funds launched since November 2018 till November 2020

Alinma's Endowment Funds	Establishment	Aims/purpose	Social impact/beneficiaries
Alinma Wareef Endowment Fund (a public open-ended endowment fund)	1 November 2018	The Fund aims at: (1) enhancing the developmental role of private endowments by participating in supporting health care (2) investing the fund for the purpose of achieving social solidarity thus benefiting the endowment disbursement channels and the endowed asset	The Fund's beneficiary: King Faisal Specialist Hospital Foundation and Wareef Charity Wareef Charity commits to meet the following objectives: (1) supporting and providing specialized medical care (2) supporting scientific and applied research related to the medical and health (3) supporting cultural and scientific activities that contribute to raising awareness of healthy living (4) Supporting the cultural and scientific activities that contribute to raising the level of awareness of health culture (5) supporting disease prevention programs (6) helping needy patients and families
Alinma Orphan Care Endowment Fund (a public open-ended endowment fund)	21 July 2019	The Fund aims at (1) enhancing the developmental role of private endowments by participating in supporting orphan care (2) investing the fund for the purpose of achieving social solidarity thus benefiting the endowment disbursement channels and the endowed asset	The Fund beneficiary: Ekhaa Charity (charitable foundation for orphanage) Ekhaa Charity commits to meet the following objectives: (1) achieving social and living stability for orphans (2) improving the psychological and social health of orphans (3) financial and social independence of orphans (4) developing the capabilities of Ekhaa's financial sustainability and excellence in institutional capital

(continued)

Table 1 (continued)

Alinma's Endowment Funds	Establishment	Aims/purpose	Social impact/beneficiaries
Alinma Endowment Fund for Mosques (an open-ended endowment mutual fund)	1 September 2019	The Fund aims at: (1) strengthening and enhancing the developmental role of private endowments by participating in supporting the care of road mosques in line with the principle of social solidarity (2) benefiting both beneficiary and the endowment asset	The Fund beneficiary: The Association for the Care of Road Mosque The Association for the Care of Road Mosques is committed in meeting the following objectives: (1) elevating the level of service and sustainability of road mosques (2) promoting volunteer work in the association's activities (3) building and activating strategic partnerships (4) infrastructure development (5) achieving financial sustainability
Alinma Enayah Endowment Fund (a public open-ended endowment fund)	15 September 2019	The Fund aims at: (1) enhancing the developmental role of private endowments by participating in supporting health care (2) investing the fund for the purpose of achieving social solidarity thus benefiting the endowment disbursement channels and the endowed asset	The Fund beneficiary: Enayah Charity (charitable health society for patients care) Enayah Charity is committed to meet the following objectives: (1) free medical service in government or private treatment institutions as well as in treatment camps and mobile clinics (2) nursing service for chronically ill and disabled patients (3) supply of prosthetic devices or diagnostic supporting aids (4) service of providing unavailable drug or available, but the price is expensive and needed by the patient for a long duration (5) health awareness and education, epidemiology, training and rehabilitation of cadres, seminars and conferences (6) preventive service and vaccinations

(continued)

Table 1 (continued)

Alinma's Endowment Funds	Establishment	Aims/purpose	Social impact/beneficiaries
Bir Al-Riyadh Endowment Fund (an open-ended endowment mutual fund)	9 September 2020	The Fund aims at: (1) helping the beneficiary in strengthening the development role of private endowments in supporting families in need through the capitalization and investment of the endowment assets while conserving the principle of social solidarity for the benefit of the beneficiary and the endowed asset	The Fund beneficiary: Al Bir Charitable Society in Riyadh. Al Bir Charitable Society in Riyadh is committed to meet the following objectives: (1) caring for families in need, (2) seeking to alleviate their suffering by providing them food, clothing, furniture, household appliances, and financial assistance (3) address the well-off individuals and raise their awareness to help fulfill the needs of the poor (4) collecting zakat, charities, expiations and others, and distributing them to the people in need (5) contribute with private and governmental bodies to help people affected by public disasters (6) establish seasonal charitable projects (school kits, feeding the fasting, Zakat al-Fitr, Eid clothing, winter clothing, and benefiting from sacrifice and continuous supply of charitable items)

Source Adapted from Alinma Investment (2020) and Arab News (2018) transparency policies. The sound regulation and supervision by the relevant authorities ensure that values for the community and its social beneficiaries are continuously served and secured. Royal encouragement and patronage given to all the endowment initiatives, in the case of Alinma, ensure that these initiatives meet the social impact as expected in Saudi's Vision 2030.

Indonesia's PT Ethis Indo Asia

Supervision and Establishment

PT Ethis Indo Asia (Ethis[6]) was established in 2015 as a fully licensed entity for real estate development, construction, and agency services in Indonesia (Ethis, 2018). Ethis is the Indonesian arm of Singapore-based Ethis Group, specializing in Islamic property crowdfunding, that matches investment opportunities to its members via its Ethis Crowd platform, i.e., EthisCrowd.com (Ethis Crowd, 2017). This platform is renowned for being the world's first real estate Islamic crowdfunding platform and one of the world's first investment Islamic crowdfunding platforms (Ethis, 2017).

The massive Indonesian population, the boom in its real estate market, the stable and fast-growing domestic-driven economy, and its huge emerging middle class led to the setting up of Ethis in Indonesia. Using its expertise in crowdfunding, Ethis focused on developing affordable housing for the poor in Indonesia as well as *Waqf* development (ClubEthis, 2021). The fundraising for affordable housing projects have positioned Ethis as the leading Islamic crowdfunding platform globally.

In fact, Ethis's decision to focus on social housing development projects was in line with the "One Million Houses Program" launched by the government of Indonesia in 2015 (Government Social Housing Program). Through this program, the government aims at providing adequate housing facilities with the target to build 700,000 houses for low-income families and 300,000 for higher-income families (Indonesia Investments, 2017).

---

[6] The word "Ethis" is a fusion of "Ethical" and "Islamic". Ethis strives to operate with the highest levels of ethics and transparency, based on the universal principles of Islam.

Investment and Business Operation

Since setting its footprint in Indonesia, Ethis's crowdfunding platform has attracted 21,000 members from 59 countries. The funds raised were channeled to affordable housing, commercial housing, and infrastructure projects. The funds raised from its members have helped fund the building of more than 9,000 houses in Indonesia. By doing so, Ethis has assisted in the implementation of the Government Social Housing Program, which aims to solve the massive shortage of affordable housing (Ethis, 2020a, 2020b, 2020c, 2020d).

In executing its investment projects in Indonesia and as part of its best practice, Ethis took steps and measures to safeguard the interests of its members (investors) and the safety of funds invested. In addition to that, Ethis ensures that the relationship with the relevant local stakeholders is appropriately managed to ensure the smooth implementation and completion of the project (Ethis, 2017). The following highlights Ethis's latest affordable housing development projects, illustrating Ethis's project management from the angles of funds' usage, project selections, and project modus operandi.

The Essential—Daru 3 (Daru 3)

Daru 3 is a premium, affordable, and subsidized housing project located in the strategic location of Daru, Tangerang, one of the fastest-growing areas in Banten. This project is developed by collaborating with two reputable property developers (PT Sentosa Membangun Bangsa (SMB) and PT Individwa Refah Kreaasi), which both form PT Esensi Prima Cipta. The funds raised by Ethis for this project are used to fund the third tranche of the development, covering the land acquisition, licensing, and working capital for the land and construction work.

Daru 3 is part of the Government Social Housing Program, which aims to provide 283 families with houses that they will fully own at the end of the project. As an incentive, project developers are given easier and faster permit approvals, whereas banks are given subsidies and targets to provide low-income families with home financing for the houses bought under this program. As in any typical home financing, upon successful completion and sale of the housing units, property developers will receive the full payment from the bank, from which payment the investors will then be paid out.

To protect the interest of Ethis investors, several mechanisms were put in place in the structure of Daru 3 project, namely:

1. The construction of this project is being taken up by a reputable project developer in Indonesia. Ethis places its sister company, SMB, as one of the developers for this project. Being a co-developer, its responsibilities include development work related to licensing, land maturation, construction, sales, and project financial management. It also ensures that the work of all the stakeholders is in accordance with the development standards and requirements. The good coordination between SMB and the contractors and sales partners has assured the project's completion.
2. The investment of this project is backed by assets, which in turn protect the investors' principal.
3. SMB and the developer signed a Musharakah Joint Operations agreement, in which the developer agreed to share profits with SMB at a rate of 14% to 86%.
4. SMB holds the power of attorney over the acquired land. The said power of attorney empowers SMB to liquidate the land in the event the developer breaches any of the contractual terms.
5. SMB also holds the land certificate on behalf of Ethis investors and will release it to its co-developer once all the housing units have been sold to end-buyers and Ethis investors are paid back.
6. A captive market of 1,000 ready buyers from Tanah Abang traders has been identified together with their executed intent of purchase letter. The overwhelming interest is due to the strategic location of the project and its modern home concept development.
7. Each unit is sold at IDR 285,000,000 (USD 20,114). With the sale of the first 283 units, investors will exit the project.

The above safeguards have assisted the crowdfunding campaign for Daru 3, which has raised almost 29% more than its targeted amount of SGD 300,000 (USD 225,903).[7] Daru 3 project also offers an attractive return for investment where Ethis investors can expect to get higher return rate than the market, reaching 19% to 20% in 18-month time (Ethis, 2020a, 2020b).

---

[7] The exchange rate is based on Bank Indonesia's rate on 29 December 2020, namely USD1 = IDR14,169 (Bank Indonesia, 2020a).

Hasanah City

Hasanah City is an affordable housing project located in Parung Panjang, one of the fastest-growing areas in Bogor. It is also part of the Government Social Housing Program, which aims to provide 156 families with accommodation that they will fully own at the end of the project. This project is developed by a reputable property developer in Indonesia, PT Hasanah Karya Abadi. The funds raised by Ethis for this project are used to finance the construction of 20 units out of 156 units.

In the Hasanah City project, Ethis investors are protected and secured through several embedded mechanisms, namely:

1. The project is constructed by a reputable project developer which owned the land and equipment. This ensures the project is completed efficiently.
2. The investment is backed by assets worth 150% above the crowdfunding amount which in turn protects the investors' principal.
3. SMB signed a Musyarakah Joint Operations agreement with the developer where the developer agreed to a profit-sharing ratio of 23.97%:76.03%.
4. The developer executed Conditional Sale and Purchase Certificate affecting 30 housing units whereby the ownership of these units was transferred to SMB. SMB will hold these units on behalf of Ethis investors until these units are sold to the end-buyers.
5. Developer's post-dated check covering an amount higher than the total value of the crowdfunded amount is kept by SMB.
6. Personal guarantee given by the developer's director.
7. The developer has secured more than 300 interested buyers. 290 of them have passed the Central Bank's assessment and some have even paid the down payment.
8. Investors will exit from the project after the sale of the 20 units of houses. The targeted price for each unit is set to be at minimum IDR 379,000,000 (USD 26,748). There is no price cap for the selling price as to allow the price to increase based on the market demand.

The above safeguards have assisted the crowdfunding campaign for Hasanah City, which has raised almost 9% more than its targeted amount of SGD 304,229 (USD 229,088). Hasanah City project also offers an attractive return for investment where Ethis investors can expect a higher return than the market rate reaching up to 14% in 12-month time (Ethis, 2020c).

As part of its best practice, Ethis published an insightful report in 2018 documenting the success and unsuccessful stories and lessons learned from its journey in funding affordable housing in Indonesia. This is the first report published by Ethis on Indonesian projects since its operation there. In addition to that, Ethis has published a preliminary report on its Social Return on Investment (SROI), which highlights the method of measuring the social impact arising from its affordable housing projects in Indonesia. Likewise, Ethis has published an introduction to Islamic crowdfunding to raise people's awareness of its products and activities.

Social Impact

The success in funding affordable and subsidized housing development projects in Indonesia has led Ethis to develop its own SROI. Ethis's SROI enables it to measure and quantify the social impact of each of its investments on the low-income families in Indonesia.

In measuring the social impact, three forms of measurement have been adopted, namely:

1. A basic financial calculation to measure clear financial changes resulting from individuals moving into affordable housing, such as different disposable income, different expenditures on health care, and the cost of moving.
2. Financial proxies to place a market cost on a change resulting from a move into affordable housing. The financial proxy method has been used in relation to changes in mental stress and feelings of security.
3. Contingent Valuation Method (CVM) to evaluate the social impacts and intangible benefits of affordable housing developments. For example, residents are asked about their willingness to accept financial compensation if they were to give up the benefit they are currently enjoying.

Though no literature can be found reporting on the actual calculation of SROI on Ethis's investment in Indonesia, the SROI measurement aided Ethis in screening projects of more significant social impact in the future (Ethis, n.d.).

All in all, Ethis is yet another exceptional example of convergence between SDG and *maqasid al-shariah*, where protection of life and wealth are fostered through matching profitable investment with social-impact projects. The adoption of advanced technology in its crowdfunding model enabled Ethis to tap new pools of investors and allowed funders to participate in sustainable investments hence unlocking the door for financial and social inclusion. The transparency and disclosures offered by its platform instill trust among its stakeholders—a recipe for success and sustainable investment initiatives.

COVID-19 Sukuk Issuance

The outbreak of the COVID-19 pandemic heralded another watershed for Islamic finance, which saw the expansion of the role of Sukuk as the COVID-19 mitigating financing tool. Several governments leveraged Sukuk as part of their public finance borrowing strategies, especially in response to the COVID-19 disruption (Parker, 2020). FitchRatings estimated that despite the unprecedented stress from the COVID-19 pandemic, the volumes of Sukuk issuance in the full-year 2020 are expected to be around the 2019 level. Sovereign Sukuk is expected to remain the major contributor to overall Sukuk volumes as they face widening fiscal deficits and high borrowing needs caused by COVID-19-related economic disruptions and lower oil prices (FitchRatings, 2020).

The above preludes the following three case studies on Sukuk. These case studies showcase the issuance of three sovereign and multilateral Sukuk, namely the Islamic Development Bank's Sustainable Sukuk, the Government of Malaysia's Sukuk PRIHATIN, and the Government of Indonesia's Cash Waqf-link Sukuk. These Sukuk were issued during the COVID-19 pandemic that aided the respective governments in attending to their deteriorating balance sheets and wider deficits due to the outbreak.

Islamic Development Bank Sustainable Sukuk

The impetus for IsDB Sustainable Sukuk Issuance

The Islamic Development Bank (IsDB) is a multilateral development bank set up in 1975 with the mandate to promote cooperation and foster development in Islamic countries. Its agenda, among others, is to assist its 57 member countries (MCs) in meeting the SDGs by 2030.

Though many of the MCs are still grappling and falling far behind on many dimensions of the SDGs, the IsDB is optimistic and continues to aspire MCs' lives and livelihoods. Many efforts have been made, and the pinnacle of the commitment was manifested in November 2019 with the inauguration of the IsDB's Sustainable Finance Framework (SFF). Under this framework, the IsDB launched its first ever green Sukuk.

The unforeseen global pandemic outbreak in early 2020 has, however, forced the IsDB to re-strategize and re-purpose some of its efforts. The IsDB swiftly introduced the 3R (Respond, Restore, and Restart) program and pledged USD2.3 billion in funding packages under the said program to support the MCs in dealing with the pandemic. To finance this program, the IsDB issued its first sustainability Sukuk under the SFF, making it the second issuance under the framework (IsDB, 2020a).

Issuance of IsDB Sustainable Sukuk

The IsDB Sustainable Sukuk was successfully issued on June 25, 2020, during which the market was recovering from the sharp COVID-19-driven volatility. The issuance of IsDB Sustainable Sukuk marked the first COVID-19-related Sukuk ever issued in the global capital markets and the first sustainability Sukuk ever rated AAA by Standard & Poor's, Fitch Ratings, and Moody's (IsDB, 2020a). The Sukuk raised USD 1.5 billion and, offered a profit rate of 0.908% per annum, payable on a semi-annual basis over a period of 5 years. The Sukuk was listed on Nasdaq Dubai, Bursa Malaysia (Exempt Regime), and Euronext Dublin and targeted investors mainly from the Middle East and North Africa (MENA) countries, Asia, and Europe (IsDB, 2020b).

The issuance of IsDB Sustainable Sukuk was made under its USD 25 billion trust certificate issuance program, which technically operates based on the following structure (Fig. 1):

Generally, as seen in Fig. 1 and elaborated in the program base prospectus (IsDB, 2019a), the proceeds raised through the Sukuk subscription will be used by IDB Trust Services Limited as the issuer cum trustee to purchase a portfolio of assets from the IsDB. This portfolio (which shall be separate and independent from all other assets of the IsDB) shall mainly comprise:

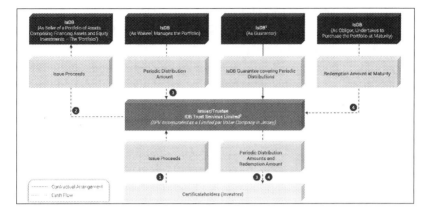

Fig. 1 Structure of IsDB Sustainable Sukuk. *Source* IsDB (2020c)

- at least 33% of tangible assets that comprised of leased assets, disbursing istisna' assets, Shariah-compliant shares, Sukuk, and/or restricted *mudhārabah* assets; and
- no more than 67% of intangible assets that comprised of istisna' receivables, loan receivables, and/or murabaha receivables.

The IsDB itself is then appointed by the trustee, as the *wakeel*, to manage the portfolio. The profit received from the portfolio will be paid to the investors as the Periodic Distributions. Interestingly, these periodic distributions and all payment obligations are guaranteed by the IsDB. In case the amount of profit generated by the IsDB exceeds the periodic distribution amount payable, the IsDB may retain the excess as an incentive fee for its performance. At maturity or upon an option call, the trustee will sell the outstanding portfolio, and the IsDB is obliged to purchase it at the exercise price, which equals the face amount plus accrued but unpaid periodic distribution amounts owing to investors. The exercise price received by the trustee then will be used to pay the dissolution amount due to the investors.

Besides IsDB's strong credit and financial position, the Sukuk garnered overwhelming investors' interest which signified the support of the investors toward the purpose of its issuance—to tackle the aftermath of the COVID-19 pandemic (IsDB, 2020b). Proceeds from the Sukuk

Table 2 Eligibility criteria for projects funded by IsDB Sustainable Sukuk

Project Category	Eligibility Criteria
Employment generation / SME financing	Providing and increasing access to finance for micro SMEs, SMEs, and providing jobs for youth or underprivileged individuals in MCs.
Access to essential services	Expanding access to free/subsidized healthcare, education and training facilities.

Source IsDB (2019b)

were allocated by the IsDB to finance eligible projects recognized under two (out of five) categories of the SFF's Social Projects Categories, namely "Employment Generation" and "Access to Essential Services." Table 2 shows the targeted sustainability goals under the mentioned Social Projects Categories and their eligible criteria.

On top of that, these potential projects must comply with international and local laws, standards, and regulations related to environmental and social risk management. Not to mention that they are also required to abide by all of IsDB's related policies, including the newly issued Environmental and Social Safeguards (ESS) policy (IsDB 2019b).

IsDB Sustainable Sukuk Socio-Economic Impact

As part of its due diligence, IsDB's SFF required all selected projects to incorporate and execute a monitoring and evaluation plan. Even at the bank's level, all the IsDB Sukuk issuances are required to be reported on an annual basis, and a special task force called the Sustainable Finance Task Force (SFTF) has been assigned to undertake this reporting task. The report employs qualitative and quantitative measurement, which evaluates the usage of the proceeds on the respective eligible projects and their impact. The following are the areas included in the said impact reporting (IsDB, 2019b):

- A qualitative description of the green or social eligible projects.
- The environmental objective of green or social eligible projects.
- A breakdown of the financial items for the green or social eligible projects includes assets, capital expenditures, and operating expenditures.

- IsDB's share of financing.
- Potential key environmental impact indicators.
- Information on the methodology and assumptions used to evaluate the impact of the green or social eligible projects.

This report is required to be reviewed by an external party, and the same is published on IsDB's website for investors and public reference.

Although it is still too early to assess the real impact of the IsDB Sustainable Sukuk, it is worth mentioning the positive impacts of its previous programs on their beneficiaries. For example, in 2019, the IsDB reported that it had built, among other things, 11,000 houses for the poor, irrigated 60,000 hectares of land, helped recover the eyesight of 10,000 people, granted 1200 scholarships, and connected electricity to 240,000 households (IsDB, 2019c). This encouraging track record indicates the strong accountability and transparency of the IsDB in ensuring the effectiveness of its programs.

However, it is noteworthy to mention that a report prepared by the Statistical Economic and Social Research and Training Centre for Islamic Countries (SESRIC) (2019) indicated that with the current pace of progression, the Organisation of Islamic Cooperation (OIC) countries as a group are most unlikely to achieve the targeted SDGs by 2030. For instance, in terms of economic growth, the average annual growth rate of GDP per capita for the OIC countries was only 2.7%, not even reaching half of the minimum 7% targeted per year. Not to mention the estimation that 10% of the total OIC population will be living in extreme poverty in 2030 should there be no substantial effort to curb this situation. On the other hand, the investment gap to realize SDGs in Islamic countries lies between USD 700 billion and USD 1 trillion per year (IsDB, 2019d). This amount will inevitably increase due to the pandemic outbreak. In this respect, the issuance of IsDB Sustainable Sukuk is absolutely appropriate and timely.

From the deliberation above, it is apparent how leveraging SDG could effectively facilitate the realization of *maqasid al-shariah*. The IsDB Sustainable Sukuk demonstrates a viable modern means to preserve life, wealth, and intellect according to the *maqasid al-shariah* and the goals of SDG. Furthermore, IsDB's practices showcase a good blend of the spirit of cooperation (*ta'awun*) and the concept of precision (*itqān*) perceived by Islam that other institutions can learn.

Malaysia's Sukuk PRIHATIN

Impetus for Sukuk PRIHATIN Issuance

COVID-19 was first detected in Malaysia in late January 2020. Since then, COVID-19 cases have grown exponentially, particularly during the third wave of the outbreak. By the end of November 2020, a total of 63,176 COVID-19 cases were reported, with 350 death reported (MRC, 2020). Due to the alarming growth of COVID-19 cases, the Government of Malaysia (GoM) was compelled to implement movement control measures which resulted in a massive economic downturn. To stem the condition, the GoM launched several economic stimulus packages amounting to RM 305 billion (USD 75 billion) to cushion the devastating impact of COVID-19 pandemic. Table 3 outlines the summary of the progressive packages announced by the GoM.

Table 3 GoM Economic Stimulus Packages announced from February till October 2020

Date	Economic Stimulus Packages
27 February 2020	**Economic Stimulus Package 2020 (ESP)** • RM 20 billion (USD4.9 billion) • Strategy: (1) Mitigating impact of COVID-19; (2) Spurring the people-centric economic growth; • and (3) Promoting quality investments
27 March 2020	**Prihatin Rakyat Economic Stimulus Package (PRIHATIN)** • RM 250 billion (USD 61 billion) (including RM 20 billion from previous package) • Welfare, supporting business including SMEs, strengthen the economy
6 April 2020	**Additional Prihatin SME Economic Stimulus Package 2020 (PRIHATIN SME+)** • RM10 billion (USD 2 billion) • Assist SMEs and micro business which include wage subsidy program and grant
5 June 2020	**National Economic Recovery Plan (PENJANA)** • RM 35 billion (USD 8.6 billion) • Provides an array of tax incentives, financial support for businesses, and wage subsidies
23 September 2020	**PRIHATIN Supplementary Initiative Package (KITA PRIHATIN)** • RM 10 billion (USD 2 billion) • Includes cash aids for struggling households, grants for micro businesses, and wage subsidy program
Total	**RM 305 billion (USD 75 billion)**

Source Malaysia Ministry of Finance (2020a), Malaysia Prime Ministry Office (2020a, 2020b, 2020c) and KPMG (2020)

Under the PENJANA package, the government aimed to accomplish three main objectives: (i) to empower the people; (ii) to propel businesses; and (iii) to stimulate the economy. Under the third objective, the issuance of Sukuk PRIHATIN has been proposed as an avenue for all Malaysians to contribute toward the recovery of the nation's economy jointly.

Issuance of Sukuk PRIHATIN
In August 2020, the GoM launched the RM 500 million (USD 123 million) Sukuk PRIHATIN, which is dubbed the country's first digital Sukuk. The retail Sukuk issuance allowed subscription with a minimum investment of RM 500 (USD 123) and no maximum limit. Such minimal subscription amount enables Malaysians, particularly individuals and SMEs, to do their bit to help the country's economic recovery efforts. A distinctive feature is incorporated into the structure of the Sukuk PRIHATIN, which grants the option to Sukuk holders to donate part or all of the subscribed principal amount when the investment period matures.[8] In return for their subscription, Sukukholders were offered a profit rate of 2% per annum to be paid every quarter over a 2-year term. (BERNAMA, 2020a).

The digitalization of the sukuk has made the subscription experience easy and smooth. Public subscribers could easily subscribe to the Sukuk via JomPAY[9] or DuitNow[10] on all the 27 distribution banks' digital (internet/mobile) banking. To boost the Sukuk uptake, Sukuk holders were accorded tax incentives through tax exemption on the profit and tax deduction on any principal amount (partial or full) waived at the maturity date. The following Diagram 2 illustrates the transaction flow of Sukuk PRIHATIN (Fig. 2).

---

[8] September 21, 2022, is the maturity date for the Sukuk PRIHATIN.

[9] JomPAY is Malaysia's national bill payment scheme established and operated by Payments Network Malaysia Sdn Bhd (PayNet), under the auspices of the Central Bank of Malaysia with the participation of banks and large billers. JomPAY establishes an accessible bill payment ecosystem for consumers, banks, and billers, where the customers of 40 banks in Malaysia can pay bills anywhere and anytime (JomPAY, 2020).

[10] DuitNow is also operated by PayNet, which allows consumers to pay instantly to any account or a DuitNow ID such as mobile number or New Registration Identity Card (NRIC) number (PayNet, 2020).

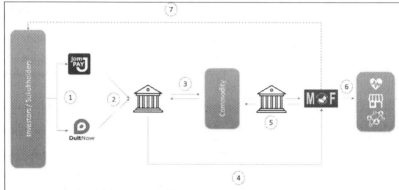

1. Investors subscribe to Sukuk PRIHATIN through Distribution Banks' internet/mobile banking via JomPAY or DuitNow.
2. The Sukukholders appoint Bank Negara Malaysia (BNM) as their agent to act on their behalf for all matters related to the Commodity Murabahah transaction.
3. BNM, on behalf of the sukuk holders, purchases commodity(ies) on spot basis.
4. BNM sells the commodity(ies) to the GoM at a cost-plus mark-up price.
5. BNM, also acting as the agent of the GoM, sells the commodity(ies) at cost price on spot basis and remits the cash to the GoM.
6. The GoM channels the proceed to the COVID-19 Consolidated Fund (Kumpulan Wang COVID-19) to finance measures announced in the economic stimulus packages and recovery plan.
7. Payment of profit will be credited directly into the Sukukholders' account quarterly by the Primary Distribution Bank (Malayan Banking Berhad or "Maybank").

Fig. 2 Sukuk PRIHATIN Transaction Flow. *Source* Adapted from Terms and conditions of Sukuk Prihatin (Malaysia Ministry of Finance, 2020b)

The subscription period for Sukuk PRIHATIN was opened for a month from August 18 to September 17, 2020. By the close of the subscription period, the Sukuk was oversubscribed with a total subscription of RM 666 million (USD 164 million), which surpassed the original target of RM 500 million. Due to the overwhelming response, the government rolled in an additional Sukuk Prihatin of RM 166 million (USD 40 million) to support the government in rebuilding the country after the pandemic (NST Business, 2020).

Sukuk PRIHATIN were subscribed by many Malaysians—individuals, companies, including the King of Malaysia, Al-Sultan Abdullah Ri'ayatuddin Al-Mustafa Billah Shah, who became the first investor for the Sukuk. Nevertheless, significant institutional funds like Employees Provident Fund, Tabung Haji (Hajj Pilgrims Fund Board), Permodalan Nasional Bhd, and even insurance companies are barred from subscribing to the Sukuk (Adilla, 2020).

The over-subscription of Sukuk PRIHATIN was unexpected, given that the country was facing a challenging economic environment. It displayed a strong show of unity, cooperation, and support from the people of Malaysia toward the government's socio-economic recovery plans. This positive spirit aptly epitomized the spirit of the term 'PRIHATIN'—care and empathy—among fellow citizens toward their nation and togetherness in building a stronger country during the COVID-19 pandemic.

Sukuk PRIHATIN Socio-Economic Impact

As mentioned earlier, Sukuk PRIHATIN, part of the PENJANA program, was launched in June 2020. As announced in the economic stimulus packages and recovery plan, the funds raised through Sukuk PRIHATIN will be channeled to initiatives and programs related to, for example (BERNAMA, 2020b, Malaysia Ministry of Finance, 2020c):

- Medical expenditure associated with COVID-19 disease. This will benefit the Ministry of Health and public research institutions as well as institutions of higher learning in their study of infectious diseases or epidemics.
- Financing and grants for micro enterprises This will support the bottom sector of society in reviving their businesses that have been badly affected by the pandemic.
- Enhance connectivity of rural schools, which will also act as hubs to connect nearby villages. This will enable telecommunications networks in rural areas to be modernized to help students' access education through digital channels.

In essence, the Sukuk PRIHATIN initiative meets the three-focus areas outlined in the nation's blueprint, Shared Prosperity Vision (SPV), launched by the government in 2019. These areas focus on restructuring the economy by ensuring development for all, addressing inequality by bridging the income gap, and building the country toward a united, prosperous, and dignified nation (BERNAMA, 2020b).

Though Sukuk PRIHATIN is still at its early stage and its delivery is yet to be known, the overwhelming response garnered by Sukuk PRIHATIN prompted the GoM to consider introducing the second round of Sukuk PRIHATIN in the future. Though the future issuance is mooted not to be as big as the first Sukuk PRIHATIN and may probably come with a 0% profit return (Adilla, 2020).

In short, the successful issuance of Sukuk PRIHATIN demonstrated its capability to be a viable vehicle to achieve the *maqsad* (objective) of *rawāj* (circulation of wealth in the economy), as well as the eighth goal of SDG. Importantly, it illustrates the effective cooperation between the government and the people in driving the government's COVID-19 agenda to ensure that no one would be left behind in the economic recovery efforts.

Indonesia Cash Waqf Linked Sukuk
Impetus for Cash Waqf Linked Sukuk Issuance
Indonesia is known as one of the most active sovereign Sukuk issuers globally. In 2019 alone, Indonesia issued sovereign Sukuk worth USD 18.15 billion, which is equivalent to 21.82% of the total global sovereign Sukuk issued that year (Bank Indonesia, 2020b). In addition, Indonesia's total outstanding sovereign Sukuk in 2019 stands at IDR 740.62 trillion (USD 52.90 billion). In general, these issuances are meant to help the country finance its budget deficit and manage its cash flow (Islamic Financial Services Board [IFSB], 2020).

In the same vein, Indonesia, as a country with the largest Muslim population and a huge-growing middle class, possesses great potential in the *Waqf* sector. *Waqf* land in Indonesia, for example, is reported to reach 51,155.57 hectares and a big chunk of it has yet to be developed as a productive, profit-generating asset (Bank Indonesia, 2020a, 2020b). As part of the government's support for the National Waqf Movement (Gerakan Wakaf National) and to maximize the *Waqf* potential, the Cash Waqf Linked Sukuk program (CWLS) was then issued in the third quarter of 2018.

Issuance of Cash Waqf Linked Sukuk
CWLS is a government social investment program in which the collection of cash *waqf* will be invested in Sukuk or Surat Berharga Syariah Negara (SBSN). CWLS provides an efficient platform for private sectors to join hands with the government in developing public infrastructure and supporting social programs. Although the scheme's primary objective is not explicit in tackling the adverse effects of COVID-19, like IsDB's Sustainability Sukuk and Malaysia's Sukuk PRIHATIN, this model certainly serves as a complementary measure in cushioning the impact of COVID-19.

It was in the midst of the pandemic outbreak that the Indonesian government issued two Sukuk under the CWLS program. The first issuance, known as Sukuk Wakaf 001 (SW001), were issued at a discount, which means that the principal of SW001 paid during the issuance is lower than the principal amount received at maturity (100%). This discount was exempted from tax, and additionally, the Sukuk offered a 5% fixed coupon rate per annum (Badan Wakaf Indonesia [BWI], 2020a). These incentives were given by the Indonesian government to attract investors' interest.

To further accommodate this issuance, the Indonesian Ministry of Finance amended its regulation on private placement issuance.[11] The new regulation namely Peraturan Menteri Keuangan (PMK) No. 139/PMK. 08/2018, reduces the minimum amount of purchase offer from IDR 250 billion (USD 50 million) for normal private placement issuance to IDR 50 billion (USD 3.5 million) for issuance through a private placement with the purpose of meeting socially responsible investment (Indonesia Ministry of Finance, 2018). However, SW001 took approximately two years to barely surpass the aforesaid minimum requirement. It was claimed that a low level of *Waqf* literacy and limited accessibility to the Sukuk were among the factors that led to the lengthy duration of time spent (Farhand, 2020).

Learning from that experience, the second issuance, called Sukuk Wakaf Ritel 001 (SWR001), was offered to the public with a minimum subscription of as low as IDR 1 million (USD 70.67) with no maximum cap. With the intense Sukuk Wakaf literacy program and the promotion of SWR001 throughout the two-month offering period, SWR001 managed to raise a total of IDR 14.91 billion (USD 1 million). However, it is believed that the amount could be higher should the subscription be made available online (Sari, 2020). This is due to Indonesia's high level of internet penetration, particularly during the pandemic outbreak. Table 4 gives a snapshot of both the SW001 and SWR001 issuances.

Five key stakeholders have joined forces to ensure the feasibility of CWLS's issuance. They are Bank of Indonesia (BI) as the accelerator and custodian bank, Badan Wakaf Indonesia (Indonesian Waqf Agency) (BWI) as the leader and *nazir* for CWLS, the Ministry of Finance as the issuer, Islamic banks, namely Bank Mualamat Indonesia, Bank BNI

---

[11] The amended regulation was PMK No. 239/PMK.08/2012 on issuing and selling Sukuk via private Placement.

Table 4 Snapshot of SW001 and SWR001

	SW001	SWR001
Issuer	Ministry of Finance	Ministry of Finance
Originator	Ministry of Finance	Ministry of Finance
Currency format	Indonesia Rupiah	Indonesia Rupiah
Structure	Wakalah	Wakalah
Sukuk rating	N/A	N/A
Underlying asset	1. State-owned properties (Barang Milik Negara (BMN)) 2. Projects under State Budget (Anggaran Pendapatan dan Belanja Negara (APBN))	1. State-owned properties (BMN) 2. Projects under State Budget (APBN)
Purpose	Discount: • Building renovation and medical equipment procurement for Ahmad Wardi Waqf Hospital in Serang, Banten Coupon: • Free cataract surgery for needy people at Ahmad Wardi Waqf Hospital • Ambulance procurement	• To fund social programs and activities that have socio-economic impact
Issuance date	10 March 2020	18 November 2020
Tenure	5 years	2 years
Maturity	10 March 2025	10 November 2022
Amount	IDR 50.85 billion (USD 3.5 million)	IDR 14.91 billion (USD 1 million)
Periodic distribution	Yield: 6.15%, fixed coupon: 5% per annum	Fixed coupon: 5.5% per annum
Listing	N/A	N/A
Tradability	Non-tradable	Non-tradable
Target investors	Institutional investors	Retail investors

Source Indonesia Ministry of Finance (2020a, 2020b)

Syariah, Bank BRI Syariah, and Bank Syariah Mandiri) as the Lembaga Keuangan Syariah Penerima Wakaf Uang (LKS PWU) or the Islamic Financial Institutions collecting cash *Waqf*, and Nazhir Wakaf Produktif (Non-LKS PWU) as BWI's *nāzir* partners to collect cash *Waqf* and manage the proceeds of the Sukuk (BWI, 2020b).

In the CWLS structure, the donor or *Wāqif* will choose whether to give out cash *Waqf* temporarily or perpetually. The former entitles

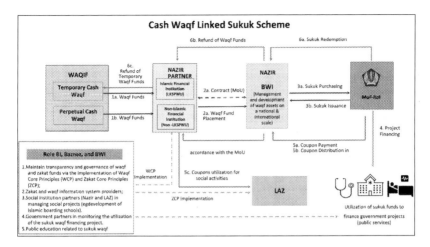

Fig. 3 Cash Waqf Linked Sukuk Transaction Flow. *Source* Adapted from Indonesia Ministry of Finance (2020c)

the *waqif* to earn his principal back upon maturity, while the latter waives his principal for *Waqf* utilization. Cash *Waqf* collected via *nāzir* partners in such LKS PWU and non-LKS PWU will then be given to BWI as *nāzir* to manage the purchase of CWLS from the Ministry of Finance. The Ministry of Finance utilizes the cash *Waqf* to finance the government's social projects, and the return from it will be channeled to BWI, which will then be distributed to *mauquf 'alayh* (*Waqf* beneficiaries) through the *nāzir* partners accordingly (Bank Indonesia, 2020a, 2020b). Figure 3 illustrates the transaction flow of CWLS and the roles of the respective stakeholders.

Cash Waqf Linked Sukuk Socio-Economic Impact

The CWLS model is unique in the sense that it enables development in both commercial and social sectors, killing two birds with one stone. The proceeds from the CWLS issuance are used to finance the government's projects while the return benefits society at large. This multiplier effect of value creation would reduce the government's fiscal burden and promote sustainable economic development.

With regard to SW001, the discount received once at the beginning of issuance is allocated for renovation and provision of medical equipment for the Retina Center at Ahmad Wardi Hospital, a *waqf*-based

Table 5 Type of social projects proposed for SWR001

Health	Education	Farming and Agriculture	MSME	Religion
• Establishment of clinics for Islamic boarding school • Hearing aid assistance • Provide financing for medication • Provide personal protective equipment for medical staff • Indonesia Mobile Clinic	• Scholarship programs for different levels of education • Capital assistance for learning institutions • Improve educators' well-being	• Support for food security programs • Support for hydroponics industry	• Capital injection, training and mentoring program for local MSMEs • Construction of affordable houses with affordable rental price	• Building mosque

Source Indonesia Ministry of Finance (2020d)

hospital managed by BWI and Dompet Dhuafa, while the coupon received monthly is utilized to sponsor cataract surgery at the same hospital. It is estimated that 2513 patients from the poor and needy category will benefit from the project throughout the five-year tenure (Indonesia Ministry of Finance, 2020c). On the other hand, returns from SWR001 are proposed by the *nāzir* partners to finance the following types of social projects (see Table 5).

The management of the social projects is held by six appointed *nazir partners*, namely, Lembaga Amil Zakat Infaq Shodaqoh Nahdlatul Ulama (LAZISNU), Lembaga Amil Zakat Infaq dan Sadaqah Muhammadiyah (LAZISMU), Yayasan Bangun Sejahtera Mitra Umat (Yayasan BSM Umat), Baitul Maal Muamalat, Wakaf Salman ITB, Yayasan Hasanah Titik, and Dompet Dhuafa. These *nazir* partners are entitled to a maximum of 10% of the Sukuk's return to cover their operational costs. Henceforth, they are obliged to provide a progress report to the monitoring parties, namely BWI, Ministry of Religious Affairs, Ministry of Finance, and Bank of Indonesia, including the *Wāqif*. However, there is no clear information on the period and the minimum requirement on the information needed to be reported back by these *nazir* partners.

In short, this model of investment introduced by the Indonesian government could be an active catalyst for sustainable economic development if its potential is fully maximized. The convergence between *maqasid al-shariah* and SDG is glaring, especially on the inclusion of the poor as the CWLS beneficiaries and the focus on health, agriculture, social, and education-based projects. Besides the worldly return that the investors enjoy, CWLS is the avenue where they can enjoy the expected heavenly reward, which is ultimately the end goal of every Muslim.

5 Recommendation

The foregoing mini-case studies have shed light on how the efforts, initiatives and best practices of these institutions have contributed to the development of a more human-centered and sustainable investment in their business approaches and practices. These ethical yet profit-making features are warranted at a time when the world is combating the social and economic adverse impact of the COVID-19 pandemic. Nonetheless, there are a number of key lessons gathered from these case studies that are worthy of consideration for better planning and implementation.

Premised on that, this study, therefore, proposed the following recommendations:

1. **Awareness gap.**
   Ethical-based investment, social-impact investment, *maqasid al-shariah* or *Waqf* for that matter are still nascent concepts to many investors including Shariah-compliant minded investors. Awareness campaigns must be activated on a large-scale basis and these campaigns must reach much bigger audiences. The narration used in these campaigns must be in a consumer-friendly style of narration that caters for every sect of society.
2. **Capacity building.**
   Structuring innovative social-impact products that appeal to Shariah compliance minded investors, other faith-based investors, ethical investors, philanthropists and millennials, and deploying advance technologies requires the right expertise. The scarce number of experts in these fields can be expanded through upscaling and upskilling individuals with experience, interest and passion in these areas. This process may include leveraging on experts from the

conventional side specially those who are Principles for Responsible Investment (PRI) signatories (Malaysia Securities Commission, 2019).
3. **Data gap and unlocking data access.**
Having easy access to accurate, reliable, relevant and current data is vital. The data facilitates ethical ventures in their due diligence process on the viability and the social-impact value of the selected investment projects. Disclosing adequate, updated and quality data on the venture's website would assist investors in making a sound and well-informed investment decision.
4. **Government support.**
To create a viable and conducive environment, the support of the government and regulator is fundamental. A clarity in the national agenda on the strategic approach and milestone in developing human-centered and sustainable investment is critical. The authorities and regulators can also play important role in showcasing the country's ethical ventures during their high-level dialogues, engagements, or meetings with their high-level counterparts. From these engagements and roadshows, they can then coordinate the interested counterparty with these ethical ventures (Malaysia Securities Commission, 2019).
5. **Enabling and conducive environment.**
A conducive regulatory framework enables the healthy growth of ethical business initiatives in the sense that it regulates and governs the initiatives in compliance with the required laws and Shariah. The legal protection given to investors offers certainty and confidence for them to invest. Favorable tax treatment and incentives would help to boost ethical business initiatives especially during the nascent stage of development.
6. **Collaborative and integrated approach among stakeholders.**
A concerted effort by ethical market players is important. Strategic formation of collaborations among the players and the relevant stakeholders help to foster closer interaction, coordination, and support to each other in growing the niche market. Joint initiatives among the players and stakeholders could be an effective platform in promoting their ethical business venture locally and internationally. Eventually, this will attract foreign investment into the country (Malaysia Securities Commission, 2019).

6 Conclusion

This study studied the convergence of the divine-based *maqasid al-shariah* and the human-based goals for sustainability or SDG, and their influence on business and investment strategies, approaches, and practices. Six case studies have been selected and highlighted. Three case studies describe the best practices of institutions like Singapore-based Warees Investment Pte Ltd, Saudi-based Alinma Investment Company, and Indonesia-based PT Ethis Indo Asia. The other three case studies illustrate the latest Sukuk issuances that enable the sovereign issuers to finance COVID-19 economic recovery measures, namely the Islamic Development Bank's Sustainable Sukuk, Malaysia's Sukuk Prihatin, and Indonesia's Cash Waqf-link Sukuk.

This study found that the propositions of *maqasid al-shariah* and SDG are almost symmetrical, except that the former involves divine intervention and reward-based motivation. The six case studies conducted have shown the positive impact of both *maqasid al-shariah* and SDG. Three of the case studies, namely the Singapore-based Warees Investment Pte Ltd, the Saudi-based Alinma Investment Company, and Indonesia's Cash Waqf-link Sukuk, utilized modern financial tools to maximize *Waqf* potential in their respective jurisdictions. They showcased innovative ways of connecting the real economy and social well-being through *Waqf*.

PT Ethis Indo Asia sets an exemplary business model that fulfills the basic needs of human beings by funding the development of affordable houses through its crowdfunding platform. Similarly, the issuance of Sukuk PRIHATIN and IsDB Sustainable Sukuk during this predicament situation is timely and commendable as they aim to preserve the *maslahah* (public interest) of the people without compromising profit and the planet.

The examination of these case studies unearths room for improvement. Recommendations have been suggested, namely, (i) awareness gap, (ii) capacity building, (iii) data gap and unlocking data access, (iv) government support, (v) enabling and conducive environment, and (vi) collaborative and integrated approach among stakeholders. It is hoped that this study will intrigue and encourage many more establishments and investments to embed the propositions of *maqasid al-shariah* and SDG in their decisions and practices. Indeed, COVID-19 has inevitably hampered efforts to achieve the universal development goals by 2030, but the realization of *maqasid al-shariah* by the vicegerent of the *Shari'* (the Law Maker) is a continuous responsibility until the end of worldly life.

REFERENCES

Abraham, S. (2020, January 16). *Alinma Investment: Building sophisticated products for the Saudi investor.* Retrieved from https://internationalfinance.com/alinma-investment-building-sophisticated-products-for-the-saudi-investor/

Adilla, F. (2020, November 9). *Govt may look into Sukuk Prihatin 2.0: Finance Minister.* Retrieved from https://www.nst.com.my/business/2020/11/639462/govt-may-look-sukuk-prihatin-20-finance-minister

Al-Fassi, A. (1993). *Maqasid al-Shariah wa makarimaha* (5th ed.). Dar Al-Gharb Al-Islami.

Al-Ghazali, A. H. M. (1937). *Al-Mustasfa min 'ilm al-usul.* Al-Maktabah al-Tijariyyah.

Alinma Bank. (2017, November 14). *Alinma Bank launches special services for endowments.* Retrieved from https://www.alinma.com/wps/portal/alinma/Alinma/MenuPages/TheBank/News/NewsItem_ar/alinma%20bank%20launches%20special%20services%20for%20endowments/!ut/p/z1/pZBf-b4IwFMW_Sv0AS28VO_ZY1IAiVCRurC9Lxwo2g0KAuWSfftUse9gfXbL7dm9-J-eegwXOsDDyoEs56MbIyu73gj5QHrjgu7C

Alinma Investment. (2020). *Endowment investment funds.* Retrieved from https://www.alinmainvestment.com/wps/portal/investmentNew/AlinmaInvestment/Menu/AssetManagement/EndowmentInvestmentFunds

Al-Naggar, A. H. (2019). *Waqf investment funds in GCC countries: A case study on Saudi Arabia.* Retrieved from https://www.researchgate.net/publication/337791873_Waqf_investment_funds_in_GCC_countries_A_case_study_on_Saudi_Arabia

Al-Shatibi, I. (1975). *Al-Muwafaqat fi Usul al-Shari'ah* (2nd ed., vol. 2). Dar al-Ma'rifah.

Arab News. (2018, September 5). *Saudi Arabia's first waqf investment fund launched.* Retrieved from https://www.arabnews.com/node/1367396/corporate-news

Badan Wakaf Indonesia. (2020a). *BWI gunakan dana hasil pengelolaan wakaf Sukuk untuk pembangunan sarana kesehatan.* Retrieved from https://www.bwi.go.id/4590/2020/03/16/bwi-gunakan-dana-hasil-pengelolaan-wakaf-sukuk-untuk-pembangunan-sarana-kesehatan/

Badan Wakaf Indonesia. (2020b). *Cash waqf linked Sukuk.* Retrieved from https://www.bwi.go.id/cash-waqf-linked-sukuk/

Bank Indonesia. (2020a). *JISDOR.* Retrieved from https://www.bi.go.id/id/statistik/informasi-kurs/jisdor/default.aspx

Bank Indonesia. (2020b). *Laporan ekonomi dan keuangan Syariah 2019.* Retrieved from https://www.bi.go.id/id/publikasi/laporan/Pages/Laporan-Ekonomi-dan-Keuangan-Syariah-2019.aspx.

BERNAMA. (2020a). *RM500 million Sukuk Prihatin launched.* Retrieved from https://www.pmo.gov.my/2020/08/rm500-million-sukuk-prihatin-launched/

BERNAMA. (2020b). *Sukuk Prihatin: Response to people's desire to help rebuild economy—PM Muhyiddin.* Retrieved from https://www.pmo.gov.my/2020/08/sukuk-prihatin-response-to-peoples-desire-to-help-rebuild-economy-pm-muhyiddin/
ClubEthis. (2021). *ClubEthis.* Retrieved from https://e27.co/startups/clubethis/
Ethis Crowd. (2017). *Salaam Citayam affordable housing in Bojong Gede—Depok, Indonesia [Campaign Facts].* Retrieved from https://ethis.co/id/wp-content/uploads/2017/10/EthisCrowd-Investment-Salaam-Citayam-Bojong-Gede-Depok-Indonesia-Campaign-Facts-oct2017.pdf
Ethis. (2018). *Ethis Islamic crowdfunding Report 2018.* Retrieved from https://cdn2.hubspot.net/hubfs/2627399/Ethis%20Islamic%20Crowdfunding%20Report.pdf?t=1531319295463&utm_campaign=Ethis%20Report&utm_source=hs_email&utm_medium=email&utm_content=64451562&_hsenc=p2ANqtz-_n2b429iQjHwC0bilGeadqzpi-LUx-9Ho319eRTV-LS9qDt6j8GfSf4bLwoZButW_2OX2pXzLKjIH-GlnOVqhqR5qER3EA&_hsmi=64451562
Ethis. (2020a). *Impact investing in real estate, supply chain and other interesting projects.* Retrieved from https://ethis.co/id/discover/
Ethis. (2020b). *The Essential Daru 3 [Campaign Highlights].* Retrieved from https://f.hubspotusercontent40.net/hubfs/2627399/THE%20ESSENTIALS%20-%20DARU%203/Essential%20Daru%203%20Campaign%20launch.pdf
Ethis. (2020c). *The Essential Daru 3 [Campaign Facts].* Retrieved from https://f.hubspotusercontent40.net/hubfs/2627399/THE%20ESSENTIALS%20-%20DARU%203/THE%20ESSENTIALS%20-%20Daru%20(Eng).pdf.
Ethis. (2020d). *Hasanah City [Campaign Facts].* Retrieved from https://cdn2.hubspot.net/hubfs/2627399/Hasanah%20village/CFS%20-%20Hasanah%20City-2.pdf.
Ethis. (n.d.). *Ethis social return on investment.* Retrieved from https://cdn2.hubspot.net/hubfs/2627399/Ethis%20SROI%20Report-2.pdf?utm_medium=email&_hsmi=79212980&_hsenc=p2ANqtz---z1Gge-Sh31ZkN-KPkBme9KCwcgOgpe2umPqHWp1ldSZUaC1BcSX4wgwt1TaYl-vffwqPWely8tlLOhlPBDeZ76X9EFvg&utm_content=79212980&utm_source=hs_automation
Farhand, M. Z. (2020). *Analisis SWOT terhadap Cash Waqf linked Sukuk Seri SW001 sebagai evaluasi penghimpunan* (Master's thesis). Retrieved from Institutional Repository UIN Syarif Hidayatullah Jakarta.
Fitch Ratings. (2020, October 21). *2020 Sukuk Volumes resilient to coronavirus stress.* Retrieved from https://www.fitchratings.com/research/islamic-finance/2020-sukuk-volumes-resilient-to-coronavirus-stress-21-10-2020

GOV.SA. (2020). *General authority of awqaf*. Retrieved from https://www.my.gov.sa/wps/portal/snp/pages/agencies/agencyDetails/AC395/!ut/p/z0/04_Sj9CPykssy0xPLMnMz0vMAfIjo8zivQIsTAwdDQz9LQwNzQwCnS0tXPwMvYwNDAz0g1Pz9L300_ArAppiVOTr7Juu H1WQWJKhm5mXlq8f4ehsbGmqX5DtHg4ATyJbYA!!/
Holmes, J. (2008). *Losing 25,000 to hunger every day*. Retrieved from https://www.un.org/en/chronicle/article/losing-25000-hunger-every-day
Idris Al-Shafii, A. A. M. (2003). *Al-Shafi'i's Risala: Treatise on the foundations of Islamic Jurisprudence* (M. Khadduri, Trans.). Islamic Texts Society.
Indonesia Investments. (2017, August 11). *Indonesia's One Million Houses Program on schedule in 2017*. Retrieved from https://www.indonesia-investments.com/news/todays-headlines/indonesia-s-one-million-houses-program-on-schedule-in-2017/item8089#:~:text=The%20one%20million%20houses%20program,facilities%20to%20low%20income%20families.&text=This%20package%20simplified%20the%20process,projects%20for%20low-income%20families
Islamic Development Bank. (2019a). *U.S.$25,000,000,000 trust certificate issuance programme [Base Prospectus]*. Retrieved from https://www.isdb.org/sites/default/files/media/documents/2020-02/Base%20Prospectus.PDF.
Islamic Development Bank. (2019b). *IsDB Sustainable Finance Framework*. Retrieved from https://www.isdb.org/sites/default/files/media/documents/2019a-11/IsDB%20Sustainable%20Finance%20Framework%20%28Nov%202019a%29.pdf.
Islamic Development Bank. (2019c). *Annual Development Effectiveness Report*. Retrieved from https://www.isdb.org/sites/default/files/media/documents/2020-05/IsDB_ADER%202019_27May2020.pdf.
Islamic Development Bank. (2019d). *The road to the SDGs: The President's programme, A New Business Model for a Fast-Changing World*. Retrieved from https://www.isdb.org/sites/default/files/media/documents/2020-06/IsDB-NBM-FINAL.pdf
Islamic Development Bank. (2020a). *The COVID-19 crisis and Islamic finance: Response of the Islamic Development Bank Group*. Retrieved from https://www.isdb.org/sites/default/files/media/documents/2020a-10/1.%20IsDB%20Group%20Report%20on%20COVID-19%20and%20Islamic%20Finance__FINAL.pdf.
Islamic Development Bank. (2020b, June 19). *Islamic Development Bank issues US$1.5 Billion Debut Sustainability Sukuk in Response to COVID-19*. Retrieved from https://www.isdb.org/news/islamic-development-bank-issues-us-15-billion-debut-sustainability-sukuk-in-response-to-covid-19.
Islamic Development Bank. (2020c). *Investor Presentation, November 2020*. Retrieved from https://www.isdb.org/sites/default/files/media/

documents/2020-11/IsDB%20Investor%20Presentation%20%28Nov%20 2020%29%20%281%29.pdf.
Islamic Financial Services Board. (2020). *Islamic financial services industry stability report 2020*. Retrieved from https://www.ifsb.org/
Islamic Religious Council of Singapore. (2019). *Annual Report 2019*. Retrieved from https://www.muis.gov.sg/-/media/Files/Corporate-Site/Annual-Reports/Muis-AR2019.pdf
Islamic Religious Council of Singapore. (2020). *Administration of wakaf*. Retrieved from https://www.muis.gov.sg/wakaf/About/Administration-of-Wakaf
Jo, Y. S. (2015). *First Islamic Endowment Villas launched to help unlock value*. Retrieved from https://www.straitstimes.com/singapore/first-islamic-endowment-villas-launched-to-help-unlock-value-of-donated-land
JomPay. (2020). *About JomPAY*. Retrieved from https://www.jompay.com.my/aboutus.html
KPMG. (2020). *Malaysia—Government and institution measures in response to COVID-19*. Retrieved from https://home.kpmg/xx/en/home/insights/2020/04/malaysia-government-and-institution-measures-in-response-to-covid.html
Lin, M. (2015). *Katong's Iconic Red House to reopen by quarter of 2016*. Retrieved from https://www.straitstimes.com/singapore/housing/katongs-iconic-red-house-to-reopen-by-second-quarter-of-2016
Masood, E. (2019). *MUIS Wakaf disbursement ceremony*. Retrieved from https://www.muis.gov.sg/Media/Speeches/CE-Speech-at-Wakaf-Disbursement-2019
Ministry of Finance, Indonesia. (2018). *Peraturan Menteri Kuangan Republik Indonesia Nomor 139*. Retrieved from https://peraturan.bpk.go.id/Home/Details/113251/pmk-no-139pmk082018
Ministry of Finance, Indonesia. (2020a). *Penerbitan Sukuk Wakaf (Cash waqf linked Sukuk – CWLS) Seri SW001 Pada Tanggal 10 Maret 2020 Dengan Cara Private Placement*. Retrieved from https://www.djppr.kemenkeu.go.id/page/load/2736/penerbitan-sukuk-wakaf--cash-waqf-linked-sukuk--cwls--seri-sw001-pada-tanggal-10-maret-2020-dengan-cara-private-placement
Ministry of Finance, Indonesia. (2020b). *Pembukaan Masa Penawaran Cash Waqf linked Sukuk (CWLS) Seri SWR001*. Retrieved from https://www.djppr.kemenkeu.go.id/page/load/2934/pembukaan-masa-penawaran-cash-waqf-linked-sukuk--cwls--seri-swr001
Ministry of Finance, Indonesia. (2020c). *Cash Waqf linked Sukuk—SW001*. Retrieved from https://img1.wsimg.com/blobby/go/4a9bc408-fd4f-4403-91e2-.f93624a4f91e/downloads/4.%20Cash%20Waqf%20Linked%20 Sukuk%20Dwi%20Irianti.pdf?ver=1607762618591

Ministry of Finance, Indonesia. (2020d). *Daftar proyek/kegiatan sosial CWLS ritel Seri SWR001*. Retrieved from https://kemenkeu.go.id/media/16570/daftar-proyek-kegiatan-sosial.pdf

Ministry of Finance, Malaysia. (2020a). *Economic stimulus package 2020*. Retrieved from https://www.treasury.gov.my/pdf/pre2020/Booklet_2020_Economic_Stimulus_Package.pdf

Ministry of Finance, Malaysia. (2020b). *Terms and conditions of Sukuk Prihatin*. Retrieved from https://penjana.treasury.gov.my/pdf/gom-sukuk-prihatin-ptc-en.pdf

Ministry of Finance, Malaysia. (2020c). *Sukuk Prihatin knowledge pack*. Retrieved from https://penjana.treasury.gov.my/pdf/gom-sukuk-prihatin-knowledge-pack.pdf

Monetary Authority of Singapore. (2020). *Exchange rates*. Retrieved from https://eservices.mas.gov.sg/Statistics/msb/ExchangeRates.aspx

MRC Centre for Global Infectious Disease Analysis, Imperial College London. (2020). *Situation report for COVID-19: Malaysia, November*. Retrieved from https://mrc-ide.github.io/global-lmic-reports/MYS/

NST Business. (2020, September 20). *Govt rolls out additional RM166 mil new Sukuk Prihatin issuance*. Retrieved from https://www.nst.com.my/business/2020/09/625893/govt-rolls-out-additional-rm166mil-new-sukuk-prihatin-issuance

Osman, Z. (2018). *Enhancing waqf instrument*. Retrieved from https://inceif.org/events/world-bank-inceif-isra-roundtable-on-waqf/

Parker, M. (2020, June 29). *The emergence of COVID-19 mitigation Sukuk—Malaysia Set to Join IsDB*. Retrieved from https://www.bernama.com/en/thoughts/news.php?id=1854830

PayNet. (2020). *Who We Are*. Retrieved from https://paynet.my/about-paynet.html

Prime Ministry Office, Malaysia. (2020, June 5). *Pelan Jana semula ekonomi negara* [Speech Text]. Retrieved from https://www.pmo.gov.my/2020/06/teks-ucapan-pelan-jana-semula-ekonomi-negara-penjana/?highlight=PENJANA

Prime Ministry Office, Malaysia. (2020, September 23). *Special announcement on KITA PRIHATIN [Speech Text]*. Retrieved from https://www.pmo.gov.my/2020/09/teks-perutusan-khas-kita-prihatin/

Prime Ministry Office, Malaysia. (2020, April 6). *Additional Prihatin SME economic stimulus Package* [Speech Text]. Retrieved from https://www.pmo.gov.my/2020/04/langkah-tambahan-bagi-pakej-rangsangan-ekonomi-prihatin-rakyat-prihatin/

Prime Ministry Office, Malaysia. (2020, March 27). *Prihatin Rakyat economic stimulus package* [Speech Text]. Retrieved from https://www.pmo.gov.my/2020/03/speech-text-prihatin-esp/

Sari, I. N. (2020, November 25). *Hasil penjualan CWLS SW001 dirasa belum maksimal.* Retrieved from https://investasi.kontan.co.id/news/hasil-penjualan-cwls-swr001-dirasa-belum-maksimal?utm_source=dable

Securities Commission, Malaysia. (2019). *Sustainable and responsible investment roadmap for the Malaysian capital market.* Retrieved from https://www.sc.com.my/upload/sri-roadmap-2019/book/sri-roadmap-2019.pdf

Statistical Economic and Social Research and Training Centre for Islamic Countries. (2019). *Towards the achievement of prioritised Sustainable Development Goals in OIC Countries.* Retrieved from https://www.sesric.org/files/article/688.pdf

United Nations. (2018). *Food.* Retrieved from https://www.un.org/en/sections/issues-depth/food/index.html

Warees. (2014). *Institutional Investments Initiative (3I) hibah disbursement ceremony.* Retrieved from https://docplayer.net/47290985-Institutional-investments-initiative-3i-hibah-disbursement-ceremony.html

Warees. (2020a). *About us.* Retrieved from https://warees.sg/

Warees. (2020b). *Home.* Retrieved from https://www.warees.sg/

Water.org. (2020). *The water crisis.* Retrieved from https://water.org/our-impact/water-crisis/#:~:text=The%20water%20crisis%20is%20a,from%20a%20water%2Drelated%20disease

World Health Organisation. (2016). *Ambient air pollution: A Global Assessment of Exposure and Burden of Disease.* Retrieved from https://apps.who.int/iris/bitstream/handle/10665/250141/9789241511353-eng.pdf?sequence=1

The Resilience of Islamic Finance Against Pandemic-Induced Future Economic Crisis

Umar A. Oseni and Sukaynah O. D. Shuaib

1 Introduction

Even though the pandemic is still ravaging the world, with different countries recording high numbers despite the availability of different vaccines, it is difficult to predict its end, given the various variants of the virus emerging from different nooks and crannies of the globe. While the world remains hopeful that the pandemic will be over soon, there is, however, a need to prepare for the post-pandemic era or even for future pandemics (Ainol-Basirah & Siti-Nabiha, 2020; Hamed, 2020).

With the protracted effect of the COVID-19 pandemic, it is now clear that there is always a silver lining in every difficult situation, as the Fourth Industrial Revolution has been significantly fast-tracked by the pandemic. One aspect of the Fourth Industrial Revolution is harnessing

---

U. A. Oseni (✉) · S. O. D. Shuaib
International Islamic Liquidity Management Corporation, Kuala Lumpur, Malaysia
e-mail: umaroseni@gmail.com

S. O. D. Shuaib
e-mail: shuaibsukaynah@gmail.com

technology to create an inclusive human-centered future (Thakur & Thakur, 2021). Although the pandemic has fast-tracked the adoption of the Internet-of-Things (IoT), the Fourth Industrial Revolution goes beyond just technology (Xu et al., 2018). According to the World Economic Forum, when it comes to the Fourth Industrial Revolution, "the real opportunity is to look beyond technology and find ways to give the greatest number of people the ability to impact their families, organizations, and communities positively" (World Economic Forum, 2021). The relevance of such human-centered connections during the pandemic could not be overstated, as the significance of the digital economy is being felt in the global economy (Sturgeon, 2021).

This study examines the impact of Islamic finance in the post-pandemic world and the policies to be put in place to ensure the resilience of the Islamic finance industry in strategizing against pandemic-induced future economic crises. It may be difficult to cast a crystal ball and predict the end of the pandemic. However, identifying key policies that can be learned from Islamic financial products, services, and institutions could provide some glimpse of hope for future-proofing the economy against pandemics and other economically destructive issues. Thus, this study seeks to address the following pertinent questions: How resilient is the Islamic finance industry against financial and economic distress? How can Islamic finance contribute to the long-term economic stability that allows countries to be able to cope with the uncertain consequences of the pandemic? What tools can the Islamic finance industry deploy to change the fortunes of emerging economies for the better as part of the post-COVID-19 economic recovery? Does Islamic social finance have any role to play in reducing the impact of the prolonged pandemic on the less privileged in society? What is the role of Islamic-driven FinTech in transforming modern economies?

The study is organized into six major sections. While Sect. 1 provides the introduction, Sect. 2 provides a brief high-level overview of the Islamic finance industry and the global economic effect of the COVID-19 pandemic. Furthermore, Sect. 3 provides some brief data on the resilience of the Islamic finance industry in the initial pandemic year, as reported by the Islamic Financial Services Board (IFSB). Section 4 takes a fresh look at Islamic social finance and long-term financial stability with a view to identifying some key policies that can be considered to future-proof the financial systems against the effects of future pandemics. In order to contextualize the analysis within the general ambit of the

Fourth Industrial Revolution, Sect. 5 explores the relevance of FinTech in Islamic finance and digitalization in the post-COVID era. Finally, Sect. 6 provides the conclusion and some key policy recommendations.

2   Islamic Finance Industry and The Global Economic Effect of COVID-19

The Islamic financial system is growing exponentially across the globe, as the total volume of its assets reached USD 3.374 trillion in 2020. This figure is expected to grow by 8% year-on-year basis (Refinitiv, 2021). Malaysia, the United Arab Emirates, Saudi Arabia, and Iran are the largest markets out of the 61 Islamic finance jurisdictions as these four leading jurisdictions. Despite the successes recorded over the years, one cannot conclusively say that the Islamic finance industry is completely immune from the effect of the COVID-19 pandemic (Ainol-Basirah & Siti-Nabiha, 2020).

The COVID-19 pandemic continues to be an unprecedented and globally shared phenomenon in the new millennium. Although COVID-19 involves a highly multi-layered experience at different levels—personal, communal, institutional, national, and global—its effects cut across wide-ranging repercussions (Yan, 2020). The pandemic has disrupted lives and economies globally since it emerged in December 2019. From the economic perspective, it negatively reduced economic growth, especially in 2020 at an annualized rate of -3.4 to -7.6%. The 2021 recovery projection ranged between 4.2 and 5.6%. It is estimated that global trade will fall by 5.3% in 2020 and is projected to grow by 8% in 2021 due to different measures introduced in various countries to boost trade and economic recovery. However, the subsequent economic rebound was not as initially estimated due to the prolonged COVID-19 impact on the global economy and health (Congressional Research Service, 2021).

Initial efforts to coordinate the economic response to the pandemic in various countries were uneven due to divisions among governments over the appropriate response. However, following the G-7 and G-20 emergency teleconferences, the most needed commitment was eventually gained (Goodman & Sobel, 2020). The international organizations, including the International Monetary Fund (IMF) and the Financial Stability Board (FSB), also played their unique roles pursuant to their respective mandates to provide economic support and advice to governments across the world (Financial Stability Board, 2020; Goodman & Sobel, 2020; Jickling, 2009).

One of the notable effects of COVID-19 is the wave of defaults across the world. This is because in the third quarter of 2019, prior to the COVID-19 outbreak, the reported global debt levels reached a record high of about USD 253 trillion, which is about 320% of the global GDP (Amaro, 2020). "Households faced a rapid increase in unemployment and a decline in remittances in many developing countries. With fewer resources and absent government intervention, corporations and households faced defaults on their debts. Such defaults could result in a decline in bank assets, making it difficult for banks to extend new loans during the crisis or, more severely, create solvency problems for banks" (Congressional Research Service, 2021, p. 105). Islamic financial institutions are (or were) not immune from such solvency issues (Congressional Research Service, 2021; Plender, 2020).

The finance ministers of the G-20 collectively agreed to suspend the servicing of debts by the poorest countries in the world until the end of 2020. Further, the Institute for International Finance (IIF) announced the commitment of private creditors toward the joint debt relief effort voluntarily with the aim of freeing up more than USD 20 billion of the debt standstills for these countries and improving their health systems and fighting the pandemic (Barbuscia, Rashad, & Shalal, 2020; Congressional Research Service, 2021).

As national governments across the globe adopt fiscal and monetary policy actions to cushion the evolving effects of COVID-19, the key Islamic finance jurisdictions are no exception (Belouafi, 2020). According to IFSB (2021), the key Islamic finance jurisdictions are the Gulf Cooperation Council (GCC), Malaysia, Indonesia, and Turkey. Several measures have been put in place by the key Islamic finance jurisdictions such as Saudi Arabia, Malaysia, Indonesia, the United Arab Emirates, Bahrain, and Turkey. From the Islamic finance perspective, the policy measures may be classified into two, namely: first, the general measures to address the effect of COVID-19, which cover other than the Islamic finance sector, and second, the specific measures to promote the stability and resilience of the Islamic finance industry amid the ravaging COVID-19 pandemic (Mansour et al., 2021).

As for the general policy measures, the approaches adopted by each jurisdiction will be briefly explained. It is important to add that the brief analysis below is not intended to be exhaustive; it merely provides some examples of some key measures taken by various jurisdictions. In Malaysia, the government has been rolling out stimulus packages, and similar steps have been taken in Indonesia, where the government has rolled out measures for a national public health emergency. The United Arab Emirates, Turkey, Kuwait, Qatar, and Saudi Arabia also introduced similar fiscal and monetary measures to address the needs of customers and Islamic financial institutions. In addition, other regulatory pushes to support local industries in Pakistan and Bangladesh have contributed significantly to developing global Islamic finance. The policy measures in these countries were meant to ensure the resilience of the Islamic finance industry amid the COVID-19 pandemic. As COVID-19 became pervasive, various policy measures were adopted, including, among others, the "eased monetary policies, regulatory forbearances, liquidity provisions, credit guarantees, and payment moratoria," which were quite effective (IFSB, 2021).

3 Resilience of The Islamic Finance Industry

The year 2020 was faced with an unprecedented event in recent history, with a global pandemic affecting not only the financial sphere but also the lives of billions of people across the world (Mansour et al., 2021). According to the IFSB (2021).

From conventional banks to institutions offering Islamic financial services (IIFS), all market participants suffered from the unexpected market sell-off, which was almost like that experienced during the 2008 Global Financial Crisis (GFC). However, Islamic banks entered the March 2020 crash better capitalized than during the GFC. The main difference between the two episodes of the financial crisis was the immediate intervention from central banks to mitigate the liquidity stress and the unknown impact of the global economic shutdown in countering the spread of the pandemic. Pricing, risk metrics, and credit exposures have been stressed, with a major impact on short-term funding, especially in the USD-denominated markets—the industry benchmark (IFSB, 2021, p. 91).

The Islamic banking sector is the biggest sector of the Islamic finance industry and accounted for nearly USD 1.84 trillion worth of assets, or 68.3% of all Islamic finance assets in the year 2020, compared to USD 1.77 trillion and 72.4% in the previous year. The IFSB (2021) stated that as of today, there are over 520 Islamic banks, including Islamic windows, operating in around 72 countries around the globe. Despite the pandemic, this sector is growing continuously, with new Islamic banks and windows entering the market and a number of them undergoing consolidation or reorganization in some jurisdictions.

The Islamic capital markets (ICM) and the Sukuk sector, in particular, are among the most resilient sectors of the Islamic finance industry. Therefore, despite the wide range and unprecedented impact of the COVID-19 pandemic, the Sukuk market was considerably resilient in 2020 and 2021, respectively. The ICM segment continues its year-on-year growth, as evidenced in several Islamic economic and financial reports. The IFSB (2021) stated that the ICM recorded 26.9% year-on-year growth, and the sector increased its size in the Islamic finance industry by 30.9%.

It is noteworthy to mention that, based on the IFSB Report (2021), takaful, which is the Islamic insurance sector, accounted for 0.9% of the total Islamic finance market as at the end of 2019, with a total asset size of USD 23.1 billion, with 335 takaful operators around the globe, including 122 windows which are providing takaful services. The takaful sector is considerably small, and concentrated mainly in key markets, even though it has great potential to grow, according to the IFSB (2021).

Beyond just considering statistics from the major sectors of the Islamic finance industry, it is important to have a more philosophical view on what could provide some resilience measures on a long-term basis for the Islamic finance industry. The resilience of the Islamic finance industry against future pandemics will be seen in its ability to return to basics by revisiting its original value proposition, which is mainly its social objective of achieving economic empowerment in an egalitarian society where the gap between the rich and the poor only depends on the ability of individuals to utilize the economic opportunities available to them (Oseni et al., 2012). This value proposition has at its core Islamic social finance institutions, products, and services that, when properly structured and deployed, have the potential to positively disrupt the global financial system (Syed Nazim Ali & Oseni, 2022).

4   Islamic Social Finance and Long-Term Financial Stability

As discussed above, the COVID-19 pandemic has had an immediate short-term fiscal impact as well as a significant long-term economic impact on various jurisdictions across the world. Both the fiscal and economic impacts have led to various socio-economic crises (Kamaruddin et al., 2021). While various governments have taken immediate measures to cushion the impact of the short-term fiscal crisis, the long-term effects have not really been the focus of policymakers. Just like long-term COVID health issues, the long-term economic impact of the pandemic is more devastating than the short-term effects. Therefore, to ensure long-term financial stability and better play their role of financial intermediation by creating value in the economy, Islamic financial institutions should explore all legitimate means to raise capital to ensure they are better capitalized. This requires financial engineering in order to explore some risk-sharing Islamic products such as *mudhārabah* and *mushārakah* (Assa'd & Albusaili, 2021; Djebbar, 2016).

Recently, we have seen a significant number of players in the Sukuk space during the pandemic. Apart from sovereigns, financial institutions have taped the capital market to raise funds to ensure long-term stability. At the peak of the pandemic, on April 4, 2021, the International Islamic Financial Market (IIFM) released its Tier 1 Sukuk Al-Mudārabah documentation template for Islamic financial institutions (International Islamic Financial Markets, 2021). It was indeed another significant milestone in the history of Sukuk issuances and efforts toward standardization in the global Islamic finance industry. It seems the implementation of the Basel III rules relating to capital requirements has led to benign innovation in the Islamic finance space (Sairally, Muhammad, & Mustafa, 2016). Such benign innovations in products and services should be encouraged and actively supported in order to deepen the development of the Islamic capital market. As a matter of fact, this is more relevant in difficult times when financial institutions are struggling to cope with the negative effects of COVID-19 and the potential for protracted liquidity stress among financial institutions. When Basel III rules introduced Core Tier 1 Capital, the Islamic financial engineers needed to go back to the drawing board to develop shariah-compliant contingent capital structures. To future-proof the Islamic finance industry against pandemics, the industry needs more of these Shariah structures and accompanying documentation that is primarily based on core Shariah principles (Sairally et al., 2016). While this is quite encouraging, it is also important to assess the level of impact of such long-term financing vis-a-vis SMEs and the average person on the street. This is where the social dimension and long-term impact are required in the final analysis.

Therefore, it is pertinent to consider the significance of Islamic social finance in the ongoing discourse. This would require a total overhaul of how Islamic social finance institutions are viewed and structured within the general realm of the finance industry (Tahiri Jouti, 2019). The age-long practice of key social institutions traditionally utilized on matters relating to distributive justice and wealth creation is key to the post-pandemic recovery in Muslim-majority countries (Faturohman et al., 2021; Umar et al., 2022). In the modern sense, this practice is called "Islamic Social Finance." Islamic Social Finance comprises key institutions such as *zakat, waqf, sadaqah*, and other charitable dispositions prescribed in Islam. Perhaps, it is possible to extend the definition of Islamic Social Finance to other financial products and services that tend to have in-built social objectives in addition to profit targets. This will encourage Islamic financial institutions to ensure that every form of financing or service provided has social dimensions to it. This is similar to the laudable practice in Malaysia with the Value Based Intermediation (VBI) introduced by the central bank, Bank Negara Malaysia.

The VBI initiatives have the potential to positively impact the Islamic finance-growth nexus and contribute to the efforts toward future-proofing the industry from pandemics. The VBI initiatives are more focused on realizing the full potential of Islamic finance, which goes beyond just economic growth. They contribute to the element of self-discipline on the part of Islamic banks. While considering the four main thrusts of the VBI initiatives—entrepreneurial mindset, community empowerment, good self-governance, and best conduct, the most important thrusts that would directly impact Islamic finance growth are entrepreneurial mindset and community empowerment, while the remaining two could potentially provide some ancillary support to the Islamic finance-growth nexus. One could therefore say that since BNM issued the "Value-based Intermediation Financing and Investment Impact Assessment Framework – Guidance Document" (VBIAF), on November 1, 2019, which is pretty recent, there has been a change in the attitudes and behaviors of Islamic financial institutions in Malaysia. Such a policy could be replicated in other jurisdictions as part of a major step toward future-proofing the global Islamic finance industry from pandemics. SME's will be the greatest beneficiaries of such initiatives if properly implemented and measured through key performance indicators.

As many jurisdictions are coming up with COVID-19 legislation, there is a need to ensure that aspects of Islamic social finance are considered as part of the funding options. Therefore, positive law is used to realize the ideals of Islamic social finance. There may also be the need to amend existing laws or enact new legislation to incorporate Islamic social finance principles into such laws to prepare for the uncertain era of post-COVID-19. The laws should cover the entire Islamic social finance ecosystem, which comprises institutions, instruments, market infrastructure, and regulatory authorities, including an efficient Shariah governance framework. It may also include the following: Islamic social finance institutions, licensing, regulatory authority and its powers, tax relief and incentives, Shariah governance, impact measurement and reporting obligations, business conduct, and dispute resolution.

The Islamic social finance ecosystem must give a prime role to Shariah advisory services to ensure that Islamic social finance institutions are Shariah compliant in form and substance. The legal framework or regulation should also include the requirement for a measurable positive social and environmental impact (Syed Azman & Engku Ali, 2019). The Impact Measurement and Management Tools should also be Shariah compliant.

5 Post-COVID Era: FinTech and Digitalization

Digitalization involves the active utilization of technologies to transform a business model, which would lead to new revenue streams and value-based opportunities (Niemand et al., 2021; Ritter & Pedersen, 2020). This is indeed relevant to the Islamic finance industry, as technologies are merely a means to an end and not the end itself (Umar A. Oseni & Ali, 2019). The ultimate end is profits and principles, but the underlying philosophy underpinning Islamic finance emphasizes principles before profit and the need to always consider the social dimension and objective of any business model (Umar A. Oseni, 2014).

One aspect of the Fourth Industrial Revolution is the IoT, in addition to artificial intelligence (Griffiths & Ooi, 2018). There is no doubt in the fact that the pandemic has accelerated the use of IoT technologies not just in social relations but also in financial intermediation (Ojo-Fafore, Aigbavboa, & Thwala, 2021). The Islamic finance industry is not left behind in the adoption of FinTech and digitalization generally. While this is a welcome development, there is a need to address ethical and governance issues. One would expect that, as part of the role of the Shariah Supervisory Boards, a continuous review of the digitalization process adopted by an Islamic bank should be considered (Yasini & Yasini, 2019).

Beyond Shariah matters, it is pertinent to also consider technology governance matters (Campbell-Verduyn & Goguen, 2018; Zhang, 2021). As the World Economic Forum noted, "Effective technology governance mitigates risks and reduces the potential harm to society while also helping to maximize the technology's positive impacts" (Marchant, 2021). Therefore, to maximize the positive impacts of FinTech in Islamic finance, regulatory and supervisory authorities should put in place relevant policies to ensure proactive, effective technology governance.

With respect to the post-COVID era, it is expected that Islamic financial institutions will leapfrog the COVID-era experiences where the adoption of IoT was rapid amidst lockdown in various countries. The Great Lockdown in 2020 did not affect financial intermediation as most transactions were still being carried on through different online channels. Just like their counterparts in the conventional space, the Islamic financial institutions were quick to innovate new ways to conduct financial and banking operations and had to upgrade their IT systems and cybersecurity protocols to be able to conduct transactions remotely.

It is expected that FinTech will evolve to become the primary means of customer engagement rather than being a supportive technology. With the use of artificial intelligence, customer behavior online and otherwise will be closely monitored and optimized through new product offerings. This will help to enhance the customer experience in the long run, as the customer's desired products are brought to them in real-time without having to make any application.

In terms of technology-driven initiatives that emerged during the pandemic, customers are now able to access some services such as "Buy Now, Pay Later" at no additional cost (Gerrans et al., 2021). This will definitely help to cushion the effect of the pandemic on consumers.

Finally, the pandemic has also provided a unique opportunity for Islamic financial institutions to explore digital banking. There are ongoing efforts among some Islamic banks to overhaul the way and manner in which they offer products and services to their customers. Some Islamic banks have concluded some strategic alliances with tech start-ups to establish digital Islamic banks jointly. As noted elsewhere, "[i]n an increasingly globalized world, there is no doubt that innovation in financial technology will continue to move at a fast pace, and regulations may try to catch up with it even though this remains a Herculean task." For the new types of banks in this era, such as digital Islamic banks, it is important to come up with some clear parameters for their operations. This is where the legal requirements for such digital Islamic banks are important to ensure consumer protection and avoid fraudulent practices" (Umar A. Oseni, 2019, p. 39). Moreover, some central banks within the Islamic finance world have introduced various regulatory frameworks for digital banks, such as the Central Bank of Bahrain, Kuwait Central Bank, and BNM (Kaur et al., 2021; Zouari & Abdelhedi, 2021).

6 Conclusion and Policy Recommendations

The first quarter of the year 2020 was a year of unprecedented health and economic challenges, as COVID-19 was declared a pandemic in March of the same year. Each country took various measures, albeit uncoordinated initially, which triggered a global economic downturn spilling out across the globe. It is noteworthy that, no doubt, decisive government intervention and digitalization can provide a major boost to this wave of defaults and keep the national and global economy on track. The Islamic finance industry, just like its conventional counterpart, harnessed technological advancement to manage unprecedented and standstill COVID-19 impacts.

This chapter concludes with the following recommendations for policymakers, industry experts, and Islamic financial institutions:

1. Islamic social finance remains an evergreen project for Muslim societies across the world. This is the time when Islamic financial institutions should be actively involved in managing Islamic social finance projects. The funds realized from *sadaqah* and *waqf* could be used to fund SMEs. Besides, Islamic financial institutions could also consider Sukuk al-Waqf, that is endowment Sukuk, to fund economic activities that will generate employment and fast-track economic recovery. This will increase the level of financial inclusion of the population, eradicate poverty, and attract more financial resources.
2. Islamic financial institutions should consider the need to utilize the IIFM Template Sukuk Al-Mudārabah Tier 1 Standard Documents to issue Tier 1 Sukuk. They should also explore the funding of green projects to ensure sustainable development and promote sustainable consumption. Beyond green projects, Islamic financial institutions should also consider funding specific projects

that are targeted at brownfield projects to create jobs and improve the environment while also creating a safer and healthier space for people.
3. Islamic financial institutions must innovate new products that are not only shariah-compliant but also highly profitable for their customers. In other words, beyond Shariah compliance, which is, of course, very important, such products and services should also be conventionally viable and competitive. This will fast-track the post-COVID-19 recovery and increase the size of Islamic finance assets globally. The VBI initiatives by BNM should be replicated in other jurisdictions to ensure that the social dimension of financing is embedded into the DNA of Islamic financial intermediation.
4. FinTech remains an important tool to fast-track economic recovery. However, one must bear in mind that FinTech is not the end itself but a means to an end. Therefore, policymakers must ensure proper governance policy and risk management are put in place to ensure ethical use of FinTech in transforming the economy. All hands must be on deck to ensure FinTech and digitalization are not abused. In most cases, this is the major role of regulators and supervisory authorities. While FinTech is ever-changing, regulation must endeavor to catch up with the developments in the FinTech space. This emphasizes the role of RegTech in the post-COVID era.

Finally, the study finds that beyond Shariah compliance, which is of course, very important, Islamic finance products and services should also be conventionally viable and competitive. Above all, financial and economic reforms can be actualized through enabling legislation to support long-term economic recovery and stability.

References

Ainol-Basirah, A. W., & Siti-Nabiha, A. K. (2020). The Roles of Islamic Social Finance in the Era of Post-COVID-19: Possible prospects of Waqf Institutions for Economic Revival. *International Journal of Industrial Management,* 7(1), 1–8.

Ali, Syed Nazim, & Oseni, U. A. (2022). *Waqf development and innovation socio-economic and legal perspectives.* (Syed Nazim Ali & U. A. Oseni, Eds.) (1st ed.). Routledge.

Amaro, S. (2020, January 14). Global debt hits new record of $253 trillion and is set to grow even more this year. *CNBC*. Retrieved from https://www.cnbc.com/2020/01/14/global-debt-hits-all-time-high-of-nearly-253-dollars--iif-says.html

Assa'd, A. M., & Albusaili, A. K. (2021). The means and pretexts and their applications in Islamic Financial Engineering. *Al-Rashad Journal of Islamic Finance*, 1(3). https://doi.org/10.46722/ajif.1.3.21c

Barbuscia, D., Rashad, M., & Shalal, A. (2020, April 15). G20 Countries agree debt freeze for world's poorest countries. *Reuters*.

Belouafi, A. M. (2020). Socio-Economic Implications of the Novel Corona Virus (COVID-19): An Islamic perspective. *Journal of King Abdulaziz University, Islamic Economics*, 33(3). https://doi.org/10.4197/Islec.33-3.2

Campbell-Verduyn, M., & Goguen, M. (2018). A digital revolution back to the future: Blockchain Technology and Financial Governance. *Banking & Financial Services Policy Report*, 37(9).

Congressional Research Service. (2021). *Global Economic Effects of COVID-19*. Washington, D.C. Retrieved from https://sgp.fas.org/crs/row/R46270.pdf

Djebbar, M. (2016). Islamic Financial Engineering: An overview. *Journal of Islamic Banking and Finance*, Jan-March.

Faturohman, T., Farras, M., Rasyid, A., Rahadi, R. A., Darmansyah, A., & Afgani, K. F. (2021). The potential role of islamic social finance in the time of COVID-19 Pandemic. *Review of Integrative Business and Economics Research*, 10(1).

Financial Stability Board. (2020, March 20). FSB coordinates financial sector work to buttress the economy in response to COVID-19. *Press Release 6/2020*. Retrieved from https://www.fsb.org/2020/03/fsb-coordinates-financial-sector-work-to-buttress-the-economy-in-response-to-covid-19/

Gerrans, P., Baur, D. G., & Lavagna-Slater, S. (2021). FinTech and responsibility: Buy-now-pay-later arrangements. *Australian Journal of Management*. https://doi.org/10.1177/03128962211032448

Goodman, M., & Sobel, M. (2020). *Time to pull the G-20 Fire Bell*. Washington, D.C.

Griffiths, F., & Ooi, M. (2018). The fourth industrial revolution—Industry 4.0 and IoT. *IEEE Instrumentation and Measurement Magazine*, 21(6).

Hamed, M. M. (2020). The role of Islamic social finance in mitigating humanitarian crises; A multi-range strategy to mitigate COVID-19 impacts. *European Journal of Islamic Finance*.

International Islamic Financial Markets. (2021, April 4). IIFM Releases New Standard for Sukuk Al Mudarabah Tier 1 to enhance the global issuance of Sukuk. *Press Release*. Retrieved from https://www.iifm.net/press-media/news-and-updates/iifm-releases-new-standard-for-sukuk-al-mudarabah-tier-1-to-enhance-the-global-issuance-of-sukuk/8

Jickling, M. (2009). Causes of the financial crisis. *Washington DC: Congressional Research Service*, 1(1), 1–12. https://doi.org/10.1080/08913810902952903

Kamaruddin, Z., Oseni, U. A., & Abdul Manaf, Z. I. (2021). Implementing the E-family expert model through a legal framework for online dispute resolution. *ICR Journal*, 12(2), 235–248.

Kaur, S. J., Ali, L., Hassan, M. K., & Al-Emran, M. (2021). Adoption of digital banking channels in an emerging economy: exploring the role of in-branch efforts. *Journal of Financial Services Marketing*, 26(2). https://doi.org/10.1057/s41264-020-00082-w

Mansour, W., Ajmi, H., & Saci, K. (2021). Regulatory policies in the global Islamic banking sector in the outbreak of COVID-19 pandemic. *Journal of Banking Regulation*. https://doi.org/10.1057/s41261-021-00147-3

Marchant, N. (2021, March 31). What is the Internet of Things? *World Economic Forum*. Retrieved from https://www.weforum.org/agenda/2021/03/what-is-the-internet-of-things/

Niemand, T., Rigtering, J. P. C., Kallmünzer, A., Kraus, S., & Maalaoui, A. (2021). Digitalization in the financial industry: A contingency approach of entrepreneurial orientation and strategic vision on digitalization. *European Management Journal*, 39(3). https://doi.org/10.1016/j.emj.2020.04.008

Ojo-Fafore, E., Aigbavboa, C., & Thwala, W. (2021). The impact of the COVID 19 Pandemic on the Development of the Fourth Industrial Revolution in Southern Africa. *Journal of Intellectual Disability - Diagnosis and Treatment*, 9(1). https://doi.org/10.6000/2292-2598.2021.09.01.7

Oseni, U.A., Kadouf, H. A., Ansari, A. H., & Olayemi, A. A. M. (2012). The value proposition of Islamic financial intermediation: Some current legal and regulatory challenges. *Australian Journal of Basic and Applied Sciences*, 6(11).

Oseni, Umar A. (2014). Toward a new socio-legal framework for faith-based and socially responsible investments. In S. Nazim Ali (Ed.), *Islamic Finance and Development* (pp. 111–134). Harvard Law School, ILSP.

Oseni, Umar A. (2019). Legal requirements for Digital Islamic Banks. In *5th Doha Islamic Finance Conference: Islamic Finance and Digital World* (pp. 23–41). Bait Al-Mashura Finance Consultations.

Oseni, U. A., & Ali, S. N. (Eds.). (2019). *FinTech in Islamic Finance: Theory and practice*. Routledge.

Plender, J. (2020, March 4). The Seeds of the next debt crisis. *Financial Times*.

Refinitiv. (2021). *Islamic finance development report 2021: Advancing Economies*.

Ritter, T., & Pedersen, C. L. (2020). Digitization capability and the digitalization of business models in business-to-business firms: Past, present, and future. *Industrial Marketing Management*. https://doi.org/10.1016/j.indmarman.2019.11.019

Sairally, B. S., Muhammad, M., & Mustafa, M. M. (2016). Additional Tier 1 Capital Instruments under Basel iii: A Sharī'ah Viewpoint. In *Arab Law Quarterly* (vol. 30). https://doi.org/10.1163/15730255-12341314

Sturgeon, T. J. (2021). Upgrading strategies for the digital economy. *Global Strategy Journal*, *11*(1). https://doi.org/10.1002/gsj.1364

Syed Azman, S. M. M., & Engku Ali, E. R. A. (2019). Islamic social finance and the imperative for social impact measurement. *Al-Shajarah*, *2019*(Special Issue Islamic Bankingand Finance 2019).

Tahiri Jouti, A. (2019). An integrated approach for building sustainable Islamic social finance ecosystems. *ISRA International Journal of Islamic Finance*, *11*(2). https://doi.org/10.1108/IJIF-10-2018-0118

Thakur, S. C., & Thakur, M. (2021). The fourth industrial revolution-COVID-19 conundrum: a periscopic view of some opportunities and challenges. *Journal of Banking, Insurance and Management Sciences*, *2*(1).

Umar, U. H., Baita, A. J., Haron, M. H. Bin, & Kabiru, S. H. (2022). The potential of Islamic social finance to alleviate poverty in the era of COVID-19: The moderating effect of ethical orientation. *International Journal of Islamic and Middle Eastern Finance and Management*, *15*(2). https://doi.org/10.1108/IMEFM-07-2020-0371

World Economic Forum. (2021). Fourth Industrial Revolution. Retrieved May 1, 2022, from https://www.weforum.org/focus/fourth-industrial-revolution

Xu, M., David, J. M., & Kim, S. H. (2018). The fourth industrial revolution: Opportunities and challenges. *International Journal of Financial Research*, *9*(2). https://doi.org/10.5430/ijfr.v9n2p90

Yan, Z. (2020). Unprecedented pandemic, unprecedented shift, and unprecedented opportunity. *Human Behavior and Emerging Technologies*, *2*(2). https://doi.org/10.1002/hbe2.192

Yasini, S., & Yasini, M. (2019). Current trends and future impacts of fintech in Islamic finance. In *FinTech in Islamic Finance*. https://doi.org/10.4324/9781351025584-20

Zhang, D. (2021). Cooperative Governance Path of Financial Technology Supervision. *Proceedings of Business and Economic Studies*, *3*(6). https://doi.org/10.26689/pbes.v3i6.1718

Zouari, G., & Abdelhedi, M. (2021). Customer satisfaction in the digital era: evidence from Islamic banking. *Journal of Innovation and Entrepreneurship*, *10*(1). https://doi.org/10.1186/s13731-021-00151-x

Emergence of Islamic Finance in the Fourth Industrial Revolution and COVID-19 Post-Pandemic Era

Mohammad Sahabuddin, Abu Umar Faruq Ahmad and Md. Aminul Islam

1 Introduction

The global financial crisis (GFC) 2007–2008 and the ongoing COVID-19 pandemic have reshaped the financial architecture and the world economy. Particularly, during the period of GFC, Islamic finance (IF) shed light as

---

M. Sahabuddin
Universiti Malaysia Perlis, Arau, Malaysia
e-mail: sahabuddingme@gmail.com

University of Science and Technology Chittagong (USTC), Chattogram, Bangladesh

A. Ahmad
Guidance College, Texas, USA
e-mail: aufahmad@gmail.com

United International University, Dhaka, Bangladesh

© The Author(s), under exclusive license to Springer Nature Switzerland AG 2023
Z. H. Jumat et al. (eds.), *Islamic Finance, FinTech, and the Road to Sustainability*, Palgrave CIBFR Studies in Islamic Finance,
https://doi.org/10.1007/978-3-031-13302-2_6

a variable alternative and more resilient financial system compared to the traditional financial system (Abdou, 2015; IMF, 2015; Kayed & Hasan, 2011). However, the scenarios of the COVID-19 pandemic are different due to their causes and effects. Even, it differs from the magnitude of previous disasters and crises in terms of endogenous and exogenous risks perspective (SRC, 2013)[1] International Monetary Fund (IMF) indicates the COVID-19 pandemic as a crisis, but at the same time, it describes it as a crisis that is like no others. The World Bank (WB) is concerned about the adverse effect of this crisis. The Economist Intelligence Unit (EIU), the research and analysis division of The Economist Group, warned that the long-term effect on the global economy would be more deadly and much worse than GFC and 1919–1946 recessions (IMF, 2020). The massive and deadly shock of this pandemic not only shrinks the developed economy but also disrupts the emerging and developing economies (The World Bank, 2020). However, the consequent effect of this crisis is acute. It may lead to low-income households in miserable conditions, jeopardizing the noteworthy development made in reducing extreme poverty in the world since the 1990s. Particularly, small and medium-sized enterprises (SMEs) have become more vulnerable, and many are already on the verge of shutdown. The facts show that SMEs contains 90% of global enterprises, generating more than 50% of employment. Under these circumstances, such a scenario will speed up the high employment globally. Therefore, there is an urgent need to explore all possible alternatives to mitigate the risk of the crisis and restart economies in the post-pandemic era. Inherently, IF is an assets-backed and low leveraged-based economy, and with its key inborn orientation toward supporting the real sector will play a vital role in sustainable development (IsDB, 2020).

It has been observed that every crisis has several positive aspects. More importantly, this is the key time to adopt new technologies and adjust to new environments that could lead to more safe and sustainable

---

[1] GFC is the real example of exogenous risk, which is derived from outside of the economy. In contrast, the COVID-19 crisis is an example of endogenous risk, which is derived from within the system. Primarily, GFC hit the financial system, whereas the COVID-19 directly hit the real economy.

M. Islam
School of Business Innovation and Technopreneurship, University Malaysia Perlis, Arau, Malaysia
e-mail: amin@unimap.edu.my

development. For example, after the GFC and even during the ongoing COVID-19 pandemic crisis, the advancement of information technology has been playing a vital role in the acceleration of financial innovation subsequently. The wave of financial innovation is challenging traditional business norms, policies, and systems (World Economic Forum, 2017). However, these innovations have brought revolutionary changes not only to the way daily life is handled by ordinary people and businesses, but the era of digitalization has also transformed the social and political systems. In recent years, the structure of media industries such as TV, magazines, and newspapers has drastically changed, and social media such as Facebook, LinkedIn, Imo, and WhatsApp have captured the central role of people's attention.

Currently, digital technological innovation such as Big Data, Blockchain, Artificial Intelligence (AI), Robotics, and the Internet of Things (IoT), on the future image of the industry value chain is expected to arise, and considerable changes will be brought to the social structure, daily lifestyle, and industrial revolution (IR). Collectively, this trend is associated with the Fourth Industrial Revolution (4IR) (Koizumi, 2019). Likewise applying technology to different aspects of it has become a trend today in IF. Starting from adopting simple automation processes of transactions to using sophisticated technology like Blockchain and AI has been tested in IF. Since the technology has no religion and no boundaries, there is potential to enhance the mechanisms used in IF.

Therefore, it is imperative to conduct comprehensive research to find out the impact of 4IR on IF. As such, the objective of this chapter is to find out the extent to which technology has been adopted in IF and to recommend the potential application of technology in IF by highlighting the challenges that IF could overcome with the adoption of appropriate technology. This study adopts a qualitative research method where the existing developments found in the subject matter are presented and reviewed to derive conclusions. It is essential to note that the development in the application of technology to IF is an area that is continuously and swiftly evolving every day. The capturing of the developments in this regard has, therefore, become a challenge, showing the paramount consideration given by the IF industry to adopt the appropriate technology. In the adoption of technology in IF, the only limitation one ought to be mindful of is not concerning the kind of technology one adopts. Instead, the focus should be to ensure that whatever aspect of the technology is adopted must comply with the underlying principles of Shariah. Given that, there is no notion of shariah-compliant technology, and technology ought to be adopted and implemented in IF without eroding its essence, which is built primarily on achieving compliance with the tenets of Shariah.

This study is divided into five sections. Followed by the introduction, Section 2 discusses the definition and background of 4IR, while Section 3 provides a brief literature of 4IR in relation to IF. Section 4 discusses the evidence of technological progress in the IF industry by highlighting the challenges and suggesting recommendations for further improvements in the IF industry using technology. The final section of the study presents the summary and conclusion of the study.

2 Definition and Background of 4IR

The notion of 4IR was first introduced in Germany in 2011. Later, this concept was publicly declared and officially announced by Schwab at the annual general meeting of the World Economic Forum, 2016 held in Geneva (Dais, 2017; Kagermann, Lukas & Wahlster, 2011; Schwab, 2015). According to a World Economic Forum Report (2015), the present industrial structure will change radically, and 80% of the world's population will be interconnected through the trillions of sensors that control the physical and cyber spaces by 2025, with an economic effect estimated to be equivalent to USD 4–11 trillion. These revolutionary changes are not only due to the impact of sectoral breath but also due to the speed of transformation (Menon & Fink, 2019).

The definition of 4IR still seems to be unclear, and it is not easy to understand what 4IR means due to its state of infancy in many ways (Um, 2019). Nonetheless, 4IR has been described as the cyber-physical system (CPS) that represents the exponential changes to the way of life and work due to the bridging of the IoT and the Internet of Systems (Drath & Horch, 2014; Fobes, 2018; Mosterman & Zander, 2017).

The scope of 4IR appears likely to be far-reaching and much more comprehensive than the three previous revolutions. It will be driven largely by the convergence of physical, biological, and digital innovations. Simultaneously, waves of further breakthroughs are occurring and moving from gene sequencing to nanotechnology, from renewable energy to quantum computing, and from automated production and IT to an automated society. This revolution is expected to have an impact on all disciplines, industries, markets, and economies (Schwab, 2017).

The industrial world stands on the brink of the era of 4IR that will radically change the human use of technology, with major implications

Table 1 Evaluation of fourth industrial revolution

Revolutions	Period	Cause	Effect	Achievements
First Revolution	1760–mid 1800s	• Steam engine powered by water	• Mechanize production • Iron and textile production	• Steam engine • Textile • Steel • Train
Second Revolution	1870–1914 (start of WWI)	• Electrical motors powered by electricity	• Mass production • Steel making process • Large scale machine tools • Manufacturing	• Internal combustion engine metallurgy • Machine building • Train • Car
Third Revolution	(1970–2011)	• Electronics circuits • Programmable logic controller (PLC) • Information and communication technology (ICT) derived by digital signals	• Production • Automation human controlled manufacturing	• Computers • Robots • Automation • Chemistry • Plane
Fourth Revolution (4IR)	(2011–ongoing)	• Cyber-physical systems (CPS) • Advanced automation and robotics • Artificial intelligence • IoT derived by smart digital signals	• Autonomous manufacturing • Connected businesses	• Internet • 3D printer • Genetic engineering • High tech industries • Electric car • Ultra-fast train

Source Adapted from Nick von Tunzelmann (2003) and Gunal (2019)

for the way people live, work, and relate to one another, which is summarized in Table 1. The first industrial revolution started after 1760 and led to the move from hand production to machines, which created many new industrial processes, including chemical manufacturing. The second industrial revolution occurred after 1870 and was initially stimulated by new methods for the mass production of steel but then spread to the development of other industries, such as chemicals and transport. The third industrial revolution (the "Digital Age") began in the 1970s with the developments in electronics, IT, and automated production. These revolutions have shaped the pharmacy practice that we recognize today (Baines et al., 2019).

The impact of the industrial revolution is profound, and in any era of industrial revolution, people, and society are the beneficiaries in one aspect and they are also the ones affected in another. Unlike the others, 4IR is not restricted to industrial production but also manifested in all aspects of human lives and society, like technology, biology, business, economics, and ethical perspectives (Gentner, 2016; Home et al., 2015; Ivanov et al., 2016; Kube & Rinn, 2014; Lalanda et al., 2017; Li et al., 2017; Qin & Cheng, 2016; Sackey & Bester, 2016; Singer, 2015; Sommer, 2015; Theorin et al., 2017; Webster, 2015; Weiss et al., 2016; Xu et al., 2013). According to Schwab, founder and EC of the World Economic Forum, 2016, the impact is profound as this revolution is evolving with greater velocity, affecting various industries, economies, and countries across the world, and calling for a total overhaul of the existing systems and processes.

3   4IR Relations to Islamic Finance

There were many previous studies conducted on 4IR. However, there has been a scarcity of conceptual and empirical studies from the IF perspectives to the best of the researchers' knowledge. Scholars suggest that industrial production can increase significantly through technological integration and data automation systems (Lasi et al., 2014; Buhr, 2015; Berawi, 2018). Dallasega et al. (2017) argued that 4IR could positively affect the industry, market supply chain, and multiple applicants. Similarly, Kamble et al. (2018) and Lu (2017) supported the arguments of Dallasega et al. (2017). They also noticed that 4IR promotes production through technological integration. Therefore, 4IR can generate more sustainable outcomes in terms of social, economic, and environmental perspectives.

On the other hand, Ibarra et al. (2018) and Pereira and Romero (2017) mentioned that 4IR carries out several disruptive technological innovations that can hamper the delivery process. Given the complexity of system integration and production, it may become a barrier to the information and industrial revolution. Islam et al. (2018) suggested that as a developing country, Bangladesh is still far behind in 4IR technologies due to its poor infrastructure facilities, lack of a skilled workforce, additional installation costs, lack of government support, and knowledge of the relevant discipline. Therefore, the strategic decision makers in Bangladesh need to adapt to 4IR so that the country can apply and utilize its benefits.

Sahabuddin et al. (2019) suggested that IF and its digitalization process create an opportunity to rebuild trust and confidence in the financial system that has to promote economic growth and sustainable development. This implies that the role of innovation and the creative use of digital technology are a powerful vision of the UN's Sustainable Development Agenda in 2030. Santoso (2019) suggested that the application of 4IR through the blockchain system can accelerate the efficiency of the zakat management system, and the efforts of digitalization steps must contribute to the development of the economy and poverty alleviation in society. Ali et al. (2019) investigated the potential impact of FinTech on the Islamic banking and IF industries in Brunei and Malaysia by employing content and semi-structured interviews. The findings indicate that FinTech has the potential to have an impact (both positive and negative) on both the IF and conventional finance industries. However, the impact of the IF industry is sluggish compared to its conventional counterparts.

Moreover, the current trend of 4IR has attracted the attention of researchers and policy-makers in the shariah-compliant financial system, particularly concerning its significant implications for the innovation and digitalization of IF products and services. Oseni and Ali (2019) found that crowdfunding platforms are being used more and more to fund shariah-compliant projects. This is especially true for small and medium-sized enterprises (SMEs), housing, and agricultural financing through FinTech. Saiti et al. (2016) gave the example of the recently introduced cross-border multi-currency-based platform known as the Investment Account Platform (IAP) to facilitate global and regional financing opportunities by a consortium of several renowned IBs in Malaysia. In addition, it describes how it has started a new online-based platform for performing liquidity management, known as commodity muarābah transactions. These initiatives are gaining momentum in different jurisdictions, particularly in the Asian, North African, and Middle East (MENA) regions. The rate of growth of online muarābah was said to be very high, and the number of transactions related to it rose by 178% from 2009 to 2014 (MIFC, 2016). Similarly, the Dubai Multi Commodities Center in the United Arab Emirates introduced the Commodity-Based *Murarbahah* Trading Platform (CMTP) in 2013 through the shariah-based tradeable warrants model. This model has made it possible to transfer ownership and process transactions on online platforms via agency (*wakālah*) investments as underlying assets on the Nasdaq Dubai Murabahah Platform. It has also made it easier and faster for its banks to offer financing services to their customers (Nazir & Lui, 2016).

Overall, studies in the area of 4IR from an IF perspective are still in their infancy stage, and it is noteworthy to highlight that IF has just started paying attention to the 4IR arena.

4 Adoption of Technology in Islamic Finance

Adoption of Technology in Islamic Banking, Takaful and Capital Markets

In essence, there are three main components of Islamic commercial finance, namely, Islamic banking, takaful, and Islamic capital markets. In all these components, technology could be used to enhance the processes, documentation, governance, and dispute resolution mechanisms. Despite digitization being adopted in Islamic banking, it is still at a developing stage as the investments needed to be made in this sector are immense. For example, some banks, like Bank Islam Brunei Darussalam (BIBD), have shown that through investing in technology and adopting technology, they have enjoyed many advantages, such as reaching out to new customers at a lower cost. Likewise, CIMB Bank in Malaysia, including CIMB Islamic, has invested RM 2 billion in technology, including data analytics, for the 2019–2023 period, which resulted in their digital users increasing to 4.9 million in 2018 (Global Ethical Banking, 2019).

As for takaful institutions, it was reported in 2019 that some UAE takaful companies had adopted blockchain technology to reduce the transaction costs and assist in having a fast and secure process of making claims (IFN FinTech, 2019). These takaful companies collaborated with an emerging InsurTech company called Addenda, which uses distributed ledger technology to streamline processes between insurance companies (Unlock, 2019). Whereas in Malaysia, it was reported in 2020 that FWD

Takaful Berhad (formerly known as HSBC Amanah Takaful (Malaysia) Berhad) has entered into an agreement with Naluri Hidup Sdn Bhd to provide a digital therapeutics program to customers of FWD Care Direct, which is its first online family takaful cancer plan (FWD Takaful, 2020). In addition, Malaysian takaful companies have adopted digital strategies and launched an application called "Click for Cover," through which the takaful companies' products are available online, and payments for subscriptions or contributions can be made using e-payment facilities (Disruptive Tech Asian, 2018).

In the area of Islamic capital markets, blockchain-based Sukuk was first introduced in 2019 by Blossom Finance, and USD 50,000 has been raised to help microfinance institutions via the blockchain-based Blossom Finance's SmartSukuk™ platform (Blossom, 2019). Similarly, in 2019, it was reported that Wethaq, a Dubai-based company, issued its first pilot blockchain Sukuk successfully under the supervision of the Dubai Financial Services Authority (DFSA). The pilot blockchain Sukuk was issued on its decentralized platform, which automates the roles of a registrar, CSD, trustee delegate, paying agent, calculation agent, and transfer agent (Ledger Insights, 2019).

Furthermore, Islamic crowdfunding platforms and Islamic peer-to-peer (P2P) lending platforms have also developed concurrently (Ethis, 2018; Lloyd, 2020), highlighting the importance of big data analytics in shariah stock screening, which is an area that ought to be explored. In 2019, it was reported that Wahed, a US-based investment fund company, had become the first globally accessible halal robo-advisor for Islamic value-based investing. This was a big step forward, since the funds were first initially available to people in the US and UK but are now available to people in over 130 countries (I-FIKR, 2019).

While the examples above have provided some insights into IF steady technology adoption over the years, there is still a need for regulatory authorities to be proactive in encouraging Islamic financial institutions (IFIs) to invest and experiment in the emerging technology. This can be achieved through devising regulatory sandbox environments, which allow IFIs to test and then implement technology-based transactions in the market. It is noteworthy that some of the regulatory authorities in many countries, such as Malaysia and the United Arab Emirates, have assumed this initiative. However, due to the lack of regulatory framework applicable to transactions made with technology, the result of those initiatives are not entirely promising. The regulatory authorities need to develop the relevant technology-related requirements applicable to the IF transactions in the hope that enough guidance in this regard can be given to the IFIs without compromising the trust factor required for stakeholders to get involved in such transactions. Furthermore, they should rethink the implications of IR 4.0 and how they reform and restructure their productivity for participating in the digital economy, which fosters diversity and increases interconnectivity among local and global key players (Al-Roubaie & Sarea, 2020).

Nonetheless, there is no one-size-fits-all approach to regulating the digital technology-enabled applications in general and virtual currencies in particular. This is mainly because the social conditions and financial investment market parameters in the regulatory jurisdictions around the world differ from one jurisdiction to another. The rule of thumb is that most jurisdictions adopt a wait-and-see approach as blockchain technology is still relatively new. Even those jurisdictions which have issued regulations or guidelines generally adhere to the do-no-harm approach by introducing policy-based regulations and guidelines for fear of stifling the potential for the development of blockchain technology in their respective jurisdictions. Also, it can be noted that most Islamic jurisdictions have warned about the bubbles and risks of investing in digital currencies. This is unsurprising given the need to protect local financial investment markets from any systemic shock which may occur if there is a sizeable public uptake of virtual currencies and then a failure of the currencies. In this regard, Muslim countries may introduce assets-backed (gold or silver, or other tangible commodities) digital currencies which meet theshariah compliance requirements for financial markets stability.

The 4IR vis-a-vis COVID-19: The Way Forward

Despite the devastating global economic effects, COVID-19 serves as a wake-up call for the IFIs' stakeholders to reassess their fundamental value proposition as the underlying dimensions, nature, causes, and effects of the ongoing crisis are different from other pandemics. A reassessment is essential for expanding and exploring the IF industry as a development-oriented financial intermediation model rather than a purely technical phenomenon-based model. This is also perhaps the timeliest notice for the IF industry to start adopting technology immediately and thoughtfully. In this context, following the COVID-19 crisis, perhaps the changes in technology over time will only yield positive results.

In the era of post-COVID-19, the 4IR, mostly FinTech, may play a more prominent role in IF since it can increase streamlining process and standardization, ensure transparency, and reduce cost, making IF instruments more competitive than conventional forms (GIFA, 2020).

Furthermore, Islamic FinTech can play a vital role in financial stability in the post-pandemic era and is expected to accelerate Islamic banking in the coming years by improving access to financial services and transforming Islamic social finance (Jakarta Post, 2020).

Although there are still debates over a few instruments of FinTech like cryptocurrencies (Hassan et al., 2020), FinTech itself is relatively new, though the prospect of Islamic FinTech is emerging. Islamic FinTech should deliver only goods and services that do not only comply with shariah rulings but also with their spirits. For example, FinTech components such as smart contracts, tokenized assets, and crowdfunding should facilitate more shariah-compliant IF instruments at the bottom of the social pyramid. Notably, this would benefit SME entrepreneurs by accelerating growth, start-up, and business recovery in the post-pandemic era.

In addition, FinTech-based Islamic social finance can aid in easing the socio-economic impact during the pandemic period. In this context, Islamic social finance can assist the affected population by facilitating zakat as short-term relief and prioritizing to invest in business activities in terms of social impact. Meanwhile, impact-based Sukuk can act as a source of long-term capital for governments and companies. Similarly, the *waqf* entities would also be able to contribute to long-term resilience. Moreover, P2P lending is another good investment tool during the post-pandemic era. It can play a fantastic role as a diversification strategy during a period of uncertainty in a pandemic crisis (Malaymail, 2020), as P2P lending allows us with a surplus to finance the borrower via an online platform without intermediaries (Piskin & Kus, 2019).

5 Summary and Concluding Remarks

The 4IR is not an exception from the other previous three revolutions. It also has some challenges that require a thorough study and understanding to find a better policy implementation. For example, the European Parliament (2016) identified some major challenges in this regard, including *inter alia* changing business models, investment decisions, data issues, legal questions of liability and intellectual property, standards, and skill mismatches. At the same time, other types of challenges have been identified in Germany, such as unemployment, social security, data privacy, disqualification, and increased stress for new kids (Manda & Dhaou, 2019). In addition, the flow of cross-broader data may bring some challenges for taking more significant benefits from 4IR. Notably, personal and sensitive information may create obstacles to drawing the benefits from 4IR. For instance, the privacy of financial transactions and health records should be maintained in a particular country. Otherwise, it may influence the other countries in terms of strategies and policies. However, the security and privacy of data do not depend on the physical location of servers. Instead, they depend on the protocols and rules in places where the data are accessed, used, and stored.

The 4IR has gained popularity due to its vast potential to improve income levels and increase the quality of life for the mass population worldwide. To date, the beneficiary groups are mostly consumers from 4IR. For example, consumers can access and achieve the gains from the digital transformation of technology. Technology has made it easy and affordable to consumers, even in remote areas. At the same time, from the industry and business sides, they are bound to concentrate on improving their quality, efficiency, and production line. People are happy in their personal lives by getting new products and services at affordable prices. As an illustration, ordering a cab, booking a flight, reading a book, watching a movie, and playing a game, can all be done with the click of a finger.

Furthermore, digital innovation will lead to the supply chain side gaining productivity and efficiency in the long term. Global logistics and supply chain management will become more efficient, which would help minimize transportation and communication costs. Therefore, the trade of costs will be controlled, and it will open a new era of business, which would accelerate the markets and economic growth (Rose, 2016). The 4IR is expected to progress in a rapid manner that would make daily life closer to exploring new areas of study. The development areas of 4IR are multi-dimensional that the human being will pose and consequently enable them to travel across the galaxy and explore the potential of leveraging other planets' resources (Al Hajri, 2019).

Muslim countries should pay attention to amending the existing rules and regulations in shariah compliance boundaries. For example, cyber laws need to be made more robust for dealing with unethical trespasses into the customers' privacy and other banks' clients (Al Ghassani et al., 2017). Nevertheless, the 4IR has been discussed from multi-disciplinary perspectives. However, to the best of researchers' knowledge, conceptual and empirical studies have been scarce from the perspectives of IF. Thus, to continue shaping the industry and organizations, a plethora of research opportunities on this topic remain untapped. Meanwhile, with the increasingly in-depth understanding of 4IR, there are more research potentials to combine conventional and IF industries of 4IR with a broader scope. Therefore, rather than defining 4IR, the need to understand its impact is far more critical in adopting and coupling it in our social, economic, political, environmental, and business life.

To sum up, from the discussions mentioned in previous sections, it can be concluded that COVID-19 has started to disrupt the paradigms of changing process. Even if scientists are able to discover a cure or vaccine for this virus, we can no longer speak of returning to our previous notion of life. Now, we are speaking of an entirely new understanding of going to the "new normal." Habits resulting from COVID-19 are expected to impact people's lives in the coming years (Neto et al., 2020). In this context, a reassessment is essential for the expansion and exploration of the IF industry as a development-oriented financial intermediation model rather than a purely technical phenomenon-based model in line with the underlying principles of shariah. This is also perhaps the timeliest period for the IF industry to focus more on technology with an immediate effect and in a serious manner. In the era of post-COVID-19, 4IR, mostly FinTech, may play a more significant role in IF. Moreover, it will increase streamlining process and standardization and ensure transparency and reduce costs, making IF instruments more competitive than their conventional counterparts.

References

Abdou, D. I. A. W. (2015). The global financial crisis and Islamic finance: A review of selected literature. *Journal of Islamic Accounting and Business Research*, 6(1), 94–106.

Ahmad, A.U.F., and Habib, F. (2020). FinTech-based Islamic social financing products: a critical evaluation. In Y. A. Albastaki, A. Razzaque & A. M. Sarea (Eds.), *Innovative strategies for Implementing FinTech in Banking* (pp. 67–82). IGI Global, Pennsylvania. https://doi.org/10.4018/978-1-7998-3257-7.ch004

Ahmad, A.U.F. (2019). The challenges and potentials of improving access to Islamic financial services in non-Muslim countries: The case of Australia. In

E. Ghazali et al. (Eds.), *Management of Sharīʿah Compliant businesses—Case studies on creation of sustainable value* (pp. 9–20). Springer. https://doi.org/10.1007/978-3-030-10907-3_2

Habib, F., & Ahmad, A. U. F. (2019). Using blockchain and smart contracts for waqf institutions. In Muhammad Anshari, M. N. Al Munawar & M. Masri (Eds.), *Financial technology and disruptive innovation in ASEAN* (pp. 225–244), IGI Global. https://doi.org/10.4018/978-1-5225-9183-2

Al Ghassani, A., Al Lawati, A., & Ananda, S. (2017). *Banking sector in Oman strategic issues, challenges and future scenarios*. College of Banking and Financial Studies, Oman. http://www.cbfs.edu.om/UploadsAll/Annexure%2013%20Edited%20Book%20on%20Bankng%20Sector%20in%20Oman%20-%202017.pdf. Retrieved 20 February 2020.

Al Hajri, H. (2019). The innovation of internet industries transformed to fourth 4th industrial revolution: Threats and challenges of the cyber-enabled industries. *International Journal of Engineering and Technology, 8*(1.12), 79–82.

Al Hilal Bank. (2018). Al Hilal Bank executes the world's first blockchain sukuk transaction. https://www.alhilalbank.ae/en/news/2018/november/al-hilal-bank-executes-the-worlds-first-blockchainsukuk-transaction.aspx. Retrieved 25 January 2021.

Ali, H., Abdullah, R., & Zaini, M. (2019). FinTech and its potential impact on Islamic banking and finance industry: A case study of Brunei Darussalam and Malaysia. *International Journal of Islamic Economics and Finance, 2*(1), 73–108.

Al-Roubaie, A., & Sarea, A. M. (2020). Rethinking economic development in Muslim societies in the context of the fourth industrial revolution. In *Joint European-US workshop on applications of invariance in computer vision* (pp. 683–695). Springer.

Anca, C. (2019). FinTech in Islamic finance: From collaborative finance to community-based finance. In U. Oseni & A. Nazim (Eds.), *FinTech in Islamic Finance* (pp. 47–63). Routledge.

Baines, D., Nørgaard, L., Babar, Z. U., & Rossing, C. (2019). The Fourth Industrial Revolution: Will it change pharmacy practice? *Research in Social and Administrative Pharmacy*. In press. https://doi.org/10.1016/j.sapharm.2019.04.003

Berawi, M. (2018). Utilizing big data in industry 4.0: Managing competitive advantages and business ethics. *International Journal of Technology. International Journal of Technology, 9*(3), 430–433. https://doi.org/10.14716/ijtech.v9i3.1948

Buhr, D. (2015). Social innovation policy for Industry 4.0. In *Friedrich-Ebert-Stiftung, division for social and economic policies*. The Friedrich-Ebert-Stiftung, http://library.fes.de/pdf-files/wiso/11479.pdf. Retrieved January 25, 2021.

Blossom. (2019). World's first primary sukuk Issuance on blockchain closes. https://blossomfinance.com/press/world-s-first-primary-sukuk-issuance-on-blockchain-closes. Retrieved 16 August 2020.

Boubyan Bank. (2018). Boubyan Bank launches AI based "Msa3ed" service to clients. https://www.pressreader.com/kuwait/kuwaittimes/20180510/282059097636779. Retrieved 17 August 2020.

Dallasega, P., Rojas, R., Rauch, E., & Matt, D. (2017). Simulation based validation of supply chain effects through ICT enabled real-time capability, in ETO production planning. *Procedia Manufacturing, FAIM, 11*(1), 846–853.

Dais, S. (2017). Industrie 4.0 Anstoß, Vision, Vorgehen. In B. Vogel-Heuser, T. Bauernhansl, M. ten Hompel (Hrsg.): *Handbuch Industrie* 4.0 Bd.4 (pp. 261–277). Allgemeine Grundlagen, Berlin: Springer Vieweg, S.

Disruptive Tech Asian. (2018). Takaful Malaysia launches seamless customer interaction with click for cover. https://disruptivetechasean.com/big_news/takaful-malaysia-launches-seamless-customer-interaction-withclick-for-cover/. Retrieved 16 August 2020.

Ethis. (2018). Islamic crowdfunding platforms in Malaysia. https://blog.ethis.co/islamic-crowdfunding-platformsmalaysia/. Retrieved 17 August 2020.

European Parliament. (2016). Industry 4.0: digitalization for productivity and growth. www.europarl.europa.eu/RegData/etudes/BRIE/.../EPRS_BRI. Retrieved 15 December 2019.

Fobes. (2018). The 4th industrial revolution is here, are you ready?. https://www.forbes.com/sites/bernardmarr/2018/08/13/the-4th-industrial-revolution-is-here-areyouready/#7459b59a628b. Retrieved 20 February 2020.

FWD Takaful. (2020). FWD Takaful partners with Naluri to offer digital therapeutics program. https://www.fwd.com.my/en/press/2020/FWD-Takaful-partners-with-Naluri-to-offer-Digital-Therapeutics-Program/. Retrieved 16 August 2020.

Gentner, S. (2016). Industry 4.0: Reality, future or just science fiction? how to convince today's management to invest in tomorrow's future! successful strategies for industry 4.0 and manufacturing IT. *CHIMIA International Journal for Chemistry, 70*(9), 628–633. https://doi.org/10.2533/chimia.2016.628

GIFA (2020). https://gifaawards.com/isfireIssues/April-2020.pdf

Global Ethical Banking. (2019). Digitising to drive growth of Islamic banks. http://www.globalethicalbanking.com/digitising-drive-growth-islamic-banks/. Retrieved 17 August 2020.

Gunal, M. (2019). Simulation and the fourth industrial revolution. *Simulation for Industry 4.0* (pp. 1–17). Springer. https://doi.org/10.1007/978-3-030-04137-3_1

Home, S., Grutzner. J., Hadlich. T. et al. (2015). Semantic industry: Challenges for computerized information processing in *Industrie 4.0. Automatisierung Stechnik, 63*(2), 74–86. https://doi.org/10.1515/auto-2014-1142

HSBC. (2019). HSBC leads Malaysia's first pilot blockchain letter-of-credit transaction, https://www.google.com/search?q=HSBC+amanah+and+blockchain+letter+of+credit&rlz=1C1GCEU_enLK819LK819&oq=HSBC+amanah+and+blockchain+letter+of+credit&aqs=chrome..69i57.13859j0j4&sourceid=chrome&ie=UTF-8. Retrieved 17 August 2020.

Ibarra, D., Ganzarain, J., & Igartua, J. (2018). Business model innovation through industry 4.0: A review, *Procedia Manufacturing, 22*(1), 4–10.

I-FIKR. (2019). Wahed becomes the first globally accessible halal robo-advisor. https://ifikr.isra.my/news/post/wahed-becomes-the-first-globally-accessible-halal-robo-advisor. Retrieved 17 August 2020.

IFN FinTech. (2019). Emirati Takaful operators adopt blockchain technology as UAE eyes insurtech hub title. https://ifnfintech.com/emirati-takaful-operators-adopt-blockchain-technology-as-uae-eyes-insurtech-hubtitle/. Retrieved 11 August 2020.

IMF (2020). A crisis like no other; an uncertain recovery, *World Economic Outlook Update*, June 2020, www.imf.org.

IMF. (2015). https://www.imf.org/en/News/Articles/2015/09/28/04/53/sores100410a.

ISDB. (2020). https://www.isdb.org/pub/reports/2020/the-covid-19-crisis-and-islamic-finance-response-of-the-islamic-development-bank-group.

Iqbal & Mabud, A. (2021). The challenge of the fourth industrial revolution in an Islamic system of governance. *Journal of Islamic Governance, 6*(1), 41–60.

Islam, M., Jantan, A., Hashim, H., Chong, C., & Abdullah, M. (2018). Fourth industrial revolution in developing countries: A case of Bangladesh. *Journal of Management Information and Decision Sciences, 21*(1), 1–9.

Ivanov, D., Dolguy, A., Sokolov, B. et al. (2016). A dynamic model and an algorithm for short-term supply chain scheduling in the smart factory industry 4.0. *International Journal of Production Research, 54*(2), 386–40.

Jakarta Post. (2020). https://www.thejakartapost.com/academia/2020/06/05/how-covid-19-will-reshape-islamic-finance-markets.html.

Javaid, M., Haleem, A., Vaishya, R., Bahl, S., Suman, R., and Vaish, A. (2020). Industry 4.0 technologies and their applications in fighting COVID-19 pandemic. *Diabetes and Metabolic Syndrome: Clinical Research and Reviews, 14*(1), 419–422.

Juris Tech. (2015). Bank Muamalat awards credit management project to juris. https://juristech.net/juristech/bank-muamalat-juris-credit/. Retrieved 17 August 2020.

Kagermann, H., Lukas, W., Wahlster, W. (2011). Industrie 4.0: Mit dem Internet der Dinge auf dem Weg zur vierten industriellen revolution. *VDI Nachrichten*, 13: 2. https://www.dfki.de/fileadmin/user_upload/DFKI/Medien/News_Media/Presse/PresseHighlights/vdinach2011a13-ind4.0-Internet-Dinge.pdf. Retrieved 20 February 2020.

Kamble, S., Gunasekaran, A., & Gawankar, S. (2018). Sustainable industry 4.0 framework: A systematic literature review identifying the current trends and future perspectives. *Process Safety and Environmental Protection, 117,* 408–425.

Kayed, R. N., & Hassan, M. K. (2011). The global financial crisis and Islamic finance. *Thunderbird International Business Review, 53*(5), 551–564.

Koizumi, S. (2019). The light and shadow of the fourth industrial revolution. In S. Lechevalier (Eds.), *Innovation beyond technology* (pp. 63–86). Creative Economy. Springer. https://doi.org/10.1007/978-981-13-9053-1_4

Kube, G., & Rinn, T. (2014). Industry 4.0-The next revolution in the industrial sector. *ZGK International, 67*(11), 30–32.

Lalanda, P., Morand, D., & Chollet, S. (2017). Autonomic mediation middleware for smart manufacturing. *IEEE Internet Computing, 21*(1), 32–39.

Lasi, H., Fettke, P., Kemper, H., Feld, T., and Hoffmann, M. (2014). Industry 4.0. *Business and Information Systems Engineering, 6*(4), 239–242.

Ledger Insights. (2019). R3's partner Wethaq issues its first blockchain sukuk. https://www.ledgerinsights.com/wethaq-blockchain-sukuk/. Retrieved 17 August 2020.

Li, G., Hou, Y., & Wu, A. (2017). Fourth industrial revolution: Technological drivers, impacts and coping methods. *Chinese Geographical Science, 27*(4), 626–637.

Liu, Y., & Xu, X. (2016). Industry 40 and cloud manufacturing: A comparative analysis. *Journal of Industrial Information Integration, 139*(3), 034701.

Lloyd, M. (2020). Islamic P2P lending platform launches in the UK. https://www.p2pfinancenews.co.uk/2020/07/13/islamic-p2p-lending-platform-launches-in-the-uk/. Retrieved 17 August 2020.

Lu, Y. (2017). Industry 4.0: A survey on technologies, application, and open research issues. *Journal of Industrial Information Integration, 6*(1), 1–10.

Malay Mail, (2020). https://www.malaymail.com/news/money/2020/06/15/p2p-financing-an-ideal-investment-portfolio-amidst-covid-19-says-funding-so/1875615.

Manda, M., & Dhaou, S. (2019). Responding to the challenges and opportunities in the 4th industrial revolution in developing countries. *ICEGOV2019: Proceedings of the 12th International Conference on Theory and Practice of Electronic Governance* (pp. 244–253). https://doi.org/10.1145/3326365.3326398

Manyika, J., & Chui, M. (2015). By 2025, Internet of things applications could have $11 trillion impact. Global Institute; repurposed in *FORTUNE*. http://fortune.com/2015/07/22/Mckinsey-internet-of-things/. Retrieved February 20, 2020.

Menon, J., & Fink, A. (2019). The fourth Industrial revolution and its implications for regional economic integration in ASEAN. *Journal of Asian Economic Integration, 1*(1), 32–47. https://doi.org/10.1177/2631684618821566

Microsoft News Center. (2018). KFH transforms customer service levels with microsoft AI and chatbot technologies. https://news.microsoft.com/en-xm/2018/08/06/kfh-transforms-customer-service-levels-with-microsoft-aiandchatbottechnologies/#:~. Retrieved 17 August 2020.

MIFC (Malaysia International Islamic Financial Centre). (2016). Islamic finance technology andinnovation. http://www.mifc.com/index.php?ch=28&pg=72&ac=172&bb=upload.pdf. Retrieved 20 February 2020.

Nazir, M., & Lui, C. (2016). A brief history of virtual economy. *Journal for Virtual Worlds Research, 9*(1), 1–23. https://doi.org/10.4101/jvwr.v9i1.7179

Neto, R. D. C. S., Maia, J. S., de Silva Neiva, S., Scalia, M. D., & de Andrade, J. B. S. O. (2020). The fourth industrial revolution and the coronavirus: A new era catalyzed by a virus. *Research in Globalization, 2*, 100024.

von Nick, T. (2003). Historical coevolution of governance and technology in the industrial revolutions. *Structural Change and Economic Dynamics, 14*(4), 365–384. https://doi.org/10.1016/S0954-349X(03)00029-8

O'Neill, A. (2021). Global gross domestic product (GDP) 2026. https://www.statista.com/statistics/268750/global-gross-domestic-product-gdp/. Retrieved 13 December 2021.

Oseni, U., & Ali, S. (2019). *FinTech in Islamic finance: theory and practice* (1st ed.) Routledge.

Pereira, A., & Romero, F. (2017). A review of the meanings and the implications of the Industry 4.0 concept. *Procedia Manufacturing, 13*(2017), 1206–1214.

Qin, S., & Cheng, K. (2016). Special issue on future digital design and manufacturing: Embracing Industry 4.0 and beyond. *Chinese Journal of Mechanical Engineering, 29*(6), 1045.

Rose, G. (ed.). (2016). *The fourth industrial revolution: A Davos reader*. Council on Foreign Relations.

Sackey, S., & Bester, A. (2016). Industrial engineering curriculum in Industry 4.0 in a South African context. *South African Journal of Industrial Engineering, 27*(4), 101–114.

Sahabuddin, M., Muhammad, J., Yahya, M., Shah, S., & Rahman, M. (2018). The co-movement between Shariah compliant and sectorial stock indexes performance in Bursa Malaysia. *Asian Economic and Financial Review, 8*(4), 515–524.

Sahabuddin, M., Muhammad, J., Yahya, M., Shah, S., & Alam, M. (2019). Digitalization, innovation and sustainable development: An evidence of Islamic finance perspective. *International Journal of Asian Social Science, 9*(12), 651–656.

Saiti, B., Bacha, O., & Masih, M. (2016). Testing the conventional and Islamic financial market contagion: Evidence from wavelet analysis. *Emerging Markets Finance and Trade, 52*(8), 1832–1849. https://doi.org/10.1080/1540496X.2015.1087784

Santoso, I. (2019). Strategy for optimizing zakat digitalization in alleviation poverty in the era of industrial revolution 4.0, *IKONOMIKA*, 4(1), 35–52.
Schwab, K. (2017). *The fourth industrial revolution* (p. 192). Crown Business.
Singer P. (2015). Are you ready for Industry 4.0? *Solid State Technology*, 58(8), 2–2.
Sommer, L. (2015). Industrial revolution—Industry 4.0: are German manufacturing SMEs the first victims of this revolution? *Journal of Industrial Engineering and Management*, 8(5), 1512–1532. https://doi.org/10.3926/jiem.1470
The Asian Banker. (2017). CIMB tests acceptance of chatbots in Malaysia. http://www.theasianbanker.com/updates-and-articles/cimb-tests-acceptance-of-chatbots-in-malaysia. Retrieved 17 August 2020.
Theorin, A., Bengtsson, K., Provost, J. Leider, M., & Johnsson, C. (2017). An event-driven manufacturing information system architecture for industry 4.0, *International Journal of Production Research*, 55(5), 1297–1311.
The World Bank, (2020). https://www.worldbank.org/en/events/2020/05/12/responding-to-covid-19-how-islamic-finance-can-help.
The World Bank, (2020). https://www.worldbank.org/en/news/press-release/2020/06/08/covid-19-to-plunge-global-economy-into-worst-recession-since-world-war-ii.
Um, J. (2019). Introduction to the fourth industrial revolution, *Drones as Cyber-Physical Systems*, Ch 1 (pp. 1–20). Springer.
Unlock. (2019). UAE based Addenda insurtech blockchain firm signs on five insurance players. https://www.unlock-bc.com/news/2019-08-06/uae-based-addenda-insurtech-dlt-firm-signs-on-fiveinsurance-players. Retrieved 11 August 2020.
Webster, S. (2015). Coming to a factory near you: industry 4.0, *Manufacturing Engineering*, 154(3), 8.
Weiss, A., Hubber, A., Minichberger, J. et al., 2016. First application of robot teaching in an existing Industry 4.0 environment: does it really work? *Societies*, 6(3), 20. https://doi.org/10.3390/soc6030020
World Economic Forum. (2015). Deep shift: technology tipping points and societal impact, *Global Agenda Council on the Future of Software and Society Deep*. http://www3.weforum.org/docs/WEF_GAC15_Technological_Tipping_Points_report_2015.pdf. Retrieved 22 February 2020.
World Economic Forum. (2016). An insight, an idea with Yao Chen. https://www.weforum.org/events/world-economic-forum-annual-meeting-2016. Retrieved 22 February 2020.
World Economic Forum. (2017). *Global Competitiveness Report* 2017–2018. https://www.weforum.org/reports/the-global-competitiveness-report-2017-2018. Retrieved 22 February 2020.
Xu, J., Huang, E., Hsieh, L. et al. (2016). Simulation optimization in the era of industrial 4.0 and the industrial internet, *Journal of Stimulation*, 10(4), 310–320. https://doi.org/10.1057/s41273-016-0037-6

Innovative Islamic Financial Tools
for Sustainable and Socio-Economic Impact

Sukuk Innovation: Powering Sustainable Finance

Mustafa Adil, Henk Jan Hoogendoorn and Zul Hakim Jumat

1 The Convergence Between ESG, Islamic Finance, and SDGs

Demand for ESG Investments

Sustainable bonds are gradually reaching the critical mass. According to data from Refinitiv, in the first half of 2021, Sustainable finance bonds were collectively worth USD 551.6 billion, representing a 76% increase from H1 2020. More specifically, a subset of these is green bond

---

M. Adil
London Stock Exchange Group, Manama, Bahrain
e-mail: Mustafa.Adil@lseg.com

H. J. Hoogendoorn
Qatar Financial Centre, Doha, Qatar
e-mail: h.hoogendoorn@qfc.qa

Z. H. Jumat (✉)
Center for Islamic Economics and Finance, College of Islamic Studies, Hamad Bin Khalifa University, Doha, Qatar
e-mail: zhakim@hbku.edu.qa

© The Author(s), under exclusive license to Springer Nature Switzerland AG 2023
Z. H. Jumat et al. (eds.), *Islamic Finance, FinTech, and the Road to Sustainability*, Palgrave CIBFR Studies in Islamic Finance, https://doi.org/10.1007/978-3-031-13302-2_7

issuance, which totaled USD 259.3 billion in H1 2021, a nearly threefold increase year on year from 2020. Similarly, ESG bonds have grown at a considerable pace since their introduction in 2007 (Refinitiv, 2021a). Moreover, according to data from the Climate Bonds Initiative (CBI), in December 2020, global green bond issuance crossed the USD 1 trillion threshold in cumulative issuance since the market started, with green bond and green loan issuances totaling USD 270 billion in 2020 alone (Sustainalytics, 2021). More broadly, ESG and socially responsible investment (SRI) funds in the United States collectively surpassed the USD 1 trillion mark in assets under management (AuM) in March 2021 (Refinitiv, 2021b).

Several qualitative factors are bolstering the current demand for ESG investments, such as increased investor appetite, the decreasing cost of ESG investments relative to non-ESG investments, and greater awareness of ESG issues. Meanwhile, governments are also tapping into the ESG space to fund their green or sustainability-themed public projects. As a result, fund managers across the globe, including at powerhouses such as Blackrock, are altering their mandates to focus more on ESG-related investments. Moreover, according to a Morgan Stanley Sustainable Signals survey of asset owners, 80% said they actively integrated sustainable investing in 2019, an increase of 10% from the previous study in 2017 (Morgan Stanley, 2020). Also, the same survey found that 95% of millennials surveyed were interested in sustainable investing (Financial Times, 2021), which bodes well for the continued rise of ESG over the medium and longer term. Collectively, as of March 2020, the signatories to the 2005 UN Principles for Responsible Investing (PRI) manage over USD 103 trillion in assets, and ESG assets have grown 22% annually since this investment theme emerged in 2006 (Bhat, 2021). Furthermore, in key markets such as the US, ESG assets now make up a considerable share of investments—33% of all assets under management in 2021 (USD 17.1 trillion out of a total of USD 51.4 trillion) (Carlson, 2020). These numbers strongly indicate that ESG investments have gone mainstream.

Principles-Based Convergence of Shariah, ESG and SDGs

For some time now, there has been a gradual shift in the financial services industry away from shareholder primacy in corporate governance toward a more inclusive view of stakeholder-led governance, culminating in increased awareness about the need for a more inclusive form of capitalism. As a result, investors and other stakeholders, such as governments and large corporations, are keen to explore more holistic models of finance that also prioritize aspects of development agendas, reducing inequality empowering women, and combating water scarcity. Within this broader context, Islamic, ethical, and development finance have emerged as the key candidates for helping this transition toward a more sustainable and equitable global financial system.

Unsurprisingly, shariah-based finance, ESG concerns (which are essentially based on ethical finance values), and the SDG goals, in addition to their broadly similar aims, share a variety of foundational principles or values that make them natural allies in the movement toward sustainable finance at the global level. These similar Islamic and ethical/ESG finance values include emphasizing fairness, transparency, and tangible concern for the greater good and balancing profitability with sustainability. In particular, the focus on sustainability links both Islamic and ethical finance seamlessly with the ethos behind the SDGs, which promotes sustainable outcomes through tangible goals and measurable targets. Moreover, data from Refinitiv's EIKON database of over 5,000 non-financial companies suggests a strong link between Shariah screening practices and higher ESG scores for companies. The data also indicates that combining ESG and Shariah screening methods could lead to better risk-adjusted returns (Refinitiv, 2019). Table 1 summarizes the similarities and differences between ESG investing and Islamic finance. From the table, we can discern that there is much in common between the two, albeit with a few points of difference that are gradually waning as convergence between the two increases (e.g., active selection and stewardship are rising in Islamic finance incrementally).

Role of Islamic Capital Markets in Fulfilling SDGs

Despite the conceptual alignment between Islamic finance and the SDGs, there remains a gap in practice for the use of Islamic capital market funding to help fulfill the SDGs. With the global infrastructure funding gap estimated at USD 15 trillion by 2040 (George et al., 2019), and with the World Bank also estimating that developing countries worldwide will need to invest close to 4.5% of their GDP to achieve infrastructure-related SDGs, there is a clear need for increased funding flows toward the SDGs (Lu, 2020). Bridging this funding gap will require improved access

Table 1 Similarities and differences between Islamic and ethical finance

Similarities/differences	ESG investing	Islamic finance
Considers environmental and social factors	Yes	Yes in principle—standard is yet to be developed
Life protection—avoids adverse effects on life	Yes	Yes
Consideration of long term goals and perspectives for stakeholders	Yes	Yes
Role in development and achieving SDGs	Yes	Yes
Exclusionary screening to avoid and exclude investments that are not aligned with their morals/criteria	Yes	Yes
Established governance	No—still at early stages	Yes—rather legalistic
Religious foundation	No—increasingly secular	Yes
Derivatives market/sale of risk	Yes	Depends—the majority of financial derivatives are prohibited
Best in class screening/active selection	Yes	No—not generally used
Stewardship	Yes	No—not generally used

Source Adapted from Aderazi (2020)

to the global investor pool. In this regard, Islamic capital markets may broaden the pool of shariah-sensitive in Muslim-majority countries, particularly in developed Islamic finance jurisdictions in the Gulf region and Southeast Asia that have surplus funding and/or technical expertise in tapping Islamic finance capital market funds. Although the Islamic funds market, worth USD 126 billion in outstanding funds in 2021 (Refinitiv, 2021a, 2021b), could help plug this gap, the focus should arguably be on patient capital that can be set aside for medium and longer-term SDG and environmental infrastructure outcomes. In that sense, and given the nature of shariah-compliant fixed income, it would make more sense to focus efforts on deploying new sukuk issuances toward expressly fulfilling SDGs. Governments and corporates across the 57 Muslim-majority countries could tap into increasing investor appetite for green and sustainable investments that provide stable returns by issuing sukuk that cater to various SDGs or positive environmental outcomes.

2 ESG Sukuk

ESG Sukuk Landscape

The ESG sukuk market size in H12021 was USD 4.05 billion (see Fig. 1), as measured by the value of outstanding sukuk. Although this segment is relatively small compared to the broader ESG market, which recently surpassed the USD 100 trillion threshold, ESG sukuk is growing at an impressive rate. As the chart below illustrates, ESG sukuk has grown over eight times in a relatively short span of four years, from USD 468 million to USD 4,051 million, at a compound annual growth rate (CAGR) of 71.5%. This augurs well for the future development of this segment. Cumulatively, since 2017, 174 ESG sukuk have been issued, with a total value of USD 14.29 billion.

In terms of geography, four countries account for almost all ESG sukuk issuers—Saudi Arabia, Indonesia, Malaysia, and the UAE, with the bulk of issuers, 73%, from just two countries: Saudi Arabia (45.3%) and Indonesia (27.7%). Interestingly, as Table 2 illustrates, the top five ESG sukuk issuances to date make up 87% of the total value of ESG sukuk issuance to date (USD 12.45 billion out of a total of USD 14.29 billion).

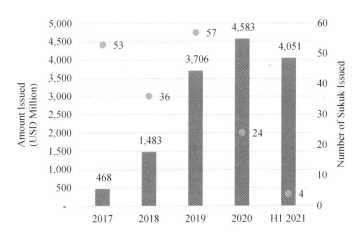

Fig. 1 Global ESG sukuk issuance by year and number of sukuk issues (*Source* Refinitiv)

Table 2 Top 5 ESG sukuk issuances by value

Issuer	Sum of issuance size (million USD)
Islamic Development Bank (IsDB)	5,182.10
Indonesian Gov	3,969.70
Saudi Electricity Company	1,300.00
Majid Al Futtaim Group	1,200.00
Malaysia Wakala Sukuk Bhd	800.00

Source Refinitiv

Development of ESG Sukuk

In 2014, the Securities Commission of Malaysia, a leading jurisdiction for Islamic finance, introduced a Sustainable and Responsible Investment (SRI) Sukuk framework. This regulatory precursor helped pave the way for market developments in Islamic green finance, namely, shariah-compliant financing of investments that focused on developing positive environmental impacts, improving energy efficiency, reducing pollution, and mitigating climate change. Subsequently, ESG sukuk emerged in the form of green sukuk in Malaysia in 2017, issued by energy companies such as Tadau Energy and Quantum Solar Park. Despite their small size (typically less than USD 10 million), these sukuk helped provide use cases for sukuk that meet ESG criteria and brought this new market to the attention of regional and global investors. Not long after, in 2019, new countries entered the market, such as Indonesia and the UAE.

Along with these new countries, another notable development was the increase in issuance size. There were 17 ESG sukuk over USD 10 million, seven between USD 20–100 million, and four ESG sukuk issuances were over the USD 500 million mark. These four "mega-issuances" in 2019 were notable not only for their sheer size but were also different from previous issuances as they were listed on exchanges rather than arranged via private placements. Also, unlike most smaller issuances in the past, these mega-issuances were typically US dollar or Euro-denominated, indicating perhaps a more global uptake by investors.

Qualitatively, the market continued to witness innovation as well. In particular, two ESG sukuk come to mind: **HSBC Amanah's SDG sukuk** and the **Islamic Development Bank (IsDB) sustainability sukuk**. HSBC Amanah's SDG sukuk in 2017 (see Table 3) was the world's first sukuk that explicitly set out to help achieve outcomes

Table 3 HSBC Amanah SDG sukuk profile

Issuer	HSBC Amanah (Malaysia)
Obligor	HSBC Bank
Size	RM 500 million (USD 120.45 million)
Type	5-year Medium Term Note (MTN)
Use of proceeds	Sustainable Development Projects
Why unique	This was the world's first sustainability sukuk by a financial institution and was a landmark issuance in that its proceeds would be used to help achieve eight out of the 17 SDG goals

Source United Nations Development Programme (2018)

Table 4 IsDB's Debut sustainability sukuk profile

Issuer	IDB trust services
Obligor	Islamic Development Bank
Size	USD 1.5 billion
Type	Dollar-denominated Eurobond
Use of proceeds	A variety of socioeconomic goals, such as: alleviating unemployment, socioeconomic advancement and empowerment, social and affordable housing, financing for SMEs, microfinance, and affordable basic infrastructure
Why unique	This was the world's first supranational AAA-rated sustainability sukuk, was listed on multiple exchanges (most ESG sukuk are done by private placements), and was notable for its large issuance size as well

Source Retrieved from Refinitiv Eikon database as of August 2021

aligned to the SDGs. More specifically, it was the first sukuk issuance by a financial institution that marked the SDGs as the beneficiary of the sukuk's proceeds (United Nations Development Programme, 2018). It focuses on eight out of the seventeen SDGs, and the issuance size is RM 500 million (USD 120.45 million).

In 2019, IsDB issued the first supranational sustainability sukuk as part of its newly formed Sustainable Finance Framework (see Table 4). The EUR1 billion issuance was the first-ever AAA-rated green sukuk globally. The profits from the issuance were earmarked for use in combating climate change and bolstering green projects across the 57 OIC Muslim-majority countries under the IsDB's remit, including projects relating to renewable energy, clean transport, and energy efficiency (Islamic Development Bank, 2019).

Table 5 Timeline of ESG sukuk and funds—key market developments

2014	2015	2016	2017	2018	2019	2020	2021
• SC Malaysia launched SRI sukuk framework			• Malaysia issued world's first green sukuk—Tradau Energy • HSBC Amanah issued first-ever SDG sukuk • ASEAN green bond standards introduced		• IsDB issues first-ever sustainability sukuk • UAE enters ESG sukuk market		• Rise of *waqf*-based ESG funds

As of writing, in 2021, the ESG market continues to grow and see innovations, such as *waqf*-based ESG funds in Malaysia and Saudi Arabia. In Malaysia, issuers of such waqf-based ESG funds include Maybank and Kenanga Investors. At the same time, in Saudi Arabia, there are currently eight waqf investment funds managed by four domestic asset managers, including Jadwa and SNB Capital (Refinitiv, 2021a). These Saudi and Malaysian waqf investment funds aim to harness the power of waqf. This Islamic social finance instrument has historically channeled philanthropic funds to further socioeconomic development and is witnessing a revival through contemporary Islamic finance. Other developments include Malaysia's first-ever sustainability sukuk, which employed an innovative underlying asset in the form of public transportation vouchers on the domestic train system. At the same time, a Sudanese bank offered what it said was Sudan's first green sukuk, which focused on renewable energy (Table 5).

3 Next-Generation Innovation Through Sukuk

One of the most exciting aspects of the risk of ESG sukuk is their potential to support the development of the next-generation economy, with a strong focus on innovation, both in terms of the Islamic finance instruments used and, more importantly, in the impact they have in bridging the funding gap in pivotal real-economy sectors such as energy and aviation. As the effects of climate change continue to intensify, the need to mitigate against them and boost the transition to a decarbonized economy is no longer optional. At an implementation level, targeting historically significant polluting sectors such as energy and aviation makes practical sense, though the imperative to reduce emissions and achieve net-zero needs to be completed across other industries to achieve the various targets set globally. In this regard, green sukuk is a welcome development. They enable the energy sector transformation in major Islamic finance markets such as Malaysia and Saudi Arabia by funding environmentally friendly projects such as solar parks, biogas plants, and wind farms.

A key concern amid the global carbon transition is that development goals should not be left behind, especially in developing economies at risk due to megatrends such as climate change, changing demographics, and rising food insecurity. At the governmental level, for these economies, raising funds through sustainability-linked sukuk is of paramount importance to help increase the flow of funds toward supporting developing and emerging economies in implementing green projects and social development initiatives. More SDG-specific sukuk like the HSBC Amanah SDG issuance are also needed to help achieve the UN's SDG goals by 2030. This will inevitably form part of the solution across economies worldwide by tackling the root causes of underdevelopment.

Furthermore, corporates can help support the transition to the new decarbonized economy by issuing transition sukuk, such as the one issued by **Etihad Airways** in 2016 (see Table 6), to help them move toward sustainable aviation. These transition sukuk can help corporates tangibly shift to a model that reduces the impact of their operations on the environment and can help them lower their carbon emissions. Although it is still early days, the start made in the aviation sector may potentially pave the way for large corporates in other sectors that are also heavily dependent on non-sustainable practices and energy sources. Some of these sectors include but are not limited to transportation, logistics, and retail.

Finally, given the importance of the world's oceans in helping to mitigate the global climate emergency, "blue sukuk" could be an exciting development to explore. Blue sukuk is essentially a variation on the environmental focus of green sukuk. This subset would focus specifically on

Table 6 Etihad Airways' transition sukuk profile

Issuer	Unity 1 sukuk
Obligor	Etihad Airways (UAE)
Size	USD 1.5 billion
Type	5-year Medium Term Note (MTN)
Use of proceeds	Sustainable Development Projects
Why unique	This was the world's first sustainability sukuk issued by an airline and was issued to help Etihad move toward sustainable aviation. It specifically links the sukuk's terms to Etihad's carbon reduction targets (Net Zero Carbon emissions by 2050, 50% reduction in net emissions by 2035, and 20% reduction in emissions intensity in the Etihad's passenger fleet by 2025)

Source Retrieved from Refinitiv Eikon database as of August 2021

financing initiatives that conserve ocean resources and facilitate the sustainable development of coastal regions. Indeed, access to capital and investment remains one of the most significant barriers to global ocean resilience and supporting the blue economy. As awareness increases about the crucial role of the oceans in our planet's ecosystem and health, investors may soon develop an appetite for blue sukuk, similar to how green sukuk are currently making inroads.

4 Conclusion and Outlook

According to the Refinitiv report (2021c) on sukuk perceptions and forecast study, green bond annual issuances reached USD 260 billion in 2020. In contrast, sukuk issuances are projected to reach USD 290 billion in 2026. Although the green sukuk are lagging in growth compared to green bonds, an increase in their annual growth was observed, but it remains a small market compared to green bonds (Bennet, 2021). The geographical locations for sukuk issuance in the future would still be dominated by Southeast Asia, the Middle East, and North Africa, as they are the top issuers today and are expected to remain so with larger issuances.

Currently, the acceptance of SDG has become widely accepted, and mature markets demand stricter regulations to prevent "green washing." It is expected the GCC and other MENA countries will accelerate their ESG frameworks to tap into the attractive pool of investors and large institutions. We hope and expect many Muslim countries to make the connection in their regulations between ESG and Islamic finance an issue in ESG sukuk. Leading Muslim countries like Indonesia and Malaysia have already issued government green sukuk. GCC countries, starting with Saudi Arabia and Qatar, are expected to follow soon, as well as core Islamic markets such as Pakistan, Turkey, and other central Asian Muslim countries.

In terms of the outlook for ESG sukuk as a driver of sustainable finance in Islamic capital markets, we anticipate three broad trends will take shape over the coming years. First, ESG sukuk will become more relevant in financing social development projects across the globe. Countries such as Malaysia and Indonesia have already issued COVID-19 recovery sukuk to help move toward a post-pandemic economic recovery. These "pandemic sukuk" follow a broader global trend that we have witnessed in pandemic bonds issued by institutions such as the World Bank. Given the continued low-rate environment and the enduring nature of the current pandemic (e.g., second and third waves), we expect pandemic sukuk and bond issuances to continue for the near future and possibly beyond.

Second, over the longer-term horizon, the global energy transformation and movement toward decarbonized economies, along with the increased importance of renewable energy on the national agendas of core Islamic finance jurisdictions (e.g., in the oil-producing GCC and SE Asia regions), are factors that point in the direction of increased uptake of green sukuk in Islamic capital markets. As issuances increase, issuance costs should also decrease, making green sukuk more attractive to Shariah-sensitive and ethical investors. We can already discern such indications via the surge in the value of ESG sukuk issued since 2020 (the first half of 2021 ESG sukuk issuances alone almost equal the whole of 2020 issuances).

Third, one of the drivers of this uptake of ESG sukuk will inevitably be the entry of new market players. Sudan has already begun issuing ESG sukuk at the corporate level, while Egypt, a major Muslim-majority economy, is seriously considering entering the ESG sukuk market to support its policy moves toward a green economy. Finally, Oman, a growing jurisdiction for Islamic finance, is developing its regulatory framework for green, blue, and social bonds at a pace that will pave the way not only for regulatory conditions in other Islamic finance markets to change similarly but also set the stage for such ESG sukuk issuances in its domestic market more immediately.

Despite these positive developments and outlooks, the challenge remains on the credential and certification of the Islamic, ESG, and SDG characters of sukuk as the global and the Islamic investors would like to be assured that it meets their criteria. We see the traditional rating agencies claiming a role in ESG issuance certification, which may well be welcomed from a global perspective. However, devising a clear convergence between sukuk and conventional ESG issuances framework and standards at the global policy level would be advisable, and we need Islamic Pillar institutions to command that role.

In addition, it is a challenge to educate the global investors that Islamic finance has always been in line with SDG. However, this challenge posed a unique opportunity for academic institutions together with Islamic Pillar institutions, such as the Islamic Development Bank and the International Islamic Liquidity Management, to fill that education gap and convince corporate Islamic debt capital markets that ESG-based sukuk will not only fulfill the SDGs funding needs but also attract both Islamic investors and international investors.

References

Aderazi, A. (2020). *Religion, philanthropy, and risk: ESG and Islamic finance.* GIB Asset Management. Retrieved 31 May 2022, from https://gibam.com/assets/Islamic-Finance_09.20_2020-09-14-164738.pdf

Alam, N., Duygun, M., & Ariss, R. T. (2016). Green Sukuk: An innovation in Islamic capital markets. In A. Dorsman, O. Arslan-Ayaydin, & M. B. Karan (Eds), *Energy and finance: Sustainability in the energy industry* (pp. 167–185). Springer.

Bennet, M. (2021). *Can Sukuk match the growth trajectory of green bonds?* World Bank Blog. Retrieved 31 May 2022, from https://blogs.worldbank.org/voices/can-sukuk-match-growth-trajectory-green-bonds

Bhat, O. M. (2021). *The risk of ESG investing.* Value Research. Retrieved 31 May 2022, from https://www.valueresearchonline.com/stories/49015/the-rise-of-esg-investing/

Carlson, D. (2020). *ESG investing now accounts for one-third of total U.S. assets under management.* MarketWatch. Retrieved 31 May 2022, from https://www.marketwatch.com/story/esg-investing-now-accounts-for-one-third-of-total-u-s-assets-under-management-11605626611

Climate Bonds Initiative. (2020a). *2019 Green bond market summary.* https://www.climatebonds.net/files/reports/2019_annual_highlights-final.pdf

Climate Bonds Initiative. (2020b). *ASEAN Green finance state of the market 2019*. https://www.climatebonds.net/resources/reports/asean-green-finance-state-market-2019

Climate Bonds Initiative. (2020c). *Green Sukuk*. https://www.climatebonds.net/projects/facilitation/green-sukuk

Ellen MacArthur Foundation. (2020). *Financing the circular economy: Capturing the opportunity*. Retrieved 30 March 2021, from www.ellenmacarthurfoundation.org/publications

Etihad Airways. (2020). *Etihad becomes first Airline to issue sustainability-linked Sukuk*. Retrieved 31 May 2022, from https://www.etihad.com/en/news/etihad-becomes-first-airline-to-issue-sustainability-linked-sukuk

Financial Times. (2021). The rise of ESG: Is this the defining moment? Retrieved 31 May 2022, from https://www.pictet.ft.com/the-rise-of-esg-is-this-the-defining-moment

George, A., Kaldany, R. R., & Losavio, J. (2019). *The world is facing a $15 trillion infrastructure gap by 2040: Here's how to bridge it*. World Economic Forum. Retrieved 31 May 2022, from https://www.weforum.org/agenda/2019/04/infrastructure-gap-heres-how-to-solve-it/

Government Launches Green Finance Strategy. (2019). Retrieved 21 March 2021, from https://www.circularonline.co.uk/insight/government-launches-green-finance-strategy/

Green Bond Market Summary. (2019). *Climate bonds initiative*. Retrieved 30 March 2021, from https://www.climatebonds.net/system/tdf/reports/2019_annual_highlights-final.pdf?file=1&type=node&id=46731&force=0

Huifang, T. (2018). Establishing green finance system to support the circular economy. In V. Anbumozhi & F. Kimura (Eds.), *Industry 4.0: Empowering ASEAN for the circular economy* (pp. 203–234). ERIA.

Islamic Development Bank. (2019). *Islamic Development Bank achieves new milestone with debut Green Sukuk worth EUR 1 billion for green financing in its member countries*. Retrieved 31 May 2022, from https://www.isdb.org/news/islamic-development-bank-achieves-new-milestone-with-debut-green-sukuk-worth-eur-1-billion-for-green-financing-in-its-member-countries

Lieder, M., & Rashid, A. (2016). Towards circular economy implementation: A comprehensive review in context of manufacturing industry. *Journal of Cleaner Production, 115*, 36–51.

Lu. J. Z. (2020). *A simple way to close the multi-trillion-dollar infrastructure financing gap*. World Bank Blogs. Retrieved 31 May 2022, from https://blogs.worldbank.org/ppps/simple-way-close-multi-trillion-dollar-infrastructure-financing-gap

Morgan Stanley. (2020). *7 Insights from asset owners on the rise of sustainable investing*. Retrieved 31 May 2022, from https://www.morganstanley.com/ideas/sustainability-investing-institutional-asset-owners

Morlet, A., Blériot, J., Opsomer, R., Linder, M., Henggeler, A., Bluhm, A., & Carrera, A. (2016). *Intelligent assets: Unlocking the circular economy potential* (pp. 1–25). Ellen MacArthur Foundation.

OECD. (2017). *Mobilising bond markets for a low-carbon transition.* OECD Publishing. https://doi.org/10.1787/9789264272323-en

Pearce, D. W., & Turner, R. K. (1990). *Economics of natural resources and the environment.* JHU Press.

Refinitiv. (2019). *Islamic finance ESG outlook 2019—Shared values.* RFI Foundation. Retrieved 31 May 2022, from https://www.refinitiv.com/content/dam/marketing/en_us/documents/reports/islamic-finance-esg-outlook-2019-report.pdf

Refinitiv. (2021a). *Reports 2021 Q2—Sustainable finance review.* Retrieved 31 May 2022, from https://thesource.refinitiv.com/thesource/getfile/index/01aee0be-58f7-4c72-bf2f-fa895cdd1b5f

Refinitiv. (2021b). *Reports 2021 Q2—Sustainable Islamic finance monitor.*

Refinitiv. (2021c). *Sukuk perceptions and forecast study 2021: Thriving amidst uncertainty.* Retrieved 31 May 2022, from https://www.refinitiv.com/en/resources/special-report/refinitiv-2021b-sukuk-survey-market-perception-growth-trends-challenges

Sustainalytics. (2021). *Sustainalytics recognized as the largest verifier for certified climate bonds by climate bonds initiative for a fourth consecutive year.* Retrieved 31 May 2022, from https://www.sustainalytics.com/esg-news/news-details/2021/04/22/climate-bonds-awards-2020

United Nations Development Programme. (2018). *HSBC Amanah Malaysia issues world's first SDG sukuk.* Retrieved 31 May 2022, from https://www.undp.org/press-releases/hsbc-amanah-malaysia-issues-worlds-first-sdg-sukuk

Mobilizing Funds for Industrialization and Development Through Islamic Value System, Capital Markets, and Social Finance

Salman Ahmed Shaikh

1 INTRODUCTION

According to the Global Humanitarian Assistance Report (2021), total humanitarian assistance, including government and private sources, has reached USD 30.9 billion in 2020. Government donors and EU institutions had contributed USD 24.15 billion, while private donors contributed only USD 6.75 billion.

Due to the economic downturn following COVID-19 and the massive deployment of funds for fighting the health emergency instigated by COVID-19, most of the rich donor countries have themselves faced an economic crisis. Moreover, the ongoing conflict between Russia and Ukraine has created a massive increase in energy and food prices. Several small economies are unable to cope up with their balance of payments situation due to heavy reliance on imports of energy and food products. For

---

S. A. Shaikh (✉)
Islamic Economics Project, Karachi, Pakistan
e-mail: salman@islamiceconomicsproject.com

© The Author(s), under exclusive license to Springer Nature Switzerland AG 2023
Z. H. Jumat et al. (eds.), *Islamic Finance, FinTech, and the Road to Sustainability*, Palgrave CIBFR Studies in Islamic Finance,
https://doi.org/10.1007/978-3-031-13302-2_8

example, Sri Lanka has defaulted, and some other countries are on the verge.

The humanitarian crisis requires not only sound policy and incentives but a strong sense of social responsibility for affirmative action. Institutions as organizations and institutions as values and norms are both vital to manage and sail through socio-economic crises. A value system that extolls affirmative action, pro-social responsibility, and environmental sustainability should be promoted more urgently now than ever before. Mobilization of funds through the private sector and beyond markets is necessary to arrest humanitarian crises when economies stagnate.

When it comes to policy incentives for market-driven industrialization, well-directed incentives are required to support industries to avert massive layoffs and poverty. *Functional inequality* is a term introduced by Haq (1963). The argument is that if a small industrial class is patronized with incentives, industrialization can be instigated, providing private profits to the industrialists and employment at a large scale to the masses. Economic growth through industrialization can trickle down to the masses eventually. However, the promised dip in inequality in the Lorenz curve (1905) after the initial burst of economic growth leading to higher inequality is not necessarily confirmed in real-world economic growth stories.

Eventually, Haq (1995) learned that human beings are 'means' as well as 'ends' of any social and development process. They are not merely inanimate inputs to the production process or greedy and self-centered utility maximizing machines. They can be responsible and compassionate if the correct values are promoted and if policies encourage pro-social behavior and abhor abuses of wrong private choices.

In fostering sustainable and inclusive development, this chapter discusses the solutions offered by Islamic finance through its underpinning value system and worldview and through its set of commercial and social finance institutions to intervene in development assistance through and beyond markets. The chapter also takes note of the ground realities of poverty and underdevelopment in Muslim majority countries in Sect. 2. Section 3 looks at the state of development assistance and debt servicing in selected Organization of Islamic Cooperation (OIC) countries. Section 4 discusses the Islamic injunctions of pure altruism, which reinforce the need for sharing and giving to poor people and social causes. Section 5 discusses the role of Islamic capital markets to help in mobilizing development funds for financing development infrastructure. Section 6 explains how Islamic redistributive institutions can mobilize and institutionalize funds in the social sector and causes. Finally, Sect. 7 looks at the potential of FinTech in Islamic finance to confront the challenges and harness the opportunities in the age of Industrial Revolution 4.0.

2 State of Underdevelopment in the Muslim World

A number of Muslim majority countries face a very high incidence of poverty. In particular, Muslim countries in the African continent have a high incidence of poverty. In at least four Muslim majority countries in Africa, the poverty headcount ratio at national poverty lines exceeds half of the total population. These countries include Guinea-Bissau (69.3%), Togo (58.7%), Sierra Leone (56.8%), and Mozambique (54.7%), as can be seen in Table 1. Muslim countries in South Asia like Afghanistan (54.5), Bangladesh (24.3%), and Pakistan (22.3%) also face a high

Table 1 Poverty Head Count Ratio (PHCR) in selected OIC countries

Country	PHCR-national (%)	Country	PHCR-national (%)
Guinea-Bissau	69.3	Egypt	32.5
Togo	58.7	Lebanon	28.6
Sierra Leone	56.8	Tajikistan	26.3
Mozambique	54.7	Bangladesh	24.3
Afghanistan	54.5	Kyrgyz Republic	22.4
Gambia	48.4	Pakistan	22.3
Senegal	46.7	Uganda	21.4
Sudan	46.5	Iraq	18.9
Guinea	43.7	Bosnia	17.9
Chad	42.3	Uzbekistan	16
Mali	42.1	Jordan	15.7
Burkina Faso	41.4	Tunisia	15.5
Niger	40.8	Turkey	14.4
Nigeria	40.1	Albania	14.3
Cameroon	39.9	Indonesia	9.8
Benin	38.5	Morocco	8.9
Syria	35.2	Malaysia	5.6
Yemen	34.8	Kazakhstan	2.5
Gabon	33.4		

Source World Development Indicators 2019

incidence of poverty. Muslim countries with the lowest poverty headcount ratio include Kazakhstan (2.5%) and Malaysia (5.6%). Table 1 illustrates that at least 26 OIC countries have a poverty headcount ratio of over 20%, and 14 such countries have a poverty headcount ratio of over 40%.

Poverty is not a single problem in isolation. It is the mother of many problems, and it creates a vicious cycle of poverty trap that may go beyond a poor person's own life and transcend to future generations. Malnutrition, stunting, low skill levels, and lack of access to drinking water, sanitation, education, and health facilities all come as a bundle in a poor person's life. Income poverty hampers socio-economic mobility. Investing in education and business is not possible for poor people since they lack funds and are unserved by commercial banks.

Table 2 shows the standing of OIC countries on the Human Development Index (HDI), both within themselves and as compared to the world at large. Ironically, no OIC country features in the top 30 countries on the HDI ranking, and as many as 24 OIC countries are listed in the bottom 39 countries. High levels of poverty are associated with a lower level of human development in OIC countries.

Also, it is worth noting that the recent geopolitical conflicts and natural calamities have resulted in an increased number of internally displaced people. For Syria, Yemen, Afghanistan, Nigeria, Sudan, Iraq, and Turkey, the number of internally displaced people due to conflicts and violence stands at 6.57 million, 3.64 million, 3.55 million, 2.73 million, 2.23 million, 1.22 million, and 1.1 million, respectively, in 2020 (Internal Displacement Monitoring Centre, 2021).

3 State of Development Assistance in OIC Countries

State of development assistance does not show a promising picture in OIC countries. Table 3 illustrates the net Official Development Assistance (ODA) obtained by OIC countries as a percentage of Gross Fixed Capital Formation (GFCF) and Gross National Income (GNI). Conflict-hit and poorer countries like Afghanistan, Syria and Yemen significantly depend on ODA. Countries with the greatest number of poor people like Bangladesh, Nigeria and Pakistan only receive 1.42%, 0.81% and 0.79% net ODA as a % of GNI, respectively.

Table 4 shows the enormous debt problem in Muslim majority countries. In populous countries like Pakistan, Indonesia and Bangladesh, as

Table 2 Overall and relative ranking of selected OIC countries on HDI

Country	HDI value	HDI rank	OIC rank	Country	HDI value	HDI rank	OIC rank
UAE	0.89	31	1	Guyana	0.682	122	29
Saudi Arabia	0.854	40	2	Iraq	0.674	123	30
Bahrain	0.852	42	3	Tajikistan	0.668	125	31
Qatar	0.848	45	4	Bangladesh	0.632	133	32
Brunei	0.838	47	5	Syria	0.567	151	33
Kazakhstan	0.825	51	6	Cameroon	0.563	153	34
Turkey	0.82	54	7	Pakistan	0.557	154	35
Oman	0.813	60	8	Comoros	0.554	156	36
Malaysia	0.81	62	9	Mauritania	0.546	157	37
Kuwait	0.806	64	10	Benin	0.545	158	38
Albania	0.795	69	11	Uganda	0.544	159	39
Iran	0.783	70	12	Nigeria	0.539	161	40
Bosnia	0.78	73	13	Ivory Coast	0.538	162	41
Azerbaijan	0.756	88	14	Djibouti	0.524	166	42
Algeria	0.748	91	15	Togo	0.515	167	43
Lebanon	0.744	92	16	Senegal	0.512	168	44
Maldives	0.74	95	17	Afghanistan	0.511	169	45
Tunisia	0.74	95	18	Sudan	0.51	170	46
Suriname	0.738	97	19	Gambia	0.496	172	47
Jordan	0.729	102	20	Guinea-Bissau	0.48	175	48
Libya	0.724	105	21	Guinea	0.477	178	49
Uzbekistan	0.72	106	22	Yemen	0.47	179	50
Indonesia	0.718	107	23	Mozambique	0.456	181	51
Turkmenistan	0.715	111	24	Burkina Faso	0.452	182	52
Egypt	0.707	116	25	Sierra Leone	0.452	182	53
Gabon	0.703	119	26	Mali	0.434	184	54
Kyrgyzstan	0.697	120	27	Chad	0.398	187	55
Morocco	0.686	121	28	Niger	0.394	189	56

Source World Development Indicators 2019

Table 3 Official Development Assistance (ODA) received in selected OIC countries

Country	Net ODA % GNI	Net ODA % GFCF	Country	Net ODA % GNI	Net ODA % GFCF
Afghanistan	22.43		Lebanon	2.97	23.84
Albania	0.19	0.78	Malaysia	0.00	0.01
Algeria	0.10	0.22	Maldives	1.43	2.75
Azerbaijan	0.26	1.24	Mali	11.18	47.85
Bangladesh	1.42	4.69	Mauritania	5.29	11.86
Benin	4.23	16.33	Morocco	0.64	1.98
Bosnia	2.30	9.13	Mozambique	2.64	27.05
Burkina Faso	7.50	31.97	Niger	11.06	37.70
Chad	6.35	29.18	Nigeria	0.81	3.09
Comoros	6.68	51.41	Pakistan	0.79	4.98
Cote d'Ivoire	2.11	10.23	Senegal	6.37	19.40
Djibouti	8.43	.	Sierra Leone	14.77	116.40
Egypt	0.60	3.15	Sudan	6.62	17.35
Guinea	4.52	17.17	Syria	46.73	.
Guinea-Bissau	8.20	41.20	Tajikistan	3.81	12.48
Indonesia	(0.06)	(0.17)	Togo	5.68	27.75
Iran	0.08	0.20	Tunisia	2.45	.
Iraq	0.95	4.05	Turkey	0.11	0.43
Jordan	6.28	51.44	Turkmenistan	0.06	.
Kazakhstan	0.03	0.11	Uganda	6.10	23.27
Kyrgyz Rep	5.55	13.99	Uzbekistan	1.91	4.59
			Yemen	36.98	

Source World Development Indicators 2019

much as 32.38%, 36.74% and 9.91% of exports proceeds are paid in debt servicing. Among the 41 countries for which these statistics are available, there are 14 OIC countries whose debt service payments are more than 5% of GNI. In addition to that, Table 3 illustrates that there are at least 14 OIC countries that receive net ODA lower than 1% of their GNI. This suggests that in some OIC countries, the inflows received in the form of development assistance would be lower than the net outflow of resources in the form of interest payments.

Table 5 reveals that out of 41 countries for which this data is available, 21 countries have a negative difference between Net ODA as a % of GNI and debt servicing payment as a % of GNI. The remaining 20 countries have a positive difference.

Table 4 Total debt service (% of exports and GNI) for selected OIC countries

Country	Debt service % GNI	Debt service % exports	Country	Debt service % GNI	Debt service % exports
Afghanistan	0.23	2.67	Maldives	8.25	15.90
Albania	7.85	29.88	Mali	1.46	4.41
Algeria	0.12	0.68	Mauritania	3.75	9.93
Azerbaijan	4.33	10.76	Morocco	4.57	13.49
Bangladesh	1.14	9.91	Mozambique	11.50	33.99
Benin	1.86	13.88	Niger	1.41	9.21
Bosnia	8.43	22.63	Nigeria	1.33	13.36
Burkina Faso	0.99	3.53	Pakistan	3.50	32.38
Chad	1.14	.	Senegal	5.58	15.18
Comoros	0.66	10.44	Sierra Leone	2.25	8.90
Cote d'Ivoire	4.10	21.19	Sudan	0.75	2.89
Djibouti	1.90	1.66	Syria	0.02	.
Egypt	3.38	29.47	Tajikistan	9.56	30.96
Guinea	0.95	1.52	Togo	1.39	5.96
Guinea-Bissau	1.36	3.56	Tunisia	8.01	19.60
Indonesia	6.55	36.74	Turkey	12.24	41.34
Iran	0.16	0.86	Turkmenistan	4.96	.
Jordan	7.13	27.58	Uganda	1.87	12.11
Kazakhstan	19.61	56.26	Uzbekistan	5.59	20.72
Kyrgyz Rep	8.49	25.59	Yemen	0.52	.
Lebanon	41.58	127.48			

Source World Development Indicators 2020

Countries with a negative difference are relatively less poor and have a better capacity to source development finance through capital markets by issuing Sukuk. In contrast, countries with a positive difference would require support from Islamic social finance and non-commercial development assistance.

In light of this, Sect. 5 explicates the use of sovereign Sukuk in sourcing development finance from the capital markets. On the other hand, Sect. 6 discusses the role of Islamic social finance in regions where governments have less capacity to undertake debt commitments and where the role of third-sector institutions is vital to complement the government in meeting development needs through non-market-based non-commercial assistance.

Table 5 Debt service (% of GNI) and net ODA (% of GNI) for selected OIC countries

Country	Net ODA % GNI	Debt service % GNI	Difference	Country	Net ODA % GNI	Debt service % GNI	Difference
Afghanistan	22.43	0.23	22.21	Maldives	1.43	8.25	(6.82)
Albania	0.19	7.85	(7.66)	Mali	11.18	1.46	9.71
Algeria	0.10	0.12	(0.02)	Mauritania	5.29	3.75	1.54
Azerbaijan	0.26	4.33	(4.07)	Morocco	0.64	4.57	(3.93)
Bangladesh	1.42	1.14	0.28	Mozambique	12.64	11.50	1.15
Benin	4.23	1.86	2.36	Niger	11.06	1.41	9.64
Bosnia	2.30	8.43	(6.13)	Nigeria	0.81	1.33	(0.52)
Burkina Faso	7.50	0.99	6.51	Pakistan	0.79	3.50	(2.71)
Chad	6.35	1.14	5.20	Senegal	6.37	5.58	0.79
Comoros	6.68	0.66	6.02	Sierra Leone	14.77	2.25	12.52
Cote d'Ivoire	2.11	4.10	(1.99)	Sudan	6.62	0.75	5.88
Djibouti	8.43	1.90	6.54	Syria	46.73	0.02	46.71
Egypt	0.60	3.38	(2.79)	Tajikistan	3.81	9.56	(5.75)
Guinea	4.52	0.95	3.56	Togo	5.68	1.39	4.30
Guinea-Bissau	8.20	1.36	6.84	Tunisia	2.45	8.01	(5.56)
Indonesia	(0.06)	6.55	(6.60)	Turkey	0.11	12.24	(12.13)
Iran	0.08	0.16	(0.08)	Turkmenistan	0.06	4.96	(4.90)
Jordan	6.28	7.13	(0.85)	Uganda	6.10	1.87	4.23
Kazakhstan	0.03	19.61	(19.57)	Uzbekistan	1.91	5.59	(3.68)
Kyrgyz Rep	5.55	8.49	(2.94)	Yemen	36.98	0.52	36.46
Lebanon	2.97	41.58	(38.60)				

Source World Development Indicators 2020

4 Role of Islamic Worldview in Fostering Responsibility and Cooperation

Faith in the single source of creation defies any genetic, racial, ethnic, or gender basis of discrimination. Islamic worldview holds that all living and non-living things are created by Allah. The Islamic principles promote the sense and feeling of stewardship in human beings regarding the use and ownership of economic and environmental resources. If this sense strengthens preferences, it can affect choices.

Islamic principles and teachings provide guidelines for morally acceptable behavior, be it in social relations with people, ecological relations with environment and biodiversity, or economic matters. From earning incomes to spending these incomes, Islamic teachings introduce moral filters in economic activities to avoid exploitation, injustice, fraud, deceit, miserliness, conspicuous consumption, and wastage.

In economics, Andreoni (1989, 1990) explains altruism in a self-interested framework. He regards altruism as an activity that is done to promote private self-interest. The private motives could be to get fame, build a reputation, and satisfy the ego. Corporate spending on social causes, as in corporate social responsibility, is looked at as a way to do indirect marketing and advertising. In contrast, Islamic teachings urge pure altruism, which is not influenced by pleasure-pain calculus (Naqvi & Qadir, 1997).

Islamic principles do not promote impure altruism to satisfy the ego and achieve fame and recognition (*Al-Baqarah*: 264; *Al-Ma'oon*: 6). Prophet Muhammad (PBUH) encouraged secrecy in charity.[1] Allah says of the ideal believers in Quran: "And they give food, despite their love for it to *Miskin* (poor), the orphan, and the captive. (Saying): 'We feed you seeking Allah's countenance only. We wish for no reward, nor thanks from you'" (*Al-Insān*: 8–9). Quran recommends Muslims to spend what they love to achieve righteousness (Al-Imran: 92), spend throughout their lives (*Al-Munāfiqūn*: 10) and it is considered best to spend in charity whatever is beyond needs (*Al-Baqarah*: 219).

Quran urges Muslims to show generosity, kindness, and benevolence to their fellow human beings. Allah says in Quran: "... Do good to parents, kinsfolk, orphans, *Al-Masākin* (the poor), the neighbor who is near to kin, the neighbor who is a stranger, the companion by your side, and the wayfarer (you meet) ..." (*Al-Nisa'*: 36). Quran says in another place: "So give to the kindred his due, and *Al-Miskin* (the poor) and the wayfarer..." (Ar-Rum: 38). Feeding the poor and orphans are considered a highly virtuous act *(Al-Balad*: 12–16). Furthermore, Quran insists Muslim to look after orphans and treat them with generosity and kindness (*Al-Fajr*: 17–20), spend honestly in their property for their needs (Al-Baqarah: 220) and avoid harsh treatment (*Al-Dhuha*: 9) as well as harsh behavior (*Al-Ma'oon*: 2). In addition, Quran strictly prohibits appropriating the wealth of orphans (*Al-Nisa'*: 2).

---

[1] Al-Muslim, Book of Zakat, Vol. 3, Hadith No. 2380.

Prophet Muhammad (PBUH) professed that the best charity is to spend in charity while you are healthy, aspiring, hoping to survive, fearing poverty, and not delaying until death comes.[2] Quran recommends avoiding miserliness (*Al-Nisa'*: 37). Instead, Islam urges Muslims to help one another in good acts and endeavors (*Al-Maida*: 2). Indeed, mutual cooperation and collective affirmative actions are needed to tackle enormous development and humanitarian challenges.

Since Islam only recognizes pure altruism, it promises due reward for pure altruism (*Al-Tauba*: 121; Al-*Fātir*: 29; *Al-Hadīd*: 7). Spending in charitable ways is compared to a good loan, which Allah will repay with a manifold increase (*Al-Hadīd*: 11; *Al-Hadīd* 18; *Al-Taghabun*: 17; *Al-Muzammil*: 20). In Ahadith, Muslims are urged to spend so that Allah also spends on them with His blessings.[3]

Thus, we observe that the Islamic moral principles emphasize moral choices in the socio-economic sphere of life, and the Islamic view of life encourages empathy, commitment, and responsibility in human behavior.

5 Role of Sovereign Sukuk in Sourcing Development Funds

In what follows, the widely used Sukuk structures in practice are briefly explained and illustrated for use by the government to mobilize development funds through Islamic capital markets.

Ijārah Sukuk

A typical *Ijārah* Sukuk would be structured like this. For example, if the government needs to build industrial zones on industrial real estate, it will use Sukuk that institutional and/or retail investors can purchase. A Special Purpose Vehicle (SPV) is usually established to issue Sukuk certificates. The government will sell industrial real estate to the SPV. The SPV will issue Sukuk to the investors. The Sukuk represents the part ownership of the Sukuk holder in industrial real estate. By purchasing

---

[2] Sunan Abu Daud, Book of Wills, Vol. 3, Hadith No. 2865. Also, Sunan An Nisai, Book of Zakat, Vol. 3, Hadith No. 2543.

[3] Al-Bukhari, Book of Commentary, Vol. 6, Hadith No. 4684. Also, in Al-Muslim, Book of Zakat, Vol. 3, Hadith No. 2308. Also in Sunan Ibn Majah, Chapters on Expiation, Vol. 3, Hadith No. 2123.

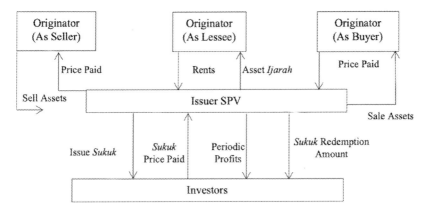

Fig. 1 *Ijārah* Sukuk structure

the Sukuk certificates, the Sukuk holders would become part owners of the industrial real estate. The SPV will use the Sukuk proceeds to pay for the price of industrial real estate purchased from the government. Then, the SPV would provide the industrial real estate on a lease basis to the government by using the Ijarah mode of financing. The rent received by the SPV from the lease of industrial real estate will be distributed among the Sukuk holders who own the industrial real estate. The maturity of the Sukuk and the lease term would usually coincide. At the end of the lease period, the SPV will sell the industrial real estate to the government on behalf of the Sukuk holders, and the sale proceeds will be distributed among the Sukuk holders. The cash flows at the end would usually enable the Sukuk holders to recoup their original investments with income arising as rents during the lease period. Figure 1 shows the structure of the Ijarah Sukuk.

Mudhārabah Sukuk

This Sukuk structure is used when there is a need to obtain financing on an equity basis rather than debt. This is suitable for countries where governments cannot meet commercial debt commitments. In this Sukuk structure, the Originator (Government in this case) requiring financing does not invest capital of its own. The structure of *Mudhārabah* Sukuk involves these steps. The SPV issues Sukuk, to which the investors

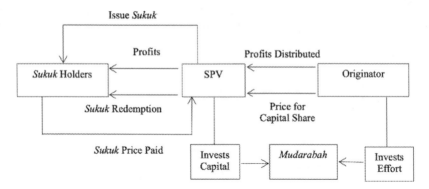

Fig. 2 *Mudhārabah* Sukuk structure

subscribe and pay the proceeds to the SPV. Then, the Originator and the SPV get into a *mudhārabah* (partnership) agreement. The SPV acts as *Rabb-al-Mal* (principal owner), and the Originator acts as *mudhārib* (working partner). Originator agrees to contribute its management skills to the *mudhārabah* enterprise. Profits generated by the *mudhārabah* enterprise are distributed between the SPV and the Originator as per the pre-agreed profit-sharing ratios stipulated in the *Mudhārabah* Agreement.

Profits earned in *mudhārabah* are distributed to the Sukuk investors by the SPV. When the *Mudhārabah* Sukuk matures, the *mudhārabah* enterprise is liquidated. The equity capital is bought by the Originator. The proceeds received by the SPV are used to redeem the investments of Sukuk holders. Figure 2 gives the structure of *Mudhārabah* Sukuk.

This Sukuk is suitable in cases where global development finance institutions like the Islamic Development Bank, Asian Development Bank, and World Bank want to provide finance for energy and transportation projects that have the potential to generate revenues from services. Such revenues can provide returns to the Sukuk holders and also achieve social impact through funding these development projects.

Mushārakah Sukuk

Like *Mudhārabah* Sukuk, the *Mushārakah* Sukuk structure is used when there is a need to obtain equity financing rather than debt. In this Sukuk

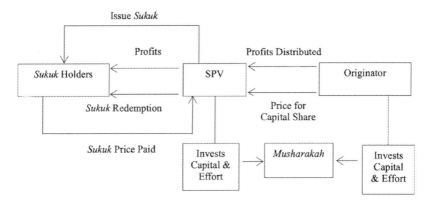

Fig. 3 Mushārakah Sukuk structure

structure, the Originator (Government in this case) requiring financing also needs capital of its own to invest in *mushārakah* (joint-partnership). This is suitable for financing development projects in the energy, transport, and communications sector with a public–private partnership. The structure of *Mushārakah* Sukuk involves these steps.

The SPV issues Sukuk, which the investors subscribe to and pay the price to the SPV to purchase *Mushārakah* Sukuk certificates. Then, the SPV enters into a *mushārakah* agreement with the Originator.

The SPV uses the proceeds from Sukuk issuance to contribute capital to the *mushārakah* enterprise and is allocated Musharakah units in proportion to capital investment.

On each periodic profit distribution date, the SPV receives a percentage share of the expected profits generated by the *mushārakah* enterprise. The loss, if any, is shared in proportion to the capital contributed by the Originator and the SPV. After receiving profits, the SPV distributes profits to the Sukuk holders.

In case, the *mushārakah* assets generate a loss, the SPV shall share that loss in proportion with its capital contribution to the *mushārakah*. Upon receiving its profit share, the SPV will share the profits with the Sukuk holders. When the *Mushārakah* Sukuk matures, the *mushārakah* enterprise is liquidated. The equity capital is bought by the Originator. The proceeds received by the SPV are used to redeem the investment of Sukuk holders. Figure 3 gives the structure of *Mushārakah* Sukuk.

6 Role of Islamic Social Finance in Sustainable Development

Islamic commercial finance involves products and services that are marketed to the clients with overall objective of profit maximization. Those clients are served in Islamic commercial finance since they have the capacity to afford the cost of financial services. For instance, if a client is not able to meet acceptable creditworthiness checks, then an Islamic bank is not compelled to provide finance to each and every client. At the end of the day, Islamic banks are intermediaries who are serving shareholders and depositors to provide asset backed financing and other financial products and services in a way so as to earn Halal returns for the shareholders and the depositors. Thus, market-based Islamic commercial finance solutions are restricted in their scope and capacity to service social ends.

For financing socially important projects, it is important to capitalize on beyond market mobilization and allocation of funds. Islamic social finance is a set of institutions which cater to the funding needs of social sector projects and enable cash transfers to poor beneficiaries without the tag of pricing. They chip in where the market fails to serve needs which are not 'demands' in the market sense of having backing of purchasing power.

Role of Zakat in Development Assistance

Zakat is an obligatory payment that every Muslim has to pay who owns wealth equivalent to the value of 612 g of silver beyond needs. The rate of zakat is 2.5% on the value of wealth subject to zakat. There is an inbuilt mechanism in the institution of zakat that the money has to flow as a direct transfer to the beneficiary who is deserving and lacking in funds. This ensures effective and systematic redistribution.

Zakat is an important institution in an Islamic economics framework for poverty alleviation and economic welfare. However, the institutionalization of zakat in contemporary economic framework and policy poses certain challenges. The challenges can be summarized from the perspective of three major stakeholders in the zakat administration, namely the *Muzakki* (Zakat Payer), *Mustahiq* (Zakat Beneficiary), and the *Āmil* (Government Zakat Agency).

From the perspective of Muzakki, the following are the important challenges identified in the current administration and system:

- Trust deficit in a centralized government run system.
- Inexact incidence in deduction at source.
- Complexity in adjustments/refunds if people wish to claim adjustment or refund in lieu of private zakat payment or in case zakat was deducted at source by deducting agency, such as banks while people were not Sāhib al-Nisāb (having minimum wealth holding which makes zakat obligatory).
- Dual burden increases tax evasion and the tendency to hide zakat payments.

From the perspective of Mustahiq, following are the important challenges identified in the current administration and system:

- Lack of impactful donation hinders socio-economic mobility. If people are paid very small and insignificant amounts, then they can at best afford consumption for a short period of time rather than using the funds more productively.
- Low autonomy in using received benefits in institutions. For example, when zakat is paid to religious schools, the recipients do not have enough autonomy in the use of funds.
- Access is hindered by ineffective targeting which results in disbursement of zakat funds even to those people who do not deserve it.
- Temporary cash assistance leads to consumption while skills and capacity remain unchanged. When there is prime focus on payment of cash to the recipients instead of looking to make them skillful and productive, then people fail to graduate to the non-poverty state in most cases.

From the perspective of government as collecting agent and regulator, following are the important challenges identified in the current administration and system:

- Low voluntary collection out of the potential zakat which can be collected. Allowing voluntary payment to accommodate juristic differences along with trust deficit and inadequate administrative capacity on the part of government result in very meager voluntary payment to the government.
- Complexity in assessment with juristic differences.
- Inadequate as well as inefficient administration for involuntary and compulsory collection.
- Unequal incidence on different forms of wealth and production.

Overcoming these challenges is vital to generating indigenous economic activity, employment, and spending. Effective mobilization and productive utilization of zakat can, directly and indirectly, support small and cottage industries by enhancing spending power in the marginalized segments and providing seed capital to engage in entrepreneurship.

To overcome these challenges, certain steps are necessary. It is important to utilize documented channels, such as ATMs, cross checks, or direct transfers, if the target beneficiary has a basic banking account or any digital wallet account. It is important that the whole process, from identification of the beneficiary to disbursement, remains free of political influence and intervention. On the top of that, using scoring-based screening can make the process of finding targets more open and objective.

In identifying beneficiaries, local zakat committees can utilize the mosque institution, which is an important community center in Muslim society. They can effectively ensure screening, enhance outreach, enable meeting points, and even help in monitoring. Mosque institutions are among the most vital community engagement institutions in a Muslim society, and Akhuwat has used mosques as a point of meeting and disbursing interest-free loans. Informally, people in need gather around mosques to seek cash assistance in our social milieu. If this informal engagement of donors and beneficiaries can be formalized under a governance framework, then it can be a valuable vehicle for community-based welfare assistance. People regularly coming to mosques are aware of people's local needs and whereabouts in their local community. Thus, they can help identify and screen deserving beneficiaries and channel charitable funds in a well-governed, impersonal, and institutionalized way.

Many people are not aware of the rulings of zakat related to contemporary forms of wealth and assets. A great majority of people are not aware of the treatment of real estate, financial assets, receivables, and debts in zakat calculation. It is important to raise awareness and urgency about zakat. It is a religious obligation, and its effective mobilization and disbursement can improve the social welfare of the masses. Hence, it is critical to raise awareness using public broadcast media, awareness seminars, mosque sermons, and other ways of engagement.

The trust deficit is the biggest hurdle in the central collection of zakat at the level of government. Periodic reporting about programs and allocation schemes and independent auditing are necessary to build trust in the system. Therefore, tax reforms and incentives related to tax liability adjustment in lieu of zakat payment can encourage people. Currently, in some countries, income tax laws allow deducting zakat as an expense to reduce taxable income rather than adjusting the tax liability itself. When zakat has been paid, like other expenses, it can be deducted against one's income. However, it would be a significant incentive to allow adjustment of tax assessed against payment of zakat.

Furthermore, under the guidance of scholars having the expertise to interpret primary Islamic sources of knowledge, it is also important to carry out *Ijtihād* (independent reasoning) in the estimation, collection, and disbursement mechanisms of zakat and *ushr* in contemporary times where possible in order to enhance the effectiveness and impact of these social finance institutions.

In addition to that, technology can aid in bringing efficiency to operations and administration. It can also help in avoiding adverse selection as well as help in generating impact assessment reports with valuable data about the beneficiaries in the database. In social crowdfunding, technology plays an important enabler in capitalizing on seasonal and impulsive charitable giving at important events. Not only can ATMs be used to disburse payments to deserving beneficiaries, but they should be utilized for mobilizing charitable giving. Likewise, banks that provide discounts and reward points should engage with institutions providing welfare services to offer point redeeming mechanisms for the provision of social services. For instance, Careem offers redemption of points for providing school books, meals, patient services, and planting trees. Likewise, Facebook offers matching incentives on "Giving Tuesday" for fundraisers. Such initiatives can enhance the effectiveness of mobilizing social crowdfunding.

It is expected that the private sector can mitigate the trust deficit and bring operational efficiencies and competencies. Public–private partnerships can scale the provision of social finance networks and services. In this regard, if the private sector shows commitment, resolve, competence, and efficiency, then this can push the government to engage in a public–private partnership.

The financial sustainability of social finance programs is also vital. The institution and infrastructure of mosque are important in Muslim society. Mosque-centered markets can help with the financial sustainability of mosques and religious schools. The infrastructure and human resources can also be employed to offer community health centers and vocational institutes. If there is more trust capital in the community about mosques, then mosques can be utilized as a vehicle to offer an extension of social services.

Role of Waqf in Mobilizing and Institutionalizing Philanthropy

Waqf is an important social institution in the Islamic framework. In a *waqf* institution, an owner donates and dedicates a movable or immovable asset for perpetual societal benefit, and the beneficiaries enjoy its usufruct and/or income perpetually. *Waqf* can be established by dedicated real estate, furniture or fixtures, other movable assets, and liquid forms of money and wealth like cash and shares.

Deaton (1991) shows that in the absence of credit markets for households, people may be able to achieve a high degree of consumption-smoothing using buffer stocks. In this regard, *waqf* provides an opportunity to institutionally share the buffer stock of resources in society for both contemporaneous and intertemporal needs.

Khan (2019) thinks that since the *waqf* funding base primarily comes from donors who are not driven by profits, the *waqf* institution can prioritize access to finance for small businesses promoting environmental friendly practices in production, packaging, logistics, warehousing, and using natural resources responsibly. In this way, waqf will also complement maqasid al-shariah (the higher objectives of shariah) as well as Sustainable Development Goals (Abdullah, 2018).

Not everyone has the resources to dedicate non-divisible property resources beyond their needs and use. However, many people would welcome the idea of donating liquid resources that are divisible, such as cash. Such funding can be used to mobilize funds for hospitals, educational institutes, and orphanages (Aziz et al., 2013; Sadeq, 2002). As compared to the specific heads in which zakat funds can be allocated, *waqf* has more flexibility in fund utilization for diverse social causes. Thus, the funds can directly flow to individuals or pool resources for establishing organizations and institutions, including financial institutions, such as w*aqf*-based microfinance (Ahmed, 2007) and socially driven banks (Mohammad, 2011).

Mukhlisin and Mustafida (2019), Musari (2019), and Fauziah et al. (2021) discuss the potential of Cash Waqf Linked Sukuk by blending altruistic and investment motives to mobilize funds for commercial or quasi-commercial projects and undertakings. From an economics perspective, there are three issues with that innovation: (i) the cost of double intermediation against the marginal benefit; (ii) loss of flexibility in fund allocation when the dual motive is involved; and (iii) increased burden on the fiscal side if the government issues it and if it is expected to fund the returns gap.

In addition to that, Shirazi (2014) suggests a global trans-national *waqf* spearheaded by the Islamic Development Bank to cater to the socio-economic needs of the Muslim Ummah through effective distribution, especially during the time of the COVID-19 pandemic.

Non-financial support in the form of skills development, better education, and nutrition are also vital (Haneef et al., 2014; Obaidullah, 2008). The institution of *waqf* has the potential to fund infrastructure or resources for infrastructure in providing these services. Such non-financial support can help social inclusion and to meet the missed targets and activities in market-based Islamic commercial finance. Socio-economic mobility through the successful provision of non-financial support can also eventually increase the demand for Islamic commercial finance.

However, there are certain challenges in Waqf administration that need to be overcome, such as:

- Cash *waqf* is riskier given the governance issues. When even land is appropriated, it is hard to ensure that there is no misappropriation and mis-utilization of cash *waqf* capital.
- *Waqf* property is not managed and invested properly. Apart from below-market value rents, property is sometimes sold at throwaway prices. There is a possibility of involvement of kickbacks in such cases.
- Properties are usurped as well by private land grabbers, with or without the connivance of officials.
- No periodic reporting of revenues and assets in some jurisdictions.
- No periodic audits on standardized parameters in some jurisdictions.
- Only the hold and rent dormant model is used with no active management. There are no specific governance and operational standards in many jurisdictions if a *waqf* is to be actively managed.

7   The Budding Industry of FinTech and Industrial Revolution 4.0

Technology provides solutions for reaching new markets, customer bases, and opportunities to cross sell as well as economize outreach and delivery of financial services. Nowadays, there are companies that specialize in doing shariah compliance checks and providing shariah advisory digitally.

For example, Wahed Invest is an American-based and halal-focused investment firm, and it is the first robo-advisor tailored for Muslim investors with a shariah-compliant platform. Algebra by Farringdon Group also offers shariah-compliant robo-advisory investment services. In addition to that, Blossom Finance provides an impact investment platform.

Furthermore, there are platforms that aim to take up the financial intermediation function through peer-to-peer (P2P) lending. Based in Dubai, Beehive is the first P2P lending platform in MENA. Using innovative technology, it directly connects businesses seeking fast and affordable financing with investors who can help fund their growth. Beehive is certified as a shariah-compliant P2P finance platform by the Shariah Review Bureau (SRB). Beehive has worked with prominent Islamic legal advisors and Islamic finance industry experts to develop a structure that allows them to process investments in a shariah-compliant way. There are other players like Maliyya, which provide a global shariah-compliant P2P financing platform as well.

Even for consumers, InsureTech companies provide insurance services. StrideUp is another FinTech app that assists consumers in purchasing property in a shariah-compliant manner.

On the top of that, in the social financial intermediation domain, there are FinTech companies providing crowdfunding platforms and the opportunity to make impact investments. Ethis Crowd platform features high-impact investments in property projects to build affordable houses supported by local government programs. On the other hand, Kapital Boost is a crowdfunding platform based in Singapore that matches SMEs in need of financing with impact investors globally looking for attractive investment opportunities that support community growth.

FinTech players in Islamic finance are also leveraging artificial intelligence and big data. MyFinB is a Big Data & Analytics company that helps banks and consultants evaluate a high volume of financial data to generate strategic insights using Artificial Intelligence. MyFinB incorporates shariah modules onto its engine to evaluate listed and unlisted companies for compliance and quality assurance. Using a RoboBanker makes bankers' jobs easier by generating sales leads, shortening processing time to evaluate credit risks, monitoring their exposure seamlessly, and detecting red flags. Banks have the potential to manage their risks effectively, which can improve their asset quality and profitability.

Also, traditional Islamic financial institutions are adopting FinTech solutions. Kuwait Finance House, Dubai Islamic Bank, and Bank Syariah

Mandiri are some of the Islamic banks that have adopted the Chatbot solution. Al-Rajhi Bank and Kuwait Finance House have adopted Robotic Process Automation (RPA) to automate the workflow system for retail financing and conduct customer due diligence.

These are some of the many examples of FinTech companies starting to play an active role in facilitating the use of financial services by embedding technology to provide convenience to both consumers as well as financial service providers. They also provide innovation, cost efficiency, and the opportunity to leverage technology to reach digitally savvy customers. Apparently, FinTech may seem to challenge traditional financial service providers. However, if the traditional financial service providers decide to join the FinTech wave, then they too can benefit from technology and achieve bigger gains with a large existing customer base, greater outreach, infrastructure, investment, and economies of scale.

8 Conclusion

Industrial Revolution 4.0 has to be welcomed, but without giving rise to environmental challenges and income inequality. The role of Islamic commercial finance and Islamic social finance is vital to support the large-scale and small-scale mobilization of funds with and without a price tag to ensure social inclusion. The state of development assistance and debt servicing in selected OIC countries shows that some countries have the capacity to source development finance by issuing sovereign Sukuk, whereas other countries require more focus on social finance institutions. Islamic principles of pure altruism and charitable giving can aid in the effective mobilization, institutionalization, and utilization of social savings as well as philanthropic and humanitarian assistance. The chapter explained that Islamic finance, through its commercial and social finance options, has both market and non-market-based solutions to mobilize development funds for effective and impactful utilization in socio-economic development needs.

References

Abdullah, M. (2018). Waqf, Sustainable Development Goals (SDGs) and Maqasid al-Shariah. *International Journal of Social Economics, 45*(1), 158–172.

Ahmed, H. (2007, 6–7 March). *Waqf-based microfinance: Realizing the social role of Islamic finance.* Presented at the International Seminar on Integrating Awqaf in the Islamic Financial Sector, Singapore.

Andreoni, J. (1989). Giving with impure altruism: Applications to charity and Ricardian equivalence. *Journal of Political Economy*, *97*(6), 1447–1458.

Andreoni, J. (1990). Impure altruism and donations to public goods: A theory of warm-glow giving. *Economic Journal*, *100*(401), 464–477.

Aziz, M. R. A, Johari, F., & Yusof, M. A. (2013). Cash Waqf models for financing in education. Proceedings of the 5th Islamic Economic System Conference (iECONS2013).

Deaton, A. (1991). Saving and liquidity constraints. *Econometrica*, *59*(5), 1221–1248.

Fauziah, N. N., Ali, E. R. A. E., & Bacha, A. M. (2021). An analysis of cash Waqf linked Sukuk for socially impactful sustainable projects in Indonesia. *Journal of Islamic Finance*, *10*(SE), 1–10.

Global Humanitarian Assistance. (2021). *Global humanitarian assistance report*. Development Initiatives.

Haneef, M. A., Muhammad, A. D., Pramanik, A. H., & Mohammed, M. O. (2014). Integrated Waqf based Islamic Microfinance Model (IWIMM) for poverty alleviation in OIC member countries. *Middle-East Journal of Scientific Research*, *19*(2), 286–298.

Haq, M. (1995). *Reflections on human development*. Oxford University Press.

Haq, M. (1963). *The strategy of economic planning: A case study of Pakistan*. Oxford University Press.

Internal Displacement Monitoring Centre. (2021). *Global report on internal displacement 2021*. Retrieved 31 May 2022, from https://www.internal-displacement.org/global-report/grid2021/

Khan, T. (2019). Venture Waqf in a circular economy. *ISRA International Journal of Islamic Finance*, *11*(2), 187–205.

Lorenz, M. O. (1905). Methods of measuring the concentration of wealth. *Publications of the American Statistical Association*, *9*(70), 209–219.

Mohammad, M. T. S. H. (2011). Towards an Islamic social (Waqf) bank. *International Journal of Trade, Economics and Finance*, *2*(5), 381–386.

Mukhlisin, M., & Mustafida, R. (2019). Can we combine Sukuk and Waqf? A case study of Indonesia. In *Revitalization of Waqf for socio-economic development* (Vol. I, pp. 169–191). Palgrave Macmillan.

Musari, K. (2019). The evolution of Waqf and Sukuk toward Sukuk-Waqf in modern Islamic economy. *International Journal of 'Umranic Studies*, *2*(1), 45–54.

Naqvi, S. N. H., & Qadir, A. (1997). The dimensions of an Islamic economic model. *Islamic Economic Studies*, *4*(2), 1–24.

Obaidullah, M. (2008). *Role of microfinance in poverty alleviation: Lessons from experiences in selected IDB member countries*. Islamic Development Bank.

Sadeq, A. M. (2002). Waqf, perpetual charity and poverty alleviation. *International Journal of Social Economics*, *29*(1/2), 135–151.

Shirazi, N. S. (2014). Integrating Zakat and Waqf into the poverty reduction strategy of the IDB member countries. *Islamic Economic Studies*, *22*(1), 79–108.

The Role of Green Sukuk in Maqasid Al-Shariah and SDGs: Evidence from Indonesia

Khairunnisa Musari and Sutan Emir Hidayat

1 Background

Climate change poses a significant risk to the United Nations Sustainable Development Goals (SDGs). It is one of the most urgent global issues to be faced, both in developed and developing countries. Climate change has sprung up to the primacy of the development agenda as the intensity of rabid weather has increased globally, starting from higher water temperatures to severe droughts and the intensity of floods that have adverse impacts on human life, people's health, social, economic, and business activities. Certainly, climate change deepens poverty. It has already

---

K. Musari (✉)
Kiai Haji Achmad Siddiq State Islamic University (UIN KHAS), Jember Regency, Indonesia
e-mail: khairunnisamusari@uinkhas.ac.id

S. E. Hidayat
Gunadarma University and National Committee for Islamic Finance and Economy (KNEKS), Depok City, Indonesia
e-mail: sutan.emir@kneks.go.id

© The Author(s), under exclusive license to Springer Nature Switzerland AG 2023
Z. H. Jumat et al. (eds.), *Islamic Finance, FinTech, and the Road to Sustainability*, Palgrave CIBFR Studies in Islamic Finance,
https://doi.org/10.1007/978-3-031-13302-2_9

imposed a high charge on low-earning and undefended people, mainly in emerging economies.

The Securities Commission (SC) and the World Bank (2019) observed a new wave in the financial community participating in sustainable development and addressing climate change after the Paris Agreement on Climate Change in 2015. Nonetheless, there are funding issues for achieving the SDGs on top of the funding gap in combating climate change (Buana & Musari, 2020; Ministry of Finance of the Republic of Indonesia (MoF) and United Nations Development Programme (UNDP) Indonesia, 2018; United Nations Economic and Social Commission for Asia and the Pacific (UN ESCAP), 2014; Yu, 2016). In this regard, countries like Indonesia require prodigious financial assistance to bridge the financial gaps between their funding necessities and currently available financial sources. UN ESCAP (2019) emphasized how important it was for countries to work together to fill the investment gap in combating climate change by encouraging fiscal space and the private sector to get involved.

In order to tackle climate change and reduce greenhouse gas (GHG) emissions, one of the most widely used Islamic financial instruments is the green sukuk. Moghul and Safar-Aly (2014) mentioned that many prominent environmentalists highlight the potential role of religion, or at least philosophical approaches originating from religion, in addressing the environmental crisis. Islamic law, also known as shariah, contains a deeply established ethical framework for caring for the environment. Hence, the main objective behind the development of green sukuk is to address Shariah's concerns concerning safeguarding the environment, as stated by Alam et al. (2016).

The International Monetary Fund (IMF) pointed out in 2015 that sukuk could help bridge the funding gap for infrastructure projects. In addition, sukuk are seen as well-suited to infrastructure financing because of their risk-sharing features, making them suitable for filling financing gaps in emerging countries. Furthermore, Kahf (1997) cited that sukuk has the potential to act as a public sector financing instrument. Musari (2009) and Sriyana (2009) also mentioned the potential of sukuk for fiscal sustainability in the long term in managing public finances. Furthermore, Ismal and Musari (2009a, 2009b, 2009c) asserted that sukuk is a superior financing instrument to debt or loan. This is further proven by Ismal's (2010) study that viewed sukuk as an effective instrument for managing liquidity and portfolio. Similarly, the study by Musari

(2013a, 2013b) also found that sukuk has a significant positive influence on the independence of the state budget if it is used for industrial working capital and developing infrastructure as well as replacing foreign debt.

As an Islamic financial instrument, green sukuk must possess *maslahah (public interest)* that is in line with *maqasid Al-Shariah*, as they are the foundations of Islamic finance and the underlying principles and values for the preservation of the environment and society. The core of environmental development in Islamic economics is to reduce the environmental risks and increase the environmental benefits. Thus, this is an opportunity for Islamic finance to bridge the investment gap through green sukuk as an Islamic green financial instrument.

Indonesia's Sovereign Green Sukuk can provide valuable lessons concerning national collaboration among state institutions in addressing climate change. As the world's first sovereign green sukuk, Indonesia's Global Sovereign Green Sukuk can serve as a case study to learn its impacts on SDGs, including its relevance to *maqasid al-shariiah*. Therefore, this study aims to address the topic of green sukuk by focusing on the following three sections: (1) Indonesia's Sovereign Green Sukuk as a national collaborative effort to tackle climate change; (2) the relevance of Indonesia's Sovereign Green Sukuk with *maqasid Al-Shariah*; and (3) the role of Indonesia's Sovereign Green Sukuk in achieving SDGs.

2 Indonesia's Sovereign Green Sukuk

Indonesia is verily dedicated to fighting climate change, considering this country is most susceptible to climate-induced catastrophes. As part of the global community that is responsible for dealing with climate change in the world, Indonesia in 2016 ratified the Paris Agreement and submitted Nationally Determined Contributions (NDCs). This shows Indonesia's seriousness in taking part in the movement of low-carbon and climate-resilient.

In order to put the commitment into action, the government needs funding to fulfill its financial needs. However, Yu (n.d.) and Tamura and Yu (2015) mentioned that there is still no mechanism that oversees the coordination of how resources might be allocated and utilized effectively among government agencies. They further asserted that climate change should be fully integrated into national and sectoral development plans and be channeled into the public financial management system, and therefore, developing countries need to develop robust national strategies for scaling up domestic climate finance.

The Indonesian Sovereign Green Sukuk is an exemplary national collaboration to face climate change. It employs the climate budget tagging mechanism results and channels investments toward and across green sectors. This is shown in Table 1, where Indonesian Green Bond and Green Sukuk Framework ensure green sectors have the most climate impacts.

The Indonesian Green Bond and Green Sukuk Framework have received a second opinion from the Centre for International Climate Research (CICERO), the foremost institute for interdisciplinary climate research in Norway, as external reviewers, and have been awarded Medium Green Shading. This shading contemplates the nations' ambitiousness for the climate and environment in making the transformation to a low-carbon society (CICERO, 2018). This shading also shows that

Table 1 Indonesia's Green Bond & Green Sukuk framework

Using the fund	Evaluating and selecting the project	Managing the fund by MoF	Reporting
Eligible Green Projects must fall into one of the nine eligible sectors	MoF and Ministry of National Development Planning/National Development Planning Agency (Bappenas) do review and approval process	The Green Bond and Green Sukuk proceeds will be distributed to appointed account of relevant ministries for financing special projects as previously assigned. Allocation is organized by MoF **Related Ministries** The related ministries which manages the proceeds will track, monitor, and report to MoF, on the environmental benefits of the Eligible Green Projects	MoF will organize and issue a Green Bond and Green Sukuk annual report on the projects list, the proceeds allocated to such projects, and the estimation of beneficial impacts

Source Adapted from MoF and UNDP Indonesia (2018)

eligible listed projects, as a reflection of the policy's work in realizing the vision of the future in lowering carbon emissions, have not reached the target yet (MoF, 2019, 2020). According to the Framework, there are nine sectors which can be financed by Green Sukuk as shown in Table 2.

The Eligible Green Sectors refer to projects which promote the transition to a low-emission economy and climate resilient growth, including climate mitigation, adaptation, and biodiversity in accordance with the criteria and process set out in this Framework. To avoid confusion, MoF (2019) stated that the Eligible Green Sectors will be exempt from the following: (1) the expenditure and capacity of new fossil fuel-based electric power generation associated with the efficiency improvement of fossil fuel-based electric power generation; (2) high scale hydropower plants (capacity > 30 MW); and (3) nuclear and nuclear-related assets.

The government of Indonesia debuted its first green sukuk in March 2018 with a USD1.25 billion offering. Then, the government issued the second sukuk of its in February 2019, generating USD 750 million of funds. Additionally, in November 2019, the government issued Savings Retail Sukuk, the first retail green sukuk in the world. The three instruments are evidence of the government's serious commitment toward climate action. The two sovereign global green sukuk have a total value of USD 2 billion. Each issuance is comprised of 51% refinancing for existing projects and 49% financing for new projects. Table 3 provides an executive summary of Indonesia's Sovereign Global Green Sukuk for the period 2018–2021.

Overall, projected environmental benefits from the issuance of Indonesia's Sovereign Green Sukuk in 2018 reduced 5,776,497.49 tonnes of CO_2 emissions and 3,218,014.41 tonnes of CO_2 emissions in 2019 (MoF, 2020). As for allocation by activity, the cumulative Indonesia's Global Green Sukuk issuance between 2018 and 2020 was 57% for mitigation and 43% for adaptation. Accordingly, allocation by sector yielded 5% for Renewable Energy (Clean Energy), 11% for Energy Efficiency (Efficient Energy Use), 41% for Sustainable Transportation (Environmental-friendly Transportation), 36% for Climate Change Resiliency of Very High-Risk Sectors and Areas and Minimize Disaster Risk, as well as 6% for Waste-to-Energy (Energy-from-Waste/Energy Recovery) and Waste Management (MoF, 2021). These results represent the continuing efforts to support sectors with green growth and maintain Indonesia's integrity and dedication to creating a low carbon and climate-resilient economy.

Table 2 The projects of eligible green sectors

Eligible green sectors	Projects
1. Renewable Energy (Clean Energy)	• Renewable energy resources for generator and transmittal of energy, comprise: onshore and offshore wind, geothermal heat, biomass, rain, tides, waves, hydropower, tidal, and solar/sunlight • Finding products or technologies for generating renewable energy through research and development, comprise: solar panels and turbines
2. Sustainability in Managing the Natural Resources	• Sustainability in managing the natural resources, primarily to elude or minimize carbon loss/escalate carbon isolation through replanting of deteriorated land, utilize of flood/temperature/drought-resistant breeds, and/or the planting of new forest zones • Conservation of biodiversity and habitat through sustainability in managing the forestry/fisheries/agriculture and land-use change, pest management, and shelter of marine environments and coastal areas
3. Energy Efficiency (Efficient Energy Use)	• The improvement for the energy efficiency infrastructures which proceeds an energy consumption leastwise 10% under the national energy consumption average of an equivalent consumption leastwise 10% under the national energy consumption average equivalent • Finding products or technologies and their practice through research and development that lower the energy consumption of underlying asset, product, technology, or systems, including improved lighting technology, improved chillers, LED lights, and diminished power utilization in manufacture industry
4. Green Tourism (Ecotourism/ Sustainable Tourism)	• Developing the resilience of tourism for climate change risk • Optimizing the supporting infrastructure to bear sustainable tourism, such as energy efficiency and/or water treatment • Developing the areas of new tourism in accordance with the Principles of Green Tourism
5. Climate Change Resiliency for Very High Risk Sector and Areas / Minimize Disaster Risk	• Managing the public health • A leading research on technology innovation with sustainability of benefits • Mitigating the flood risk • Securing the food system • Managing for drought
6. Green Buildings (Green Construction/ Sustainable Building)	Establishing green buildings refer to Greenship constructed by Green Building Council (GBC) Indonesia with six categories: material and resources cycle, development of appropriate site, energy conservation and efficiency, water conservation, environment and building management, and leisure air and air quality (water indoor comfort and health)
7. Sustainable Transportation (Environmentally Transportation)	• Intensifying the transport network to have the highest resilience design standards of climate • Expanding the clean transportation system

(continued)

Table 2 (continued)

Eligible green sectors	Projects
8. Sustainable Agriculture (Sustainable Farming/ Sustainable System of Plant and Animal Production)	• Expanding the sustainability of agriculture management and methods, as research and development on climate resilient germ, deficient pesticides, organic farming, and energy efficient in the agricultural sector • Developing a mechanism of subvention for agriculture insurance
9. Waste-to-Energy (Energy-from-Waste/ Energy Recovery) & Waste Management	• Rehabilitating the landfill areas • Rectifying the waste management • Converting waste toward a renewable energy resource

Source Adapted from MoF and UNDP Indonesia (2018), MoF (2019, 2020)

Table 3 Indonesia's Sovereign Global Green Sukuk (2018–2021)

Date		March 1, 2018	June 20, 2019	June 23, 2020	June 9, 2021
Volume		USD 1.25 billion	USD 750 million	USD 750 million	USD 750 million
Tenor		5 years	5.5 years	5 years	30 years
Yield		3.75%	3.9%	2.3%	3.55%
Allocation by Sector	Renewable Energy (Clean Energy)	8%	5%	0%	n.a
	Energy Efficiency (Efficient Energy Use)	8%	27%	0%	n.a
	Climate Change Resiliency for Very High Risk Sector and Areas /Minimize Disaster Risk	22%	11%	83%	n.a
	Sustainable Transportation (Environmentally Transportation)	55%	48%	7%	n.a
	Waste-to-Energy (Energy-from-Waste/ Energy Recovery) & Waste Management	7%	9%	11%	n.a

Source Adapted from MoF (2020, 2021)

3 Green Sukuk and *Maqasid Al-Shariah*

SC and the World Bank (2019) reported that Islamic finance offers huge potential in promoting the agenda for climate change and the development of a green economy across numerous economic sectors. In principle, the greener the economy, the better climate change can be tackled. Also, it would need well-balanced economic development programs that work well with the core principles of Islamic finance, which are based on the values of maqasid Al-Shariah.

Regarding the existence of green sukuk as an Islamic green financing instrument, it is important to note that *maqasid Al-Shariah* must be the main objective, and therefore, the allocation and impact of green sukuk should be the manifestation of the *maqasid Al-Shariah*. Wahab and Naim (2020) argued that the consequences of ignoring *maqasid Al-Shariah* and *maslahah* would cause Islamic financial products to lose their intrinsic values and would become unacceptable in the global market.

Therefore, the approach to assessing the relevance of green sukuk in achieving *maqasid Al-Shariah* should be through the quality of allocation and impact of green sukuk. In general, the quality of allocation and impact of green sukuk is expected to improve environmental quality within the limits of regeneration and assimilation. Musari (2020c) wrote that the environment as a resource has limited regeneration and assimilation. If this limit is exceeded, natural resources will suffer damage because they are exploited as factors of production and consumption. Figure 1 shows how green sukuk as an Islamic financial instrument works to combat climate change.

Economic policies that favor short-term growth have triggered aggressive, exploitative, and expansionary patterns of production and consumption, resulting in a decline in the carrying capacity and function of the environment. One of which is the acceleration of climate change. In the Quran (2:29; 15:19—20; 16:14, 66; 42: 4; 67:15), Allah has mentioned that Allah is the owner of the earth and Allah created everything on earth, including the sea and livestock, which the earth is spread to and smoothed out for humans to move, eat, and fulfill all their needs of life. However, the Quran (11:61) also reminds us of the obligation of humans to maintain the environment and nature.

Various studies such as Rohmah et al. (2020), Utama et al. (2019), Maimunah (2018), Suryani (2017), Pratama (2015), Iswanto (2013),

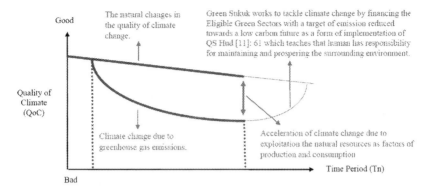

Fig. 1 Green Sukuk in tackling climate change (*Source* Adapted from Musari [2020c] and Musari and Zaroni [2021])

and Ghufron (2010) showed multiple encouraging examples for the five of *maqasid Al-Shariah* to be developed into new interpretations which reconstruct these universal principles to suit the times. One thing that needs to be echoed is environmental preservation *(hifz al-bi'ah)*. It is important to note that the current environmental damage will threaten the sustainability of all living things. Earlier, Yafie (2006, 2007) also sounded the need to add *hifz al-bi'ah* in addition to the rules of *hifdzul an-nafs* (life preservation), *hifdzul al-aql* (life preservation), *hifdzul an-nasl* (progeny preservation), *hifdzul al-māl* (wealth preservation), and *hifdzul ad-'din* (religion preservation).

The same thing was also conveyed by Al-Qardhawi's (2001, 2002) writings that state protecting the environment as *riayatu al-bi'ah* (preserving the environment) is the same as preserving the five objectives of *maqasid Al-Shariah*, as it provides *maslahah* (public interest) and prevents *mudharrah* (harms). Any behavior that leads to environmental destruction will threaten *an-nafs, al-aql, an-nasl, al-māl,* and *ad 'din* so that *riayatu al bi'ah* is in line with *maqasid Al-Shariah*.

Additionally, within *ushul fiqh (principles of Islamic jurisprudence)*, there is an established shariah maxim that states, "*mā lā yatim al-wāǧib ilā bihi fahūwa wāǧib*," which means that without which an obligatory command cannot be accomplished, it also becomes obligatory.

In order to ensure that all green sukuk project financings in Indonesia comply with *hifdzul al-bi'ah* or *riayatu al-bi'ah* and *maqasid*

Al-Shariah, several references need to be followed, namely Government Regulation of the Republic of Indonesia Number 56, year 2011 on Project Financing through the Issuance of Sovereign Shariah Securities and Decision of the National Shariah Council-Indonesian Ulema Council (DSN-MUI) Number 01/DSN-MUI/III/2012 on Criteria of Projects in accordance with Shariah Principles. In addition, referring to Suminto (Ed.) (2015), the two regulations also regulate all utilization of projects not for purposes related to implementation and/or their contribution to the activities of destructive and dangerous (harm) against morals and the environment *(al-bi'ah)*.

Referring to the Eligible Green Sectors and the projects during 2018–2019, Table 4 sums up the relevance of Indonesia's Sovereign Green Sukuk with *maqasid Al-Shariah*. As such, the projects were financed by green sukuk and must manifest the allocation and proceeds of green sukuk, which is in accordance with the *maqasid Al-Shariah*.

Furthermore, Sodikun (2012) noted that there are approximately 94 verses of the Qur'an concerning the environment and the prohibition of causing damage to it. This shows the importance of nature and the environment in Islam, where it gives warnings to the people to preserve and safeguard the environment from any calamity. The preservation of the five of *maqasid Al-Shariah* requires Muslims to create a balance, harmony, and conformity in the order of life, including nature and the environment *(al-bi'ah)*.

According to Sayadi (2012), there are chapters *(surah)* in the Qur'an that are named after animals, such as *al-Baqara* (The Cow), *al-An'aam* (The Cattle), *an-Nahl* (The Bee), *an-Naml* (The Ant), *al-'Ankaboot* (The Spider), *al' Aadiyaat* (The Courser), *al-Fīl* (The Elephant), and names of plants such as at-Tīn (The Fig), and other names such as al-Hadīd (The Iron), adh-Dhāriyat (The Winnowing Winds), an-Najm (The Star), ash-Shams (The Sun), al-Layl (The Night), al-Fajr (The Dawn). One of the wisdom behind the names is to serve as a sign to humans to realize that their existence is tied to the natural environment, and they are obliged to preserve it.

As for the relevance of green sukuk in achieving *maqasid Al-Shariah*, it is noted by Çizakça (2007, 2011, 2014) that all innovations on Islamic financial products must meet at least three requirements:

1. The innovation must not represent *rib*.
2. It must lead the risk sharing, not risk shifting.

Table 4 Relevance of Green Sukuk in *maqasid Al-Shariah*

Eligible green sectors	The characterize of project	Maqasid al-Shariah
1. Renewable Energy (Clean Energy)	Generating and transmitting the energy from renewable energy sources	• *Hifdzul al-bi'ah*, can be mentioned also as *ri'āyah al-bī'ah*, is to preserve nature and the environment
2. Sustainability in Managing the Natural Resources	–	• It is in accordance with *maqasid al shariah* and in line with the preservation of *dīn* (religion), *nafs* (self), *'aql* (intellect), *nasl* (progeny), and *māl* (wealth)
3. Energy Efficiency (Efficient Energy Use)	Improving the energy efficiency of infrastructure	
4. Green Tourism (Ecotourism/Sustainable Tourism)	–	
5. Climate Change Resiliency for Very High Risk Sector and Areas/ Minimize Disaster Risk	Mitigating flood	
6. Green Buildings (Green Construction/Sustainable Building)	–	
7. Sustainable Transportation (Environmentally Transportation)	Developing the systems of clean transportation	
8. Sustainable Agriculture (Sustainable Farming/ Sustainable System of Plant and Animal Production)	–	
9. Waste-to-Energy (Energy-from-Waste/Energy Recovery) & Waste Management	Improving the management of waste	

Source MoF and UNDP Indonesia (2018), MoF (2020), Al-Qardhawi (2001, 2002), Yafie (2006, 2007), modified

3. It must be good to encourage the society toward the al-Ghazali and Shatibi Optimum.

By adopting Pareto's insight, it can be explained that any policy which contributes to one of *maqasid Al-Shariah* without undermining any of the other four would be desirable. Furthermore, each policy has to lead the society toward al-Ghazali and Shatibi Optimum. The al-Ghazali and Shatibi Optimum would be reached when it is no longer possible to improve any components without undermining one of the *maqasid Al-Shariah*.

4 GREEN SUKUK AND SDGS

Indonesia is among the leading countries in adopting the SDGs agenda. According to Musari (2022a, 2022b), Indonesia, as a major global economy in Asia, is engaging in financial inclusion as a strategy to achieve inclusive growth and SDGs. Through Islamic philanthropy, Indonesia has been recognized as the most generous country. In addition, through the various innovations that have developed in recent years, Indonesia is now seen as an emerging force in Islamic finance globally. The country has a great opportunity to eradicate poverty and achieve the SDGs through the untapped potential of Islamic finance and funding, which has now become a vital and innovative financing modality to close the funding gap for the SDGs as well as climate change.

Buana and Musari (2020) and Musari (2020a) mentioned that there must be a gradual change to pull money back into real economies through innovative financing, and Indonesia has realized this pathway, which among others is green sukuk. Despite being innovative in their own stature, the three greens (green economy, green financing, and green instruments) exclude certain sectors from their framework. This, as a result, can trigger new constructs, one of which is the blue economy, which in the future could take the form of Blue Sukuk and White Sukuk.

All in all, the role of green sukuk in achieving SDGs can be indicated by the allocation of Indonesia's Global Green Sukuk projects and their impacts on achieving the SDGs. Table 5 shows the financing and refinancing projects by Global Green Sukuk in 2018, their results, and their impacts on SDGs achievement in Indonesia.

Then, in 2019, the role of green sukuk in achieving SDGs in Indonesia can also be indicated by the allocation of Global Green Sukuk projects and their impacts on achieving the SDGs. Table 6 shows the financing and refinancing projects by Global Green Sukuk in 2019, their results, and their impacts to SDGs achievement in Indonesia.

Undoubtedly, Indonesia's Sovereign Green Sukuk can be a lesson as a national collaborative effort to tackle climate change through Islamic green financing. This instrument has paved the way for the enforcement of *hifdzul al-bi'ah/riayatu al-bi'ah* and *maqasid Al-Shariah* as

Table 5 Projects of Global Green Sukuk 2018, its results and impacts to SDGs

Sector	Projects' name	Brief description	Result	SDGs
Renewable Energy (Clean Energy)	Developing the Infrastructure of New, Renewable Energy, and Energy Conservation	Developing infrastructures for new and renewable energy as well as energy conservation, by focusing off-grid areas to escalate the electrification ratio. Power plants are sourced from biofuel, micro-hydropower, mini-hydro, solar power, biogas communal, biogas power plant by Palm Oil Mill Effluents (POME)	Minimize GHG emissions by 2,122 tonnes CO2e per year; improves electrification ratio; 4,639 kW power generated; 60 m³ biogas communal	7, 8, 9, 11, 13
	Developing the Minihydro Power Plants	Improving the electrification ratio in off-grid areas in Papua Provinces and replacing the existing diesel generators	Minimize GHG emissions by 101,483,080,670 tonnes CO2e per year; improves electrification ratio, 1,700 kW power	7, 8, 9, 11, 13
	Developing the Energy Infrastructure through Renewable Energy Usage	Developing the renewable energy facilities and infrastructure to serve rural electrification in off-grid areas, especially in small islands and remote areas	Minimize GHG emissions by 13,044.474 tonnes CO2e per year; 8,180 kW power generated	7, 9, 13
	Biofuels Usage	Constructing the infrastructure and facilities for biofuels storage to overcome the obstacles in the Biofuels Mandatory Program implementation and make sure the facile distribution along with all areas	Minimize GHG emissions by 3,830,609 tonnes CO2e per year; distributing 2,571,569 kiloliter of biodiesel	7, 9, 13
	Developing the Infrastructure for NonElectricity Bioenergy	Constructing the communal biogas power plants to promote the renewable energy utilization to meet the energy needs of the community	Minimize GHG emissions by 11,814 tonnes CO2e; 10 units of digester with biogas production of 36 m³/day	7, 13
	Developing the Infrastructure of Bioenergy Power Plant	Constructing the biogas power plants by POME and seaweed	Minimize GHG emissions by 57,666 tonnes CO2e per year; potential producing power capacity at 7,340 MW	7, 11, 13
Energy Efficiency (Efficient Energy Use)	Installing the Energy-Saving Solar Energy Lights in the Rural Area	Distributing the solar-powered LED lighting	Minimize GHG emissions by 127,048,262.4 tonnes CO2e per year; 172,996 unit solar saving lamp to restricted villages	7, 11, 13
	Installing the Device for Energy Efficiency	Installing the intelligent public street lighting integrated with solar power plants	To be confirmed for minimizing GHG emission per year; 7,180 kW power generated	7, 8, 9, 11, 13
Energy Efficiency (Efficient Energy Use)	Clean and Efficient Energy Technology	Installing the intelligent public street lighting integrated with solar power plants and retrofitting LED lights on existing public street lighting systems	Minimize GHG emissions by 2,325,611 tonnes CO2e per year	7, 11, 13
	Constructing the Aid of Navigation Facilities	Provide the navigation facilities with solar photovoltaic-based, such as for fog signals, buoys, day beacons, and conventional lighthouses	Minimize GHG emissions by 141,800 tonnes CO2e per year; 2 flare towers; 18 flare buoys, and 111 beacon signs	7, 9, 13
	Procuring and Installing the Equipment for Road	Installing the equipment for road with solar photovoltaic-based, such as for warning lights system and public street lighting	Minimize GHG emissions by 615 tonnes CO2e per year; eliminate the use of conventional electricity	7, 11, 13

(continued)

Table 5 (continued)

Sector	Projects' name	Brief description	Result	SDGs
Waste-to-Energy (Energy from-Waste/Energy Recovery) & Waste Management	Improving the Management System of Municipal Solid Waste	Improving the decent basic infrastructure services by developing the final disposal sites with city area-scale	To be confirmed for minimizing GHG emission per year; 1,457,428 households received the benefit	7,11, 13
		Improving the decent basic infrastructure services by developing the final disposal sites with city, regional, and special area-scale	To be confirmed for minimizing GHG emission per year; 110,000 households received the benefit	7,11, 13
Sustainable Transportation (Environmentally Transportation)	Constructing & Managing the Infrastructure & Supporting Facilities of Railways	Constructing the Trans Sumatra Railways from Aceh to Lampung Province	Minimize GHG emissions by 206,470 tonnes CO2e per year; to be confirmed for other results	To be confirmed
		Constructing the double-double track railway in Greater Jakarta	Minimize GHG emissions by 169,003.9 tonnes CO2e per year; to be confirmed for other results	
	Operating the Double Track Railways in Java's North Path	Constructing 727 km double-track railway project transforms the existing single-track railway Jakarta-Surabaya	Minimize GHG emissions by 613,434 tonnes CO2e per year; reducting the fuel usage	8, 9, 11, 13
	Constructing the Trans Sumatra Railways	Constructing the Trans Sumatra line facilities and infrastructure as well as covering the development of new tracks and revitalisation of existing tracks, developing the new stations, and electric signals system	Minimize GHG emissions by 235,458 tonnes CO2e per year; shifting mode for logistics transportation	8, 9, 11, 13
	Developing the Urban Train in Greater Jakarta	Improving the facilities of passengers by raising the capacity of power supply; land acquisition; constructing the pedestrian bridges, flyovers, and underpasses of the urban railway network in Greater Jakarta	Minimize GHG emissions by 856,828 tonnes CO2e per year; shifting mode for passengers	8, 9, 11, 13
	Procuring for medium-size Bus Rapid Transit	Providing the 381 units of medium-sized buses under Bus Rapid Transit system	Minimize GHG emissions by 165,704 tonnes CO2e per year; minimize the crowded public transportation and also develop the feeder transportation	8, 9, 11, 13
Sustainable Transportation (Environmentally Transportation)	Procuring the Equipment for Road and Installing the ICT-based traffic control system	Installing the two packages of area traffic control system to secure a facier traffic flows at intersection area	Minimize GHG emissions by 203,116 tonnes CO2e per year; the consumption of fuel is more efficient as fewer traffic jams and the controlled speed of vehicles	9, 11, 13
	Developing the pioneer sea transport	Modernizing the 100 vessels with the engines more energy efficient	Minimize GHG emissions by 5,868 tonnes CO2e per year; improving the connectivity of sea transportation and reduce the fuel consumption	7, 9, 11, 13

(continued)

Table 5 (continued)

Sector	Projects' name	Brief description	Result	SDGs
Climate Change Resiliency for Very High Risk Sector and Areas / Minimize Disaster Risk	Constructing the surface irrigation networks authorized by the Central Government	Developing and rehabilitating the dams and the networks of surface irrigation	Fulfilling the need for irrigation water service for flowing the rice fields in 54,111.21 ha area	3, 5, 6, 8, 10, 11
	Constructing the Facilities for Flood Control	With the increased rainfall intension, some regions become more inclined to have flooding risk. This is added by the changes in land use and the narrowness of the river leads to higher run-off/stormwater	Setting the technical planning and environmental documents for constructing the 23 ha flood control; improving the flood infrastructure and facilities for 285 ha of area	3, 5, 6, 8, 10, 11

Source Adapted from MoF (2019, 2020, 2021)

Table 6 Projects of Global Green Sukuk 2019, its results, and impacts to SDGs

Sector	Projects' name	Brief description	Result	SDGs
Renewable Energy (Clean Energy)	Planning, Developing, and Supervising the Infrastructure of the New, Renewable Energy and Energy Conservation	Constructing infrastructures for new and renewable energy as well as energy conservation, by focusing on districts that are out of coverage of current electricity to escalate the electrification ratio. Power plants are sourced from solar and biogas	To be confirmed for minimizing GHG emission per year; and other results	7, 8, 9, 11, 13
		Constructing infrastructures for new and renewable energy, by focusing on districts that are out of coverage of current electricity to escalate the electrification ratio. Power plants are sourced from micro-hydropower, mini-hydro, and solar	Minimize GHG emissions by 134,872.41 tonnes CO2e per year; electricity for 15,607 households; 7,429 kW power generated; 48 m3 biogas communal, 930 unit public street and battery	7, 8, 9, 11, 13
	Installing the Energy-Saving Solar Energy Lights in the Rural Area	Installing the energy saving solar-powered lamps in areas with limited or no electricity facilities. These lamps would improve accessibility to lighting for off-grid areas while reducing use of diesel generators	Minimize GHG emissions by 1,184,748 tonnes CO2e per year; 79,556 units installed; households with lighting	7, 11, 13
Sustainable Transportation (Environmentally Transportation)	Constructing & Managing the Infrastructure & Supporting Facilities of Railways in Sumatera	Financing the Trans Sumatra Railways construction from Aceh to Lampung Province	Minimize GHG emissions by 206,470 tonnes CO2e per year; streamlining the goods and passengers flow; shifting mode in logistics transport	8, 9, 11, 13
		Refinancing the Trans Sumatra Railways construction from Aceh to Lampung Province	Minimize GHG emissions by 235,438 tonnes CO2e per year; 343.2 km of railways, shifting mode in logistics and passenger transport	8, 9, 11, 13
	Constructing & Managing the Infrastructure & Supporting Facilities of Railways in Java Line and Java North Line	Constructing the double track railway project in the Trans Java railway's northern and southern sections	Minimize GHG emissions by 917,103 tonnes CO2e per year; accelerating train travel; streamlining the goods and passengers flow to minimize the consumption of fuel	8, 9, 11, 13
		Constructing the double track railway project in the Trans Java railway's northern section	Minimize GHG emissions by 613,434 tonnes CO2e per year; upgrading the 338.6 km of doubletrack railway, reduce the time for traveling; minimize the consumption of fuel	8, 9, 11, 13
	Developing the Urban Train in Greater Jakarta	Constructing the double-double track of the urban railway network in Greater Jakarta	Minimize GHG emissions by 856,828 tonnes CO2e per year; shifting mode to public transport	8, 9, 11, 13

(continued)

Table 6 (continued)

Sector	Projects' name	Brief description	Result	SDGs
Waste-to-Energy (Energy-from-Waste/Energy Recovery) & Waste Management	Improving the Management System of Municipal Solid Waste	Financing the improvement of basic infrastructure services by developing the final disposal sites with city, regional, and special area-scale	To be confirmed for minimizing GHG emission per year; 150,701 households received the benefit	11, 13
		Refinancing the improvement of basic infrastructure services by developing the final disposal sites with city, regional, and special area-scale	In order to achieve 48,000,000 tonnes target set; 2,036,660 households received the benefit	11, 13
Climate Change Resiliency for Very High Risk Sector and Areas / Minimize Disaster Risk	Constructing the Facilities for Flood Control	Constructing the retention ponds, check dam, canals of the flood, dikes, and river normalization and preservation to decrease the flooding risk due to the changes in land use and rainfall intensity	Controlling the sediment of 0.32 million cubic m; improving the facilities and infrastructure of flood area for 27,998.5 ha	3, 5, 6, 8, 10, 11
Energy Efficiency (Efficient Energy Use)	Installing the Facilities of Navigation	Constructing, rehabilitating, and replacing the aids of marine navigation as well as installing the solar cells for marine navigation aids	Minimize GHG emissions by 141,800 tonnes CO2e per year; 2,459 units constructed; improving the safety of marine transport	7, 9, 13
Energy Efficiency (Efficient Energy Use)	Improving the Services for Managing the Traffic of Land Transportation	Installing the equipment of road traffic as well as navigation aids for river and lake crossings with energy-saving sensors	Minimize GHG emissions by 203,116 tonnes CO2e per year; minimize traffic congestion and improve safety in river and lake crossings	7, 9, 13
	Constructing, Rehabilitating, & Maintaining the Infrastructures of Airports	Installing the solar-powered street lights and plants to improve the energy efficiency of airports through renewable sources for electricity	Minimize GHG emissions by 10,478 tonnes CO2e per year; usage of renewable energy for lighting in airports	7, 9, 13

Source Adapted from MoF (2020, 2021)

well as also to achieving the SDGs. Green Sukuk also can be a gateway to finding innovative sustainable financing instruments to diversify risks through Islamic borrowing public. In the future, in line with a study by Morea and Paggio (2017), it is necessary to provide incentives for issuing sukuk to provide appropriate and sustainable investments to tackle climate change and GHG emissions. In addition, Musari (2020a, 2020d, 2022c) recommended the integration between perpetual cash *waqf* linked sukuk (CWLS) with green sukuk as a new socially responsible investment (SRI) alternative in the form of Perpetual Green CWLS. Perpetual Green CWLS is expected to link the real and financial sector as well as Islamic commercial and social finance by serving exponential benefits for tackling climate change. In addition, *esham* structured sukuk (Çizakça, 2011, 2014; Musari, 2019, 2021, 2022b) are also worth proposing to be developed as an alternative to sukuk.

5 Conclusion and Recommendations

This chapter shows that Indonesia has addressed climate change as one of its national priorities. It is imperative to ensure that policy transformation, an enabling environment, and financial investment go hand in hand to support this national agenda. As an Islamic financial instrument, Green Sukuk can serve the enforcement tool for *hifdzul al-bi'ah/riayatu al-bi'ah* and *maqasid Al-Shariah*. Regarding the SDGs, the allocation and impact of Indonesia's Sovereign Green Sukuk have roles not only to support the achievement of SDGs for Climate Action (Goal 13) but also for Good Health and Well-Being (Goal 3), Gender Equality (Goal 5), Clean Water and Sanitation (Goal 6), Affordable and Clean Energy (Goal 7), Decent Work and Economic Growth (Goal 8), Industry, Innovation, and Infrastructure (Goal 9), Reduced Inequalities (Goal 10), Sustainable Cities and Communities (Goal 11), and Peace, Justice and Strong Institutions (Goal 16).

Several recommendations related to the issuances of Sovereign Green Sukuk in Indonesia are: **First**, sovereign green sukuk issuance is still irregular and relatively done in small size due to the limited number of available green projects in the country as the underlying assets to issue green sukuk. Therefore, the government needs to increase the number and size of green projects as part of the commitment to the Paris Agreement. **Second**, at the moment, it takes a longer time to issue green sukuk than regular sukuk due to the lack of standardized guidelines on domestic green sukuk issuance. Preparation of the guidelines will speed up the issuance process and will also encourage corporations in Indonesia to issue green sukuk. **Third**, the government at the moment mainly focuses on attracting domestic investors to invest in all government securities, including green sukuk. As a result, a lot of potential global investors in green sukuk, especially in Europe, have not yet been well explored. Therefore, marketing green sukuk to those investors needs to be intensified. **Fourth**, as Islamic commercial finance, green sukuk can collaborate with Islamic social finance toward a new blended Islamic finance. CWLS and esham structured sukuk are worth a proposal for being integrated with green sukuk as an SRI instrument. **Fifth**, public involvement in tackling climate change is rational to fill the financing gap. Therefore, Islamic public borrowing must have attention and meet at least the three requirements: it does not represent riba, lead the risk-sharing, and encourage society toward the al-Ghazali and Shatibi Optimum. Hence, Perpetual Green CWLS can be an alternative scheme to be explored.

References

Al-Qardhawi, Y. (2001), *Ri'ayatu al-bi`ah fi as-syari'ah al-islamiyah*. Kairo: Dar Asy-Syuruq.
Al-Qardhawi, Y. (2002). *Islam agama ramah lingkungan*. Pustaka Al-Kautsar.
Alam, N., Duygun, M., & Ariss, R. T. (2016). Green sukuk: An innovation in Islamic capital markets. In A. B. -Dorsman, Ö. Arslan-Ayaydin, & M. B. ¬Karan (Eds.), *Energy and finance* (pp. 167–186). Springer International Publishing.
Buana, G. K., & Musari, K. (2020, December 28). A new sphere of sukuk: Linking pandemic to Paris agreement. *The World Financial Review, November-December Edition*, Islamic Finance, 59–61. https://worldfinancial-review.com/a-new-sphere-of-sukuk-linking-the-pandemic-to-the-paris-agreement/
CICERO. (2018). *'Second opinion' on the republic of Indonesia's green bond and green sukuk framework*. A report by Centre for International Climate Research (CICERO), January 23, Oslo.
Çizakça, M. (2007). Democracy, economic development and maqasid al-shariah. *Review of Islamic Economics*, *11*(1), 101–118.
Çizakça, M. (2011). *Islamic capitalism and finance: Origins, evolution, and the future*. Edward Elgar Publishing.

Çizakça, M. (2014). *Can there be innovation in islamic finance? Case study: Esham.* Paper to be presented at the 11th IFSB Summit, Knowledge Sharing Partner Session: "New Markets and Frontiers for Islamic Finance: Innovation and the Regulatory Perimeter", to be convened on May 20th in Mauritius.

Ghufron, M. (2010). Fikih lingkungan. *Jurnal Al-Ulum Juni, 10*(1), 159–176.

IMF. (2015, April). *Islamic finance: Opportunities, challenges, and policy options.* International Monetary Fund (IMF) Staff Discussion Note SDN/15/05, Washington.

Ismal, R., & Musari, K. (2009a, April 1). Menggagas sukuk sebagai instrumen fiskal dan moneter. *Bisnis Indonesia Daily.* Opini, p. 4.

Ismal, R., & Musari, K. (2009b, April). Sukuk, menuju instrumen fiskal dan moneter. *SHARING Magazine*, Edition 28 Year III, Wacana, p. 58.

Ismal, R., & Musari, K. (2009c, March 23). Sukuk menjawab resesi. *Republika Daily Newspaper*, Ekonomia.

Ismal, R. (2010, July). *The management of liquidity risk in Islamic banks: The case of Indonesia.* PhD (Doctoral) Theses, Durham Islamic Finance Program (DIFP) School of Government and International Affairs, Durham University, UK.

Iswanto, A. (2013). Relasi manusia dengan lingkungan dalam al-Quran upaya membangun eco-theology. *ṢUḤUF: Jurnal Kajian Al-Quran dan Kebudayaan, 6*(1), 1–18.

Kahf, M. (1997). *Instruments of meeting budget deficit in Islamic economy* (Research Paper No. 42 1417 H). Islamic Research and Training Institute (IRTI)—Islamic Development Bank (IDB), Jeddah.

Maimunah. (2018, June). Politik Islam perspektif maqashid syariah. *El-Maslahah Journal, 8*(1), 16–29.

MoF. (2019). *Green sukuk, allocation and impact report—February 2019.* Ministry of Finance (MoF) Republic of Indonesia.

MoF. (2020). *Green sukuk, allocation and impact report—March 2020.* Ministry of Finance (MoF) Republic of Indonesia.

MoF. (2021). *Green sukuk, allocation and impact report—May 2021.* Jakarta: Ministry of Finance (MoF), Republic of Indonesia.

MoF, & UNDP Indonesia. (2018). *Indonesia's Green Bond & Green Sukuk initiative.* Ministry of Finance (MoF) Republic of Indonesia.

Moghul, U. F., & Safar-Aly, S. H. K. (2014). Green sukuk: The introduction of Islam's environmental ethics to contemporary islamic finance. *The Georgetown International Environmental Law Review, 27*(1), 1–60.

Morea, D., & Poggi, L. A. (2017). An innovative model for the sustainability of investments in the wind energy sector: The use of green Sukuk in an Italian case study. *International Journal of Energy Economics and Policy, 7*(2), 53–60.

Musari, K. (2009, October 20). Penerbitan Sukuk Negara Berpotensi untuk Menjaga Kesinambungan Fiskal. *Kontan Daily*, Opini, p. 23.

Musari, K. (2013a). *An analysis of the issuance of sovereign Sukuk and its impact on the autonomy of state financial and well-being of society in the kingdom of Bahrain and Malaysia and republic of Indonesia.* PhD (doctoral) theses, Postgraduate Program, Airlangga University.

Musari, K. (2013b, June). Analysis of the influence of issuance of sovereign Sukuk to the autonomy of state financial and well-being of society in the kingdom of Bahrain and the republic of Indonesia. *Australian Journal of Islamic Banking and Finance* (AJIBF), 2(1), 59–84.

Musari, K. (2019, August 28–29). *Esham for fiscal sustainability, an alternative to Sukuk in Islamic finance perspective: Historical experience.* A paper was presented at Researcher Day 2019 "The 2019 International Conference on Fiscal Policy and Input-Output Modeling" at Auditorium of Fiscal Policy Agency Building, Ministry of Finance (MoF) of Republic of Indonesia, Jakarta.

Musari, K. (2020a, January 7). Menakar peluang sukuk putih untuk SDGs. *Bisnis Indonesia Daily Newspaper*, Opini, p. 2.

Musari, K. (2020b, June 14–20). *Cash Waqf linked Sukuk, a new blended finance of fiscal instrument for sustainable socio-economic development: Lesson learned from Indonesia.* A paper was presented at 12th International Conference on Islamic Economics and Finance (ICIEF) "Sustainable Development for Real Economy" with hosted by Istanbul Sabahattin Zaim University (IZU) and jointly organized by Islamic Research and Training Institute (IRTI)—Islamic Development Bank (IDB) and International Association of Islamic Economics (IAIE) with the collaboration of Statistical, Economic and Social Research and Training Centre for Islamic Countries (SESRIC) and Hamad Bin Khalifa University, Istanbul.

Musari, K. (2020c, June 14–20). *Waste bank, a local wisdom of circular economy and Islamic Nanofinance in Indonesia.* A paper was presented at 12th International Conference on Islamic Economics and Finance (ICIEF) "Sustainable Development for Real Economy" with hosted by Istanbul Sabahattin Zaim University (IZU) and jointly organized by Islamic Research and Training Institute (IRTI)—Islamic Development Bank (IDB) and International Association of Islamic Economics (IAIE) with the collaboration of Statistical, Economic and Social Research and Training Centre for Islamic Countries (SESRIC) and Hamad Bin Khalifa University, Istanbul.

Musari, K. (2020d, November 22). Paris agreement: Joe Biden, ekonomi syariah, dan adopsi hutan. *Portal Jember, Pikiran Rakyat Media Network*, Esai. https://portaljember.pikiran-rakyat.com/opini/pr-16996041/paris-agreement-joe-biden-ekonomi-syariah-dan-adopsi-hutan

Musari, K. (2021, April). Esham, the origin of Sukuk for facing the crisis: Historical experience. *Iqtishoduna: Jurnal Ekonomi Islam, 10*(1), 45–58.

Musari, K., & Zaroni. (2021). Reverse logistics in the age of digital transformation for circular economy and Halal logistics through the leadership of Asia.

In P. Ordoñez de Pablos, Xi Zhang, & M. N. Almunawar (Eds.), *Handbook of research on disruptive innovation and digital transformation in Asia* (pp. 83–103). IGI Global.

Musari, K. (2022a). P2P lending & philanthropy platform: A new face of asian digital financial inclusion (evidence from Indonesia). In M. N. Almunawar, Z. Islam, and P. Ordóñez de Pablos (Eds.), *Digital transformation management: Challenges and futures in the asian digital economy* (pp. 185-206). Routledge. https://doi.org/10.4324/9781003224532

Musari, K. (2022b). A comparative study of Islamic fiscal instrument securitization in history to modern ages: Esham, sukuk, cash waqf linked sukuk (CWLS). In Ş. Akkaya and B. Ergüder (Eds.), *Handbook of research on challenges in public economics in the era of globalization* (pp. 397-418). IGI Global. https://doi.org/10.4018/978-1-7998-9083-6.ch021

Musari, K. (2022c). Integrating green sukuk and cash waqf linked sukuk, the blended Islamic finance of fiscal instrument in Indonesia: A proposed model for fighting climate change. *International Journal of Islamic Khazanah*, 12(2), 133-144. https://doi.org/10.15575/ijik.v12i2.17750

Pratama, L. K. A. (2015). *Lingkungan hidup dalam pandangan hukum Islam (perspektif maqashid al-syariah)*. Fakultas Syariah dan Hukum, UIN Alauddin, Makassar.

Rohmah, R., Rohim, A., & Herianingrum, S. (2020, July). Sovereign green Sukuk Indonesia dalam tinjauan maqashid shariah. *Jurnal Penelitian IPTEKS*, 5(2), 259–269.

Sayadi, W. (2012). Hablun minal 'alam: Memakmurkan lingkungan hidup. In LPLH&SDA MUI. *Kumpulan khutbah jum'at dan ied: Perlindungan dan pengelolaan lingkungan hidup dan sumber daya alam* (pp. 77–82). Environmental and Natural Resources Board The Indonesian Council of Ulema (LPLH&SDA MUI).

SC & World Bank. (2019). *Islamic green finance development, ecosystem and prospects*. Securities Commission (SC) Malaysia.

Sodikun. (2012). Jihad lingkungan. In LPLH&SDA MUI (Eds.), *Kumpulan khutbah jum'at dan ied: Perlindungan dan pengelolaan lingkungan hidup dan sumber daya alam* (pp. 147–152). Environmental and Natural Resources Board The Indonesian Council of Ulema (LPLH&SDA MUI)

Sriyana, J. (2009, October 8–9). *Peranan sukuk negara terhadap peningkatan fiscal sustainability*. A paper was presented at Simposium Nasional IV Sistem Ekonomi Islam 2009 'Strengthening Institutions on Islamic Economic' at Universitas Islam Indonesia (UII) Yogyakarta, Yogyakarta.

Suminto (Ed.). (2015). *Sukuk negara: Instrumen keuangan berbasis syaria* (2nd ed.). Directorate of Islamic Financing, Directorate General of Budget Financing and Risk Management, Ministry of Finance (MoF) of Republic of Indonesia.

Suryani. (2017, November). Pengarusutamaan ḥifdh al-ʿalam sebagai bagian dari maqāṣid al-sharīʾah. *Al-Tahrir, 17*(2), 353–370.
Tamura, K., & Yu, Y. (2015). Cycles for strengthening mitigation and support. In Institute for Global Environmental Strategies (IGES) (Eds.), *The Paris climate agreement and beyond: Linking short-term climate actions to long-term goals* (pp. 33–58). IGES.
UN ESCAP. (2014, June 10–11). *Sustainable development financing: Perspectives from Asia and the Pacific*. A paper prepared by the United Nations (UN) The Economic and Social Commission for Asia and the Pacific (ESCAP) Secretariat for the Regional Outreach of the Intergovernmental Committee of Experts on Sustainable Development Financing for the Asia-Pacific Region, Jakarta.
Escap, U. N. (2019). *Economic and social survey of Asia and the Pacific 2019: Ambitions beyond growth*. United Nations Publication.
Utama, R. W. A., Muhtadi, R., Arifin, N. R., & Mawardi, I. (2019, November). Tinjauan maqashid syariah dan fiqh al-biʾah dalam green economy. *Jurnal Ekonomi Islam, 10*(2), 242–259.
Wahab, M. Z. H., &, Naim, A. M. (2020). Sustainable and responsible investment: Concept and the commonalities with Islamic financial institutions. *Etikonomi, 19*(1), 141–154.
Yafie, A. (2006). *Merintis fiqh lingkungan hidup*. Ufuk Press.
Yafie, A. (2007, February 9). Menjaga alam wajib hukumnya. *Republika Daily Newspaper*, Interview. https://www.republika.co.id/berita/q4uzc9430/saat-kh-alie-yafie-bicara-soal-fikih-lingkungan-hidup
Yu, Y. (2016, March 30–31). *Climate finance in and beyond the Paris agreement: Implementing climate finance commitments in Asia and the Pacific*. A Discussion Paper of Macroeconomic Policy and Financing for Development Division at First High-Level Follow-up Dialogue on Financing for Development in Asia and the Pacific, Incheon.
Yu, Y. A. (n.d.). Climate finance gaps and challenges. *United Nations (UN) The Economic and Social Commission for Asia and the Pacific (ESCAP)*. https://www.unescap.org/sites/default/files/Session%205.%20Climate%20finance%20gaps%20and%20challenges.pdf

Is Islamic Microfinance a Resilient Business Model During Periods of Crisis? Empirical Evidence from Arab Countries

Asma Ben Salem, Ines Ben Abdelkader and Sameh Jouida

1 Introduction

The COVID-19 pandemic is the latest crisis that has led regulators, policymakers, and scholars to question the business model prevailing in the microfinance sector, particularly the risks associated with microcredits provided by conventional institutions (Sotiriou, 2020).[1] One of the

[1] Can be accessed at: https://www.cgap.org/blog/microfinance-and-covid-19-insolvency-horizon.

A. Ben Salem
Higher Institute of Theology, Ez-Zitouna Universiy, Tunis, Tunisia

A. Ben Salem (✉)
MoFiD Lab, University of Sousse, Tunis, Tunisia
e-mail: asmabensalem@isth.u-zitouna.tn

I. Ben Abdelkader
Laremfiq's Lab, University of Sousse, Sousse, Tunisia

S. Jouida
Institut Supérieur de Gestion de Sousse, University of Sousse, Sousse, Tunisia

© The Author(s), under exclusive license to Springer Nature Switzerland AG 2023
Z. H. Jumat et al. (eds.), *Islamic Finance, FinTech, and the Road to Sustainability*, Palgrave CIBFR Studies in Islamic Finance,
https://doi.org/10.1007/978-3-031-13302-2_10

main risks to MFI solvency is a decline in portfolio quality as suggested by the sharp increases in non-performing loans during the early months of the pandemic. The foremost purpose of microfinance institutions is to reach the poorest individuals excluded from the formal financial system. Nevertheless, the high interest rates charged by conventional microfinance institutions encourage their clients, particularly Muslims, to request the services of Islamic MFIs that provide interest-free financial services. The core idea is to identify the product design in microfinance that is associated with lower credit risk.

There is a fundamental question about the relative stability of Islamic microfinance compared to conventional microfinance. Many banking studies consider the risk of Islamic banks during periods of crisis compared to the risk of conventional banks. However, we could not find studies that consider the Islamic microfinance business model and the financial stability of microfinance institutions. Accordingly, there is still a gap in microfinance literature regarding the effect of diversification strategies on the risk of Islamic MFIs compared to the risk of conventional institutions. Therefore, the limitations in previous studies encourage us to analyze the different effects of diversification on the solvency risk of MFIs before, during, and after the financial crisis. To accomplish this aim, we use data from 68 conventional MFIs and 13 Islamic institutions in the Middle East and North Africa due to their high percentage of Islamic MFIs compared to other regions (Fan et al., 2019).

The aim of this study is to test whether the microfinance business model has a different effect on the solvency risk of conventional MFIs compared to the stability of Islamic MFIs. Based on the arguments of previous literature that specifically reviews the Islamic microfinance business model, we guess that the effect of diversification on the solvency of conventional MFIs might be different to the impact on Islamic MFI stability. Comparing the solvency risk of MFIs and banks, Schulte and Winkler (2019) find that the relative riskiness of MFIs depends on the risk measure employed. Accordingly, we consider different measures of risk in microfinance.

The study is organized as follows: Sect. 2 summarizes the related literature guiding our hypotheses. Section 3 introduces our datasets, and the econometric methodology. Results and robustness checks are presented in Sect. 4. The study ends with Sect. 5 discussing the results and drawing policy conclusions.

2 Related Literature and Hypotheses Development

While there is no empirical evidence regarding the relationship between income diversification and the risk in microfinance, the findings of the banking literature on the subject matter are mixed. Several studies analyze the impact of income diversification on the risk and performance of banks, few studies like Zamore (2018) and Zamore et al. (2019) consider the effect of diversification in microfinance. Zamore (2018) finds little evidence of income diversification gains on the profitability and sustainability of MFIs. Zamore et al. (2019) examine the impact of geographic diversification on the credit risk of MFIs. They find higher credit risk for MFIs with greater geographic diversification. Their results indicate that group-based financing mitigates the negative effect of geographic diversification on credit risk. Most of the studies do not include data from Islamic MFIs to provide evidence of the gains from diversifying into non-interest income and from the geographic expansion of MFIs providing shariah-compliant services. Although a large amount of literature in banking tried to assess the effects of income diversification on the performance of Islamic banks comparatively to their conventional counterparts, there is no empirical evidence regarding the Islamic microfinance industry.

One strand of banking literature suggests that diversification reduces the risk of banks. The idea is that when banks expand their operations across a wide range of products and services, they benefit as they reduce their risks. Studying diversification in European banking, Köhler (2015) shows that increasing the share of non-interest income activities reduces the risk of retail-orientated banks. Likewise, Shim (2019) finds a positive impact of loan diversification on the financial strength of US commercial banks over the period between 2002 and 2013. Consistent with these results, Kim et al. (2020) show that excessive bank diversification increases the risk of banks while a moderate degree of bank diversification is related to low risk.

Similarly, regarding the effect of income diversification on the risk of Islamic institutions, the results from the banking literature are mixed. For instance, Nguyen et al. (2012) find lower risk for Islamic windows of diversified commercial banks, operating in four South Asian countries. Focusing on the insolvency risk of 160 conventional banks and 57 Islamic banks in eighteen Middle Eastern and North African countries during 2006–2015, Albaity et al. (2019) find higher risk-adjusted returns for diversified banks. Consistent with these results, Rufai et al. (2019) show that greater diversification reduces the risk of banks, with evidence from ten MENA countries from 2008 to 2016. This evidence indicates diversification benefits for commercial and Islamic banks. Zamore (2018) provides empirical evidence on the positive effect of revenue diversification in microfinance through an improvement in the sustainability and the profitability of MFIs. As suggested by Zamore (2018), we presume MFIs are like banks. So, we hypothesize that:

Hypothesis 1a: Diversification reduces the credit risk of MFIs

In contrast to the literature above, an array of other studies suggest that bank diversification increases risks. The study by Li and Zhang (2013) for the period of 1986–2008 suggests that income diversification worsens the risk/return adjustment for the Chinese banks (Li & Zhang, 2013). Another study by Kabir and Worthington (2017) for the period of 2000 and 2012 using accounting-based measures of banking risk concludes that riskier banks have higher income diversification in both the Islamic and the conventional banking systems. Based on the data of 76 banks in the GCC region from 2000 to 2013, Alqahtani and Mayes (2018) find that income diversification increases the risk of banks, also the Islamic banks are riskier than conventional banks (Alqahtani & Mayes, 2018). Focusing on the insolvency of banks in eighteen MENA countries during 2006–2015, Albaity et al. (2019) show a positive relationship between income diversification and risk-adjusted returns (Albaity et al., 2019).

The negative effect of revenue diversification is confirmed by the results of Yang, Liu and Chou (2019) for a sample of US listed banks between 2000 and 2013 show a higher systematic risk. This effect of revenue diversification on the systemic risk is more significant for large and medium sized banks during periods of crisis. For instance, the systematic risk increases during the 2007–2009 credit crunch and the 2010–2013 European Debt crisis. In microfinance, Zamore et al. (2019), find that geographic diversification increases the credit risk of MFIs. Their results show that the negative effect of geographic diversification on credit risk is lower for MFIs using the group-lending approach. Therefore, following previous studies like Zamore (2018), Schulte and Winkler (2019), and Zamore et al. (2019), we consider microfinance institutions like banks. Bearing in mind the above-mentioned issues and diversification implications on bank risk-taking, we guess that:

Hypothesis 1b: Revenue diversification is associated with higher MFI risk

Like banks, Islamic MFIs provide shariah-compliant services while conventional institutions give microcredits to the poor. Although conventional MFIs (CMFIs) charge interest on loans, which are prohibited by shariah law, Islamic MFIs provide alternative instruments based on profit-and-loss sharing (PLS) schemes. Besides religion, Islamic MFIs use a range of debt-based (Istisna and Ijarah), equity-based (Mudaraba and Musharaka), and sales-based products (Murabaha and Salam) while conventional MFIs offer debt-based products (Abedifar et al., 2015).

In terms of income, financing income is derived from traditional (deposit/lending) activities whereas non-financing income includes any fees or charges on services, and micro insurance. Hence, financing income is equivalent to interest income in conventional microfinance, and non-financing income corresponds to non-interest income. While conventional MFIs are more debt-oriented, with income derived from traditional (deposit/lending) activities, Islamic MFIs are expected to have a higher share of non-interest income which characterizes non-traditional activities. It is noteworthy that the income of Islamic microfinance largely results from fees as well as gains associated with shariah-compliant financings whereas CMFIs fund most of their activities through customer deposits, and essentially provide loans. Despite exhaustive literature on this area, Abdelkader and Salem (2013), Mobin et al. (2017), and Fan et al. (2019) examined the effect of religion on the performance of MFIs in many regions; little is known about whether MFIs should diversify to shariah-compliant services or focus only on conventional microfinance.

Given these considerations, we expect the risk of Islamic MFIs and conventional MFIs to be affected differently by their diversification activities, and the overall impact for each MFI group to be conditioned by the scope of the diversification efforts. Accordingly, we hypothesize as follows:

Hypothesis 2: Income diversification differs between conventional and Islamic MFIs

The positive (negative) effect of income (geographic) diversification on credit risk and the resilience of microfinance institutions is different for Islamic MFIs during periods of crisis. Differences between conventional and Islamic MFIs in terms of income diversification and geographic expansion are driven by their poverty outreach, reflecting their business models.

3 DATA AND METHODOLOGY

We use annual data from MIX Market with about 81 MFIs (68 conventional MFIs and 13 Islamic MFIs) in the Middle Eastern and North African region and from Word development indicators, over the period 1999–2018. Both datasets provide information on institutional characteristics and macroeconomic variables as determinants of solvency risk in the microfinance literature. Following Abdelkader and Salem (2013) and Fan et al. (2019), we define Islamic MFIs as MFIs that fully and partially provide shariah-compliant products and services. We find that 22.75% of the observations are from Islamic MFIs and 77.25% of the observations are from conventional MFIs.[2] In the MENA region, we identify ten MFIs with Islamic windows that provide shariah-compliant products and services and three fully Islamic MFIs, namely *Al Takadum* (Iraq), *Azal* (Yemen) and *Reef* (Palestine).

Risk Measures

As suggested by previous studies like Fan et al. (2019) and Zamore et al. (2019), we consider three measures of risk in the microfinance literature: (1) PaR30 (Portfolio at Risk > 30 days); (2) Loan Loss Rate and (3) Z-score as a proxy for the global risk of MFIs (Schulte & Winkler, 2019).

Portfolio at risk (PAR30) is the percentage of a gross loan portfolio that has been unsettled for more than 30 days. It is noteworthy that PAR30 is generally used as a measure of portfolio quality in microfinance since most loans have a duration of around 12 months (Zamore et al.,

---

[2] The share of Islamic MFIs in Middle East and North Africa (MENA) is higher than other regions as shown in previous studies. For example, Fan et al. (2019), find that only 12.50% of the observations are linked to Islamic MFIs for a sample of MFIs operating in three regions, including South Asia, MENA and Eastern Europe and Central Asia, over the period of 1998–2014.

2019). As suggested by Mersland and Strom (2010), PAR30 denotes the nonperforming loans rate as a common measure of credit risk in microfinance.

Loan Loss Rate is the ratio of the difference between write-offs and loans convalesced to the gross loan portfolio. A higher proportion of loan deferral, write-off and loss suggests higher credit risk (Fan et al., 2019).

Z-score measures the number of standard deviations of a MFI's return-on-assets that it would have to fall in order to deplete the sum of its equity and income (Ashraf et al., 2016). Schulte and Winkler (2019) view that the Z-score has become the appropriate measure of MFI solvency risk, indicating the unlikeliness of microfinance failure. As per Schulte and Winkler (2019), the Z-score is calculated as:

$$Z - \text{score}_{it} = \frac{ROA_{it} + ETA_{it}}{\partial(ROA)_{ip}}$$

The Z-score as a global measure of the risk of MFIs, the Z-score is the suitable risk measure for MFIs as they provide a larger range of services to clients than just credit. Similarly, for Islamic MFIs, the Z-score has the advantage over other accounting-based financial stability measures that it captures both interest and fee-based income streams.

ROA is calculated as the net income divided by the annual average total assets; the standard deviation is calculated based on observations for a period p defined as t to $t-n$. Assuming a normal distribution of ROA, the Z-score measures the distance to default. Accordingly, a rising Z-score indicates a decline in risk.

Descriptive statistics (Table 1) reveal that based on the Z-score; conventional MFIs are riskier than Islamic MFIs on average. The average MFI has a Z-score of 4.88 compared to 6.39 for Islamic MFIs. Figure 1 shows that the Z-score value for MFIs decreases significantly after the GFC for the period from 2010 to 2013 whereas the value of the Z-score remains higher for Islamic MFIs in the same period.

However, using the PAR 30 to measure the solvency risk suggests that Islamic MFIs haver higher risk than conventional MFIs. The average MFI has a PAR30 of 0.04 compared to 0.14 for Islamic MFIs. Although Islamic MFIs have a higher solvency risk, conventional MFIs are riskier after the GFC from 2011 to 2013 (Fig. 2). While the solvency risk of Islamic MFIs declines significantly during the global financial crisis, it rises from 2012 onwards to high levels compared to conventional MFIs.

Table 1 Descriptive statistics

Variables	All MFIs N	Mean	SD	Conventional MFIs N=574 Mean	SD	Islamic MFIs N=169 Mean	SD
Key Variables							
NONI	245	0.097	0.148	0.107	0.171	0.073	0.054
GDIV	318	0.874	0.332	0.906	0.293	0.770	0.424
SCP (Islamic MFIs)	743	0.227	0.419	N=574		N=169	
Dependent variables							
PAR30	611	0.063	0.128	0.044	0.087	0.135	0.207
Z-score	514	0.232	3.099	4.881	5.239	6.396	2.834
LLR	598			0.015	0.059	0.971	6.460
Control variables							
Size	709	3,14E+07	6,46E+07	3.40E+07	7.16E+07	2.24E+07	2.92E+07
Age	743	12.791	9.909	13.272	10.670	11.160	6.469
Loan	708	0.714	0.217	0.718	0.208	0.701	0.245
Equity	708	0.528	0.448	0.488	0.480	0.664	0.280
GroupLending	644	0.337	0.473	0.343	0.475	0.317	0.467
Indv_lending	330	0.973	0.163	0.972	0.165	0.975	0.158
Macroeconomic variables							
GDP_G	719	4.465	4.562	4.493	3.398	4.370	7.207
Inflation	690	5.778	5.899	5.805	5.562	5.683	6.967
PoliticS	716	0.261	0.053	0.254	0.040	0.285	0.078

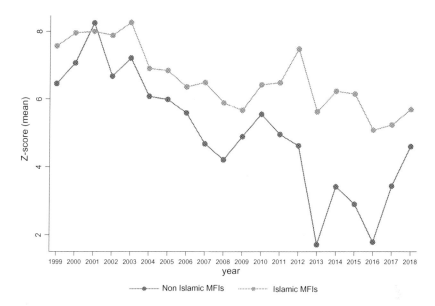

Fig. 1 Average Z-score developments over time, 1999–2018 (*Source* Authors' calculations based on Mix Market sample)

Variables Definitions

Diversification Measures: Income Diversification and Geographic Expansion

- **Income Diversification**

  Consistent with previous banking literature, we consider the NONI as a proxy for income diversification. The variable NONI is equal to the percentage of non-interest income[3] in total operating income (Rufai et al., 2019). Descriptive statistics reveal that conventional

---

[3] The definition of the different components of non-interest income are drawn from the MIX market's glossary of terms, which can be found in the MIX Market website (www.Mixmarket.org). Non-interest income includes penalties, commissions and other fees earned on the loan portfolio, other than penalty fees for late payment and revenue under Islamic finance methods.

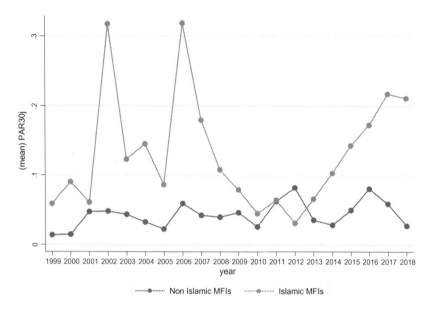

Fig. 2 Average PAR 30 developments over time, 1999–2018 (*Source* Authors' calculations based on Mix Market sample)

MFIs have a higher share of non-interest income than Islamic MFIs (10.7% vs 7.3%). While the average MFI has a NONI of 9.7%, Islamic MFIs have a lower NONI ratio (7.3%) that suggests a low degree of income diversification compared to conventional institutions. However, the NONIs of Islamic and conventional MFIs show differences in patterns during the global financial crisis and the post-crisis period (Fig. 3). While the NONI for Islamic MFIs fell slightly from 2009 to 2012 after a rise in 2008, the NONI declined for conventional MFIs from 2012 after a rise in 2010. Before the crisis, the NONI ratio for conventional MFIs drops significantly while the average NONI ratio rises for Islamic MFIs in 2007. After 2012, conventional MFIs continue to see a decline in the NONI ratio, while the ratio for Islamic MFIs rises again to higher levels in 2015. These differences in the patterns are consistent with the view that Islamic MFIs respond more strongly to business cycle fluctuations than conventional MFIs by increasing their share of

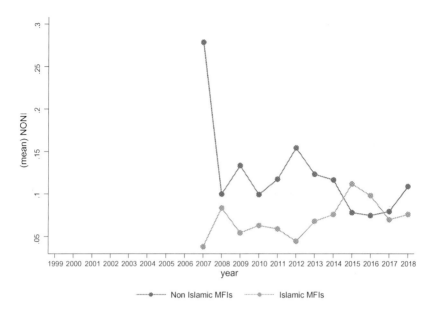

Fig. 3 Average NONI developments over time, 1999–2018 (*Source* Authors' calculations based on Mix Market sample)

non-interest oriented based financing. For example, the interest income ratio drops significantly between 2010 and 2015 (Fig. 4).

- **Geographic Expansion**
  We define a geographic diversification index to understand the specific dimension in relation with microfinance institutions, whose main objective is to reach the poorest individuals. While previous research studies focus on asset and revenue banking diversification, we expand our interest to investigate geographic diversification as an important dimension for the outreach of MFIs. Following Zamore (2018), we identify the MFIs that target both urban and rural clients. These institutions are likely to have higher geographic diversification than those who only focus on rural areas. Accordingly, we define GDIV as a proxy for geographic diversification using the Gross Loan Portfolio of the MFI in rural and urban areas. GDIV takes a value of 1 when the MFI has a positive gross loan portfolio in rural and urban areas, and zero, when the MFI focuses only on a rural or an urban area.

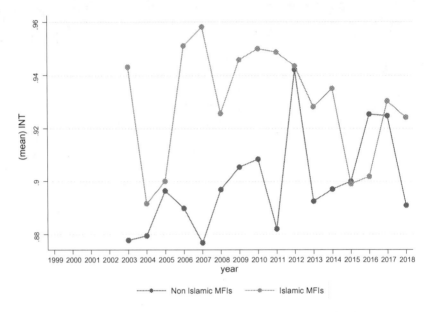

Fig. 4 Average interest income developments over time, 1999–2018 (*Source* Authors' calculations based on Mix Market sample)

With regards to geographic diversification, descriptive statistics suggest that conventional MFIs are more diverse than Islamic MFIs (0.906 vs 0.77). They confirm that Islamic MFIs are more oriented to rural markets than conventional institutions as they target rural clients (0.365 vs 0.288)

In contrast, the GDIV for both conventional and Islamic MFIs follows a similar pattern before, during, and after the global financial crisis (Fig. 5). Before and during the crisis, the GDIV drops significantly, while the average value of the GDIV rises since 2010 for both types of MFIs. Since 2010, the average value of the GDIV has risen for Islamic MFIs to a higher level than that for conventional institutions. After 2013, Islamic MFIs continue to see a decline in the GDIV, although the index for conventional MFIs continues to rise then stabilize.

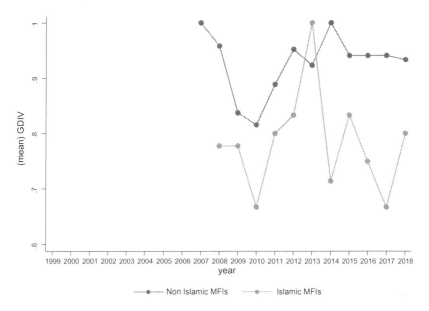

Fig. 5 Average GDIV developments over time, 1999–2018 (*Source* Authors' calculations based on Mix Market sample)

Control Variables
- **Age**
  Age controls for differences in experience across MFIs (Hermes & Hudon, 2018). Mature (experienced) MFIs are more likely to have lower risk than new institutions. Learning curve theory suggests that older firms become better practiced and learn their business better through constant repetition of their operations (Zamore et al., 2019). Adelkader and Salem (2013) show that over time, conventional microfinance institutions become more efficient than Islamic MFIs. The descriptive data confirms that conventional MFIs are more experienced than Islamic MFIs. Hence, the risk of Islamic MFIs is likely to be higher than that of conventional MFIs that have well-established dealings with customers. Following previous studies Fan et al. (2019) and Zamore et al. (2019), we consider *Age* as a control variable measuring the experience of MFIs.

- **Size**
  As an indicator for the size of MFIs, we consider the LogAssets of MFIs to control for economies of scale in microfinance, in line with previous studies. Empirical studies in microfinance suggest that there is a negative effect of MFI size on credit risk Fan et al. (2019) find that larger institutions have a higher credit risk. Banking literature suggests that a growing size increases the risk of moral hazard behaviour as "government bail-outs are more likely" (Köhler, 2015). Although Ibrahim and Rizvi (2017) find that larger Islamic banks are more stable, others studies suggest that size has negative effects on the risk of Islamic banks. Alqahtani and Mayes (2018) show that Islamic banks are more stable when they operate at a small scale and they lose this stability when they increase their scale of operations. Thus, we assume that the size of MFIs has a negative impact on their risk. The descriptive data shows that Islamic MFIs are much smaller than conventional MFIs.
- **Loan**
  We consider the ratio of the loan portfolio to total assets as a measure of financing activity. While previous studies suggest that the size of an MFI's loan portfolio has a positive impact on the financial performance of conventional MFIs, there is still a gap in the empirical evidence for credit risk in microfinance. Mobin et al. (2017) confirm the positive relationship between average loan size and the performance of Islamic MFIs in the MENA region. Conversely, it is noteworthy that the credit risk for MFIs is higher for the institutions that have large loan portfolios.
- **Equity to Assets Ratio**
  We control for differences in capital structures by including the equity-to-total assets ratio as suggested by Zamore et al. (2019). This variable indicates whether different stakeholders of MFIs may influence the "risk-taking behavior" of these institutions (Fan et al., 2019). Zamore et al. (2019) find that an increase in equity capital is associated with lower credit risk, however the relationship for Islamic MFIs is ignored.
- **Financing Models**
  There are three main lending strategies in microfinance: individual lending, the group-based financing model and the "village banks". Hermes and Hudon (2018) argue that lending methods may affect the performance of MFIs. Similarly, MFIs with different lending

methods may have dissimilar credit risks. Group-based financing and individual lending are the most common practices used in MENA countries. The group-based financing model was established to mitigate insolvency risk as suggested by the Grameen bank model. The repayment of credit is likely to be higher for this financing model since there is peer pressure between group members that are mutually responsible for the default of one member. Hence, MFIs that are more reliant on group-based financing models will have lower credit risk. We define two variables as proxies for the financing models of MFIs. *Group_lending* is a dummy variable that takes a value of one if the MFI uses group-based financing. Indv-lending is the second variable that takes a value of one for the MFIs that use individual lending as a financing model to reach the poorest individuals.
- **SCP**
To understand the Islamic microfinance business model, we consider SCP as a dummy variable. It takes a value of one for MFIs with Islamic windows that offer shariah-compliant products and 0 otherwise. Hence, this variable takes 0 for conventional MFIs (CMFs). Contrary to CMFs that offer exclusive microloans, MFIs with Islamic windows are diversified institutions, which combine conventional microcredit products and shariah-compliant microfinance services. As suggested by Mobin et al. (2017) and Abdelkader and Salem (2013), MFIs with Islamic Windows, which partially provide shariah-compliant products, have different business models compared to fully conventional MFIs and fully-fledged Islamic microfinance institutions. These differences in terms of business models might distinguish the risk of MFIs. Accordingly, we predict that the credit risk of institutions offering shariah-compliant products will be different from that of conventional MFIs.
- **Macroeconomic Factors**
Rising inflation is linked with high risk if measured by the Z-score (Köhler, 2015), while economic development is associated with lower credit risk (Zamore et al., 2019). As a part of the institutional context of the country, political factors are key determinants of the performance of MFIs (Hermes & Hudon, 2018). Thus, we investigate the effect of political stability on the risk of microfinance using the variable (*PoliticS*) as an indicator of political stability and absence of violence and terrorism. Although the demand

for services from MFIs might decline in politically instable countries as doing business becomes more difficult, political instability may also be an incentive for economic activity in the informal sector (Hermes & Hudon, 2018). Hence, the demand for microfinance services increases in politically instable countries. The mixed results from previous literature suggest that the coefficient of (*PoliticS*) can be both positive and negative. Empirical studies on bank risk also include country controls such GDP growth, inflation and political stability.

Methodology

Our econometric approach follows previous literature, exploring risk differences among financial institutions that pursue unique business models (Beck et al., 2013; Köhler, 2015; Schulte & Winkler, 2019). The main objective of our study is to investigate the effect of diversification strategies on the risk of microfinance institutions. We test whether income and geographic diversification in microfinance improve the portfolio loan quality of MFIs and their resilience during periods of crisis, and whether the effects are different for Islamic microfinance.

We test our hypotheses by estimating a Generalized Moments Method (GMM) panel regression (Eq. 1), which explains the solvency risk of the institution i in the country j at time t by a set of diversification variables (DIV), and institutional and country control variables (Controls).

We use a Generalized Method of Moments (GMM) estimator system on a dynamic panel, proposed by Arellano and Bond (1991). The dynamic GMM estimator was chosen due to its robustness as a regression estimator. It is more efficient in resolving the endogeneity problem of diversification strategies. More specifically, we adopt the improved procedure of Blundell and Bond (1998).

The first test used is the Sargan test, in order to validate the matrix of the instruments. It checks the independence between the instruments and the equation residuals, which means that if there is a correlation the model is not used.

The second review verifies the assumption that the error term has no autocorrelation in the AR tests (1) Arellano and Bond (1991). Residuals of the GMM estimators are assumed to be correlated with the order 1.

Following previous literature Fan et al. (2019) and Zamore et al. (2019), we adopt six control variables based on MFI characteristics and key macroeconomic factors that influence their credit risk: *MFI's* experience (*Age*), Size, funding structure (*Equity*), financing models (*Group_Lending, Indv_lending*), loan portfolio (*Loan*), *economic activity (GDPG)*, inflation rate (*infl*) and political stability (*PoliticS*).

To answer the main question of this study, whether Islamic MFIs are more resilient during different phases of the crisis, we construct the following panel data model:

Equation 1 presents our basic specification, consistent with previous studies:

$$Risk_{ij,t} = \beta_0 + \beta_1 * Risk_{ij,t-1} + \beta_2 * Div_{ij,t} + \beta_3 * SCP_{ij,t} + \beta_4 * Controls_{ij,t} + \varepsilon_{ij,t} \quad (1)$$

where

$Risk_{ij,t}$ is a measure of the insolvency risk in microfinance using the Z-score while PAR30 and LLR measure MFI credit risk in line with Fan et al. (2019) and Schulte and Winkler (2019).

$Div_{ij,t}$ is the proxy for diversification in microfinance measuring two dimensions: geographic (*GDIV*) and income diversification (*NONI*).

$SCP_{ij,t}$ is the proxy for the Islamic microfinance model.

To investigate the Islamic microfinance business model along with diversification strategies and their effect on the risk of MFIs, we test different specifications as extensions of Eq. 1.

$$Risk_{ij,t} = \alpha + \beta_1 \times Risk_{ij,t-1} + \beta_2 \times Div_{ij,t} + \beta_3 \times SCP_{ij,t} + \beta_4 \times Div_{ij,t} \times SCP_{ij,t} + \beta_5 \times Controls_{ij,t} + \varepsilon_{ij,t} \quad (2)$$

where $SCP_{ij,t}$ is a dummy variable that takes a value of 1 if the microfinance institution (MFI) *i* is offering shariah-compliant services (as fully-fledged Islamic MFIs and Islamic windows) and 0, otherwise. In addition to the dummy variable that reflects the differences in terms of business models between Islamic and conventional MFIs, we include an interaction variable [*Div*SCP*], in Eq. 2. This variable test whether the Islamic microfinance business model influences the relationship between diversification strategies and the risk in microfinance.

To consider the crisis effect on the relationship between diversification and the risk of MFIs, we develop different specifications as an extension of Eq. 1,

$$Risk_{ij,t} = \alpha + \beta_1 \times Risk_{ij,t-1} + \beta_2 \times Div_{ij,t} + \beta_3 \times Crisis_{ij,t} + \beta_4 \times SCP_{ij,t} \\ + \beta_5 \times Controls_{ij,t} + \varepsilon_{ij,t} \quad (3)$$

where $Crisis_{ij,t}$ is a dummy variable that takes a value of one for the years 2008–2009 as the financial crisis period, in line with Kim et al. (2020).

Moreover, we consider whether the relationship may vary depending on the business model of the MFI in terms of Islamic microfinance products. Thus, we include an interaction variable $[Div_{ij,t} \times SCP_{ij,t}]$, as an extension of Eq. 3.

$$Risk_{ij,t} = \alpha + \beta_1 \times Risk_{ij,t-1} + \beta_2 \times Div_{ij,t} + \beta_3 \times Crisis_{ij,t} + \beta_4 \times SCP_{ij,t} \\ + \beta_5 \times Div_{i,t} \times SCP_{ij,t} + \beta_6 \times Controls_{ij,t} + \varepsilon_{ij,t} \quad (4)$$

4 Empirical Results and Discussion

Descriptive Statistics

Table 1 summarizes the descriptive statistics for all of the variables for an unbalanced sample of 81 MFIs over the sample period (1999–2018) in the MENA region.

Islamic MFIs show a lower non-interest income share than conventional MFIs. While conventional MFIs have on average a share of non-interest income equal to 11%, Islamic MFIs show a lower value for this ratio (7.3%). Hence, conventional MFIs show a higher income diversification index (13.1%). In addition, Islamic MFIs are less diverse than conventional MFIs, which exhibit a larger geographic diversification index (GDIV).

In terms of income diversification, our data provides evidence of a trivial degree of diversification across non-interest sources. This evidence of small income diversification for MFIs is consistent with previous studies in different regions. For instance, Zamore (2018) shows that the share of non-interest income is equal on average to 8% for a larger sample of MFIs in six regions. On average, about 9% of an MFI's total operating income (9.7%) is from non-interest sources. The descriptive data shows that conventional MFIs have an average value of this variable (NONI) that is higher than ten%. For MFIs that provide shariah-compliant products, the share of non-interest income (7.3%) is lower than the average of the sample. This evidence indicates that Islamic windows show a lower degree of diversification across non-interest revenue sources than conventional MFIs in the MENA region. It is noteworthy that the business models of MFIs providing shariah-compliant products, which are mostly Islamic Windows, are more reliant on traditional activities (lending/deposit) with a higher share of debt-based activities. This evidence corroborates the inference of Mobin et al. (2017) that most Islamic MFIs offer both conventional and Islamic products, excluding the case of Sudan and Iran where only Islamic products are allowed.

Contrary to our expectations, Islamic MFIs have a higher credit risk than conventional MFIs. On average, 14% of the total loan portfolio of Islamic MFIs is overdue for more than 30 days compared to only 4% for conventional MFIs. On average, more than 90% of the portfolio of Islamic MFIs is reserved in anticipation of future loan losses whereas this ratio is lower than 2% for conventional institutions. These results suggest that clients of shariah compliant services are more likely to settle their debts while borrowers from conventional MFIs are insolvent. With regards to MFI solvency risk, descriptive statistics elucidate that Islamic MFIs are more resilient than conventional institutions when the MFI solvency risk is measured by the Z-score.

Conventional MFIs are larger and older than Islamic MFIs. Descriptive statistics suggest that there are no significant differences between conventional and Islamic MFIs in terms of the size of their loan portfolios. On average, the share of loans is about 70% of assets for both types of MFIs. Islamic MFIs have more than 66% of their assets financed by equity capital while the equity ratio for conventional MFIs is lower than 50%. The differences between the two types of MFIs in terms of geographic strategies are significant. Although Islamic MFIs are more oriented towards the rural market, conventional MFIs show high geographic diversification.

With regards to financing models, descriptive statistics indicate that the solidarity group-based financing model is widespread for CMFIs (34.3% vs 31.7%). Although the two types of MFIs have a high percentage of individual lending, Islamic MFIs are more reliant on individual lending (97.5%).

Financial Stability of MFIs

For the Z-score, our baseline regression results show a positive relationship between the NONI and the MFI Z-score. This evidence suggests that income diversification reduces MFI solvency risk. However, the results reveal that the relationship between geographic diversification and the Z-score in microfinance is insignificant. Regarding the solvency of Islamic MFIs, (Table 2, column2) the positive coefficient of the SCP interaction term with the GDIV suggests that Islamic MFIs have lower risk when diversifying geographically.

In terms of income diversification, our result confirms the positive effect of income diversification on MFI risk. The positive coefficient of SCP suggests that Islamic MFIs have a higher Z-score and hence lower solvency risk than conventional MFIs. Whereas the negative coefficient of the interaction term (NONI_SCP) indicates that diversified Islamic MFIs have a higher solvency risk. This result suggests that the gains of income diversification and reduced solvency risk are less evident for Islamic MFIs.

For the control variables, our results suggest that experienced MFIs are more resilient however the positive effect of the size of MFIs appears insignificant. The results reveal that NGOs are riskier. We find that rising equity capital is associated with lower solvency risk. This result is consistent with the findings of Zamore et al. (2019). With large loan portfolios, MFIs are likely to have a higher Z-score and hence lower risk. Contrary to our expectations, the group based-financing model is associated with high solvency risk while relying on the Individual lending method reduces the risk of MFIs. GDP growth is associated with lower risk. This result suggests that MFIs operating in developed countries have lower solvency risk.

Credit Risk and Diversification in Microfinance

Turning to the regressions that capture credit risk by the PAR30 and LLR, the results show that geographic and income diversification have a negative effect on MFI risk. This evidence suggests that the credit risk increases for MFIs that increase their geographic diversification. This result confirms the findings of Zamore et al. (2019) that geographic diversification increases credit risk in microfinance. However, our results are inconsistent with the theoretical argument of the microfinance

Table 2 Solvency Risk

	(1)	(2)	(3)	(4)
Variables	LZscore	LZscore	LZscore	LZscore
L.LZscore	0.067	0.083	0.021	0.028
	(0.286)	(0.192)	(0.644)	(0.538)
SCP	−0.262	−1.432**	0.076	0.170**
	(0.205)	(0.014)	(0.067)	(0.075)
GDIV	0.078	−0.042		
	(0.477)	(0.736)		
GDIV_SCP		1.191**		
		(0.031)		
NONI			0.260*	0.327**
			(0.066)	(0.025)
NONI_SCP				−0.957*
				(0.055)
Size	0.072	0.055	0.025	0.012
	(0.202)	(0.342)	(0.438)	(0.715)
Age	0.003	0.006	−0.015***	−0.014**
	(0.650)	(0.416)	(0.008)	(0.012)
Equity	2.420***	2.416***	1.998***	2.009***
	(0.000)	(0.000)	(0.000)	(0.000)
NGO	−0.181*	−0.310***	−0.239***	−0.226***
	(0.064)	(0.007)	(0.000)	(0.001)
loan	0.054	0.047	−0.041	−0.033
	(0.788)	(0.814)	(0.754)	(0.803)
group_lending	0.003	0.021	−0.198**	−0.218**
	(0.971)	(0.780)	(0.022)	(0.012)
indv_lending	0.622	1.441**	−0.151	−0.068
	(0.316)	(0.049)	(0.510)	(0.769)
GDP_G	0.007	0.008	0.001	0.000
	(0.139)	(0.131)	(0.849)	(0.954)
inflation	0.001	0.001	0.003	0.002
	(0.829)	(0.868)	(0.276)	(0.510)
PoliticS	−1.724	−1.573	−1.315*	−0.876
	(0.103)	(0.142)	(0.051)	(0.219)
Constant	−1.242	−1.615	1.088	1.119
	(0.233)	(0.130)	(0.141)	(0.131)
Observations	205	205	122	122
Number of MFIs	51	51	41	41
Wald chi2(13)	393.47	390.25	1084.62	1086.88
P	0.000	0.000	0.000	0.000
Sargan test	143.019	135.515	77.134	73.338
P	0.021	0.0498	0.0566	0.0845

Note This table reports panel regression results of MFIs' solvency risk in the sample period 1999–2018. For the dependent variable, Solvency Risk is measured by the Z-score. NGO a binary variable that takes the value 1 for Non-Governmental Organizations. p values in parentheses. ***$p<0.01$, **$p<0.05$, *$p<0.1$

literature Steinwand (2000) that MFIs reduce their loan portfolio risks by diversifying geographically.

Regarding income diversification, we find a higher credit risk for MFIs that expand their share of non-interest income. This result suggests a diversification discount when measuring the credit risk by the loan loss ratio (LLR). This evidence indicates that higher income diversification of microfinance institutions is associated with higher credit risk. Our results are consistent with the findings of the banking literature that income diversification increases the risk of financial institutions as reported in Alqahtani and Mayes (2018), Yang, Liu and Chou (2019), Albaity et al. (2019) and Rufai et al. (2019). The Hansen test (p-value Sargan test is significant at the 5%) does not reject the hypothesis of varying validity lagged in level and difference as an instrument.

There is an adjustment cost in the MFIs because the credit risk lag remains positive and significant at the 5% even with the introduction of the variable calculated by the PAR30 (values are around 0.187 and 0.249).

The patterns of conventional and Islamic MFI risk are different when measuring credit risk by the PAR 30 and LLR. Our results show that Islamic MFIs have a higher credit risk, measured by the PAR30. This evidence is inconsistent with the findings of Fan et al. (2019) that Islamic MFIs have lower credit risk than conventional MFIs. However, the results suggest that Islamic MFIs have a lower credit risk when the effect of geographic diversification on credit risk, measured by LLR, is considered. This evidence confirms the assumption that "religious belief encourages Muslim borrowers to fulfil their obligations under Islamic loan contracts" resulting in reduced credit risk (Abedifar et al., 2015). The negative effect of geographic diversification on MFI risk may be overcome by Islamic microfinance (Table 4).

On the other hand, Islamic MFIs have a higher credit risk as shown in the regressions that include the effect of income diversification on MFI credit risk. Regarding the effect of geographic diversification on the credit risk of Islamic MFIs (Table 3, column 2), the coefficient of the SCP interaction term with the GDIV suggests that this effect is insignificant when measuring the credit risk by PAR30. Likewise, the results of the regressions measuring the credit risk by LLR (Table 4, column 2) confirm this evidence that the effect of geographic diversification on the risk of Islamic MFIs is insignificant. In contrast, our results provide evidence of diversification gains for Islamic MFIs through reduced credit

Table 3 Credit risk

Variables	(1) PAR30	(2) PAR30	(3) PAR30	(4) PAR30
L.PAR30j	0.249**	0.265**	0.197*	0.187*
	(0.014)	(0.013)	(0.062)	(0.076)
SCP	0.0505*	0.0283	0.00864	0.0735
	(0.0299)	(0.0525)	(0.0336)	(0.0478)
GDIV	0.080**	0.073*		
	(0.024)	(0.063)		
GDIV_SCP		0.036		
		(0.606)		
NONI			−0.025	−0.008
			(0.685)	(0.900)
NONI_SCP				−0.179
				(0.269)
Size	−0.019*	−0.016	−0.023*	−0.028*
	(0.063)	(0.169)	(0.088)	(0.051)
Age	−0.003	−0.003	0.001	0.002
	(0.229)	(0.207)	(0.754)	(0.508)
Equity	0.142***	0.145***	0.248***	0.263***
	(0.001)	(0.001)	(0.000)	(0.000)
NGO	0.107***	0.111***	0.100**	0.107**
	(0.003)	(0.003)	(0.019)	(0.013)
Loan	−0.101**	−0.102**	−0.031	−0.035
	(0.032)	(0.031)	(0.633)	(0.581)
group_lending	−0.038*	−0.038*	−0.047	−0.057*
	(0.097)	(0.096)	(0.106)	(0.059)
indv_lending	0.048	0.049	0.037	0.049
	(0.284)	(0.274)	(0.466)	(0.335)
GDP_G	−0.003**	−0.003**	0.000	0.000
	(0.017)	(0.015)	(0.917)	(0.931)
inflation	0.001	0.001	0.002	0.001
	(0.599)	(0.572)	(0.182)	(0.247)
PoliticS	0.264	0.230	−0.429	−0.346
	(0.189)	(0.280)	(0.113)	(0.216)
Constant	0.171	0.143	0.332	0.353
	(0.433)	(0.527)	(0.245)	(0.215)
Observations	203	203	137	137
Number of MFIs	53	53	49	49
Waldchi2	135.01	133.06	89.83	92.31
P	0.000	0.000	0.526	0.000
Sargan test	129.442	127.046	63.590	163.264
P	0.060	0.070	0.000	0.502

Note This table reports panel regression results of MFIs' credit risk in the sample period 1999–2018. For the dependent variable, PAR30, the percentage of loan portfolio that is overdue for more than 30 days is the proxy of MFI's credit risk

risk. When measuring MFI credit risk by PAR30 (Table 3, column 4), the negative coefficient of the SCP interaction term with the NONI suggests that a rising share of non-interest income of Islamic MFIs may reduce their risk.

Regarding financing models, we find that group lending reduces credit risk, measured by the percentage of loan portfolio overdue for more than 30 days. Conversely, group-based financing is related to higher risk when measuring the credit risk by LLR. In terms of control variables, larger MFIs have lower credit risk measured by PAR30 and LLR. This evidence is inconsistent with the results of Fan et al. (2019). NGOsand MFIs with higher equity have higher risk, measured by PAR30. However, they are likely to have low risk when the LLR is used as the proxy for MFI credit risk (Table 4). Similarly, MFIs with large loan portfolios are more likely to have reduced credit risk. The results suggest that the effect of an MFI's experience on their credit risk is insignificant while there is a negative coefficient for Age in all of the credit risk regressions.

Regarding macroeconomic conditions, MFIs operating in countries with high GDP growth are likely to have a lower credit risk. However, the positive effect of political stability on MFI risk and the negative effect of inflation are insignificant.

The Resilience of Islamic MFIs During Crisis

Regarding the effect of a crisis on the resilience of MFIs, our results show that the negative coefficient of Crisis is economically insignificant in the regressions of the Z-score (Table 5). This evidence suggests that the negative effect of the GFC on the financial stability of MFIs is less evident. As reported in Table 5, the negative coefficient of SCP in regression 2 suggests that Islamic MFIs have lower financial stability when considering the effect of the GFC. Nonetheless, with greater geographic diversification, Islamic MFIs reduce their risk during the GFC as suggested by the positive coefficient of the interaction variable (GDIV*SCP). While our results provide evidence of a positive effect of geographic diversification on the financial stability of Islamic MFIs, they show that diversification gains are less evident for other business models.

Regarding income diversification, the positive coefficient of NONI (column 3, Table 5) suggests higher resilience during financial crises for MFIs expanding their activities to those generating non-interest

Table 4 Credit Risk

Variables	(1) LLR	(2) LLR	(3) LLR	(4) LLR
L.LLR	0.215**	0.212**	−0.117**	−0.129**
	(0.016)	(0.023)	(0.026)	(0.015)
SCP	−0.093**	−0.018	0.095**	0.066
	(0.041)	(0.97)	(0.040)	(0.048)
GDIV	−0.060*	−0.060*		
	(0.084)	(0.085)		
GDIV_SCP		−0.077		
		(0.938)		
NONI			0.065*	0.052
			(0.057)	(0.138)
NONI_SCP				0.266**
				(0.031)
Size	0.014	0.013	0.008	0.014
	(0.160)	(0.181)	(0.415)	(0.185)
Age	−0.002	−0.002	−0.001	−0.001
	(0.218)	(0.220)	(0.792)	(0.491)
Equity	−0.060	−0.060	−0.106***	−0.137***
	(0.158)	(0.165)	(0.005)	(0.001)
NGO	−0.007	−0.008	−0.034	−0.062**
	(0.880)	(0.867)	(0.211)	(0.042)
Loan	0.009	0.010	−0.039	−0.030
	(0.827)	(0.818)	(0.216)	(0.348)
group_lending	0.030	0.030	0.057***	0.069***
	(0.116)	(0.127)	(0.002)	(0.000)
indv_lending	0.525	0.601	0.070	0.192
	(0.393)	(0.602)	(0.822)	(0.547)
GDP_G	−0.000	−0.000	0.001	0.001
	(0.840)	(0.836)	(0.569)	(0.534)
inflation	−0.001	−0.001	−0.000	−0.000
	(0.384)	(0.391)	(0.735)	(0.704)
PoliticS	0.049	0.047	−0.182	−0.193
	(0.840)	(0.847)	(0.365)	(0.340)
Constant	−0.615	−0.687	−0.085	−0.265
	(0.380)	(0.553)	(0.843)	(0.545)
Observations	205	205	131	131
Number of mfiname2	51	51	45	45
Waldchi2	87.68	87.06	89.85	93.47
P	0.000	0.996	0.245	0.375
Sargan test	69.881	69.376	71.395	65.931
P	0.996	0.000	0.000	0.000

Note This table reports panel regression results of MFIs' credit risk in the sample period 1999–2018. For the dependent variable, LLR, is the third proxy of MFI's credit risk

Table 5 Crisis effect on solvency risk in microfinance: conventional vs Islamic MFIs

Variables	(1) LZscore	(2) LZscore	(3) LZscore	(4) LZscore	(5) PAR30	(6) PAR30
L.LZscore	0.067 (0.287)	0.083 (0.191)	0.021 (0.649)	0.027 (0.545)		
L.PAR30					0.255** (0.012)	0.267** (0.012)
L.LLR						
GDIV	0.085 (0.446)	−0.034 (0.784)			0.080** (0.023)	0.075* (0.052)
GDIV_SCP		1.243** (0.026)				0.030 (0.674)
NONI			0.266* (0.063)	0.334** (0.024)		
NONI_SCP				−0.958* (0.057)		
SCP	−0.273 (0.194)	−1.505** (0.011)			0.051* (0.085)	0.033 (0.538)
Size	0.072 (0.204)	0.053 (0.361)	0.027 (0.414)	0.014 (0.682)	−0.019* (0.067)	−0.016 (0.169)
Age	0.002 (0.760)	0.004 (0.557)	−0.016*** (0.006)	−0.015*** (0.009)	−0.002 (0.288)	−0.003 (0.279)
Equity	2.418*** (0.000)	2.416*** (0.000)	1.973*** (0.000)	1.984*** (0.000)	0.140*** (0.001)	0.143*** (0.001)
NGO	−0.180* (0.065)	−0.315*** (0.007)	−0.240*** (0.000)	−0.226*** (0.001)	0.106*** (0.004)	0.109*** (0.004)

(continued)

Table 5 (continued)

Variables	(1) LZscore	(2) LZscore	(3) LZscore	(4) LZscore	(5) PAR30	(6) PAR30
Loan	0.038	0.019	−0.071	−0.062	−0.099**	−0.101**
	(0.852)	(0.927)	(0.605)	(0.649)	(0.038)	(0.037)
group_lending	0.002	0.020	−0.193**	−0.213**	−0.036	−0.037
	(0.976)	(0.790)	(0.027)	(0.016)	(0.119)	(0.116)
indv_lending	0.632	1.499**	−0.161	−0.079	0.045	0.047
	(0.310)	(0.042)	(0.485)	(0.738)	(0.312)	(0.300)
GDP_G	0.008	0.008	0.001	0.000	−0.003**	−0.003**
	(0.130)	(0.110)	(0.885)	(0.989)	(0.017)	(0.016)
inflation	0.001	0.001	0.003	0.002	0.001	0.001
	(0.822)	(0.852)	(0.222)	(0.426)	(0.604)	(0.578)
PoliticS	−1.668	−1.463	−1.135	−0.694	0.241	0.218
	(0.120)	(0.177)	(0.108)	(0.352)	(0.251)	(0.318)
Crisis	−0.016	−0.028	−0.038	−0.038	0.004	0.003
	(0.685)	(0.479)	(0.349)	(0.347)	(0.719)	(0.804)
Constant	−1.235	−1.611	1.087	1.119	0.167	0.143
	(0.237)	(0.131)	(0.145)	(0.135)	(0.443)	(0.529)
Observations	205	205	122	122	203	203
Nber MFIs	51	51	41	41	53	53
Waldchi2	392.27	390.49	1065.00	1061.69	135.01	133.06
P	0.000	0.000	0.000	0.105	0.065	0.0753
Sargan test	142.358	134.953	74.798	70.692	128.827	126.486
P	0.024	0.0533	0.0680	0.000	0.000	0.000

(continued)

Table 5 (continued)

Variables	(7) PAR30	(8) PAR30	(9) LLR	(10) LLR	(11) LLR	(12) LLR
L.LZscore						
L.PAR30	0.198* (0.060)	0.187* (0.073)				
L.LLR			0.220** (0.018)	0.217** (0.024)	−0.130** (0.014)	−0.146*** (0.006)
GDIV			−0.060* (0.084)	−0.060* (0.086)		
GDIV_SCP				−0.117 (0.907)		
NONI	−0.033 (0.592)	−0.016 (0.800)			0.062* (0.069)	0.046 (0.186)
NONI_SCP		−0.179 (0.268)				0.306** (0.013)
SCP			−0.092** (0.027)	0.023 (0.981)		
Size	−0.028** (0.048)	−0.032** (0.026)	0.013 (0.175)	0.013 (0.204)	0.006 (0.573)	0.012 (0.260)
Age	0.002 (0.526)	0.003 (0.335)	−0.002 (0.307)	−0.002 (0.317)	−0.001 (0.771)	−0.002 (0.427)
Equity	0.263*** (0.000)	0.277*** (0.000)	−0.060 (0.156)	−0.062 (0.161)	−0.107*** (0.004)	−0.143*** (0.000)
NGO	0.093** (0.029)	0.101** (0.019)	−0.009 (0.848)	−0.011 (0.826)	−0.030 (0.276)	−0.060** (0.044)

(continued)

Table 5 (continued)

Variables	(7) PAR30	(8) PAR30	(9) LLR	(10) LLR	(11) LLR	(12) LLR
Loan	−0.034	−0.039	0.010	0.012	−0.036	−0.025
	(0.591)	(0.540)	(0.803)	(0.786)	(0.252)	(0.431)
group_lending	−0.051*	−0.061**	0.031	0.031	0.059***	0.074***
	(0.079)	(0.043)	(0.115)	(0.125)	(0.001)	(0.000)
indv_lending	0.030	0.043	0.522	0.636	−0.133	−0.032
	(0.544)	(0.398)	(0.399)	(0.584)	(0.686)	(0.923)
GDP_G	0.000	0.000	−0.000	−0.000	0.001	0.001
	(0.959)	(0.973)	(0.830)	(0.822)	(0.587)	(0.547)
inflation	0.001	0.001	−0.001	−0.001	−0.000	−0.000
	(0.189)	(0.255)	(0.380)	(0.386)	(0.657)	(0.606)
PoliticS	−0.688**	−0.605*	0.041	0.038	−0.014	0.007
	(0.028)	(0.058)	(0.866)	(0.878)	(0.949)	(0.976)
Crisis	0.032	0.032*	0.002	0.002	−0.023*	−0.027**
	(0.102)	(0.099)	(0.831)	(0.819)	(0.059)	(0.025)
Constant	0.445	0.465	−0.609	−0.717	0.116	−0.053
	(0.129)	(0.110)	(0.388)	(0.539)	(0.792)	(0.906)
Observations	137	137	205	205	131	131
Nber MFIs	49	49	51	51	45	45
Waldchi2	93.19	96.18	86.80	87.06	89.85	93.47
P	0.000	0.000	0.000	0.000	0.000	0.000
Sargan test	61.401	61.331	69.104	68.649	68.542	62.414
P	0.569	0.536	0.997	0.997	0.294	0.461

Note This table reports panel regression results of MFIs' credit risk in the sample period 1999–2018. For the dependent variables, Z-score measuring the resilience of MFIs; PAR30, Write-Off and LLR are proxies of MFI credit risk incomes. Conversely, the negative coefficient of the interaction term (NON_SCP) indicates that Islamic MFIs diversifying their income into non-interest income are likely to be less resilient during financial crises.

With regards to credit risk, our results provide evidence of the negative effect of financial crises on MFI risk (column 8, Table 5). We find that MFIs are likely to have a higher PAR30 during periods of crisis. On the other hand, our results show a diversification discount in terms of higher credit risk, measured by PAR30, when MFIs expand their activities to urban and rural markets. The positive coefficients of GDIV in regressions 5 and 6 suggest that MFIs are likely to have higher credit risk when they increase their geographic diversification. The positive coefficient of SCP (column 5) indicates that Islamic MFIs are likely to have higher credit risk, measured by PAR30. Considering LLR as a proxy for MFIs' risk, the results are mixed regarding the crisis effect. The positive coefficients of Crisis are insignificant in regressions 9 and 10. However, the negative coefficient of Crisis (column 11 and 12, Table 5) suggests that the LLR decreases during periods of crisis. This evidence indicates lower MFI risk in terms of the percentage of reserves to cover the estimated losses that it may suffer due to default loans. The negative coefficient of SCP in regression 9 suggests that Islamic MFIs have lower LLR. Conversely, the negative coefficient of GDIV indicates that MFIs with higher geographic diversification are likely to have a lower LLR. The positive coefficient of NONI suggests that higher non-interest income is related to higher LLR. Hence, our results provide evidence of a negative effect of income diversification on MFI risk, measured by LLR.

5 Conclusion

In this chapter, we investigate whether and to what extent the business models and diversification strategies of MFIs influence their risk. With regards to business model orientation, we analyze whether income and geographic diversification have different effects on conventional and Islamic MFIs. Using an unbalanced sample of 81 conventional and Islamic MFIs active in Arab countries over the period of 1999–2018, we consider the patterns of diversification strategies in microfinance.

A noteworthy detail about our study is that we provide evidence on the business models of the MFIs that provide shariah-compliant products in terms of revenue and geographic diversification. We find that Islamic Windows show a lower degree of income diversification than conventional MFIs in the MENA region. In terms of business models, our findings show that Islamic MFIs are more reliant on traditional activities (lending/ deposit) with a higher share of debt-based activities. This evidence corroborates the conclusion of Mobin et al. (2017) that most Islamic MFIs offer both conventional and shariah-compliant products, namely Islamic windows.

In terms of the risk standpoint, we find that income diversification of MFIs reduces their solvency risk, measured by the Z-score, while there is a negative effect of income diversification on the management of credit risk in microfinance. Our results suggest a diversification discount for MFIs that diversify their revenues. This evidence is consistent with the findings of the banking literature that shows a positive effect of income diversification on the risk of financial institutions. We find that Islamic MFIs that increase geographic diversification of their activities have a higher Z-score than their conventional counterparts. Hence, geographic diversification is related to lower solvency risk of Islamic MFIs. However, our findings show a lower Z-score for Islamic MFIs that expand their share of non-interest income. This evidence suggests that higher solvency risk is linked with increasing the share of non-interest income in Islamic microfinance. Conversely, higher income diversification reduces the credit risk of Islamic MFIs, measured by PAR30.

From the geographic diversification viewpoint, our findings are mixed. We find that higher geographic diversification is related to higher MFI credit risk, measured by PAR30 while MFIs are likely to have lower LLR when they expand their outreach to urban and rural clients. Our results suggest that there is a negative relationship between geographic diversification in Islamic microfinance and solvency risk. This positive effect of geographic diversification is insignificant when measuring credit risk. This evidence corroborates the hypothesis of the microfinance literature Steinwand (2000) that suggests that geographic diversification could reduce credit risk yet is inconsistent with the findings of Zamore et al. (2019).

In terms of differences between the business models of conventional and Islamic MFIs, our results support this hypothesis. We find diversification benefits in terms of lower risk for Islamic MFIs and a diversification discount on the solvency risk, measured by the Z-score. Our results show that income diversification may mitigate the credit risk in Islamic microfinance by reducing the percentage of loan portfolio outstanding over 30 days for diversified Islamic MFIs. Conversely, we find that income diversification is positively associated with higher MFI risk measured by LLR. The findings suggest a diversification discount in terms of credit risk for microfinance institutions that increase their non-interest generating activities and diversification gains when they expand their activities to shariah-compliant services.

Regarding the resilience of Islamic MFIs during the global financial crisis, our results show that Islamic MFIs have lower financial stability. Similarly, Islamic MFIs show a higher credit risk that confirms the negative effect of crises on their risk. However, these institutions increase their financial stability and hence reduce their solvency risk with greater geographic diversification. Likewise, our findings provide evidence of diversification benefits from expanding to non-interest income in terms of higher financial stability of MFIs during periods of crisis.

Hence, our results show differences between conventional and Islamic MFIs in terms of the effect of income and geographic diversification on financial stability and credit risk in microfinance. These findings corroborate our second hypothesis.

Our analysis of the patterns of diversification strategies may contribute to an improved understanding of how business model orientation in microfinance defines the development of Islamic windows. Likewise, the results of our study may help different stakeholders of MFIs in the decision-making process about whether expanding to shariah-compliant activities should reduce credit risk and increase their resilience during crises. Our research provides an empirical insight into how income and geographic diversification may affect the solvency risk of conventional and Islamic MFIs differently.

Overall, the conclusions from this study are essential for microfinance regulators that need to judiciously monitor the credit risk in microfinance given the ongoing policy effort for greater financial sector diversification in the MENA region.

References

Arellano, M., & Bond, S. (1991). Some Tests of Specification for Panel Data: Monte Carlo Evidence and an Application to Employment Equations. *The Review of Economic Studies, 58*, 277–297.

Abdelkader, I. B., & Salem, A. B. (2013). Islamic vs conventional microfinance institutions: Performance analysis in MENA countries. *International Journal of Business and Social Research, 2*(5), 219–233.

Abedifar, P., Ebrahim, S. M., Molyneux, P., & Tarazi, A. (2015). Islamic banking and finance: Recent empirical literature and directions for future research. *Journal of Economic Surveys, 29*(4), 637–670. https://doi.org/10.1111/joes.12113

Albaity, M., Saadaoui, R., & Hanifa, A. (2019). Competition and bank stability in the MENA region: The moderating effect of Islamic versus conventional banks. *Emerging Markets Review, 38*(June 2018), 310–325. https://doi.org/10.1016/j.ememar.2019.01.003

Alqahtani, F., & Mayes, D. G. (2018). Financial stability of Islamic banking and the global financial crisis: Evidence from the Gulf Cooperation Council. *Economic Systems, 42*(2), 346–360. https://doi.org/10.1016/j.ecosys.2017.09.001

Ashraf, D., Rizwan, M. S., & L'Huillier, B. (2016). A net stable funding ratio for Islamic banks and its impact on financial stability: An international investigation. *Journal of Financial Stability, 25*, 47–57. https://doi.org/10.1016/j.jfs.2016.06.010

Beck, T., Demirgüç-kunt, A., & Merrouche, O. (2013). Islamic vs conventional banking: Business model, efficiency and stability. *Journal of Banking and Finance, 37*(2), 433–447. https://doi.org/10.1016/j.jbankfin.2012.09.016

Blundell, R., & Bond, S. (1998). Initial conditions and moment restrictions in dynamic panel data models. *Journal of Econometrics, 87*(1), 115–143. https://doi.org/10.1016/S03044076(98)00009-8

Fan, Y., John, K., Hong, F., & Tamanni, L. (2019). Security design, incentives, and Islamic microfinance: Cross country evidence. *Journal of International Financial Markets, Institutions & Money, 62*, 264–280. https://doi.org/10.1016/j.intfin.2019.08.002

Hermes, N., & Hudon, M. (2018). Determinants of the performance of microfinance institutions: A systematic review. *Journal of Economic Surveys, 32*(5), 1483–1513. https://doi.org/10.1111/joes.12290

Ibrahim, M. H., & Rizvi, S. A. R. (2017). Do we need bigger Islamic banks? An assessment of bank stability. *Journal of Multinational Financial Management, 40*, 77–91. https://doi.org/10.1016/j.mulfin.2017.05.002

Kabir, N., & Worthington, A. C. (2017). The 'competition – stability / fragility' nexus: A comparative analysis of Islamic and conventional banks. *International Review of Financial Analysis, 50*, 111–128. https://doi.org/10.1016/j.irfa.2017.02.006

Kim, H., Batten, J. A., & Ryu, D. (2020). Financial crisis, bank diversification, and financial stability: OECD countries. *International Review of Economics and Finance, 65*(January 2019), 94–104.

Köhler, M. (2015). Which banks are more risky? The impact of business models on bank stability. *Journal of Financial Stability, 16*, 195–212. https://doi.org/10.1016/j.jfs.2014.02.005

Li, L., & Zhang, Y. (2013). Are there diversification benefits of increasing noninterest income in the Chinese banking industry? *Journal of Empirical Finance, 24*, 151–165. https://doi.org/10.1016/j.jempfin.2013.10.004

Mersland, R., & Strom, R. (2010). Microfinance mission drift? *World Development, 38*(1), 28–36. https://doi.org/10.1016/j.worlddev.2009.05.006

Mobin, M. A., Masih, M., & Alhabshi, S. O. (2017). Religion of Islam and microfinance: Does it make any difference? *Emerging Markets Finance and Trade, 53*, 1547–1562.

Nguyen, M., Skully, M., & Perera, S. (2012). Market power, revenue diversification and bank stability: Evidence from selected South Asian countries. *Journal of International Financial Markets, Institutions and Money, 22*(4), 897–912. https://doi.org/10.1016/j.intfin.2012.05.008

Rufai, A. M., Bin Hidthiir, M., & Alias, B. M. N. (2019). Impact of corruption on banking sector stability: Evidence from Middle East and North African countries. *Academic Journal of Economic Studies, 5*(2), 125–132.

Schulte, M., & Winkler, A. (2019). Drivers of solvency risk—Are microfinance institutions different? *Journal of Banking and Finance, 106*, 403–426. https://doi.org/10.1016/j.jbankfin.2019.07.009

Shim, J. (2019). Loan portfolio diversification, market structure and bank stability. *Journal of Banking and Finance, 104*, 103–115.

Sotiriou, A. (2020), Microfinance and COVID-19: Insights from CGAP's Global Pulse Survey, CGAP, https://www.cgap.org/blog/microfinance-and-covid-19-insolvency-horizon.

Steinwand, D. (2000). A risk management framework for microfinance institutions. Eschborn, Germany: GTZ, Financial Systems Development.

Yang, L., Hermes, N., & Meesters, A. (2019). Convergence of the performance of micro finance institutions: A decomposition analysis. *Economic Modelling, 81*(October 2018), 308–324. https://doi.org/10.1016/j.econmod.2019.05.014

Yang, H., Liu, C. L., & Chou, R. Y. (2019). Bank diversification and systemic risk. *The Quarterly Review of Economics and Finance, 77*, 311–326.

Zamore, S. (2018). Should microfinance institutions diversify or focus? A global analysis. *Research in International Business and Finance, 46*(October 2017), 105–119. https://doi.org/10.1016/j.ribaf.2017.12.001

Zamore, S., Beisland, L. A., & Mersland, R. (2019). Geographic diversification and credit risk in microfinance. *Journal of Banking and Finance*, 105665. https://doi.org/10.1016/j.jbankfin.2019.105665

FinTech Role in the Road to Sustainability

Digital Finance and Artificial Intelligence: Islamic Finance Challenges and Prospects

Dawood Ashraf

1 INTRODUCTION

During the 1990s, a growing body of literature began to emerge around access to banking services. The term "financial exclusion" (the opposite of financial inclusion) was coined to describe a situation where individuals and businesses are hindered with limited access to the financial services (Kempson & Whyley, 1999; Leyshon & Thrift, 1996). According to the World Bank Group, "Financial inclusion means that individuals and businesses have access to useful and affordable financial products and services that meet their needs – transactions, payments, savings, credit, and insurance – delivered in a responsible and sustainable way" (Worldbank, 2022).

Access to financial services helps families and businesses to save for long-term goals like children's education or emergency needs. Achieving financial inclusion is a critical component of both poverty reduction and

D. Ashraf (✉)
Islamic Development Bank Institute, Islamic Development Bank Group, Jeddah, Saudi Arabia
e-mail: dashraf@isdb.org

© The Author(s), under exclusive license to Springer Nature Switzerland AG 2023
Z. H. Jumat et al. (eds.), *Islamic Finance, FinTech, and the Road to Sustainability*, Palgrave CIBFR Studies in Islamic Finance, https://doi.org/10.1007/978-3-031-13302-2_11

the expansion of economic opportunities. In contrast, inaccessibility to financial services stifles economic growth and exacerbates inequality since it prevents the talented poor from investing in physical and human capital, thereby impeding the economic growth (Banerjee & Newman, 1993; Galor & Zeira, 1993), instigates social conflict, expropriation, and rent seeking behavior (Acemoglu & Robinson, 2000; Alesina & Perotti, 1996; Alesina & Rodrik, 1994; Benabou, 1996; Benhabib & Rustichini, 1996).

Financial market development does not guarantee access to financial services for everyone. To ensure financial inclusion, it will be crucial that various sectors of society have their needs addressed, appropriate technologies are used, and enabling policies are in place. A major obstacle to financial inclusion is the lack of access to services for saving and investing on the one hand and to credit, particularly for raising capital, on the other.

There are several reasons highlighted in literature for hindrance in access to financial services and may include on both demand and supply side and include:

1. **On the supply side**
   - Operational cost: Formal financial institutions do not find it cost-effective to devote extensive resources to a diverse group of opaque and high operating cost sectors that have relatively smaller transaction sizes.
   - Adverse selection: It is extremely challenging for banks to assess the creditworthiness of businesses from the informal sector, leading to delays in access to finance and often financing on restricted terms. These factors render existing financial intermediation models exclusionary.
2. **On the demand side**
   - Lack of formal identity, informal sector, fear of taxman, and informationally opaque (borrowers).

2 Digital Finance: Artificial Intelligence

An increasing number of economic and political events, such as the financial crisis of 2008 and, more recently, the COVID-19 pandemic, have encouraged the use of financial technology (FinTech) to solve wicked problems. FinTech solutions are widely available and now cover

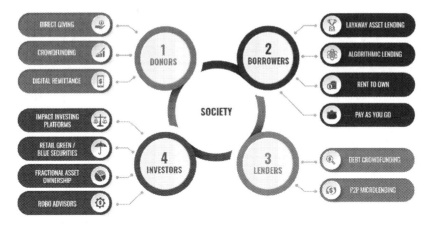

Fig. 1 Artificial intelligence application in finance: A global perspective (*Source* The United Nations Secretary Task Force of Digital Financing of the Sustainable Development Goals [2020])

the full spectrum of finance. Figure 1 illustrates various areas of finance where AI is gaining quick traction, resulting in better outreach and efficiency for society.

The rise in computing power and availability of alternative data created unique opportunities to apply Artificial intelligence (AI) to solve a number of problems associated with credit and investment decisions. The COVID-19 pandemic accelerated the application of digital solutions harnessing the AI power and big data to a number of challenges associated with credit and investment products.

Digital financial services are essential for enhancing financial inclusion. The use of technology can resolve some major pain points. Access to saving and investment products, for example, has seen significant improvement through the use of technology between 2014 to 2017. With mobile banking, a transaction can be conducted without having to leave the comfort of home is highly beneficial for achieving last mile inclusion.

By connecting small businesses with fintech companies, financial inclusion is enhanced both in terms of access to finance and savings. Globally, financial inclusion is increasing. According to the Global Findex 2017, 1.2 billion adults have opened accounts since 2011, which includes 515 million adults since 2014. Globally, the share of adults who have an account with a financial institution or use a mobile money service has increased from 62 to 69% between 2014 and 2017. This percentage increased from 54 to 6% in developing economies.

The rapid digitalization of finance during the COVID-19 pandemic accelerates the adoption of new flexible, highly networked, adaptable, and more intelligent operating models. On the deposits and saving sides, mobile phone banking played a key role in enhancing financial inclusion. FinTech offers financial services in almost all domains, including financial intermediation (challenger banking), alternative financing (platform lending and P2P crowd funding), asset management (robo-advisory), and insurance. The AI supports each of these companies in terms of fraud prevention on the deposit and savings side while avoiding adverse selection on the lending side.

3 Access to Finance: Challenge for Microentrepreneurs and SMEs

Microentrepreneur success is a function of business skills, attitude, willingness, and ability to take risks and grow the business. Several emerging economies have found that financing MSME growth has become an increasingly important development tool. However, financial products and services that meet their needs, including transactions, payments, savings, credit, and insurance, remain challenging to find at affordable rates.

The majority of MSMEs do not have access to formal financial institutions to finance their operations. The greatest barrier for MSMEs to obtain formal financing is information asymmetry. Consequently, a huge portion of the global population went unserved because of the absence of a regular source of income and an established credit history, and the lack of collateral.

It is challenging for banks to assess the creditworthiness of MSMEs, resulting in lengthy delays and often restrictive financing terms. All in all, the existing financial models are exclusionary, creating individuals who are "invisible," "unscorable," and "thin file" rated. In addition, formal financial institutions are reluctant to allocate vast resources toward opaque and high-cost sectors when they can offer relatively smaller loans to a wide variety of firms.

Major stakeholders, including governments, donors, and financial institutions, have used microcredit as the primary tool for reaching capital-strapped microenterprises and alleviating the poverty of financially and socially excluded people. However, the empirical evidence suggests that microcredit has little or no impact on the financial performance of microenterprises, leading to sub-optimal growth during microenterprise evolution because of a heavy cash outflow burden on microenterprises. Microfinance has helped MSMEs access to credit but has often resulted in suboptimal strategies to mitigate their default risk, such as:

- asymmetric pricing often at very unfavorable terms.
- offering standardized short-term loan products with minimal amounts and often involving bullet payments at the end.
- non-availability of insurance products for hedging.

While on the supply side, microfinance institutions face a very high operational cost as the volume of transactions is high while the amounts are small. The challenges faced by MSMEs in getting access to finance require a holistic approach, especially thin-file microenterprises.

For poverty alleviation and ensuring the success of microenterprises, access to finance is not sufficient. The microfinance approach is an oversimplified approach to solving a multilayered problem. In order to properly identify and prescribe the appropriate solution at the various stages of entrepreneurial financing, it is important to understand the role of government policies, donors, technology, and financial infrastructure. With a one-size-fits-all approach, there has been a proliferation of players in a market focused on a small number of micro-borrowers, resulting in unnecessary competition among credit suppliers and over-indebtedness of borrowers.

An important tool in assessing the creditworthiness of individuals and MSMEs is credit scoring, which can be done effectively and efficiently with easy-to-understand criteria for accepting or rejecting a loan application. Due to the advent of new technologies and increased computing power gained during the last couple of decades, there has been a race to learn, adapt, and use data venues that have never been used before, and credit risk assessment is no exception (see Fig. 2). With greater access to a broader range of data, increased computing power, and more and more demands for efficiency improvements, the method of assessing credit risk has evolved from traditional credit scoring models to a new breed of models that utilize AI to assess credit risk, especially for thin files.

The adoption of AI results in an objective, better-informed faster (backed by data), more accurate credit risk assessment of businessworthy

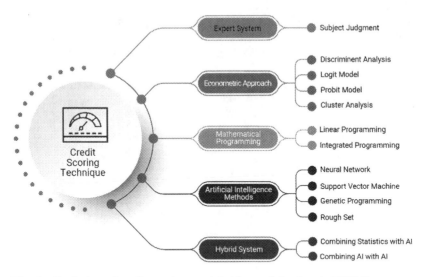

Fig. 2 Evolution of credit scoring models (*Source* Ashraf et al. [2021])

MSMEs lacking credit history. AI's application has started using big data obtained from multiple sources, including mobile phones, social media, rental payments, and psychometrics. AI models often use low-value digital footprint (features) not directly relevant to the assessment of creditworthiness by applying more complex methods for credit risk assessment. There are several financial institutions and lending platforms that now use alternative data and AI algorithms for credit risk evaluation.

The benefits of using alternative data and AI for credit scoring include greater financial inclusion through better access to credit, improved accuracy of the underlying models, efficiency gains from the automation of processes, and potentially improved customer experience. While the application of artificial intelligence using the alternative data may enable the developing of more accurate algorithms to assess creditworthiness, predict failure, and develop tailored pricing and products/services, simultaneously, it brings challenges related to a shortage of resources and possible consequences of the adoption of AI regarding fairness that is discrimination among borrowers, data privacy and security. Table 1 reports the major differences in the traditional credit scoring models and new credit scoring approaches using the AI techniques.

Table 1 Benefits and limitations of traditional credit scoring versus AI based scoring

	Benefits	Limitations
Traditional Credit Score	• A systematically developed approach: consistent, effective easy to understand numeric value for banks to decide whether to grant a loan or not • Historical information like loan repayment history, income, existing loan contribute to final score • Encourage financial discipline—reward for longer term good behavior both in terms of amount and rate	• Create invisibles due to intensive information requirement and historical data • Backward looking approach where future economic outcomes are not considered such as the global financial crisis • Take longer time for underwriting • Loan underwriting often involve expert judgment leading to judgment error perpetuation • Further enhancement is stalled • Take long time to build credit in case of a bad event in life • Hard to calibrate with new data
AI—based credit assessment	• Greater access: provide credit beyond those with credit history and financial information • Improved accuracy of default prediction: secure, holistic, and multidimensional credit assessment based on personal traits, business acumen, and networking minimizes risk for lenders • Better customer experience—efficient loan processing • Leading-edge tech capabilities: self-learning credit scoring model • Efficient and faster outcomes—human bias is minimized • Automated decisioning prevent sociological bias in factors like age or demographics from creeping in due to human involvement at the time of decision making • Personalized structuring—customer segmentation is possible with reward to specific group e.g. professional graduate pursuing entrepreneurship • Use of real time data	• Black box system: lack of transparency due to some degree of models' autonomous self-learning • Consumer protection and reputation risk • Limited interpretation of credit scores due to hidden layers in the complex models • Fairness—inbuilt data biases due to unintentional proxy discrimination • Accountability • Data privacy and security • Governance of model • Unintended consequences—exploitation of financially fragile leading to higher indebtedness and financialization • Disparity in maturity across market • Hinders effective risk management due to opaqueness of AI techniques • Systemic risk due to increasing interconnectedness across domestic and cross-border systems (World Economic Forum & Deloitte, 2018)

Source Ashraf et al. (2021)

Table 2 AI and access to finance—products, data, and models

	Structured data	Unstructured data
Debt	Linear Regression (Forecast Default) Logistic Regression (Classification of Loan Applicants) Recurrent Neural Network (RNN) Deep neural networks	Regression & Classification Deep neural networks for unstructured data
Equity	Linear Regression (Forecast Business Success/Failure) Logistic Regression (Classification of Business partners) Convolutional Neural Network (CNN) Deep neural networks	Regression & Classification Deep neural networks for unstructured data
Grant	Unsupervised Clustering (exploring) Logistic regression (Multiclass Classification of Grant Seekers) Convolutional Neural Network (CNN) Deep neural networks	Clustering & Classification Neural networks

Source Ashraf et al. (2021)

Several digital lending platforms employ artificial intelligence and leverage structured and unstructured data in a variety of models to offer a variety of products (see Table 2). These platforms are said to have provided loans to millions of borrowers in China, Hong Kong, the Philippines, Indonesia, Kenya, Nigeria, India, and Latin America. The default rates of the majority of these platforms are comparable with the default rates of developed models. Recently, companies have begun to offer products catering to socially responsible and faith-based entrepreneurs. For example, Fintek Syriah in Indonesia offers asset-backed financing, while See Out in Pakistan provides interest-free financing to entrepreneurs (Ashraf, 2022).

Concerns with Digital Financing

Despite the rapid growth of digital lending, there are several concerns regarding the use of AI for credit screening, especially concerning financial inclusion. It is common for platforms to offer short-term loans at predatory interest rates, more often in the form of consumption loans. Further,

AI primarily focuses on debt creation and credit expansion, which leads to rapid societal debt accumulation in the name of financial inclusion in developing countries and efficiency enhancement in developed countries. To prevent the financialization of fringe borrowers, it is necessary to review the credit granting practices of such platforms critically.

For financial intermediation, big data and AI provide better infrastructure. The infrastructure enables better and more efficient delivery of financial services but does not address the shortcomings of the financial system resulting in problems such as financialization. Therefore, a holistic approach is needed, considering the microentrepreneurs' poverty level and risk-sharing abilities.

4 Financial Inclusion and the Islamic Finance: Digital Adoption Backed by AI and Alternative Data

For access to finance, a recent report by the Islamic Development Bank Institutes (2021)[1] proposes a detailed infrastructure-led scheme based on Islamic finance principles and governed by Islamic financial institutions (see Fig. 3). In theory, the two-pillar approach could lead to easy access to capital more efficiently at the lowest possible cost for everyone.

First, a sustainable and inclusive policy must be developed based on a staggered approach that maps the macroeconomic requirements of microentrepreneurs at different stages of development. Graduated approaches exploit the risk-sharing ability of microentrepreneurs and rely on recent field experiment literature for application support.

Second, institutional arrangement to execute the policy framework. Islamic finance offers a comprehensive set of institutional arrangements and a variety of products that can help solve the issue of access to credit.

Based on Islamic finance principles, this framework is potentially able to create a policy framework that enables all segments of society to access finance without increasing indebtedness, which is often a criticism of debt-based interventions such as microcredit.

The Islamic Finance Framework for Digital Finance

In Islamic finance, interventions are meant to support productive activities by raising capital. Although this framework is primarily intended for

---

[1] Can be accessed at: https://irti.org/product/artificial-intelligence-and-islamic-finance/.

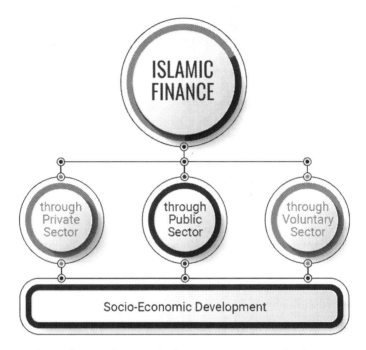

Fig. 3 Islamic finance framework for socio-economic development (*Source* Ashraf et al. [2021])

entrepreneurship development, it has the ultimate goal of reducing poverty. The proposed framework exerts access to finance to those individuals/firms who are business-worthy to undertake the venture as profitable to compensate both. Organizational life cycle theory provides the basis for the framework and is supported by working capital management and owners' liability management.

The framework is reinforced by empirical studies using field experiments in different regions of the world, wherein researchers explore three broad interventions for accessing capital for the financially excluded population to alleviate poverty. These include grants, loans, and equity.

Islamic finance framework for access to capital recognizes the need for a multiplicity of intuitions and diversity of products to suit the capital requirements of MSMEs as these grow in size and complexity. Accordingly, for each stage of development, there is an optimal instrument and optimal institutional arrangement. Figure 4 depicts the Islamic

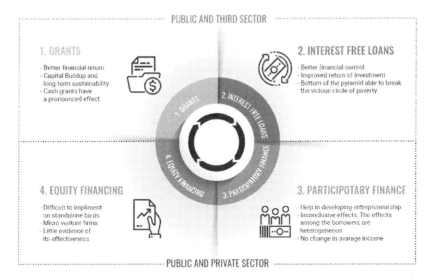

Fig. 4 Islamic finance framework for financial inclusion (*Source* Ashraf et al. [2021])

finance framework with four instruments for capital development under three different institutional arrangements involving the voluntary sector, public sector, and private sector.

Grants

Grants are like seed capital, and the grantee is not required to pay back anything to the grantor. There are several filed experiment studies highlighting the effectiveness of grants in building capital for microentrepreneurs. In aggregate, these studies suggest that grants, especially unrestricted cash grants, help microentrepreneurs grow capital and hire more people. Based on the consistency of results across regions and a variety of demographic features, it can be assumed that the impact of the grant is robust to both context and implementation variations.

However, it is important to be cautious because grants are easy to disburse but are also easy to misallocate by beneficiaries, either from a lack of self-control or family pressure. Providing in-kind grants is a better option due to the illiquidity of assets that are built on grants. The downside is that this may impede investment options that could help the microenterprise grow. The provision of grants by external agencies to entrepreneurs in developing countries without any expectation of a stake in the business or share in its profits is an essential step toward promoting social equity. However, the problem with this approach is that it relies heavily on donations and subsidies from the government, development agencies, and philanthropists, which may not be sustainable in the long run.

Interest Free Financing
In the financial market, interest-free lending is not as popular as grants or microcredit. Possible explanations may include the nonremunerative nature of the transaction. There is, however, some evidence that interest-free loans can be beneficial to the poor at the bottom of the pyramid as a way to build capital as well as increase consumption. A benefit of interest-free loans is their better financial control, as borrowers are required to make regular payments in order to qualify for a higher amount and build their credit score. The borrower can keep all the upside of the return, which helps microentrepreneurs build capital faster, ultimately breaking the vicious cycle of poverty. A large number of NGOs providing interest-free loans rely on social capital as collateral, and these firms face very low default risk. As an example, defaults on loans by Akhuwat Foundation in Pakistan are virtually nonexistent.

Micro Loans Through Microfinance Institutions
Microcredit is the most common form of access to credit worldwide. Entrepreneurs are disciplined with microcredit since they are required to repay the principal and pay interest. Financial discipline allows microenterprises to be streamlined and effective. Based on our literature review, we can conclude that microcredit promotes entrepreneurship. However, the benefits for households differ significantly.

In summary, microcredit does not completely transform people's lives; however, it may give them greater flexibility and choice by enabling them to borrow. The impact on social indicators such as schooling is virtually zero, though one study in Bosnia found a decline. In Mexico, another study shows that women's decision-making power, happiness, and trust are on the rise.

Microfinance advocates praise of the financial discipline associated with microloans for establishing credit histories and allowing enterprises to qualify for larger amounts of financing (Pretes, 2002). However, the financial discipline hypothesis ignores the fact that in difficult times, such as the COVID-19 pandemic, microenterprises have a limited ability to absorb financial risk. Several studies have suggested that low-income borrowers often refinance with moneylenders, sell household items, and move from their native villages to urban areas to work as laborers to make the loan payments (Chen et al., 2010; Francis et al., 2017). Inherently, microfinance schemes lack empathy and underestimate the risk capacity of microentrepreneurs.

Micro Loan: Participatory Finance

The participatory finance proposed in the Islamic finance framework offers similar benefits as microcredit while addressing both concerns of indebtedness and risk sharing in a time of crisis. The diversity of Islamic finance instruments provides flexibility to both financier and borrower, and the clause of no change in price due to credit default provides a ceiling since the inception of the transaction.

Micro-Equity Financing

The entrepreneur and financier share risk in equity financing, which lowers transaction costs. Poor entrepreneurs could start a business or adopt innovative ideas that they might not have considered if they had borrowed money. Equity financing entails a return on investment linked to the success of the micro-enterprise. However, the microcredit provider is entitled to receive the interest income regardless of the microenterprise's ability to sustain such expenses.

Risk-sharing is at the core of micro-equity financing. As a capital provider becomes a partner in micro-enterprise, the bond between the financier and entrepreneurs grows as they share business risks and know-how, expertise, and experience in order to ensure venture success.

In developed countries, startup grants and equity financing are successful alternatives to micro-equity financing for microenterprise development through institutions similar to venture capital firms, where investors decide which microenterprise deserves funding. The joint venture structure is superior because it allows piecemeal transactions under shared ownership and control, thus substantially reducing the costs of valuing complementary assets. The risk-sharing feature of financing can spur innovation since venture capital firms can assist high-performing microentrepreneurs in funding projects that microfinance institutions are not able/willing to support. Microfinance institutions can turn over their successful and growing clients to traditional lending institutions or venture capital firms to continue their growth trajectory.

5 FINANCIAL INFRASTRUCTURE: INSTITUTIONAL ARRANGEMENT

Having a policy framework in place helps all partners to follow a strategy to promote innovation and entrepreneurship. However, without developing a financial infrastructure that recognizes access to capital as a need of the economy, the positive outcome of the policy framework would be impossible to achieve. Developing a resilient infrastructure necessary for efficient delivery of financial services is the second pillar of policy intervention.

In this context, infrastructure includes both physical and intellectual capabilities. The infrastructure pillar aims to capture, store, and make available all available touch points necessary to reduce information asymmetry and increase access to capital. A financial technology contribution could include improved data storage, faster analysis and use of alternative data, and the application of AI to make decisions. Digital infrastructure plays the most crucial role in overall financial infrastructure, particularly for financial inclusion, because data inclusion leads to financial inclusion.

Figure 5 outlines a basic infrastructure for financial risk assessment highlighting the tools needed at various stages of business development. For example, using AI to screen microentrepreneurs is possible in the case of interest-free financing to assess their skills, business know-how, entrepreneurial traits, and ability to network. The following methods can be used to avoid adverse selection in such a situation: a psychometric analysis, a network analysis, a credit screening (financial management history), and business worthiness of microenterprises.

While in the case of grants, credit risk assessment may not be a big concern, however, grant providers often have social causes to invest. By enhancing transparency and avoiding adverse selection, AI can help find better fund suitors. AI can be used in the grant process to determine the entrepreneurial abilities of applicants by using psychometrics and network analysis to determine the breadth of the network necessary to support a microenterprise's operation. Additionally, digitalizing transactions can reduce monitoring costs even further.

Next, the high-level framework needs to be aligned with stakeholder incentives both on the demand side and on the supply side. It provides a healthy competition environment between traditional financial institutions and fintech financial service providers by allowing suppliers of financial services for responsible financial innovation. Mutual cooperation

DIGITAL FINANCE AND ARTIFICIAL ...   255

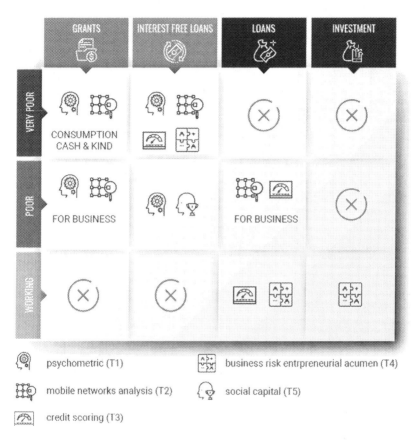

Fig. 5 Application of AI for the financial assessment of microentrepreneurs (*Source* Ashraf et al. [2021])

can be more beneficial. Financial services providers, for example, may find it challenging to integrate AI and big data due to a number of reasons, such as legacy systems and insufficient staff training. Similarly, without access to real customers or financial resources, a fintech company with a successful proof of concept may fail in the market. A regulatory sandbox and development of open API programs, which would allow fintech companies and financial institutions to work together more closely to advance the industry's understanding and enhance financial inclusion through the use of AI and big data, can help fill this void.

An effective financial policy framework must incorporate financial innovation. Along with the cost of acquiring the data, one should also consider who the potential users are, what kind of abilities they possess, and what kind of data they generate. A digital finance ecosystem cannot be successful without good data. However, without an appropriate data governance system, it will be challenging to achieve the socio-economic benefits of digital finance. Besides the biased application of data in AI, which creates and excludes a segment of society, data privacy is a major concern. A good governance system should encourage financial innovation while simultaneously keeping a check on systemic risk.

The ability of the regulators to keep up with evolving markets, and maintain the stability of the financial system, is an important success factor. Regulators who are informed can create an environment that facilitates financial innovation via AI, big data, and enhancing financial inclusion. Due to the capacity challenge, regulators may not have a clear understanding of how innovation aligns with society's needs or the capability of service providers to deliver digital products safely. It may result in unreasonable demands from the regulators, which may hamper innovation. Regulators' hesitation to adopt digital finance can hinder efforts and prolong suffering for those who are financially excluded, preventing countries from reaching their potential with artificial intelligence.

6 Summary and Conclusion

For credit risk assessment of creditworthy MSMEs lacking credit history, fintech companies using the AI and alternative data results in an objective, better-informed (backed by data), faster, more accurate credit scoring (entrepreneurial scoring). AI models often use low value digital footprint (features) not directly relevant to the assessment of creditworthiness by applying more complex methods for credit risk assessment. AI's application has started using big data obtained from multiple sources, including mobile phones, social media, rental payments, and psychometrics. There are several financial institutions and lending platforms that now use alternative data and AI algorithms for credit risk evaluation.

Despite the efficiency gains, the application of AI cannot resolve systemic issues of financialization and overindebtedness. A policy framework is proposed considering Islamic finance principles. The framework is based on two pillars. One is developing a sustainable and inclusive policy using a staggered approach that maps the macroeconomic requirements of microentrepreneurs at different stages of development. The financial instrument aligned with Islamic finance maps at each stage of the business development includes grants, interest-free financing, participatory finance, and equity financing. The second is a conducive institutional arrangement to execute the policy framework. Islamic finance offers a comprehensive set of institutional arrangements that include philanthropic, public, and private sectors that can help solve the issue of access to credit.

AI and big data can provide better financial infrastructure. AI has the potential to benefit both suppliers and users of financial services. Financial services can be offered with high quality without discrimination against consumers, and the providers can access markets that would otherwise be inaccessible due to the higher cost of resolving information asymmetry. AI helps these companies improve efficiency and reduce operating costs while providing better access to financing (terms, costs, and amounts) to entrepreneurs, as well as improving socio-economic development in society.

Disclaimer I would like to thank Professor Syed Nazim Ali and Zul Hakim Jumat for their helpful comments and suggestions that improved the quality of this paper considerably. The views expressed in this paper are those of the authors and do not necessarily reflect the views of the Islamic Development Bank Institute or the Islamic Development Bank Group. All errors are the responsibility of the author.

References

Acemoglu, D., & Robinson, J. A. (2000). Political losers as a barrier to economic development. *American Economic Review, 90*(2), 126–130.
Alesina, A., & Perotti, R. (1996). Income distribution, political instability, and investment. *European Economic Review, 40*(6), 1203–1228.
Alesina, A., & Rodrik, D. (1994). Distributive politics and economic growth. *The Quarterly Journal of Economics, 109*(2), 465–490.
Ashraf, D., Khedher, A. B., Moinnuddin, M., Obaidullah, M., & Syed Ali, S. (2021). *Artificial Intelligence and Islamic finance: A catalyst for financial inclusion.* https://irti.org/product/artificial-intelligence-and-islamic-finance/ on 16 September 2021.
Ashraf, Z. (2022). *Empowering people to change lives.* Retrieved 31 May 2022, from https://www.seedout.org/

Banerjee, A. V., & Newman, A. F. (1993). Occupational choice and the process of development. *Journal of Political Economy, 101*(2), 274–298.

Benabou, R. (1996). Inequality and growth. *NBER Macroeconomics Annual, 11*, 11–74.

Benhabib, J., & Rustichini, A. (1996). Social conflict and growth. *Journal of Economic Growth, 1*(1), 125–142.

Chen, G., Rasmussen, S., & Reille, X. (2010). *Growth and vulnerabilities in microfinance*. World Bank Group. https://policycommons.net/artifacts/1502046/growth-and-vulnerabilities-in-microfinance/2161160/ on 13 May 2021. CID: 20.500.12592/1p8856.

Francis, E., Blumenstock, J., & Robinson, J. (2017). *Digital credit: A snapshot of the current landscape and open research questions* (CEGA White Paper). 1739–1776.

Galor, O., & Zeira, J. (1993). Income distribution and macroeconomics. *The Review of Economic Studies, 60*(1), 35–52.

Kempson, H. E., & Whyley, C. M. (1999). Understanding and combating financial exclusion. *Insurance Trends, 21*, 18–22.

Leyshon, A., & Thrift, N. (1996). Financial exclusion and the shifting boundaries of the financial system. *Environment and Planning A: Economy and Space, 28*(7), 1150–1156. https://doi.org/10.1068/a281150

Pretes, M. (2002). Microequity and microfinance. *World Development, 30*(8), 1341–1353.

Worldbank. (2022). *Overview*. Retrieved 31 May 2022, from https://www.worldbank.org/en/topic/financialinclusion/overview#1

World Economic Forum and Deloitte (2018) The New Physics of Financial Services Part of the Future of Financial Services. *World Economic Forum*. Available at: http://www3.weforum.org/docs/WEF_New_Physics_of_Financial_Services.pdf

Open Banking for Financial Inclusion: Challenges and Opportunities in Muslim-Majority Countries

Nasim Shah Shirazi, Ahmet Faruk Aysan and Zhamal Nanaeva

1 Introduction

In 2015, the United Nations accepted a blueprint for sustainable development for the next 15 years. The document envisioned achieving 17 Sustainable Development Goals (SDGs), such as eradicating poverty, gender equality, access to education, and clean water. With 9.5% of the world's population (around 700 million people) living in extreme poverty (UN, 2021), poverty eradication occupies the special attention of the global community. Moreover, the ongoing COVID-19 pandemic has forced additional 120 million people into extreme poverty, further

N. S. Shirazi (✉) · A. F. Aysan · Z. Nanaeva
College of Islamic Studies, Hamad Bin Khalifa University, Doha, Qatar
e-mail: nshirazi@hbku.edu.qa

A. F. Aysan
e-mail: aaysan@hbku.edu.qa

Z. Nanaeva
e-mail: zhna33940@hbku.edu.qa

© The Author(s), under exclusive license to Springer Nature Switzerland AG 2023
Z. H. Jumat et al. (eds.), *Islamic Finance, FinTech, and the Road to Sustainability*, Palgrave CIBFR Studies in Islamic Finance,
https://doi.org/10.1007/978-3-031-13302-2_12

delaying the achievement of the first SDG. Thus, the goal to "end poverty in all its forms everywhere" remains on the agenda of governments and multilateral communities (UN, 2021).

Consultative Group to Assist the Poor ([CGAP], 2020), among other organizations, promotes financial inclusion among the means to address poverty. Furthermore, one of the seven targets within the poverty eradication goal is to ensure universal access to the appropriate technology and financial services. Moreover, financial inclusion is identified as a target in six more SDGs (Table 1).

While the COVID-19 pandemic disrupted the global economy and resulted in social and economic deterioration, it has also led to certain positive changes. Among new opportunities created by the pandemic is the digitalization of different sectors of the economy. This process has facilitated new business models and enabled innovation in various sectors, including financial services. The rapid advancement of FinTech promotes competition in the financial services sector leading to more affordable financial products and services. Open Banking, in turn, simplifies the process of market entry for FinTechs and their integration into an existing system.

Moreover, through an easier exchange of consumers' financial data, Open Banking supports further innovation, diversification, and personalization of banking and other financial products. Thus, several international financial institutions recognize that Open Banking facilitates financial inclusion and may play a pivotal role in poverty eradication (The World Bank, 2021).

The issue of poverty eradication is among the top priorities in Muslim-majority countries. While the population of these countries represents about one-fourth of the global population, their total GDP is less

Table 1 SDGs in which financial inclusion is included as one of the targets

SDG number	SDG name
1	No poverty
2	Zero hunger
3	Good health and well-being
5	Gender equality
8	Decent work and economic growth
9	Industry, innovation, and infrastructure
10	Reduced inequalities

Source Extracted from UNCDF (2021)

than nine% of the global GDP (COMCEC, 2019). Moreover, around 214 million people in Muslim-majority countries lived in extreme poverty in 2017. At the same time, several Muslim-majority countries have introduced the Open Banking framework, and many others are planning to follow suit. Thus, discussion of the effects of Open Banking on financial inclusion is timely for the Muslim-majority countries. Therefore, this study attempts to identify the advantages and risks of Open Banking from the lens of financial inclusion and in the context of Muslim-majority countries.

The study is composed of five sections. Firstly, it introduces the methodology. Section two discusses the topic of financial inclusion and its importance for poverty eradication. The next section presents the concept of Open Banking, including its pros and cons. The contribution of Open Banking toward financial inclusion is presented in section four. Recommendations for Muslim-majority countries are summarized in a concluding section of the chapter.

2 Methodology

The chapter aims to understand how Open Banking can facilitate financial inclusion in Muslim-majority countries and develop suitable recommendations. In doing so, the study presents a review of extant academic literature on financial inclusion, Open Banking, and possible effects of Open Banking on financial inclusion. Similarly, the study describes the financial inclusion and status of Open Banking in Muslim-majority countries.

The multistage process was applied to systematically analyze the literature on the relationship between Open Banking and financial inclusion. The study used the Scopus database due to its reputation as a robust metadata repository to search for extant publications on Open Banking and financial inclusion (Biancone et al., 2020). The search was conducted on October 30, 2021. When searching the database, a topic search (in titles, abstracts, keywords) was performed with the following keywords: "open banking" AND "financial inclusion" (3 results Scopus), "open banking" (74 results), "financial inclusion" (2,260 results). The initial sample consisted of 2,337 articles.

The Scopus filters were applied in the second stage to extract the top 20 most cited papers from the following sub-areas: "open banking" and "financial inclusion." The objective was to balance the breadth and depth of the papers in both sub-areas, and the result was a list of 43 papers (Appendix).

In the third stage, since the results of the search using a combination of "open banking" AND "financial inclusion" revealed a limited number of publications (see Appendix 1, Table 4, 5 and 6), the review was enhanced by including the reports and webinars of the Consultative Group to Assist the Poor (CGAP), Open Banking Implementation Entity (OBIE), and the World Bank. Furthermore, the Global Findex Database report was used to study financial inclusion worldwide and, in the Muslim-majority countries. Finally, to describe the status of adoption of Open Banking regulations in Muslim-majority countries, the information published on the websites of Central Banks of select Muslim-majority countries was utilized. This allowed to mitigate the gap in the extant literature and incorporate the Muslim-majority countries into the discussion.

3 Financial Inclusion and Poverty Eradication

The term "financial inclusion" gained popularity in the late 1990s (Kim et al., 2018). The World Bank (WB) defines financial inclusion as a possibility to have access to affordable financial products, such as savings, transactions, and payments (The World Bank, 2021). The payments usually represent an initial step of financial inclusion, leading to credit, insurance, and other financial services. Conversely, the absence of financial inclusion disrupts the regular life of the population, increasing poverty and decreasing economic development (The World Bank, 2021).

After 2000, the academic literature has been observed to be linking financial inclusion and economic development (Kim et al., 2018). The study of Boukhate (2016, as mentioned in Kim et al., 2018), for example, demonstrated that the advancement of financial services directly affected poverty reduction. Scopus identified the most cited document on "financial inclusion" being the paper by Sarma and Pais (2011). The findings of empirical analysis in the paper demonstrate a co-movement in the levels of financial inclusion and human development. Moreover, such factors as income, literacy, and inequality play a crucial role in determining the extent of financial inclusion. The later publications on the given topic discuss how digital finance can improve financial inclusion, especially in emerging and developing economies (Gabor & Brooks, 2017; Ozili, 2018). Lastly, in their article, Kim et al. (2018) examine a correlation between economic growth and financial inclusion in OIC member countries. The authors revealed a positive correlation between the two variables using the dynamic panel estimations.

In this regard, the introduction of the Findex database by the World Bank is an essential step in assessing the relationship between financial inclusion and other economic variables. The Global Findex data set describes global population savings, borrowings, and payments (Global Findex, 2018). The data set is based on the global surveys of the adult population conducted every three years. For example, according to the last survey, 69% of adults had a bank account in 2017 (see Fig. 1).

To address the issue of financial inclusion, it is essential to understand what part of the population is excluded from financial services or classified as unbanked. According to Findex (Global Findex, 2018), unbanked are usually a low-income population without enough proceeds to open a bank account, seasonal workers with irregular incomes, people out of the labor force, women, people without proper identification documents, people with religious concerns. Each of these subcategories faces specific obstacles to overcome to access financial services. According to CGAP (2020), the low-income part of the population is excluded from financial

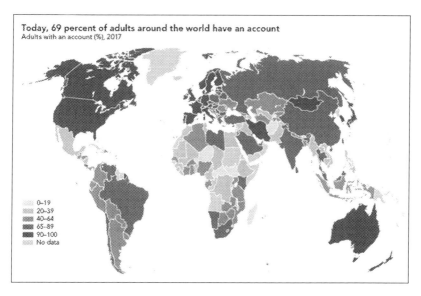

Fig. 1 Percentage of adults with an account worldwide (*Source* Global Findex database)

services due to irregularity and high-income volatility. Moreover, almost all of their income is used for essential expenses, leaving nothing for savings. Findex report revealed that half of 1.7 billion unbanked adults are women who usually live in rural areas or are unemployed. Women are typically restricted in their access to financial services due to social and cultural norms leading to a gender gap in ownership of bank accounts of about 9% in developing countries.

Data related to the OIC member countries (Organization of Islamic Cooperation) was extracted from the Findex report (2018) to analyze financial inclusion in Muslim-majority countries (see Fig. 2; Appendix 2). The 57 members of the OIC represent diverse economies with varying levels of financial inclusion. As presented in Appendix in the chapter "Islamic Specialized FinTech for Inclusive and Sustainable Growth in Sub-Saharan Africa" and Fig. 1 in the chapter "Islamic Finance, FinTech and the Road to Sustainability: Reframing the Approach in the Post-Pandemic Era—An Introduction", Iran achieved the highest level of financial inclusion, with 94% of adults holding bank accounts. Malaysia and Gulf countries follow next, with more than 80% of the population holding bank accounts. Understandably, financial inclusion in countries involved in political or military conflicts, such as Sudan and Afghanistan, is very low (9 and 15% correspondingly). Overall, as demonstrated in Table 2, the average level of financial inclusion in Muslim-majority countries is 44.3%, which is lower than the global average of 69% and the level of developing countries of 63%.

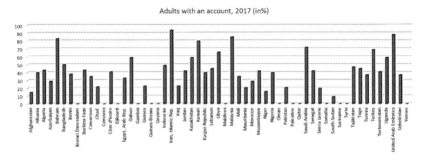

Fig. 2 Financial inclusion in Muslim-majority countries (*Source* Created by the author using Findex [2018] data)

Table 2 Comparison of financial inclusion

Countries	Adults with an account (%)	Gender gap (% point)
Global	69	7
Developed	94	–
Developing	63	7
OIC	44.3	14.5

Source Extracted from Findex (2018)

Similarly, a gender gap of 14.5% points in OIC member countries is higher than the global average and average for developing countries (7% points in both cases). In summary, financial inclusion in Muslim-majority countries is low and, as discussed earlier, may imply a lower financial resilience of the population to the economic or environmental crises.

4 The Concept of Open Banking

While still in the nascent stage, Open Banking has already affected how we make payments, open accounts, transfer funds, and make savings. However, despite its growing popularity, Open Banking still lacks a unified definition. One way to describe it is as being a process when banks share their customers' financial data with third-party providers (TPPs). Such data sharing should be performed with the customers' consent safely and securely (Euro Banking Association, 2016). In addition, Open Banking allows for the development of innovative financial services and products, thus, enabling more affordable and more accessible access to financial services.

Data is the crucial resource of Open Banking (Premchand & Choudhry, 2019). Traditionally, banks have been exclusive owners of the customers' financial data. Open Banking transfers the ownership of financial data to customers and enables data sharing among different financial service providers. Exchange of the customers' data is facilitated by opening application programming interfaces (APIs). APIs, in turn, allows for communication between two software through a set of codes built into applications (Zachariadis & Ozcan, 2017). Banks can open their APIs to TPPs voluntarily or mandatory under the legislative framework. For example, the industry initiated the introduction of Open Banking in countries like the US, Singapore, and India. At the same time, the EU and UK are the famous regulatory-driven pioneers of Open Banking.

Open Banking shifts the traditional banking business model into a platform-based system, where different financial service providers offer a variety of products in a single platform (see Fig. 3).

The introduction of Open Banking creates new opportunities for financial service providers while enhancing customers' experience. Benefits of Open Banking for FinTechs include faster and cost-effective market entry, more symmetric distribution of the customers' data, and avoiding certain expenses when joining various banking platforms

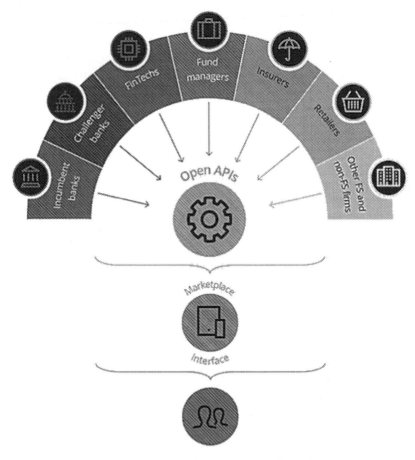

Fig. 3 Open Banking as a platform (*Source* Deloitte [2017])

(Gardner & Leong, 2020). Thus, FinTechs can start providing financial services within a relatively short period and at a more competitive price by employing these benefits.

At the same time, customers become a central part of the Open Banking framework. Open Banking implies that customers own and manage their financial data and decide which TPPs will access their personal information. Access to the customers' data, in turn, encourages innovation and customization of financial products, reducing the cost of product creation and offering more affordable financial services. Moreover, customers may be able to better manage their financial resources due to the ability to aggregate all financial information, such as accounts and loans in different banks, on a single screen (Premchand & Choudhry, 2019).

Traditionally, financial institutions, such as banks, have the advantage of collecting and storing customers' financial data, while FinTechs often employ a more advanced data analysis algorithm (He et al., 2020). Thus, by combining the strengths of incumbents and newcomers, Open Banking can ensure better financial screening ability. Similarly, Open Banking facilitates easier regulation of FinTechs through their integration into financial ecosystems.

Nevertheless, according to Premchand and Choudhry (2019), Open Banking carries certain challenges. For example, while Open Banking allows easy switching between different financial service providers, it increases pressure on banks and FinTechs. Thus, under the Open Banking regulation, incumbents and newcomers expect to work harder to attract and retain customers. Customers' loyalty, in turn, can be achieved through constantly addressing their financial needs while providing competitive financial products.

Similarly, Open Banking involves sharing sensitive financial data, thus accentuating security and cybersecurity threats. Furthermore, easier access to financial resources increases the possibilities of fraud and misuse. Moreover, there is an ethical question related to the possible use of customer data as a tool to manipulate their spending decisions. The situation might deteriorate when the big tech companies, such as Amazon and Facebook, decide to leverage their access to customer data. Combining financial data with the data available on social media platforms may allow such companies to build a complete profile of customer preferences and abilities.

The importance of data security and privacy are discussed in several articles about Open Banking. For example, in their paper "Blockchain-based data privacy management with Nudge theory in open banking," Wang et al. (2020) suggest addressing the issue of security through the application of blockchain technology to protect financial data privacy. Another popular subject in Open Banking-related articles is the regulation of the new ecosystem and the issues of trust, data privacy, and protection of customers' interests (Buckley et al., 2020; Fett et al., 2019; Mansfield-Devine, 2016). While the banking sector has been traditionally heavily regulated, the rapid development of FinTech outpaced the advancement of RegTech and SupTech. One of the ways to address this issue can be through deregulation of the new financial ecosystem. In this way, Zetzsche et al. (2020) examine the connection between DeFi (decentralized finance) and Open Banking. They argue that DeFi does not eliminate a necessity of regulation but rather requires specific regulatory approaches that could be built into the design of DeFi to provide a more effective outcome.

Given the above, financial and digital literacies may be among the critical challenges of modern customers. Therefore, regulators, financial service providers, and customers must work together to build a clear understanding of the concept of Open Banking, including its advantages and disadvantages. Finally, the technological readiness of financial institutions can pose additional challenges for the introduction of Open Banking, especially in developing countries.

As shown in Table 3, most Muslim-majority countries have not introduced Open Banking regulations. Nevertheless, some countries, such as Bahrain, Saudi Arabia, Indonesia, Nigeria, Turkey, and Iran, have already launched the Open Banking regulatory frameworks. Industry-led initiatives, such as banks opening their APIs, are present in Malaysia and the UAE. The generally slow introduction of Open Banking in OIC member countries might be due to technological challenges and limited resources available to develop open API technologies (Reddish, 2021). However, there is evidence that financial regulators in many OIC member countries have prioritized the introduction of Open Banking. Therefore, it is essential to understand the challenges of Open Banking to avoid mistakes of earlier adopters and maximize the advantages.

Table 3 Open Banking development in some Muslim-majority countries

Organization/country	Regulation	Industry initiatives	Remarks
AAOIFI			In January 2020, AAOIFI issued a compliance certificate to the iMAL—a core banking platform specifically created to support the shariah banking operations
Azerbaijan	In progress	In progress	Central Bank launched a roadmap to introduce the Open Banking regulations. As a result, some banks have opened their APIs
Bahrain	Yes	In progress	In October 2020, the Central Bank of Bahrain (CBB) launched the Open Banking Framework, mandating the local banks to comply by June 2022
Bosnia	No	No	
Egypt	No	No	
Indonesia	Yes	Yes	In August 2021, the Bank Indonesia launched the Open Banking Framework mandating the local banks to comply by June 2022
Iran	In progress	Yes	In 2019, the Central Bank of Iran launched the Open Banking platform. The launch of regulations is in progress
Kazakhstan	In progress	No	The National Bank of Kazakhstan launched the initiative to determine the open API standards for local banks
Malaysia	In progress	Yes	In 2019, Bank Negara Malaysia published a policy document to encourage the local banks' adoption of open API standards
Nigeria	Yes	Yes	In February 2021 Central Bank of Nigeria issued the Open Banking Framework

(continued)

Table 3 (continued)

Organization/ country	Regulation	Industry initiatives	Remarks
Pakistan	No	Yes	Banks and Neobanks opened their APIs to TPPs
Qatar	In progress	No	In 2021, the Central Bank of Qatar launched the payment regulations. More regulations are expected within 2021
Saudi Arabia	In progress	Yes	The Saudi Arabian Monetary Agency plans to launch the Open Banking Framework during the first half of 2022
Turkey	Yes	Yes	In January 2020, payment regulations (based on PSD2 principles) were adopted. Full adoption of Open Banking is pending the launch of the secondary legislation
UAE	In progress	Yes	In 2020, Dubai Financial Services Authority launched the AISP and PISP licenses

Source Authors' own compilation

5 Role of Open Banking in Facilitating Financial Inclusion

While the term "financial inclusion" has been around for some time and the term "open banking" gains popularity, merging these two terms is a relatively new phenomenon in the academic literature. The gap in the extant literature is exemplified by the fact that Scopus identifies only three articles when searching for a combination of these two terms (as of October 30, 2021).

An example of such an article is the analysis by Rastogi et al. (2020), who identify financial inclusion as a tool to improve India's economic situation. Moreover, their analysis of consumers' data suggests that Open Banking can facilitate broader financial inclusion and better economic development with additional efforts to improve financial literacy.

The paper by Podkolzina (2021) examines the effect of UK regulators on promoting and supporting innovation in the financial sector. In particular, the author analyzes how regulation can enable financial inclusion by facilitating increased competition in Open Banking. Finally, Kokkinis and Miglionico (2020) discuss how Open Banking and cryptocurrencies affect inclusive financial development and examine the regulators' challenges in providing secure and reliable ways to share customers' data.

Similarly, international financial institutions, such as the World Bank, accentuate Open Banking as an enabler of financial inclusion (The World Bank, 2021). Importance of the Open Banking and open APIs in addressing financial inclusion is also highlighted in the recent CGAP report (CGAP, 2020).

As discussed in previous parts, easier access to customer data enables FinTechs to develop innovative financial products, including products for previously un- and under-banked population categories. Thus, as evidenced by the example of the UK, Open Banking allows for a reduction in fees, permitting access of the vulnerable population to financial products and services (CGAP, 2020).

At the same time, Open Banking enables financial inclusion through improved financing of micro, small, and medium enterprises (MSMEs), which are often overlooked by the incumbents (Chaib, 2020). For example, "Open accounting" technology used by the UK FinTech Codat enables MSMEs to link their accounting platforms with financial accounts, allowing access to real-time data to provide faster lending decisions (Gardner & Leong, 2020).

Moreover, according to OBIE (2021), Open Banking leads to financial inclusion due to faster loan processing and lending, borrowing, and transfer procedures. Furthermore, OBIE (2021) indicates that Open Banking can assist customers who face issues related to their mental health (communal approach to the account) and inheritance (through the aggregation of all accounts on one screen). Both features allow for further inclusion of vulnerable parts of the population.

Another benefit of Open Banking is its ability to aggregate multiple accounts on a single screen. Using this feature, FinTechs can offer special services to help low-income customers to manage their finances and save. Since the lower-income population usually spends entire income on essential expenditures, some FinTechs have already introduced financial calculators and built them into expenditure tracking applications. Such services advise customers on reducing their expenditures and saving regardless of their income. By facilitating such savings, Open Banking increases customers' financial resilience to potential economic shocks.

Furthermore, when financial data shared by incumbents is combined with nonfinancial data (such as telecommunications or utility companies), financial inclusion can be accelerated by the onboarding of customers without credit history or collaterals. Moreover, access to such data may help include such categories of the population as refugees who often lack the means of identification. As such, UK FinTech Canopy uses customers' rental payments to define their credit scores (CGAP, 2021). Ultimately, innovations and competition induced by Open Banking facilitate low-cost business models that turn the previously unprofitable population into profitable customers. Thus, the customer base of financial institutions expands, improving overall financial inclusion (Gardner & Leong, 2020).

Nevertheless, there is a possibility that the advancement of Open Banking may also lead to the exclusion of certain population segments. For example, senior citizens may be excluded due to mistrust or inability to use new technologies. Another category includes the poor population, who are often restricted from accessing mobile data or owning smart devices. According to Lloyds Bank, in 2018, 12% of the UK's population remained digitally disengaged (Gardner & Leong, 2020). Similarly, while digitalization and closure of physical branches might help banks save expenses, it may lead to the financial exclusion of customers representing an older generation (Gardner & Leong, 2020). The regulators and practitioners should address such adverse effects of Open Banking.

6 Recommendations for Muslim-Majority Countries

Financial inclusion in Muslim-majority countries is significantly lower than the global average. According to CGAP (2020), it implies that the population in OIC member countries may not be able to build sufficient resilience to escape the "cycle of poverty" or face future crises. Moreover, since several OIC member countries have already initiated the implementation of Open Banking, it is advisable to design it to facilitate financial inclusion.

One of the main advantages of implementing Open Banking can be enabling shariah-compliant financial services through Islamic FinTechs. Doing so may lead to the financial inclusion of religiously conscious customers. Even in countries where banking regulations do not provide for Islamic Banking licenses, Islamic FinTechs can deliver shariah-compliant financial services through joining the existing Open Banking platforms. For example, Islamic digital bank Insha can deliver shariah-compliant services in Germany using a conventional banking license of Solarisbank (Bank-as-a-service platform) (Salaam gateway, 2020; Solarisbank, 2021).

Furthermore, Muslim-majority countries might consider the benefits of enabling charity and social assistance applications. For example, the UK's Open Banking for Good (OB4G) initiative unites charities, academics, and FinTechs to use Open Banking technology to support the most vulnerable parts of the population (Gardner & Leong, 2020). Similarly, Open Banking platforms in Muslim-majority countries might include *zakat* and waqf FinTechs along with the applications on government assistance funds. By doing so, the distribution of social benefits among lower-income populations may become more accessible, transparent, and less prone to corruption. Moreover, FinTechs can advise the recipients of social benefits about managing their received funds and saving or investing them.

Furthermore, Muslim-majority countries should be clear about the challenges and risks of Open Banking. First, OIC member countries should be aware of the expected transition of Open Banking to Open Finance and Open Data, which may happen when customer data will also include data from utilities and telecom companies, among others (CGAP, 2020). Certain economies, such as the UK and Australia, are working in this direction. Understanding the future transition as well as its benefits and challenges is essential when planning for the implementation of Open Banking.

Second, the increasing volume of financial data shared among financial service providers may become overwhelming at a certain point. Processing large volumes of data may complicate the loan assessment process and delay access to finance. Furthermore, access to detailed financial information of customers may penalize them due to easier identification of possible risks that are common among more vulnerable customers. For example, the UK defined price discrimination cases based on the customers' ethnicity or race (Gardner & Leong, 2020).

Third, the possibility of using customers' data in an unethical manner to manipulate their decision-making is of particular concern. Such manipulation can be more ubiquitous when customers are vulnerable, which is often the case with a low-income population.

In conclusion, to facilitate financial inclusion, the Muslim-majority countries are advised to consider the following aspects when implementing Open Banking:

- To require complete transparency in how customers' financial data is used. If the data is used to access customers' credibility, all criteria should be defined and stated clearly. Doing so may help prevent misuse of information and customer manipulation;
- To ensure the provision of equal opportunities for all customers. The policy-makers and financial service providers should pay special attention to the inclusion of low-income population, senior citizens, and people with disabilities through providing adequate financial and technical training;
- To consider subsidies for the poorest segments of the population to enable their access to the Internet and suitable electronic devices;
- To facilitate inclusion of social funds, such as zakat and waqf funds, into Open Banking platform;
- To develop and enforce the standards of digital ethics.

This study represents an attempt to analyze the benefits and challenges of Open Banking and its effect on financial inclusion. Extant literature suggests that Open Banking can be an effective tool to enable financial inclusion. Consequently, the study proposes introducing Open Banking in Muslim-majority countries to help eradicate poverty and build a financial resilience of the population. However, the gap in extant literature necessitates empirical research to assess the effects of Open Banking on financial inclusion. In this regard, the upcoming Findex report can be of particular interest. Furthermore, comparing changes in financial inclusion in 2017 and 2020 may help guide a future academic discourse. Finally, the experience of developing countries, such as Brazil, may be more practical for Muslim-majority countries due to possible similarities.

Appendix

Extant Literature on the Topic of Open Banking and Financial Inclusion

See Tables 4, 5 and 6.

Financial Inclusion in Muslim-Majority Countries

See Table 7.

Table 4 Scopus results on "Open Banking" and "financial inclusion"

Authors	Title	Year	Cited by	Document type
Rastogi S., Sharma A., Panse C.	Open banking and inclusive growth in India	2020	2	Article
Podkolzina I.A.	The UK's government and regulatory policy responses to FinTech	2021		Article
Kokkinis A., Miglionico A.	Open banking and libra: A new frontier of financial inclusion for payment systems?	2020		Article

Table 5 Scopus results on "Open Banking"

Authors	Title	Year	Cited by	Document type
Wang H., Ma S., Dai H.-N., Imran M., Wang T.	Blockchain-based data privacy management with Nudge theory in open banking	2020	26	Article
Kane E.J.	The dialectical role of information and disinformation in regulation-induced banking crises	2000	14	Article
Buckley R.P., Arner D.W., Zetzsche D.A., Weber R.H.	The road to RegTech: the (astonishing) example of the European Union	2020	11	Article
Fett D., Hosseyni P., Kusters R.	An extensive formal security analysis of the openid financial-grade API	2019	9	Conference paper
Mansfield-Devine S.	Open banking: opportunity and danger	2016	8	Article
Ashofteh A., Bravo J.M.	A conservative approach for online credit scoring	2021	6	Article
Premchand A., Choudhry A.	Open banking and APIs for transformation in banking	2019	6	Conference paper
Dratva R.	Is open banking driving the financial industry towards a true electronic market?	2020	5	Article

(continued)

Table 5 (continued)

Authors	Title	Year	Cited by	Document type
Sgard J.	Crise financière, inflation et currency board en bulgarie (1991–1998): Les leçons d'une transition indisciplinée	1999	5	Article
Ramdani B., Rothwell B., Boukrami E.	Open Banking: The Emergence of New Digital Business Models	2020	4	Article
Ma S., Guo C., Wang H., Xiao H., Xu B., Dai H.-N., Cheng S., Yi R., Wang T.	Nudging data privacy management of open banking based on blockchain	2019	4	Conference paper
Long G., Tan Y., Jiang J., Zhang C.	Federated Learning for Open Banking	2020	3	Book chapter
Kellezi D., Boegelund C., Meng W.	Towards Secure Open Banking Architecture: An Evaluation with OWASP	2019	3	Conference paper
Basso A., Bon J., Tasker B., Timan N., Walker M., Whitcombe C.	Recent Developments at the CMA: 2017–2018	2018	3	Article
Gozman D., Hedman J., Sylvest K.	Open banking: Emergent roles, risks & opportunities	2018	3	Conference paper
Daiy A.K., Shen K.-Y., Huang J.-Y., Lin T.M.-Y.	A hybrid mcdm model for evaluating open banking business partners	2021	2	Article
Zetzsche D.A., Arner D.W., Buckley R.P.	Decentralized finance	2020	2	Article
Mol-Gómez-Vázquez A., Hernández-Cánovas G., Koëter-Kant J.	Do foreign banks intensify borrower discouragement? The role of developed European institutions in ameliorating SME financing constraints	2020	2	Article
Dong C., Wang Z., Chen S., Xiang Y.	BBM: A Blockchain-Based Model for Open Banking via Self-sovereign Identity	2020	2	Conference paper
Rastogi S., Sharma A., Panse C.	Open banking and inclusive growth in India	2020	2	Article

Table 6 Scopus results on "financial inclusion"

Authors	Title	Year	Cited by	Document type
Sarma M., Pais J.	Financial inclusion and development	2011	248	Article
Allen F., Demirguc-Kunt A., Klapper L., Martinez Peria M.S.	The foundations of financial inclusion: Understanding ownership and use of formal accounts	2016	189	Article
Soederberg S.	Debtfare states and the poverty industry: Money, discipline and the surplus population	2014	184	Book
Demirgüç-Kunt A., Klapper L.	Measuring financial inclusion: Explaining variation in use of financial services across and within countries	2013	158	Article
Gabor D., Brooks S.	The digital revolution in financial inclusion: international development in the fintech era	2017	147	Article
Ozili P.K.	Impact of digital finance on financial inclusion and stability	2018	133	Article
Chibba M.	Financial inclusion, poverty reduction and the millennium development goals	2009	130	Article
Zins A., Weill L.	The determinants of financial inclusion in Africa	2016	126	Article
Maurer B.	Mobile Money: Communication, Consumption and Change in the Payments Space	2012	124	Article
Swamy V.	Financial Inclusion, Gender Dimension, and Economic Impact on Poor Households	2014	114	Article
Klapper L., Lusardi A., Panos G.A.	Financial literacy and its consequences: Evidence from Russia during the financial crisis	2013	112	Article

(continued)

Table 6 (continued)

Authors	Title	Year	Cited by	Document type
Kim D.-W., Yu J.-S., Hassan M.K.	Financial inclusion and economic growth in OIC countries	2018	109	Article
Fungáčová Z., Weill L.	Understanding financial inclusion in China	2015	106	Article
Leong C., Tan B., Xiao X., Tan F.T.C., Sun Y.	Nurturing a FinTech ecosystem: The case of a youth microloan startup in China	2017	103	Article
Munyegera G.K., Matsumoto T.	Mobile Money, Remittances, and Household Welfare: Panel Evidence from Rural Uganda	2016	101	Article
Leyshon A., Thrift N., Pratt J.	Reading financial services: texts, consumers, and financial literacy	1998	86	Article
Chakravarty S.R., Pal R.	Financial inclusion in India: An axiomatic approach	2013	84	Article
Okello Candiya Bongomin G., Ntayi J.M., Munene J.C., Malinga C.A.	Mobile Money and Financial Inclusion in Sub-Saharan Africa: the Moderating Role of Social Networks	2018	83	Article
Hassan M.K., Aliyu S.	A contemporary survey of islamic banking literature	2018	82	Article
Mishra V., Singh Bisht S.	Mobile banking in a developing economy: A customer-centric model for policy formulation	2013	80	Article

Table 7 Financial inclusion in Muslim-majority countries

OIC member countries	Adults with an account, 2017 (in%)	The gap between men and women (in% points)
Afghanistan	15	15
Albania	40	4
Algeria	43	27
Azerbaijan	29	–
Bahrain	83	11
Bangladesh	50	29
Benin	38	20
Brunei Darussalam	–	–
Burkina Faso	43	17
Cameroon	35	9
Chad	22	14
Comoros	–	–
Côte d'Ivoire	41	11
Djibouti	–	–
Egypt, Arab Rep	33	12
Gabon	59	10
Gambia	–	–
Guinea	23	8
Guinea-Bissau	–	–
Guyana	–	–
Indonesia	49	–5
Iran, Islamic Rep	94	5
Iraq	23	6
Jordan	42	30
Kazakhstan	59	–
Kuwait	80	10
Kyrgyz Republic	40	–
Lebanon	45	24
Libya	66	11
Maldives	–	–
Malaysia	85	5
Mali	35	20
Mauritania	21	11
Morocco	29	25
Mozambique	42	18
Niger	16	9
Nigeria	40	24
Oman	–	–
Pakistan	21	28
Palestine	–	–
Qatar	–	–
Saudi Arabia	72	22

(continued)

Table 7 (continued)

OIC member countries	Adults with an account, 2017 (in%)	The gap between men and women (in% points)
Senegal	42	8
Sierra Leone	20	9
Somalia	–	–
South Sudan	9	8
Suriname	–	–
Syria	–	–
Tajikistan	47	10
Togo	45	15
Tunisia	37	17
Turkey	69	29
Turkmenistan	41	10
Uganda	59	13
United Arab Emirates	88	16
Uzbekistan	37	–
Yemen	–	–
Average	44.3	14.5

Source Extracted from Findex (2018)

REFERENCES

AAOIFI. (2020). *AAOIFI and path solutions sign an agreement to pursue and maintain certification.* Retrieve from: https://aaoifi.com/announcement/aaoifi-and-path-solutions-sign-agreement-to-pursue-and-maintain-certification/?lang=en on November 18, 2020

Biancone, P. P., Saiti, B., Petricean, D., & Chmet, F. (2020). The bibliometric analysis of Islamic banking and finance. *Journal of Islamic Accounting and Business Research, 11*(9). https://doi.org/10.1108/JIABR-08-2020-0235

BIS. (2020). *Payment aspects of financial inclusion in the fintech era.* Available at: https://www.bis.org/cpmi/publ/d191.pdf. Accessed on November 10, 2021.

Buckley, R. P., Arner, D. W., Zetzsche, D. A., & Weber, R. H. (2020). The road to RegTech: The (astonishing) example of the European Union. *Journal of Banking Regulation, 21*(1), 26–36.

CBB. (2020). *CBB launches the Bahrain Open Banking Framework.* Available at: https://www.cbb.gov.bh/media-center/cbb-launches-the-bahrain-open-banking-framework/

CGAP. (2020). *Open Banking: How to design for financial inclusion* (Working Paper). Available at: https://www.cgap.org/sites/default/files/publications/2020_10_Working_Paper_Open_Banking.pdf

CGAP. (2021). *About CGAP*. Available at: https://www.cgap.org/about/governance

Chaib, I. (2020). *How can Open Banking accelerate financial inclusion?* OpenBankingProject. Available at: https://www.openbankproject.com/how-can-open-banking-accelerate-financial-inclusion/. Accessed on November 3, 2021.

COMCEC, (2019). COMCEC POVERTY OUTLOOK 2019. Available at: https://www.sbb.gov.tr/wp-content/uploads/2019/11/COMCEC-POVERTY-OUTLOOK_October-2019.pdf

Deloitte. (2017). *How to flourish in an uncertain future*. Open banking. Available at: https://www2.deloitte.com/jp/en/pages/financial-services/articles/future-banking-open-banking-flourish-uncertainty.html

Euro Banking Association. (2016). Understanding the business relevance of Open APIs and Open Banking for Banks. *Euro Banking Association, Version 1.0.*

Fett, D., Hosseyni, P., & Küsters, R. (2019, May). An extensive formal security analysis of the open id financial-grade api. In *2019 IEEE Symposium on Security and Privacy (SP)* (pp. 453–471). IEEE.

Gabor, D., & Brooks, S. (2017). The digital revolution in financial inclusion: International development in the fintech era. *New Political Economy, 22*(4), 423–436.

Gardner, J., & Leong, E. (2020). Open Banking in the UK and Singapore: Open possibilities for enhancing financial inclusion. *Journal of Business Law*. 2021, 5, 424–453.

Global Findex. (2018). *About*. Available at: https://globalfindex.worldbank.org/

He, Z., Huang, J., & Zhou, J. (2020). *Open Banking: Credit market competition when borrowers own the data* (No. w28118). National Bureau of Economic Research.

Kim, D. W., Yu, J. S., & Hassan, M. K. (2018). Financial inclusion and economic growth in OIC countries. *Research in International Business and Finance, 43*, 1–14.

Kokkinis, A., & Miglionico, A. (2020). Open banking and libra: A new frontier of financial inclusion for payment systems? *Singapore Journal of Legal Studies, 2020*, 601–629.

Mansfield-Devine, S. (2016). Open banking: Opportunity and danger. *Computer Fraud & Security* (10), 8–13.

OBIE, (2021). Annual report. Available at: https://assets.foleon.com/eu-west-2/uploads-7e3kk3/48197/obie-ra-artwork-10096a5716bf30-2.5853a6c2c203.pdf

OIC. (2021). *Organization of Islamic Cooperation*. About. Available at: https://www.oic-oci.org/page/?p_id=52&p_ref=26&lan=en

Ozili, P. K. (2018). Impact of digital finance on financial inclusion and stability. *Borsa Istanbul Review, 18*(4), 329–340.
Podkolzina, I. A. (2021). The UK's government and regulatory policy responses to FinTech. *World Economy and International Relations., 65*(2), 45–52.
Premchand, A., & Choudhry, A. (2019). Open banking and APIs for transformation in banking. *Proceedings of the 2018 International Conference on Communication, Computing and Internet of Things, IC3IoT 2018*, pp. 25–29. https://doi.org/10.1109/IC3IoT.2018.8668107
Rastogi, S., Sharma, A., & Panse, C. (2020). Open banking and inclusive growth in India. *Indian Journal of Ecology, 47*, 75–79.
Reddish, A. (2021). *Open Banking hasn't failed, but Open Finance might do if we don't learn from it*. Finextra. Available at: https://www.finextra.com/blogposting/21172/open-banking-hasnt-failed-but-open-finance-might-do-if-we-dont-learn-from-it. Accessed on November 2, 2021.
Salaam gateway. German Islamic fintech Insha releasing new app in July, eyes Europe expansion. June 16, 2020. Retrieved from: https://www.salaamgateway.com/story/german-islamic-fintech-insha-releasing-new-app-in-july-eyes-europe-expansion on November 4, 2020.
Sarma, M., & Pais, J. (2011). Financial inclusion and development. *Journal of International Development, 23*(5), 613–628.
Solarisbank. (2021). Retrieved from: https://www.solarisbank.com/en/about on November 4, 2020.
The World Bank. (2004). *The consultative group to assist the poor*. Retrieved from: https://ieg.worldbankgroup.org/sites/default/files/Data/reports/gppp_cgap_wp.pdf. Accessed on November 5, 2021.
The World Bank. (2021). *Financial inclusion*. Available at: https://www.worldbank.org/en/topic/financialinclusion/overview#1. Accessed on October 24, 2021.
UN. (2021). *SDGs*. Available at: https://sdgs.un.org/goals
UNCDF, (2021). Financial Inclusion and the SDGs. Available at: https://www.uncdf.org/financial-inclusion-and-the-sdgs
Wang, H., Ma, S., Dai, H. N., Imran, M., & Wang, T. (2020). Blockchain-based data privacy management with nudge theory in open banking. *Future Generation Computer Systems, 110*, 812–823.
Zachariadis, M., & Ozcan, P. (2017). The API economy and digital transformation in financial services: The case of Open Banking. *SSRN Electronic Journal*. https://doi.org/10.2139/ssrn.2975199
Zetzsche, D. A., Arner, D. W., & Buckley, R. P. (2020). Decentralized finance. *Journal of Financial Regulation, 6*(2), 172–203.

Islamic Specialized FinTech for Inclusive and Sustainable Growth in Sub-Saharan Africa

Jamila Abubakar and Ahmet Faruk Aysan

1 INTRODUCTION

The African[1] economy has been experiencing steady growth for the last ten years, credited to the emergence of digitalisation on the continent. Unfortunately, the growth is not spread equally across countries, sectors, and other socio-economic divides. As the continent struggles to cope with growing socio-economic inequalities, the health and economic disruption caused by the COVID-19 pandemic have exacerbated these inequalities. The 2021 African development report shows that for the first time in 25 years, African economies will be plunged into a recession as

[1] The use of "Africa" in the paper refers to Sub-Saharan Africa and North Africa combined.

J. Abubakar (✉) · A. F. Aysan
College of Islamic Studies, Hamad Bin Khalifa University, Doha, Qatar
e-mail: Jaab27835@hbku.edu.qa

A. F. Aysan
e-mail: aaysan@hbku.edu.qa

© The Author(s), under exclusive license to Springer Nature Switzerland AG 2023
Z. H. Jumat et al. (eds.), *Islamic Finance, FinTech, and the Road to Sustainability*, Palgrave CIBFR Studies in Islamic Finance,
https://doi.org/10.1007/978-3-031-13302-2_13

growth in 41 of the 54 countries is expected to contract (AUC/OECD, 2021). More prosperous Sub-Saharan African (SSA) economies face a possible contraction of 1.4% in GDP, with smaller economies facing up to −7.8% (Grace, 2020). Even though Africa's health crisis was not as catastrophic as the rest of the world, the total shut down of economies globally caused African economies to take a big economic hit due to their dependency on international trade, tourism, and health supplies from the rest of the world. Additionally, falling oil prices worsened the scenario for some SSA countries for whom crude oil represents at least 70% of total exports (AUC/OECD, 2021).

The COVID-19 pandemic has also stalled implementing the African Continental Free Trade Area (AfCFTA), promoting cross-border trade among African countries to boost local firms and entrepreneurs' ability to compete globally. Digitalisation is key on the agenda for harnessing the full potential of the AfCFTA along with cooperative regional policies that enhance digital trade (Songwe, 2020) and empower local businesses.

Digitalisation is at the forefront of the African Union's (AU) strategy to achieve its AU2063 vision, which puts forward science, technology, and innovation as the main drivers of sustained development in agriculture, clean energy, education, and health for the region (African Union Commission, 2014). In the future, the equitable distribution of digital technologies and skills will increase financial inclusion, improve access to global markets, increase transparency and accountability, and create more inclusive, resilient, and efficient economies (Cangul et al., 2020).

According to the IMF (2020), SSA faces several hurdles that hinder the growth of its digital economy, such as inadequate and unreliable access to essential infrastructure and high cost of ICT and mobile services and devices, especially for those in low-income brackets. Furthermore, African countries face financial constraints and cannot independently finance the post-COVID recovery and the region's digital transformation for sustainable development (EIB, 2020). The AUC/OECD (2021) reports a drop in public revenue (10%), national savings (18%), foreign direct investment (40%), remittances (25%) for at least 22 African countries (AUC/OECD, 2021). Overcoming these financial constraints will involve robust public–private partnerships to strengthen the funding ecosystem towards financing infrastructure, skills development, and empowerment of start-ups and SMEs for the digital economy.

On the upside, the economic and physical barriers created by the COVID-19 pandemic created opportunities on the digital front and accelerated the digital transformation globally. For SSA countries, this was no different. Aside from improving connectivity with the rest of the world, SSA's digital economy quickly responded to the crisis with innovative solutions to enhance communication internally, strengthen healthcare response, monitor the pandemic's evolution (EIB, 2020), and most notably, improve e-commerce and e-learning. For example, in Rwanda, anti-epidemic robots monitor patients, delivering food and medication. At the same time, Nigerians used e-consultation services to remotely assess their risk for contracting the virus and request tests (IMF, 2020). In Kenya, specialized fintech companies offer life and health insurance to help households cope with the impact of the pandemic.

Africa's digital success is most prominent in the financial sector with fintech solutions and other tech solutions in niche segments embedded with financial services (specialized FinTech). These digital innovations have disrupted both supply and demand side of goods and services and, by doing so, enhanced productivity and growth. They have contributed to human capital development by bringing disruptive innovations in education, health care, agricultural, and financial services sectors that create new market segments and job opportunities. The positive externalities from these innovations have contributed to overall economic growth (Myovella et al., 2020).

The digital economy has brought about greater national and global connectivity and easier access to financial services. Still, rural dwellers, people with low education and skills, and those working in informal sectors have not had equal access to these services. Financial exclusion is amplified for SSA's Muslim population as Islamic finance (IF) is generally scarce in the region. According to Moody's, despite SSA accounting for about 16% of the world's Muslim population, its shariah-compliant banking assets only account for 1% of the world's total Islamic banking assets.

SSA's growing Muslim population currently stands at 339 million, representing about 30% of its total population (WPR, 2021). There is a need to create sustainable, inclusive livelihoods by increasing their access to financial inclusion.

This study fills a gap in FinTech literature by distinguishing between FinTech solutions and specialized FinTech solutions. Existing studies categorise specialized FinTech solutions either as FinTech or as their core segment (i.e., Agri-tech, Health-tech, Insure-tech, Wealth-tech etc.). Differentiating them and studying their unique characteristics presents more nuanced findings on the impact of specialized FinTech on inclusive and sustainable growth in Sub-Saharan Africa. The study shows how specialized FinTech solutions have better potential to reduce inequalities than other FinTech segments in SSA by delivering targeted digital solutions to local problems across sectors and linking the digital economy to the real and informal sectors. The study also highlights the potential for Islamic finance to broaden its reach in Africa through specialized FinTech models and accelerate the drive towards achieving the SDGs in a post-covid world. It identifies the challenges for scaling and mass adoption and proffers recommendations for harnessing the digital economy's full potential for inclusive and sustainable growth in the region.

The rest of the study is organised as follows: First, the study discusses SSA's Muslim population and their experience of financial exclusion. Secondly, the study presents the current state of FinTech in SSA and analyses specialized FinTech solutions and their contribution to inclusive growth and the SDGs. Thirdly, the implication of the specialized fintech model for Islamic finance in SSA is discussed. After that, the study addresses critical challenges hindering SSA's digital economy growth, and finally, the study concludes with recommendations for overcoming these challenges.

2 Sub-Saharan Africa Muslims and Religious Financial Exclusion

Sub-Saharan Africa has a Muslim population of approximately 339 million, representing about 30% of its population (WPR, 2021). SSA's Muslim population represents almost 16% of the world's Muslim population and is projected to reach 27% by 2060, making it the 2nd most populous Muslim region, preceded only by Asia-Pacific (McClendon, 2017).

Out of 54 countries in the region, 22 are members of the Organisation of Islamic Corporation (OIC), which holds membership to countries with a large or majority Muslim population. The UN classifies 19 out of the 22 SSA OIC member states as "Least developed countries" (SESRTCIC, 2007). As of 2005, SESRIC estimated that 72% of the OIC member states in SSA lived in rural areas. The inequitable access to infrastructure and services between urban and rural areas in SSA will cause these OIC member countries to be worse-off in socio-economic growth.

The World Bank estimates that in 2018 account ownership in OIC member states stood at 41%, which is lower than the SSA average (45%), indicating more significant financial exclusion for the Muslims in the region. The 2017 Global Findex survey finds that the most common barriers to financial inclusion in SSA are having a formal bank account, lack of money, and distance to a bank. The survey also finds that 6% of people without a bank account cited religious reasons. In addition, the reason for not having an account being "religious" is 5% higher in OIC member countries (World Bank, 2020).

Given the size of its Muslim population, SSA is a region in which Islamic finance, in general, should gain acceptance. Despite this, Islamic banking penetration in SSA has been slow and limited to a few countries within the region. According to the 2020 Islamic finance stability report, Africa accounts for 1.6% of total Islamic banking assets (IFSB, 2020). The spread of Islamic finance in SSA is hindered by poor regulations, low levels of financial inclusion, inadequate funding of the regions' Islamic banks, and a lack of awareness and access to Islamic banks and essential infrastructure, especially in rural areas.

The median age for the world Muslim population is 24 years old (Pew Research Center, 2011). In addition to that, Africa has the youngest population globally, with a median population of 19 years (Gates, 2018). Due to the continent's various health challenges, SSA has an estimated 56 million orphaned population, some of which are heads of households and have to work and provide for their families (Kavak, 2014; UNCD, 2019). The financial exclusion faced by youth worldwide due to the legal rigidity of traditional financial services, lack of appropriate financial products, and low income makes it difficult for these youths to escape poverty and be empowered (UNCD, 2019).

Increasing access to (IFinTech) solutions in the region as a compliment or alternative to conventional fintech solutions would address religious/non-religious financial exclusion. It could be a significant game-changer for the underserved population. IFinTech's have the potential to increase financial inclusion and social impact for the following groups in SSA:

1. Muslims who voluntarily exclude themselves from financial services due to religious reasons.
2. Rural dwellers with no access to formal bank account regardless of religious preference
3. Young tech-savvy population regardless of religious preference.
4. Informal workers who do not participate in the digital economy.

3 Specialized FinTech, Inclusive Growth, and the SDGs

Although slower than the rest of the world, Africa's digital transformation has had a leapfrogging effect in the region, growing tenfold in the last 20 years (IMF, 2020). About 72% of Africans now have regular access to mobile phones (AUC/OECD, 2021), and 45% of mobile users subscribe to mobile services. The spread of Internet and mobile connectivity has had a tremendous impact on the reach of financial services.

SSA is leading the charge in digital financial technologies (FinTech) globally (Cangul et al., 2020), resulting in the mobile money revolution that has caused a paradigm shift in the financial services industry. Mobile money pioneered in the region with Kenya-based M-Pesa. M-Pesa started as a fintech company bringing mobile banking solutions to the unbanked and underbanked in Kenya. M-Pesa is credited with narrowing the gender financial inclusion gap and lifting 194,000 Kenyans out of poverty (Aysan, Bergigui et al., 2021). Today, there are over 500 fintech companies and 300,000 mobile money accounts in Africa (AUC/OECD, 2021). Mobile money transactions make up close to 25% of GDP in the region (Cangul et al., 2020). Figure 1 represents the share of registered mobile money accounts globally. The graph shows that between 2007 and 2016, registered mobile money accounts in SSA were more than that of the rest of the world combined.

Nigeria, Kenya, and South Africa are leading the tech revolution in SSA and boast cities that rank among the top 100 fintech ecosystems worldwide (AUC/OECD, 2021). Young entrepreneurs in these countries understand the nature of the region's social problems and are striving to solve them. Their network and skills give them an edge and enable them to innovate solutions tailor-made to solve the region's social challenges.

Without a doubt, FinTech has been a great success story for SSA. Payments, lending, insurance, and investments are the most mature and fastest growing fintech spaces in Africa. They make up about 40, 38, and 11% of the fintech ecosystem, respectively (Tellimer, 2020). Figure 2 shows the market share held by different fintech spaces in SSA. These spaces have been expanding because the companies can offer cheaper and easier access to financial services for the unbanked, underbanked, and Micro, Small, and Medium Enterprises (MSMEs) and are tapping into a dynamic range of opportunities the traditional sectors left untapped.

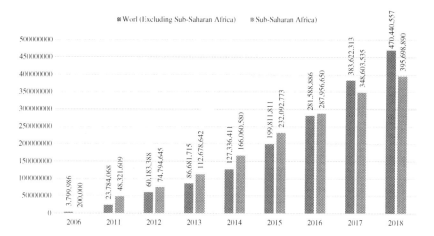

Fig. 1 Registered mobile money account 2006–2017 (*Note* The figure compares the number of registered mobile money accounts per year for Sub-Saharan Africa and the rest of the world, excluding Sub-Saharan Africa. *Source* Authors' creation based on data from World Bank [2017])

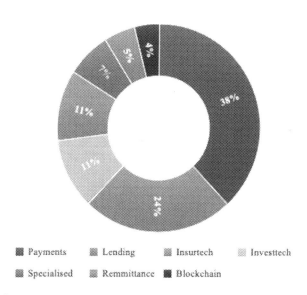

Fig. 2 Africa FinTech Segments. *Note* The chart shows the percentage of the FinTech space occupied by each FinTech segment in Africa (*Source* Authors' representation based on information from Tellimer [2020])

A key success factor for mobile money platforms in SSA is that they have reduced the formality and rigidity of the financial services sector. For some living in SSA, traditional financial services providers can seem intimidating and act as a barrier to financial inclusion. Moreover, traditional banks in SSA do not offer products for the mass market.

The vast and easy adoption of mobile money in SSA created an opportunity for other tech innovations to leverage on and develop specialized FinTech solutions for unique and niche markets. Sub-Saharan Africa's specialized fintech start-ups are perhaps doing more to bridge financial inclusion and socio-economic gaps within the region and addressing SDG goals more holistically by bringing the digital economy to Africa's real and informal sectors.

A specialized fintech is a digital solution with a distinct ecosystem and integrated financial services and e-commerce capabilities (Tellimer, 2020). Africa's specialized fintech companies have successfully solved multi-dimensional problems faced by the continent's most vulnerable people through unique digital innovations. They leverage FinTech and embed services such as payments solutions, mobile money wallets, credit transfers, short-term loans, asset financing, and insurance into their product offering. The success of these start-ups lies in their ability to first draw in their users through a niche market and then offer financial or e-commerce services to them through integrated fintech solutions on the same platform.

Financial inclusion is key to addressing SDG goals, and as such, it is a target in 8^2 of the 17 goals (UNCDF, 2019). Evidence supports fintech solutions' ability to benefit the underserved and unbanked at the bottom of the socio-economic pyramid, consequently spurring economic growth. As a result, embedding financial services into digital solutions tackling socio-economic problems serves the SDGs agenda to accelerate growth and development better. Such specialized FinTech solutions have been implemented in several sectors in SSA.

Agrocenta, an Agri-tech start-up in Ghana, used a digital platform to connect local farmers to an online marketplace to sell their produce at fairer prices directly to the buyer. They handle logistics for the farmers

---

[2] These include SDG1, no poverty; SDG 2 zero hunger; SDG 3 good health and well-being; SDG 5 gender equality; SDG 8 on decent work and economic growth; SDG 9 on supporting industry, innovation, and infrastructure; SDG 10 on reduced inequalities; and SDGs 17 partnerships for the goals (UNCDF, 2019).

and ensure the efficient delivery of crops to buyers. Agrocenta handles payment processing as an add-on service, offers mobile money services, micro-lending, and even crop insurance to the farmers on its platform. This digital solution has improved the entire value chain and enabled the farmers to be financially independent. The business model has also created multiple jobs along the value chain, from the company's direct employees to farmer recruitment and logistic agents and farm input suppliers.

Unexploited opportunities exist across the SSA agricultural sector value chain that can improve efficiency and food security. Achieving the SDGs goal of Zero hunger will entail innovative solutions that deliver necessary services to 60% of the region's population that earn their livelihood through agriculture.

Accessibility to and affordability of healthcare remains a significant concern in SSA. In Uganda's healthcare sector, Clinic Pesa provides health insurance and financial services to the poor through microtransactions from as little as $0.35 per transaction with a monthly target of $15. Users can invest in health insurance by sending a USSD code from their mobile phones. Users can also save and earn annual interest, incentivising developing a savings culture.

African digital start-ups also provide access to public goods such as electricity through mobile platforms. One Lamp facilitates access to clean energy for East African households in rural areas and urban slums with no electricity access on a pay-per-use basis. Through an SMS/USSD enabled technology, users may order solar systems, pay through mobile money, and accept doorstep delivery. One Lamp also offers individuals and MSMEs asset financing options for solar-powered appliances. Its project offers blended returns by sustainably addressing energy poverty, enabling financial inclusion, creating jobs and economic returns.

Table 1 shows other examples of these innovations already delivering multi-dimensional services that address SDG goals for people, prosperity, and the planet. Along with the SDG goals mentioned in Table 1, all the innovations accelerate the drive towards achieving SDGs 8 for reduced inequalities and 9 for industry, innovation, and infrastructure.

FinTech and specialized FinTech innovations in Africa disrupt incumbents and exert competitive pressure on traditional institutions to revise their business models to serve the underserved more efficiently. This competition creates more choices for the underserved segments and ensures that customers get better deals and services.

Unlike in developed economies, FinTech was not merely a disruptor of the financial industry in SSA. It came to fill a gap and provide services to an entirely neglected and underserved market segment. The social impact of specialized fintech start-ups in Africa has shown a strong link between these innovations, inclusive growth, and sustainable development.

Specialized FinTech has leveraged these fintech solutions to deliver innovative digital solutions with blended returns. However, IFinTech has been largely absent from this digital revolution in SSA, causing the region's Muslim population's financing needs to remain underserved. FinTech can support the delivery of Islamic financial services while at the same time protecting Islamic finance values such as transparency, equitable access, and risk-sharing (Aysan & Unal, 2021). Embedding Islamic financing within these solutions will help reach Africa's underserved Muslims and create spill-over effects in Muslim majority SSA regions that maximise their potential across markets, enhance the post-covid recovery mobilisation, inclusive growth, and sustainable development.

4 Potential for Islamic FinTech in Sub-Saharan Africa

Islamic finance, or shariah-compliant finance, is a form of finance rooted in Islamic ethics "where financial institutions offer financial services based on the principle of shared risk and reward" (SESRIC, n.d.). This form of finance aims to safeguard the interest of all parties and prohibits excessive risk-taking, gambling, and usury/interest. Islamic finance "encourages a partnership-based approach that develops robust businesses and eventually leads to an increase in the wealth of related individuals and SMEs" (World Bank, 2020).

Islamic finance, though termed "Islamic" and based on the principles of shariah, is not only accessible to Muslims. It is merely a form of participatory finance with ingrained ethical values representing an alternative to conventional finance.

The core objective of Islamic finance is to provide an ethical alternative to wealth creation and management (Rabbani, Ali et al., 2021). It promotes equity and justice and ensures that no one is left behind (Aysan, Abubakar et al., 2021). In essence, its goal is to achieve blended returns of profitability, social impact, and sustainability.

Aside from aligning with the SDGs goals for prioritising people, prosperity, peace, and partnership, Islamic beliefs also align with SDGs environmental sustainability goals for the planet. Islamic theology considers human beings to have been given guardianship of the earth and expected to treat that which has been entrusted (the environment) with respect and only take what is needed for survival. As such, promoting initiatives with positive environmental impact are fully aligned with Islamic principles and encouraged. Islamic finance can play a significant role in transitioning the world into a more circular economy through digital innovations (Aysan & Bergigui, 2021).

These shariah principles, if fully applied, make the Islamic finance industry more inclusive, impactful, profitable, sustainable, and aligned with the core principles of the SDGs.

IFinTech is still at its developmental stage globally, unlike its conventional counterpart, which has seen much growth and innovation in recent years (Rabbani, Bashar et al., 2021). The global Islamic fintech report, 2021 reports gaps across nine IFinTech[3] services in Sub-Saharan African. Nevertheless, the report estimates that global IFinTech will grow to $128 billion by 2025 from the current $49 billion at a 21% CAGR, surpassing conventional FinTech at 15% CAGR (Global Islamic FinTech Report, 2021).

These gaps represent untapped opportunities for IFinTech companies to stake a claim on a share of the industry. With the penetration of Islamic finance low in SSA, Specialized fintech solutions could prove an effective way for innovating Islamic finance products fit for increasing financial inclusion for the Muslims and non-Muslims in SSA. IFinTech can accelerate growth in SSA by targeting, at the minimum, the 335 million Muslims living in these economies and position itself to appeal to a broader target group, especially those at the bottom of the pyramid.

The COVID 19 pandemic presents a unique opportunity for Islamic finance and the halal industry to innovate unique digital solutions in sectors that the digital economy has neglected in SSA and for groups that have been excluded from the benefits of digitalisation. With the restrictions imposed by the pandemic around the world, people have experienced the benefit of the digital economy and how it can improve value chains and efficiency of service delivery. Technology's role during the pandemic has undoubtedly increased the acceptance of technology as an enabler. IFinTech must seize this opportunity to move on the African market.

---

[3] Alternative finance, digital assets, capital markets, payments, raising funds, deposits and lending, wealth management, insurance, and social finance.

Techlogical Experience	Shariah Principles and Standards	Strong Links to Real and Informal Sectors
• Appropriate tailor made technology experience that addresses the needs, educational and skills level of the target group.	• Strict adherence to shariah financing rules to maximise social justice and economic resilience.	• Innovative solutions linking the digital economy to the real and informal sectors thereby solving daily socio-economic problems faced by the most vulnerable.

Fig. 3 The 3 pillar of specialized Islamic FinTech Solutions (*Source* Authors' exposition[4])

IFinTech, as compared to the conventional, has the potential to pool together large amounts of social financing funds through zakat, waqf, and sadaqah and channel them towards providing much-needed financial assistance and start-up funds to individuals and MSMEs. The global annual Zakat potential has been estimated at between $200 billion to 1 trillion dollars (UNDP, 2018). IFinTech can improve the collection and distribution efficiency of ISF funds to create value and promote growth across different sectors in SSA. ISF funds provide more financing options as tools like zakat, waqf and sadaqah can overcome the challenges of lending to groups with inadequate credit profiles due to their benevolent nature.

Suppose IFinTech is to facilitate an inclusive, sustainable, growth-friendly economy in Africa. In that case, it must adopt outside-the-box thinking that innovates unique solutions for real socio-economic problems the most vulnerable in those economies face. The 2021 global Islamic FinTech report agrees that IFinTech has the potential to be "the world's next great success story" if it can harness profitable opportunities in emerging markets (Global Islamic FinTech Report, 2021). This study proposes that the strategy used by specialized fintech companies may be the game-changer for Islamic Finance in SSA. Specialized FinTech

---

[4] Proposed theoretical pillars upon which Islamic specialized FinTech solutions should be constructed to ensure social impact, sustainability, and compliance with Islamic economy values. These together are what will distinguish Islamic Specialized FinTech from its conventional counterparts. Upholding these three pillars will "harness the beautiful values of Shariah with far-reaching social impact and empowerment" (Global Islamic FinTech Report, 2021). It will represent an opportunity for SSA's Islamic Finance Industry to simultaneously expand the reach of its services and help bridge the funding gap for achieving the SDGs in the region.

models can propel growth for Islamic finance in the region while providing socially impactful solutions for real sectors. Embedding these solutions with ethical financing will have a significant impact and open opportunities for more underserved groups in the region.

Three interconnected pillars must hold up Specialized Islamic FinTechs to ensure they deliver value to their users: the technological experience, Shariah Compliance, and links to real and informal sectors (Fig. 3).

5 Challenges for Specialized Islamic FinTech in Africa

The challenges for specialized FinTech, whether Islamic or Conventional, are generally the same except for a few issues that are unique to Islamic financing. The challenges relate to factors that affect the diffusion of technology and hinder the growth of Islamic finance in the region.

Firstly, the lack of adequate infrastructure is one of the significant hindrances of growth in SSA. Despite the significant progress made in ICT, especially in Internet and mobile-cellular coverage, there is still a long way to ensure equitable access to ICT infrastructure and services. Internet penetration rates in SSA vary between 12 to 51% (Schelenz & Schopp, 2018). Nevertheless, mobile solutions are significantly developed in the financial services sector, where SSA is a global leader in mobile money transactions (Cangul et al., 2020).

Investment in ICT infrastructure was the key driver for economic development in the early years of Africa's digital transformation. African tech start-ups have leveraged the existing ICT and mobile infrastructure to create multi-sectoral value-addition. Current evidence shows that ICT infrastructure is necessary but insufficient to continue pushing the digital economy's growth. The main infrastructure gaps in SSA's that hinder the growth of its digital economy are access to reliable and affordable electricity, data, and Internet-enabled devices.

Less than 30% of the population in the region has access to reliable and affordable electricity, which negatively affects the regular use of the Internet and mobile devices (Myovella et al., 2020). According to the AUC/OECD (2021), a lack of electricity access can significantly limit Africa's population from benefiting from digital solutions.

AUC/OECD (2021) survey shows that 36% of respondents claim affordability as a barrier to using the Internet, while 26% say they cannot afford an Internet-enabled device. Similarly, the high cost of telecommunication services faced by FinTech affects their efficiency and makes it harder to survive and scale-up. Often, these costs are transferred to the users. Investment in ICT infrastructure will only be sufficient for driving economic growth if the population can afford to use the Internet and own the devices to connect to it.

Secondly, the population's capacity to engage the digital economy is influenced by the level of human capital in the continent. Donou-Adonsou (2019) examines whether access to education influences the relationship between technological progress and economic growth in Sub-Saharan Africa. The results indicate that education level does not hinder the productive use of mobile phones. The adoption of mobile services in areas with low or no education in SSA corroborates these results. Nevertheless, enjoying the benefits of investing in the digital economy and improving the region's global competitiveness will entail educating the 20 million youth joining the workforce annually for the next 20 years (Cangul et al., 2020).

The significant gap in education and skills levels is partly responsible for the digital divide in SSA (ITU, 2018; Nour, 2017). According to Choi et al. (2019), 60% of the SSA's labour force lacks the skills and education to participate in the region's digital economy. The jobs created by the digital economy do not match the current skills and education level of a large portion of the workforce. As investment in digital solutions for inclusive and sustainable development increases, higher-skilled jobs in the services industry will be created. Specialized FinTech companies will need skilled workers to serve the market.

Thirdly, the governments of SSA countries are not proactive with policies to steer the digital economy. Digital solutions disrupt traditional industries and present immense opportunities for new products and business models. However, policies are still stuck in the Third Industrial Revolution and are more fit for traditional institutions (Mavadiya, 2019). The current policies may be appropriate to some extent. Still, they do not address the legal and regulatory challenges peculiar to products and services offered by the digital economy, such as blockchain, cryptocurrencies, peer-to-peer lending, and Robo advisory (Mavadiya, 2019). The growth of the sector will require updating and amending policies, legal and regulatory frameworks, and supervisory practices (Cangul et al., 2020), formerly governing the traditional sectors to those more appropriate to govern the digital economy.

For IFinTech, aside from regulatory hurdles on the tech side, they also face Islamic finance regulatory challenges. Few countries in SSA have systems that accommodate shariah-compliant financing. Islamic finance faces multiple barriers (legal, capital, and operational requirements) to entry and growth in SSA markets. On a global level, Islamic FinTech also lacks regulatory supervision (Global Islamic FinTech Report, 2021). Without standardised regulations and an authority to enforce them, players in the fintech market may exploit opportunities that go against shariah values and ethics.

Additionally, cybercrime is rising in Africa, creating barriers for operating on a regional and global level. According to World Bank data, there are 571 secure servers per 1 million Internet users in SSA compared to the world average of 3511. The continent's cybersecurity investment is low, leading to cybercrimes costing an estimated $3.7 billion in 2017 (Kshetri, 2019). Furthermore, most African countries do not have updated privacy laws (Friedrich-Ebert-Stiftung Rwanda, 2019). With Internet use and e-commerce growing, consumers and users are more exposed to data theft and cybercrimes. A lack of proactive and appropriate regulation and enforcement in this area will slow the growth of the digital economy. Trust is a significant deterrent for growth, especially for fintech companies.

FinTech innovations are growing in SSA. On the other hand, governments lag in policies to support these innovations. Demand for specialized fintech companies' services will only sustain the growth for some time. Consequently, there is a need for targeted policies that create incentives to invest in underserved sectors, reduce the cost of adoption by users, and facilitate competition and innovation. Public policy plays a crucial role in technology transition, how it takes effect, and reducing any adverse impact (Cangul et al., 2020).

Lastly, funding for the private sector, SME's, and start-ups are critical for pushing the digital economy's growth and has been precarious. The South African central bank Governor, Rashid Cassim, has mentioned that fintech companies find it more challenging to access financing than traditional firms. This funding challenge has been made worse by the COVID-19 induced economic downturn. The AUC/OECD (2021) reports a drop in public revenue (10%), national savings (18%), foreign direct investment (40%) and, remittances (25%) for at least 22 African countries (AUC/OECD, 2021). Also, several SSA governments are having difficulty meeting their debt obligation. FitchRatings (2020) estimated debt to GDP for 19 fitch-rated SSA sovereigns to increase from 57% in 2019 to 71% at the end of 2020. With SSA governments challenged to raise funds domestically and an expected decline in foreign flows, financing the digital economy will involve most of the funds raised by the private sector.

6 Conclusion and Recommendations

Are specialized fintech models the solution to drive the growth of Islamic finance in SSA? Can SSA's Specialized fintech companies accelerate inclusive growth and sustainable development? This study has shown how specialized fintech companies have created opportunities for inclusive growth by bringing about disruptive innovations in the health care, agriculture, commerce, and financial services sectors. We have shown how they have addressed multiple deprivations faced by the poor through a single platform. Inclusive growth and sustainable development through specialized fintech companies and digital innovations depend on adequate funding and growth-friendly policies. Given a suitable and enabling policy environment, adopting the specialized fintech models will allow Islamic finance to reach a broader group in SSA and accelerate the drive towards financial inclusion and sustainable development. The study makes the following recommendations:

- IFinTech can collaborate with local and international incumbents to leverage existing infrastructure, knowledge, and expertise to reduce penetration costs and enhance scalability.
- Islamic Development Bank (ISDB) and other stakeholders in the Islamic development industry should nurture Islamic specialized fintech innovations with the potential for socio-economic impact and mass adoption.
- The Islamic finance industry should invest in innovations that improve the collection and distribution of social finance funds to better mobilise for a post COVID recovery.
- Governments should create a good and enabling policy environment that addresses the needs of both conventional and halal industries to ensure inclusive and sustainable development in SSA. These policies should: promote cooperative competition, create fair

advantages for Islamic finance to operate within SSA conventional financial systems, incentivise green and sustainable innovation, promote transparency and management of cybersecurity risks, promote open data to build SSA's statistical capacity, and facilitate access to funding.
- Education programmes for preparing the future workforce in SSA need a targeted upgrade to support digital, creativity, and analytical skills. SSA will need to invest in technologies that promote human capital services such as education, health, and food security to improve human capital quality for the future. Highly skilled workers will innovate creative solutions that enhance lives and livelihoods and create greater inclusiveness and growth.
- Governments must ensure that ICT infrastructures are made available in "low-technology" areas and effectively regulate service providers to provide end-user services at fair, affordable prices. As part of the infrastructure drive, there needs to be equitable access to clean and reliable energy in urban and rural areas.
- The continent must accelerate its efforts towards expanding and integrating regional and national capital markets. Strengthening SSA's capital markets will enable the region's specialized fintech companies to attract long-term funding to scale up. Reliable and affordable financing will make African companies more competitive, which will foster job creation, inclusive socio-economic growth, and sustainable development.
- Furthermore, SSA governments need to deliver policies that facilitate innovative competition for digital solutions with the potential for multi-dimensional service delivery, scalability, and spill-over effects to other sectors.

Appendix

See Table 1.

Table 1 Analysis of implemented specialized FinTech solutions in Sub-Saharan Africa, their social impact, and contribution to the SDGs

Tech Startup	Sector	Technology	Value Proposition	Social Impact	SDG Indicator
Agrocenta, Ghana	Agri Tech	Mobile App	• The platform offers an online market to match the demand and supply of farming produce • It offers e-payment solutions for the settlement of transactions on the platform • They handle the delivery of produce between seller and buyer • The platform facilitates the rentals of farming equipment for farmers • The platform has a financial services app that allows farmers to save using a mobile wallet • Enables farmers to access financing for farm input and offers financial advisory services • The platform enables access to crop insurance • It enables a pension scheme for workers in the informal sector • Agrocenta is also improving agricultural data collection • Facilitating women access to land and increasing their participation in agriculture	• The business model is curbing the exploitation of farmers who are desperate to sell by providing access to structured markets with fairer prices • The model has improved the entire value chain for farmers. From seed to market, including financing • It has provided financial inclusion for the farmers	• 1 (No Poverty) • 2 (Zero Hunger) • 5 (Gender Equality) • 8 (Decent work and economic growth)

(continued)

Table 1 (continued)

Tech Startup	Sector	Technology	Value Proposition	Social Impact	SDG Indicator
Clinic Pesa, Uganda	Insurtech	Web App, Mobile App, USSD App	• The platform enables users to save for future healthcare needs, and these savings attract annual interest as a bonus • It allows users to receive a medical top-up in the form of micro-loans • Users can pay for health care bills via the platform • Health care providers can use the platform to receive payment from patients and to access business loans • MSMEs can provide their employees with health insurance via the app	• Enhancing financial inclusion for businesses and individuals • Enabling cheaper and more guaranteed access to healthcare services when in need • Reducing inequalities in health care access • Improves household resilience in dealing with health care crisis while freeing up emergency funds for other needs	• 1 (No Poverty) • 2 (Zero Hunger) • 3 (Good Health and Wellbeing)
One Lamp, Uganda	Energy Tech	Mobile (USSD)	• This platform provides access to asset financing for solar systems and solar-powered appliances • Provides access to clean energy on a pay-per-use basis • Customer service support via SMS making it easy for those in rural areas to access user support	• Fifty thousand households have benefited from clean energy and reliable electricity access in rural areas and urban slums through the platform • Users have reported improved quality of life • It is actively reducing CO_2 emissions • It is saving households the cost of fossil fuels	• 1 (No Poverty) • 7 (Affordable and Clean Energy) • 8 (Decent Work and Economic Growth) • 11 (Sustainable Cities and Communities)

(continued)

Table 1 (continued)

Tech Startup	Sector	Technology	Value Proposition	Social Impact	SDG Indicator
Twiga Foods, Kenya	Agriculture & Logistics (Agritech)	Web Platform Mobile App Mobile USSD	• This platform connects farmers to a market to sell produce at transparent, fair prices • It improves the efficiency in the value chain by ensuring convenient collection and delivery of produce from farmers to vendors • It partners with M-Pesa to provide payment services to partners (vendors and farmers) • The platform facilitates access to credit for its partners	• The start-up has created 1000 direct jobs so far • Partners with over 4000 farmers and 35,000 vendors • The business model is curbing the exploitation of farmers who are desperate to sell by providing access to structured markets with fairer prices • The model has improved the value chain for farmers and vendors • It has enhanced financial inclusion for partners on the platform	• 1 (No Poverty) • 2 (Zero Hunger) • 8 (Decent Work and Economic Growth)

(continued)

Table 1 (continued)

Tech Startup	Sector	Technology	Value Proposition	Social Impact	SDG Indicator
Cellulant/ Growth Enhancement Support Scheme, Nigeria	FinTech/ Agritech	Mobile (USSD)	• The project provides an efficient and transparent e-distribution channel for agricultural inputs • Through the platform, farmers can access e-vouchers to purchase fertilisers and other farm inputs at prices subsidised by the government • It enhances financial inclusion for farmers and Agro-dealers • It improves efficiencies along the agricultural value chain • It is partnering with the federal government to provide grants/subsidies to farmers in the form of e-vouchers that are redeemable for agricultural inputs • Through the app, farmers get connected to suppliers and financial institutions	• Through the platform, 15 million farmers made equity contributions to empower 2500 agro-dealers • 4million households impacted annually in Nigeria • Four million farmers are benefiting from subsidies via the platform annually • 11,000 direct job creation in Nigeria • $1 billion dollars' worth of agricultural inputs processed yearly • The subsidies and improved value chain have enhanced the farmers' yield and consequently their income	• 1 (No Poverty) • 2 (Zero Hunger) • 8 (Decent Work and Economic Growth)

(continued)

Table 1 (continued)

Tech Startup	Sector	Technology	Value Proposition	Social Impact	SDG Indicator
M-Kopa, Kenya	Energy tech	Mobile App	• The platform provides access to financing for environmentally friendly energy systems (solar-powered) and home appliances • It provides access to electricity on a pay-per-use basis • It provides green asset financing to the unbanked and underbanked • It allows micro-payments making them accessible to the poor • It provides quick cash loans to users • During the COVID-19 pandemic, the platform added life insurance and health insurance to its services	• The platform has solved energy poverty for 3.7 million users • It has provided $400 million worth of financing to 1 million users for energy-efficient products and services • It is estimated to have saved $475 m in the cost of fossil fuels to its users • It has enabled users to transition from toxic fuels to clean energy, thereby preventing CO_2 and black carbon emissions • It has connected 47,000 people to the Internet for the first time • It has been able to scale to and provide services in 3 SSA countries	• 1 (No Poverty) • 7 (Affordable and Clean Energy) • 8 (Decent Work and Economic Growth) • 11 (Sustainable Cities and Communities)

Source Authors' compilation based on publicly available information on the companies' websites, reports and other Internet sources

References

'ABOUT US: AHI - Central & East Africa'. (n.d.). Available at: http://sautiafrica.org/about-us/. Accessed 27 April 2021.

Adamovich, K. (2020). 'The difference between an', p. 2010. Available at: https://payspacemagazine.com/fintech/the-difference-between-fintech-techfin/. Accessed 1 April 2021.

African Union Commission. (2014). *STISA-2024 science, technology and innovation strategy for Africa 2024.* 52.

AUC/OECD. (2021). *Africa's development 2021.*

Aysan, A., & Unal, I. M. (2021). Is Islamic finance evolving Into FinTech and blockchain: A bibliometric analysis. *Efil Journal of Economic Research.* https://hal.archives-ouvertes.fr/hal-03351153

Aysan, A. F, Abubakar, J., & Aysan, A. (2021). *The ascent of Islamic social finance reserach.* https://hal.archives-ouvertes.fr/hal-03341729

Aysan, A. F., & Bergigui, F. (2021). Sustainability, trust, and blockchain applications in Islamic finance and circular economy: Best practices and FinTech prospects. In S. N. Ali & Z. H. Jumat (Eds.), *Islamic finance and circular economy: Connecting impact and value creation* (pp. 141–167). Springer Singapore. https://doi.org/10.1007/978-981-16-6061-0_9

Aysan, A. F., Bergigui, F., & Disli, M. (2021). Blockchain-based solutions in achieving SDGs after COVID-19. *Journal of Open Innovation: Technology, Market, and Complexity, 7*(2). https://doi.org/10.3390/joitmc7020151

Cangul, M., Diouf, M. A., Esham, N., Gupta, P. K., Li, Y., Mitra, P., Miyajima, K., Ongley, K., Ouattara, F., Ouedraogo, R., Sharma, P., Simione, F. F., & Tapsoba, S. J. (2020). Chapter 3. Digitalisation in Sub-Saharan Africa. *Sub-Saharan Africa Regional Economic Outlook, April 2020.* April, 1–19.

Choi, J., Dutz, M., & Usman, Z. (2019). The future of work in Africa digital technologies for all. In *A Companion to the World Development Report 2019 on the Changing Nature of Work.* https://openknowledge.worldbank.org/handle/10986/32124

Donou-Adonsou, F. (2019). Technology, education, and economic growth in Sub-Saharan Africa. *Telecommunications Policy, 43*(4), 353–360. https://doi.org/10.1016/j.telpol.2018.08.005

EIB. (2020). *Africa's digital solutions to tackle COVID-19* (Issue July).

FitchRatings. (2020). *Debt distress rising in Sub-Saharan Africa.* https://www.fitchratings.com/research/sovereigns/debt-distress-rising-in-sub-saharan-africa-30-06-2020

Friedrich-Ebert-Stiftung Rwanda. (2019). What is digitalization? https://Innolytics-Innovation.Com/, pp. 1–16. https://innolytics-innovation.com/what-is-digitalization/

Gates, B. (2018). *The world's youngest continent.* Gates Notes. https://www.gatesnotes.com/Development/Africa-the-Youngest-Continent

Global Islamic FinTech Report. (2021). Global Islamic FinTech Report. *Cdn. Salaamgateway.Com*, 56. https://cdn.salaamgateway.com/special-coverage/islamic-fintech-2021/Global-Islamic-FinTech-Report-2021-Executive-Summary.pdf

Grace, G. (2020, July). Assessing the impact of COVID-19 on Africa's economic development. *United Nations Conference on Trade and Development*, 3, 1–21.

IFSB. (2020). *Islamic Financial Services Industry Stability Report 2020. December*, pp. 1–54. www.cbb.gov.bh

IMF. (2020). Digitalizing Sub-Saharan Africa: Hopes and Hurdles. https://www.imf.org/en/News/Articles/2020/06/15/na061520-digitalizing-sub-saharan-africa-hopes-andhurdles

Kavak, Z. (2014). Report on World's Orphans. *IHH Humanitarian and Social Researches Center, July*, 1–48.

Kshetri, N. (2019). Cybercrime and cybersecurity in Africa. *Journal of Global Information Technology Management, 22*(2), 77–81. https://doi.org/10.1080/1097198X.2019.1603527

Mavadiya, M. (2019). *African FinTech and regulation: What's the holdup?* https://www.forbes.com/sites/madhvimavadiya/2019/11/30/african-fintech-and-regulation-whats-the-hold-up/?sh=6637741f2f19

McClendon, D. (2017). *Sub-Saharan Africa will be home to growing shares of the world's Christians, Muslims | Pew Research Center.* Pew Research Center. https://www.pewresearch.org/fact-tank/2017/04/19/sub-saharan-africa-will-be-home-to-growing-shares-of-the-worlds-christians-and-muslims/

Mohamed Nour, S. S. (2017). Africa bridging the digital divides. Retrieved from Nordiska Afrikainstitutet website: http://urn.kb.se/resolve?urn=urn:nbn:se:nai:diva-2142

Myovella, G., Karacuka, M., & Haucap, J. (2020). Digitalisation and economic growth: A comparative analysis of Sub-Saharan Africa and OECD economies. *Telecommunications Policy, 44*(2), 101856. https://doi.org/10.1016/j.telpol.2019.101856

Pew Research Center. (2011). The future of the global Muslim population—Pew Research Center. In *The future of the global Muslim population*. https://www.pewforum.org/2011/01/27/the-future-of-the-global-muslim-population/

Rabbani, M. R., Ali, M. A. M., Rahiman, H. U., Atif, M., Zulfikar, Z., & Naseem, Y. (2021a). The response of Islamic financial service to the covid-19 pandemic: The open social innovation of the financial system. *Journal of Open Innovation: Technology, Market, and Complexity, 7*(1). https://doi.org/10.3390/JOITMC7010085

Rabbani, M. R., Bashar, A., Nawaz, N., Karim, S., Ali, M. A. M., Rahiman, H. U., & Alam, M. S. (2021b). Exploring the role of Islamic FinTech in combating the aftershocks of covid-19: The open social innovation of the islamic financial system. *Journal of Open Innovation: Technology, Market, and Complexity, 7*(2). https://doi.org/10.3390/joitmc7020136

Schelenz, L., & Schopp, K. (2018). Digitalisation in Africa: Interdisciplinary perspectives on technology, Development, and Justice. *International Journal for Digital Society, 9*(4), 1412–1420. https://doi.org/10.20533/ijds.2040.2570.2018.0175

SESRIC. (n.d.). *Participation finance—SESRIC*. Retrieved August 12, 2021, from https://www.sesric.org/activities-participation-finance.php

SESRTCIC. (2007). *Poverty in Sub-Saharan Africa: The situation in OIC member countries*. 44. http://www.sesrtcic.org/files/article/233.pdf

Songwe, V. (2020). *The role of digitalization in the decade of action for Africa*. United Nations Conference on Trade and Development. https://www.tralac.org/news/article/14900-the-role-of-digitalization-in-the-decade-of-action-for-africa.html

Tellimer. (2020). *The ultimate guide to Africa fintech—Tellimer*. https://tellimer.com/article/the-ultimate-guide-to-african-fintech

UNCD. (2019). Financial inclusion of youth. *United Nations Youth*.

UNCDF. (2019). Financial inclusion and the SDGs—UN Capital Development Fund (UNCDF). *Financial Inclusion and the SDGs—UN Capital Development Fund (UNCDF)*. https://www.uncdf.org/financial-inclusion-and-the-sdgs

UNDP. (2018). *Zakat for the SDGs | UNDP*. https://www.undp.org/blogs/zakat-sdgs

World Bank. (2017). Technology adoption—Our World in Data. *Our World in Data*. https://ourworldindata.org/technology-adoption

World Bank. (2020). Leveraging Islamic FinTech to improve financial inclusion. *Leveraging Islamic FinTech to Improve Financial Inclusion*. https://doi.org/10.1596/34520

WPR. (2021). *Muslim population by country 2021*. World Population Review. https://worldpopulationreview.com/country-rankings/muslim-population-by-country

The Role of Technology in Effective Distribution of Zakat to Poor and Needy

M. Kabir Hassan and Aishath Muneeza

1 Introduction

Zakat (alms) is the third pillar of Islam. In zakat management, different countries adopt different approaches. As such, the effectiveness of zakat management depends on the way it is managed. With industry 4.0, technology has become an integral part of the lives of human. Technology has no religion and Islam does not prohibit the use of technology for beneficial purposes. Therefore, to enhance zakat administration, technology can be utilized. The classical zakat management process has three stages. The first stage is the zakat collection stage where the zakat administrator will collect the zakat from its payers and then will keep that money collected in a separate account as a trust. The second stage is managing the received zakat fund in an effective way so that the benefit

---

M. K. Hassan (✉)
University of New Orleans, New Orleans, LA, USA
e-mail: mhassan@uno.edu

A. Muneeza
International Center for Education in Islamic Finance (INCEIF), Kuala Lumpur, Malaysia

© The Author(s), under exclusive license to Springer Nature Switzerland AG 2023
Z. H. Jumat et al. (eds.), *Islamic Finance, FinTech, and the Road to Sustainability*, Palgrave CIBFR Studies in Islamic Finance,
https://doi.org/10.1007/978-3-031-13302-2_14

of the zakat will be enjoyed by its recipients mentioned in the Quran (legal recipients) in an effective way. The final stage is where the zakat is distributed to the selected legal recipients.

In the classical zakat management process, there are number of issues detected. Some of these issued detected are specific to some countries while other issues are general to all countries. Habib (2020) states that the issues detected in zakat administration include lack of transparency, accountability, public disclosure and poor governance with greater intermediation with manual processes. Habib (2020) believes that using the successful cases of crypto philanthropy where blockchain technology has been used such as Pineapple fund and UNICEF Crypto-Fund, there is room to use innovation to enhance the administration of zakat too. Already there are institutions that are using blockchain technology to manage zakat such as Global Sadaqah of Malaysia and Blossom Finance of Indonesia where using cryptocurrency zakat payment is accepted (Habib, 2020). However, though enhancement of zakat collection has been discussed extensively by researchers using technology, zakat distribution stage is not given much attention. As such, there is need to conduct research to find out the ways in which technology could be used to enhance the zakat distribution process.

Implementation of effective zakat distribution system is important to achieve its objectives which include elimination of poverty. The potential of zakat in elimination of poverty has been tested and proved in the history of Muslim civilizations. For instance, it has been said that during the era of Caliph Umar bin Abdel Aziz, his administration could not find a single poor nor a needy who wanted to receive zakat (Nadzri et al., 2012). Therefore, if zakat distribution is managed effectively and efficiently, there is no doubt that even today the eradication of poverty would be possible. As such, the objective of this research is to explore the potential of technology in enhancing the function of zakat distribution. This is a desk research where the outcome of the research would assist zakat administrators and zakat payers to comprehend the importance of using the appropriate technology to effectively manage zakat distribution targeting the most deserved recipients.

This study is divided in to five sections. Followed by this introduction, Sect. 2 deals with the shariah parameters of zakat and the approaches used in the world for zakat administration followed by Sect. 3 where the existing issues in zakat administration is discussed with special reference to hiccups in zakat distribution. Section 4 discusses recommendation followed by conclusion.

2 Zakat Administration

Though *zakat* is the third pillar of Islam, it does not mean that the payment of *zakat* is compulsory for all Muslims and any Muslim can opt to receive it. There are shariah parameters applicable to the zakat payer as well as the receiver that ought to be followed. However, in case of normal charity like sadaqat and infaq, there are no such rules as anyone can give any amount at any time to any one selected with the intention of giving charity. Therefore, it is imperative to understand the type of zakat, rules of zakat and the conditions that need to be met by the receivers who accepts zakat. Quran, 9: 60 states the legal recipients of zakat which are *faqīr* (poor), *masākin* (needy), *amilīn* (collectors of zakat), *muallafat al qulūb* (whose hearts are aligned towards Islam), *riqāb* (to free slaves), *gharimīn* (debtors), *fi sabilillah* (fighters who fight for the cause of Allah (SW)) and *ibn sabīl* (needy travellers).

At the inception of zakat, the administration of it was made by the state (Sabahuddin, 2014). However, when Ottoman Empire fell in 1925, many Muslim states made zakat as a personal obligation of individuals (Anis & Kassim, 2016). Today, by looking at the way in which zakat is managed in different countries in the world, it can be said that there are three approaches used in zakat administration. The first way is through centralization method whereby there is a central or a single zakat administrator in the country to manage zakat and it is through this zakat administrator, the zakat payers will distribute the money to the deserved legal recipients. In this approach, the zakat administrator is responsible to manage the zakat fund and manage it in an effective manner to ensure that the collections and disbursements are made in an effective way to ensure there is retributive justice maintained in the society via zakat system. This method of zakat administration is popular in Muslim countries like Maldives where the majority of the population are Muslims. The second way is through decentralization method whereby there are various entities in the society who has the authority to collect zakat from the payers and distribute it within the legal and shariah parameters put by these individual organizations responsible for this within the governance framework established for such activities in the country. This method of zakat administration is popular in secular countries with Muslim minority populations like India. The final approach of zakat administration which is found in the world is there is no single body or an organization that will be responsible for zakat collection, but it is the personal responsibility of the individuals to calculate zakat on their own and give that amount directly to a deserved legal recipient of it. This approach is found in those countries where there is no specific legal framework for zakat and those countries where the zakat payers have lack of trust to those handling zakat funds. Apart from these three ways of zakat administration, in Malaysia, there is an innovative zakat administration way which is called "zakat wakalah scheme" implemented by some of the state zakat administrators whereby zakat payers when they pay the zakat amount to the organization, a certain portion of the money they paid as zakat will be refunded back to the zakat payer for them to personally distribute the amount within one year to those who deserve it except for the category of *āmil* (person helping to collect zakat) (Abd Hamid et al., 2020). In this zakat wakalah scheme there are reports that need to be submitted to the zakat administrator on how the money was disbursed and if any money is left it must be given back to the zakat administrator as well.

There are number of issues that has been detected over years on zakat administration such as lack of public awareness in giving zakat where the Muslims are not aware of when and how much to pay as zakat and not being able to identify the deserved recipients of zakat in the society (Sabahuddin, 2014). Irrespective of the way in which zakat is administered, one issue which has been common to all types is lack of governance such as not having enough trust in the zakat administrator due to lack of transparency and accountability in handling the zakat fund. There are three main stages of zakat administration. They are, handing of zakat collection, managing of zakat fund and dealing with zakat disbursements. Apart from these three main stages of zakat administration, there are other functions such as creating awareness and finding the most deserved recipients to receive zakat by application by the recipient or by finding them using the resources of zakat administrator are some of the other functions performed by the zakat administrator. In this regard, registering and verifying the poor and needy and finding out the eligibility of other legal categories of zakat recipients also involves the resources of the zakat administrator. When there is lack of transparency and the procedures followed by the zakat administrator are opaque to the stakeholders of zakat, it created doubt in their mind, eventually losing their trust in the system. As such, following good governance is imperative for any zakat administrator and this is crucial to be followed in all stages of zakat administration. To make this simple, it simply means that at least, the zakat payer should be made known how the zakat administrator collects their funds and handled it in the year and whether the beneficiaries received them and whether they benefited from these funds. Likewise, the potential recipients should be made known how they could apply to receive zakat funds or receive zakat in kind if they think they are eligible to receive it. Stating this is very simple, but implementing a transparent procedure for this with good governance is something which is difficult but not impossible to do.

For example, Maldives is a 100% Muslim country and zakat is administered by Ministry of Islamic Affairs (MoIA). MoIA each year announces poor and needy to register with the Ministry by submitting a form with documents to prove what is being claimed. This exercise is conducted every year and the data received in the previous year is not used in the subsequent year to understand the impact of zakat given to the poor and needy and it is impossible to gather simple information like how many new or old poor and needy are registered. Once the zakat distribution comes, physically the recipients who has been successfully registered as poor will have to physically come to the premise where the zakat is being distributed and then they will have to collect cash. If the recipient himself/herself is unable to come physically, they can send a person with their national identity card to collect the amount and one person may carry up to 50 identity cards to collect the zakat and there are issues facing in detecting the same identity card being using more than one time to collect zakat due to manual system followed (Muneeza, 2017). Fortunately, due to this pandemic, zakat distribution in Maldives has been changed from physically collecting of it to MoIA depositing the amount to the bank accounts of the recipients. The application form that need to be completed by the applicant to apply for zakat money in the category of poor and needy has 10 sections to be completed with 12 kind of supporting documents and a part that need to be endorsed by the bank of the applicant and the Island Council of the applicant (Ministry of Islamic Affairs, 2020).

The arrangement of the sections of the said application form are as follows: section 1 of the form deals with the personal information of the applicant; section 2 deals with marital status; section 3 deals with family details; section 4 deals with the information of all members of family who applied to register as a poor; section 5 deals with step children's information, section 6 deals with information about the aids received from national social protection schemes; section 7 deals with household information; section 8 deals with income and expense information; section 9 deals with providing the personal reasons of the applicant why he/she is unable to meet his/her expenses with the income received; and the final section is the personal declaration made by the applicant. The supporting documents that need to be submitted by the applicant is the applicant's valid national identity card copy (if the applicant is below 18 years of age, then the birth certificate copy is required), bank account details of the applicant with bank statement of those accounts for the past 6 months, if the applicant is applying to receive zakat for a legal dependant then the required authorized letter giving legal guardianship shall be submitted, if the applicant is married, the copy of marriage certificate shall be submitted, if the applicant is a divorcee, then the copy of the certificate of divorce shall be submitted, if the applicant is a widow/widower then the copy of the death certificate of the spouse shall be submitted, if the applicant's spouse is convicted for a crime and is currently in prison, a letter from the required authority prove this must be submitted, if the applicant is working, the detail of the work with salary details shall be submitted, if the applicant is living for rent, the tenancy agreement with rent details or a letter from the landlord proving that the applicant is a tenant shall be submitted, even if the applicant is above 18 years of age and is currently studying in any educational institute, a letter from the institute must be submitted to prove that the applicant is an active student and if the applicant has become poor due to an irrecoverable disease or due to change in the circumstance, a letter shall be submitted to prove that the applicant has such a disease or has become poor due to change in circumstance. It is evident that the number of supporting documents that need to be submitted depends on the applicant's individual circumstance. All family members of the applicant who apply to register as a poor to MoIA's information needs to be reflected in the designated place of the form where the information of them having a bank account is being verified by their bank. Furthermore, the local council of the respective applicant needs to give a statement about the living standard of the applicant in the form as well. This application form needs to be submitted in hardcopy; but due to the pandemic email submissions are also accepted. Every year, the registration of poor and needy will be opened by MoIA.

There is no doubt that since the supply of zakat per year is limited, there should be a fair and transparent mechanism to determine its deserved recipients in the country especially in identifying the poor and needy. However, the question is how rigid or flexible this process should be? For instance, in the case of Maldives as discussed above, is it the most convenient and fair way to register poor and needy for zakat purpose and is there no other obligation on MoIA to post monitor how zakat money impacts the society especially the lives of those who receive the zakat? By looking at this practice, it can be presumed that zakat organizations are worried about giving of zakat to a person who does not deserve it and in the struggle to ensure this, it might be causing hardship to even a genuine poor and needy to apply for zakat. One important hadith that should be continuously reminded to zakat organizations in this regard is that there is no harm in giving zakat to a thief or an adulteress or a rich person as evident from the hadith below narrated by Abu Huraira (R.A.) (Chapter 24, 502 in Bukhari [1966]):

> Allah's Apostle (SAW) said, "A man said that he would give something in charity. He went out with his object of charity and unknowingly gave it to a thief. Next morning the people said that he had given his object of charity to a thief. (On hearing that) he said, O Allah! All the praises are for you. I will give alms again." And so he again went out with his alms and (unknowingly) gave it to an adulteress. Next morning the people said that he had given his alms to an adulteress last night. The man said, "O Allah! All the praises are for you. (I gave my alms) to an adulteress. I will give alms again." So he went out with his alms again and (unknowingly) gave it to a rich person. (The people) next morning said that he had given his alms to a wealthy person. He said, "O Allah! All the praises are for you. (I had given alms) to a thief, to an adulteress and to a wealthy man." Then someone came and said to him, "The alms which you gave to the thief, might make him abstain from stealing, and that given to the adulteress might make her abstain from illegal sexual intercourse (adultery), and that given to the wealthy man might make him take a lesson from it and spend his wealth which Allah has given him, in Allah's cause."

Al Haq et al. (2017) have identified some gaps in zakat distribution in Kedah, Malaysia and these gaps include delay in distribution of zakat and lack of studies conducted on zakat distribution has been highlights as an issue that has led to information gap in this regard to resolve the issues facing zakat organizations in this regard. From the literature review conducted by Al Haq et al. (2017) it was found that there is need to manage zakat effectively to reduce the hardships faced and still the researchers who has conducted research on the effectiveness of zakat is not satisfied with the impact of zakat. They have also suggested that further research can be conducted to find out effective ways in which zakat distribution can be made. Lubis et al. (2011) have also stated that there are issues in the practice of zakat management and due to this a large number of zakat recipients as well as zakat payers are dissatisfied with the services provided by the zakat organizations and it has been said that every year the number of zakat recipients have been increasing but 15% of zakat is not even distributed. These findings were made by the researchers in the context of Malaysia and to have an effective zakat management system they have proposed a Geographical Information System for monitoring of zakat recipients by mapping statistic application and spatial data infrastructure in distribution characteristic analysis (Lubis et al., 2011).

Today, with Industry 4.0, there is no doubt that even sophisticated types of technology can be adopted to enhance the zakat administration system in the world. One of these innovations which is recently recommended is to explore the potential of crypto zakat which is an ethereum platform where blockchain technology is used to facilitate zakat contributions that offers an alternative solution, with decentralized and direct transactions that may assist zakat organizations to receive zakat money and disburse it to the specified recipients efficiently (Muneeza, 2020). It is said that in this proposed platform all stages of zakat will be automated and the owner of this platform could be a registered information technology firm and the service will be provided in affiliation with a regulatory authority or organization that deals with zakat management. The advantages of such a platform includes in real time the zakat payer could directly pay the zakat money to the intended recipients via the platform as the platform allows the zakat administrator to shortlist the deserved zakat recipients and pre-register them with their crucial information in the platform. This enables the zakat payer to directly pay the amount they desire as per the rules set by the zakat administrator directly to the recipient by eliminating the stage where the money they are first kept in the zakat fund before it is disbursed. Therefore, this platform shortens the process of zakat money reaching its recipients and make the procedure transparent and immutable via the use of blockchain technology which is a decentralized, distributed ledger where provenance of a digital asset is recorded. If crypto zakat platform is used, it is said that the resources of the zakat administrator can be channelled in creating awareness and finding the most deserved recipients of zakat. The modus operandi of crypto zakat platform is summarized in Fig. 1.

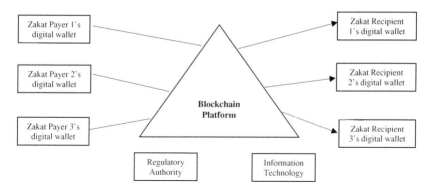

Fig. 1 Modus Operandi of Crypto *Zakat* (*Source* Authors'own)

As shown in Fig. 1, in crypto zakat platform, the regulatory authority which is the zakat administrator will supervise the operation while information technology firm will be directly responsible for the formation and maintenance of the platform. The information technology firm may charge a fee for its service and this is how they may cover the operational cost as well as the maintenance cost of the platform. It is the zakat administrator who will have to verify the poor and needy who are eligible to receive zakat. Once the poor and needy who can receive zakat is confirmed, a digital wallet to receive money will be created for each of them and the individual recipients can access to their accounts created in the platform. The zakat payer will have to register in the platform for the first time and then will have to create a digital wallet. In crypto zakat, the zakat payers directly pay the money to the zakat recipient he/she chooses and the maximum amount that could be transferred by each individual will be determined by the rules set by the zakat administrator. To avoid duplication of payment made to a single recipient in a particular year or a period, the system will show only those who did not receive any assistance in that particular time where the zakat payer is paying zakat. Once all the registered recipients are paid one time, then only the second round of assistance for the same recipient could be made possible. There will be a feature in the platform for the zakat payers to give the power to the system to choose whom to pay zakat to and the system based on its rules will choose the recipients and how much each will receive. This function will be useful for this who would not want to select their own recipients. The zakat administrator will have to find a way in which the money received by the recipients can be withdrawn or to be used while it is in the digital wallet.

Apart from crypto zakat using blockchain technology, there are also other technology linked innovations that is proposed and also used by the zakat administrators. Potential of zakat collection and distribution using zakat digital wallet (Salleh et al., 2019), rice Atms, payments of zakat using crypto currency, using big data and artificial intelligence (Muneeza, 2019; Muneeza & Nadwi, 2020; Obaidullah, 2020) have been explored. However, blockchain technology is the most frequently linked technology with zakat so far that has been explored and as well as implemented (Abojeib, 2020; Adam, 2020; Adinugroho, 2020; Habib, 2020; Obaidullah, 2020). Habib (2020) states that blockchaining zakat which means to have a complete platform with blockchain for zakat administration and introducing zakat decentralized applications (DApps) funders retain agency in the allocation and management of the funds they provide can also be used. However, the detail explanation of how these two types can be used has not been discussed by Habib (2020). Adam (2020) has identified four key areas in zakat which are zakat payment, zakat management, zakat distribution, and reporting and impact measurement of zakat where blockchain technology could be used to enhance it. In this regard, Adam (2020) presented the case study of Binance Charity which is a blockchain charity foundation of which the objective is to achieve sustainable development goals by using blockchain technology (Binance Charity, n.d.). Binance Charity practically shows the efficiency of using blockchain in managing charity in a transparent manner where without an intermediary, the beneficiaries receive funds in cryptocurrency without an intermediary. Obaidullah (2020) states that technology can be used in the context of zakat to identify the zakat payer and the legal recipient and to find out the satisfaction level of the payer as well as to specifically focus or target on legal recipients using blockchain technology as seen in the case of AID:Tech which is the world's first web based platform to deliver international aid to Syrian refugees residing in Lebanon (Ma, 2018). AID Tech with the Irish Red Cross and local development experts, provide individuals and households with a unique identity, in the form of QR code printed smart cards, and deliver aid packages remotely (Ma, 2018). From the innovative ideas proposed by the researchers and practitioners, it is evident that in future, the zakat administrators will start integrating technology more than what is seen now to enhance zakat administration. International Shariah Research Academy for Islamic Finance (ISRA) is developing a blockchain solution for zakat (Abojeib, 2020) and Baznas is developing a blockchain application for zakat management in Indonesia as well (Adinugroho, 2020).

3 Using Technology for Zakat Distribution

Often administrative process of zakat distribution is not explored in academic research from a practical perspective. The shariah parameters and the attributes of the legal recipients of it derived from Quran are discussed. However, there is a gap in understanding in practice how this is done by the zakat administrators. In zakat disbursement, the zakat administrators need to ensure that zakat money if transferred to a bank account, there should be no service charge for it imposed and charged from zakat money as this type of service charges on operational costs are not allowed to be charged from zakat (Furber, 2017). In Table 1 shown are some of the obstacles that could arise from shariah perspective in distributing zakat as identified by Furber (2017).

Zakat distribution is one stage of zakat administration and the focus of this research is on how zakat distribution could be enhanced with technology. There are many hiccups faced in zakat administration and some of these include governance issues such as inability of zakat administrators to have a transparent and convenient process to identify and validate the recipients and to disburse money or in kind zakat to those recipients in a timely manner without the zakat recipients being physically present to collect the zakat. As such, this section of the study focuses on these two hiccups of zakat distribution.

Inability to Identify and Validate the Zakat Recipients in a Transparent and Convenient Manner

As the trustee of zakat funds, it is the role of the zakat administrator to choose the most deserved recipients of zakat. The process of selecting the most deserved recipient could be a tough and complex process for both zakat administrator and the potential recipient as well. This is because, when selecting the recipient, the goal of the zakat administrator would be to choose the most deserved recipient. Therefore, the criteria applied for choosing of each legal recipient of zakat are enacted and adequate processes are put in place to ascertain them in a reasonable

Table 1 Possible Shariah obstacles in *Zakat* distribution

Obstacle	Detail
Transporting *Zakat*	The issue here is whether *zakat* should be distributed locally or can be distributed regionally. There is difference of opinion among different school of thoughts on this issue Shafi & Hanafi School—does not allow *zakat* to be transported from one locale to another Maliki & Hanbali—allows *zakat* to be transported from one locale to another
Giving to Non-Muslims	There is consensus among all scholars that *zakat* recipients shall be Muslims. However, Maliki and Hanbali school of thought allows the *zakat* to be given to a non-Muslims who fall within the legal category of *zakat* recipient mentioned as: "those whose hearts are to be reconciled."
Distributing *Zakat* via an intermediary	In this issue, there is difference of opinion among the scholars Maliki—It is allowed to distribute *zakat* via an agent provided that there is trust in him that he will deliver *zakat* as a trust to its recipients Shafi—It is allowed to appoint a Muslim-agent. If the agent is a non-Muslim then the donor will have to identify the recipient Hanafi—It is allowed to appoint whether a Muslim or a non-Muslim agent and it is not a requirement to identify the recipient even if the agent is a non-Muslim Hanbali—It is allowed only to use Muslim agents who are trustworthy for the purpose
Distribution Across and Within the Categories of *Zakat* Recipients	In this issue also, there is difference of opinion among scholars Hanafi, Maliki, Hanbali—*Zakat* can be given to one single individual Shafi—With the exception of *zakat* workers—*zakat* must be distributed equally to whichever of the categories are present and the *zakat* given to each category must be distributed to at least three of its members; it does not have to be equal, though it is recommended

Source Extracted from Furber (2017, pp. 7–8)

manner. However, the challenge in this regard is to conduct the process of identification and verification of potential zakat recipients in a convenient and timely manner without engaging in too much paper work or by conducting on-site inspections to the level the poor and needy might feel offended or to ensure that the face to face or phone interviews conducted in this process with the poor and needy does not cause humiliation to the potential receivers of zakat. If the registration for poor in the same manner is made every year, then again it might cause hardship to them.

In a research conducted by Ahmad et al. (2015) on satisfaction level of zakat recipients about zakat management, it was revealed that the legal recipients of zakat who belonged to the category of poor and needy were dissatisfied with the service of zakat administrator's approach to register and verify poor. The poor and needy said that waiting time for them is too long as the registration process with interview takes one or two hours and after finishing this process for them to know whether their application to receive zakat is successful, they have to wait another three weeks.

In this regard, it is imperative to consider the psychology of a poor and needy and the procedures set to verify their poverty status should not in any way cause humiliation to them. For example, in this process, they should not be asked unnecessary questions to belittle them. Any poor and needy must be able to go through this process in an honourable manner. Though the written procedures in this regard could be perfect, most of the times whether it is done in the manner written or not will depend on the person who implements it. Therefore, not being able to uniform and control the methods of asking questions to confirm and verify like their voice tone and the way they phrase questions may be the reason why some poor and needy might feel shameful to come forward and declare that they need zakat. To overcome this situation, there is a possibility to use Artificial intelligence (AI) technology to confirm and verify the poor and needy used AI chatbots or robo officers to gather the information required.

Imagine a situation whereby, the poor or needy family whose household head is a single mother and she goes to a zakat administration office to apply for zakat money. If she meets a male zakat officer who has no sympathy and empathy towards poor and interrogate her in a harsh manner, what would be the psychological impact on her in this situation?

Instead if a chatbot or a robo officer can replace the function of this zakat officer, that would provide a win-win situation to both the zakat administrator whose intention to identify and verify the most deserved zakat recipients and needy and poor who are in dire need of zakat money as well.

Obaidullah (2020) states that Machine Learning (ML) is a self-improving algorithm which is a type of AI technology that can be used without being explicitly programmed and this ML technology can be used to determine the amount of zakat one need to pay and can be used for clustering and anomaly detection in the process of zakat administration. He also states that using AI, the human intervention in the process can be eliminated and Natural Language Processing (NLP) could be used to do sentimental analysis from text or speech; to have a fully interactive voice assistance system for zakat advisory or estimation; and also to establish a fully interactive voice assistance systems for the legal recipients of zakat (Obaidullah, 2020). Today, having an AI based zakat chatbot with NLP is not a mere idea. In 2018, BAZNAS, the Indonesian zakat authority has launched a chatbot called "Zaki" which is an NLP based virtual assistant that has the ability to: converse with customers; analyze the questions asked by them; and to provide answers to them (*The Jakarta Post*, 2018). Customers can access to Zaki via LINE messenger application using the username: "@zakibaznas" and in future it would be available via Facebook live chat application too. Since, chatbots have been developed to facilitate the zakat payment purposes, there is no reason why a chatbot can be developed to facilitate the registration of poor and needy to register to receive zakat.

Distribution of Zakat Without the Recipient Being Physically Present in Zakat Administrator's Office

Not all recipients may have a bank account and may live in areas where there are formal financial institutions. Some zakat administrators require the zakat recipients to come physically to their office to collect the zakat money while others reach out to them and distribute it. To overcome this challenge there are certain lessons that could be learnt from the experience of some jurisdictions who has used innovation to overcome this challenge.

The first solution could be introducing zakat card which could be used in zakat rice Automated Teller Machines (ATM) machines which will be installed in areas where the poor and needy can easily access to it. Indonesia and Malaysia have successfully implemented this approach (Muneeza, 2019). Therefore, this could be one approach to ensure that enough food is in a household and for the poor and needy to use the service when they feel the need to so without asking a person for it. Rice ATM could be purchased and installed easily and this machine could be a useful way to disburse zakat to those who are poor and needy. Abidin and Utami (2020) observes that the use of rice ATM machines increase welfare index of zakat. The modus operandi of the rice ATMs is provided in Fig. 2.

The second solution is personal delivery to the zakat recipient. This approach is effective and convenient to the zakat recipient as this way they do not have to spend money on travelling to a specific place to receive the zakat. Furthermore, long queues can be avoided by doing this. Zakat House of Kuwait states in their website that they deliver in kind contribution made as Zakat to its recipients (Zakat House of Kuwait, n.d.).

United Nations High Commissioner for Refugees (UNHCR) has reported it has put in place a system to register refugees where irises of the refugees are scanned and used to disburse money to them from the special ATMs put for them to receive their aids (Furber, 2017). They have stated that the zakat money will to poor and needy refugees will also be disbursed via this iris scan enabled ATM machines specially installed for poor and needy refugees (UNHCR, n.d.). This is also a possible innovation that could be adopted in remote areas to disburse zakat money to needy and poor. The modus operandi of an iris ATM is shown in Fig. 3.

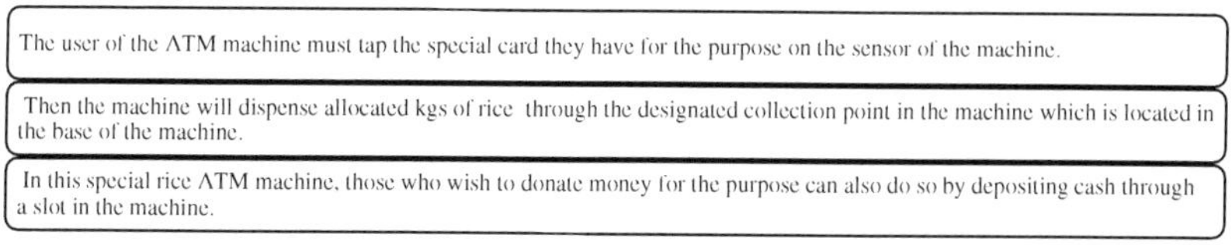

The user of the ATM machine must tap the special card they have for the purpose on the sensor of the machine.
Then the machine will dispense allocated kgs of rice through the designated collection point in the machine which is located in the base of the machine.
In this special rice ATM machine, those who wish to donate money for the purpose can also do so by depositing cash through a slot in the machine.

Fig. 2 Modus Operandi of Rice ATMs (*Source* Muneeza and Nadwi [2020])

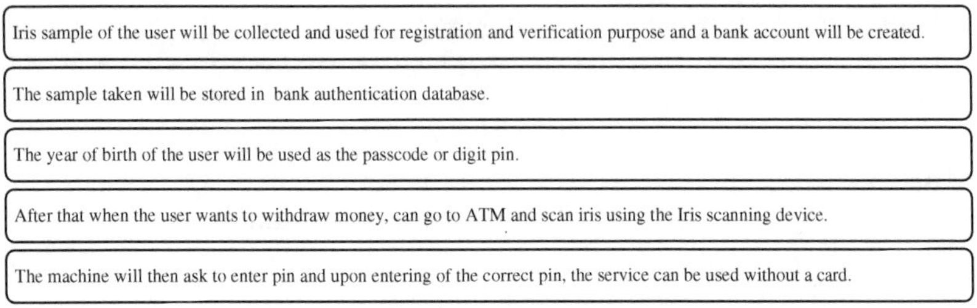

Iris sample of the user will be collected and used for registration and verification purpose and a bank account will be created.
The sample taken will be stored in bank authentication database.
The year of birth of the user will be used as the passcode or digit pin.
After that when the user wants to withdraw money, can go to ATM and scan iris using the Iris scanning device.
The machine will then ask to enter pin and upon entering of the correct pin, the service can be used without a card.

Fig. 3 Modus Operandi of Iris ATM (*Source* Sainis and Saini [2015])

4 Recommendation: Towards a Technology Based Zakat Disbursement System Using Internet of Things (IOT)

This study recommends to be utilized by the zakat administrators a full-fledged 100% technology based zakat distribution system to ensure that zakat recipient's identification and validation process is made in a transparent and a convenient manner and to establish a zakat distribution system without the zakat recipient being physically present in the zakat administrator's office. Through IoT, there is scope to change the existing approach used for zakat disbursement by the zakat administrators in the world.

IoT refers to the billions of physical devices around the world that are now connected to the Internet that can collect and share data. By using an IoT approach for zakat, the zakat administrators will choose a data driven approach and it will enable zakat payers to pay directly to the recipients without having an intermediary. What will be required is the gadget and the Internet connection to enable this process. Therefore, financial resources of zakat administrators shall be focused to ensuring this in remote or poor areas where some intervention to provide the gadget and Internet is required. How IOT works is sensors and intelligence will be added to the objects used and this will enable to collect data without the intervention of humans.

So far there is no study conducted to find out the potential of IoT in relation to zakat distribution. However, in relation to charity distribution, the role of IoT has been explored which could be relevant to understand to enhance the zakat distribution. Some of the limitations in the existing way in which donations are managed is cited by Alshammari et al. (2017) using the example of Makkah Charity Organisation (MCO) where it is stated that what MCO does is that it helps poor and needy by collecting donations at their office on a specific time allocated for that or by bank transfer. To help the poor and needy they customized several programs to provide assistance and the limitations they have in the existing way of management is that they can only display the projects and their bank account details in their website; donators will have to visit physically to their office to make donation in kind; there is no communication between the donors and MCO; the poor and needy is unable to register on their own to receive donation in an easy and convenient way; the registered poor and needy cannot update their location if there location changes; and the poor and needy cannot set their priorities of needs as they have to accept what is available or given. Alshammari et al. (2017) have discussed the ways in which these issues faced by MCO and other charity organizations could be resolved by IoT using a system called Smart Charity (SC) system where it is stated that a smart charity box could be made with sensors and Internet collecting its information to ensure that without physically monitoring the charity box placed in different parts of the country, using IoT, the charity organizations would be enabled to have information about the status of each of these donation box as to whether they are full or reached certain level as expected by the charity organizations so that they could take actions accordingly. The smart charity box allows donations to be made without being physically present to a particular office and when the poor and needy register, the employees of the charity organization could deliver the required donations to them by just locating them using map page using GPS based on the information used for the registration. Figure 4 describes the way in which smart charity works.

As shown in Fig. 4, the device used in this system is a smart charity donation box device. The first step to start it would be to Arduino Uno will start the connection with the charity organization website server and check the status of the box if it is full or reached its target will be checked using the sensors and will be notified accordingly to the charity organization. Arduino Uno is an open-source microcontroller board based on the Microchip ATmega328P microcontroller and developed by Arduino.cc and the board is equipped with sets of digital and analog input/output pins that may be interfaced to various expansion boards and other circuits. Infrared IR Sensor is used to determine the status of

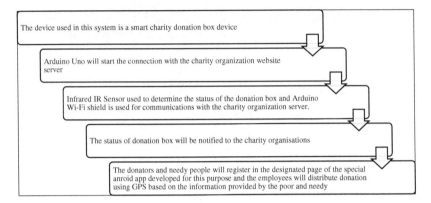

Fig. 4 How smart charity operates (*Source* Developed from Alshammari et al. [2017])

the donation box and Arduino Wi-Fi shield is used for communications with the charity organization server. If the low-level sensor is cut and the high level are cut also that means the donation box is full, in this case, the system will update the status of the donation box to full. Otherwise, if only the low level sensor is cut the donation box status will update it half full and connection with the server close. The donators and needy people will register in the designated page of the special android app developed for this purpose and upon successful registration, they will be notified accordingly. The employees of the charity organization can collect this information and then using GPS find out the location of the poor and needy and can deliver the donation accordingly without poor and needy physically coming to them.

In the context of zakat, to enhance zakat distribution using IoT, there could be various advantages that could be enjoyed. Among these include: measuring poverty level of the household without physical inspection; understanding the financial condition of the household and the essential things lacking in the household without conducting surveys; locating the poor and needy physically; having the ability to deliver the zakat to them without their physical sense; and continuous monitoring of the status of poor and needy without cumbersome paper work and submission of documents. With technological advancements that is seen today, all of these things could happen without the physical involvement of humans and what is required is innovate such ways using the available technology. Therefore, this study recommends as an innovative solution to employ IoT to enhance zakat distribution to resolve the existing hiccups in zakat distribution to poor and needy which is common and general to all zakat organizations.

Using IoT it is possible to determine the human behaviour (Saralegui et al., 2017) and mental stress level of human (Can et al., 2019). Therefore, without physically asking questions or surveying the situation of a poor and needy by on-site presence, using IoT, the poverty level of a person or his/her household can be determined. A device that could be used for this purpose could be smart phones or smart watches (Can et al., 2019). However, in collecting such kind of information using IoT, it is a must to obtain consent from the zakat recipients to monitor their stress level or behaviour. If not, ethical issues will arise from such information gathering by zakat organizations. Once the stress level of a zakat eligible household or a person from the household is within the acceptable level to receive zakat determined by the zakat organization upon first time registration as a poor or a needy, the continuous monitoring of the household could be made using IoT via smart phone used by the person or by using the smartwatch given to him by the zakat organization. In this regard, there is an investment required by the zakat organizations to obtain such customized smart watches and to give them to the first time registered poor and needy. In the subsequent year, zakat organization can distribute the zakat to the same registered poor and needy based on the result of their stress level measured. Using their actual location received from the smart device using GPS map service, zakat organizations can physically locate them and distribute the zakat directly to the person without an intermediary. The modus operandi of this is illustrated in Fig. 5.

In delivering zakat, the most classical way would be for the employees of zakat organization to do the physical delivery. For remote areas where there are no shops or banks/financial institutions nearby, this could be the only option available. Without physical delivery, the zakat organization could issue a QR Code (a type of matrix barcode first designed in 1994 for the automotive industry in Japan) via the smart device to the recipient. Then, the zakat recipient could present the QR Code to the nearest shop or a designated vendor near to his location and withdraw money or buy things using it.

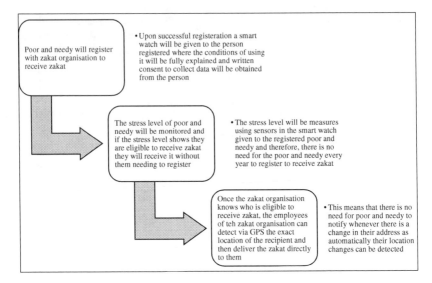

Fig. 5 Application of IoT to enhance *Zakat* distribution for poor and needy (*Source* Author's own)

The proposed approach of zakat distribution by adopting IoT will be a swift and a convenient way for both zakat organizations and the recipients of zakat. However, in collecting personal data of the recipients and using that information, the zakat organizations should strictly adhere to the personal data protection laws and the information obtained should not be misused in any way. Furthermore, in information fetching process, the personal space and privacy of the zakat recipient shall not be infringed. To ensure this, the countries using IoT should enact a legal framework to set the parameters of its use and if such framework is not available in a jurisdiction in which the zakat organization adopts it, then internationally available best practice in this regard needs to be followed.

Abidin and Utami (2020) state the significance of regulating zakat digital technology to provide benefit to the society and also to avoid any possible ethical issues that may arise from the use of such technology. In regulating zakat digital technology, it is imperative to have a proper legal framework that not only deal with the ethical issues in using of technology; but the shariah parameters to use technology that aligns with the objectives of Shariah must be formulated too. This way, maslahah (interest) of all stakeholders will be protected.

5 Conclusion

There is no doubt that technology can be linked with zakat to enhance its administration. There are various types of technology that could be used in an innovative way in this regard. It is evident from the foregoing discussion that numerous researches have been conducted to enhance zakat administration using technology. However, there is a gap in research focusing on enhancing zakat distribution as most of the available research focus on the function of zakat collection. As such, in this study, ways in which zakat distribution can be enhanced using technology is discussed. It is found that using IoT, zakat distribution can be enhanced by ensuring that by having a single registration with the zakat administrator, the poor and needy can be subsequently monitored to determine whether they are eligible to receive zakat or not. Furthermore, since the location of the recipient can be traced in real time in a convenient manner either via physical delivery of zakat or using QR code approach, the zakat administrator can distribute zakat in an effective and timely manner. However, in collecting data required for the purpose, it is important to obtain consent of the recipients and it would be prudent to have a legal and regulatory framework put in place to regulate the technology use specifically for zakat administration purpose. It is anticipated that the findings of this research will motivate the zakat administrators to link zakat administration especially the zakat distribution part with technology. In this regard, there is need to conduct further research on the technical aspect of implementing IoT based zakat system.

References

Abd Hamid, N., Othman, R. D., Arshad, R., Sanusi, S., & Rashid, N. (2020). A comparison of wakalah zakah monitoring by Lembaga Zakat Selangor (LZS) and Pusat Zakat Melaka (PZM). *Journal of Critical Reviews*, 7(11), 318–325.

Abd Rahman, A., Asrarhaghighi, E., & Ab Rahman, S. (2015). Consumers and Halal cosmetic products: Knowledge, religiosity, attitude and intention. *Journal of Islamic Marketing*, 6(1), 148–163.

Abidin, A., & Utami, P. (2020). The regulation of zakat digital technology in creating community welfare impact on economic development. *Journal of Legal, Ethical and Regulatory Issues*, 23(5), 1544-0044-23-5-543.

Abojeib, M. (2020). *Blockchain technology for Zakat institutions*. Presentation at 4th International Conference on Zakat. https://www.puskasbaznas.com/publications/video/blockchaintechnology-for-zakat-institutions-theory-practices-dr-moutaz-abojeib

Adam, F. (2020). *Blockchain technology for Zakat institutions*. Presentation at 4th International Conference on Zakat. https://www.puskasbaznas.com/publications/video/plenary-session-speaker-mufti-faraz-adam

Adinugroho, A. S. (2020). *Implementation of blockchain technology in BAZNAS: Concept and practices*. Presentation at 4th International Conference on Zakat. https://www.puskasbaznas.com/publications/video/implementation-of-blockchain-technology-in-baznas-achmad-setio-adinugroho

Ahmad, R. A. R., Othman, A. M. A., & Salleh, M. S. (2015). Assessing the satisfaction level of zakat recipients towards zakat management. *Procedia Economics and Finance, 31*, 140–151.

Al Haq, M. A., & Abd Wahab, N. (2017). Effective Zakat distribution: Highlighting few issues and gaps in Kedah, Malaysia. *Al-Iqtishad: Journal of Islamic Economics, 9*(2), 259–288.

Alshammari, M. O., Almulhem, A. A., & Zaman, N. (2017). Internet of Things (IOT): Charity automation. *International Journal of Advanced Computer Science and Applications, 8*(2), 166–170.

Anis, F. M., & Kassim, S. H. (2016). Effectiveness of zakat-based programs on poverty alleviation and economic empowerment of poor women: A case study of Bangladesh. *Journal of Islamic Monetary Economics and Finance, 1*(2), 229–258.

Binance Charity. (n.d.). *About Us*. https://www.binance.charity/about

Bukhari, M. I. (1966). *Sahih Bukhari*. Muhammad Sarid.

Can, Y. S., Chalabianloo, N., Ekiz, D., & Ersoy, C. (2019). Continuous stress detection using wearable sensors in real life: Algorithmic programming contest case study. *Sensors, 19*(8), 1849. https://doi.org/10.3390/s19081849

Furber, M. (2017). *UNHCR zakat collection and distribution*. https://reliefweb.int/sites/reliefweb.int/files/resources/TR-1-UNHCR-Zakat-Collection-And-Distribution-English.pdf

Habib, F. (2020). *Zakat on Blockchain*. Presentation at 4th International Conference on Zakat. https://www.puskasbaznas.com/publications/video/zakat-on-blockchain-speaker-dr-farrukh-habib

Lubis, M., Yaacob, N. I., Omar, I., & Dahlan, A. A. (2011). Enhancement of Zakah distribution management system: Case study in Malaysia. In *International Management Conference 2011 Proceedings*. University Sultan Zainal Abidin. http://irep.iium.edu.my/4261/1/IMAC2011_EnhancementZakatDistribution.pdf

Ma, G. (2018). *Blockchain based digital identity by AID:Tech*. United Nations. https://ideas.unite.un.org/blockchain4humanity/Page/ViewIdea?ideaid=399

Ministry of Islamic Affairs. (2020). *Application form for Zakat by poor and needy*. https://www.gov.mv/en/files/fageerunge-form-2020-final-1441.pdf

Muneeza, A. (2017). Administration of Zakat on wealth in Maldives. *International Journal of Management and Applied Research, 4*(1), 58–71.

Muneeza, A. (2018). Enhancing the Zakat framework of Maldives: A one hundred percent Muslim country. *International Journal of Zakat, 3*(3), 1–12.

Muneeza, A. (2019). Rice ATMs: Technology based innovations for enhancement of zakat. *Islamic Finance Hub, 2,* 8–15.

Muneeza, A. (2020). *The potential of crypto Zakat.* Presentation at 4th International Conference on Zakat. https://www.puskasbaznas.com/publications/video/the-potential-of-crypto-zakat-speaker-assoc-prof-aishathmuneeza

Muneeza, A., & Nadwi, S. (2020). The potential of application of technology-based innovations for Zakat administration in India. *International Journal of Zakat, 4*(2), 87–100.

Nadzri, F. A. A., Abd Rahman, R., & Omar, N. (2012). Zakah and poverty alleviation: Roles of Zakah institutions in Malaysia. *International Journal of Arts and Commerce, 1*(7), 61–72.

Obaidullah, M. (2020). *Use of technology in zakat management.* Presentation at 4th International Conference on Zakat. https://www.youtube.com/watch?v=Ku9skvKyLaQ

Sabahuddin. (2014). *Analytical study of challenges of zakat distribution in India.* Research Paper Submitted for Master of Science in Islamic banking and finance, International Islamic University Malaysia.

Sainis, N., & Saini, R. (2015). Biometrics: Cardless secured architecture for authentication in ATM using IRIS Technology. *International Journal of Innovative Research in Computer and Communication Engineering, 3*(6), 5423–5428.

Salleh, W. N. A. W. M., Abdul Rasid, S. Z., & Basiruddin, R. (2019). Towards transforming Zakat collection and distribution roles using digital wallet in support of social justice and social financing. *Open International Journal of Informatics (OIJI), 7*(2), 95–103.

Saralegui, U., Anton, M. A., & Ordieres-Meré, A. (2017). An IoT based system that aids learning from human behavior: A potential application for the care of the elderly. MATEC Web of Conferences 125, 05010. https://www.matec-conferences.org/articles/matecconf/pdf/2017/39/matecconf_cscc2017_05010.pdf

The Jakarta Post. (2018). BAZNAS launches zakat virtual payment assistance for alms donors. https://www.thejakartapost.com/adv/2018/05/28/baznas-launches-zakat-virtual-payment-assistant-for-alms-donors.html

United Nations High Commissioner for Refugees (UNHCR). (n.d.). *Dedicate your zakat.* https://zakat.unhcr.org/en

Zakat House of Kuwait. (n.d.). *Local Charity Projects.* https://www.zakathouse.org.kw/zakathouse_Detaileng.aspx?id=661&codeid=3

Notion of Value-Added in RegTech Research Work: What Is There for Islamic Finance?

Muslehuddin Musab Mohammed

1 Introduction

The global RegTech market was worth USD 2.87 billion in 2018. Similarly, RegTech is expected to have a market value of USD 6.5 billion by 2020. The global RegTech market is expected to be worth USD 55.28 billion by 2025, growing at a 52.8% CAGR (Grand View Research, 2019). While reviewing the papers, we are interested in understanding the precise notion of RegTech in the context of the financial sector. We are also interested in knowing the necessity of adopting RegTech and its benefits to different stakeholders of the economy. It would be more interesting to know about the technologies supporting RegTech, and the relationship between RegTech and FinTech. Eventually, we will try to identify the opportunities for Islamic finance

M. M. Mohammed (✉)
College of Islamic Studies, Hamad Bin Khalifa University, Doha, Qatar
e-mail: momohammed@hbku.edu.qa

in RegTech. To move forward, we will try to solve the following primary questions of the literature review:

1. What is RegTech in finance or financial RegTech?
2. What are the supporting technologies for financial RegTech?
3. What is the value in financial RegTech?
4. What are the existing structures of financial RegTech?
5. What are the opportunities for Islamic finance in RegTech?

2 Financial RegTech

During an extensive literature review by three university professors in Germany, it was found that the term 'regulatory affair' is not only used in the financial industry but also in the biomedical and pharmaceutical industries, for example, frequently use the term in combination with drug testing as it was evident in the 422 results of Web of Science were exclusively addressing biomedical topics. Whereas FinTech, which is inherently financial in nature, RegTech has the potential to be utilized in a wide range of regulatory applications. Further possibilities include monitoring firms' compliance with environmental standards and tracking the location of airliners in real time, which portrays the potential of RegTech, which may be utilized to better regulation and the regulated industry itself (Arner et al., 2018) (Fig. 1).

In general, RegTech refers to "technological solutions that streamline and improve the regulatory process" (Arner et al., 2018). The term RegTech is further described as "the use of technology, particularly IT, in the context of regulatory monitoring, reporting, and compliance"

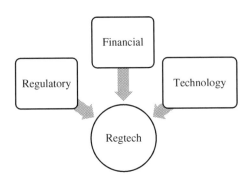

Fig. 1 Three main coverages of RegTech (*Source* Author's own)

(Becker et al., 2020). The Institute of International Finance defines RegTech "as the use of new technologies to solve regulatory and compliance requirements more effectively and efficiently" (Becker et al., 2020). The World Bank Group (2020) defines World Bank as "Regulatory technology (RegTech) a term used for the application of technology in managing regulatory processes within the financial industry."

In the context of the financial industry, IFSB defines RegTech "as the use of technology by financial institutions to enhance compliance with prudential regulations, while SupTech is the use of technology by regulatory and supervisory authorities to enforce prudential regulations" (IFSB, 2020). Thus, we can infer that the reference to RegTech in the financial industry shall cover the three aspects of regulatory, financial, and technology; otherwise, in the case of missing any aspect, the term would be relevant to any other industry, but not to the financial industry.

3 Relavance of Web 3.0 to RegTech

It is apparent from Fig. 1 that the technology is one of the core elements of RegTech, therefore understanding the direction in which technology is advancing would be equally important for capturing the sense of value-added in the RegTech. The evolution of web represents a big paradigm shift and Web 3.0 is the next phase of the evolution of the web/internet which is built upon the core concepts of decentralization, openness, and greater user utility. Berners-Lee expounded upon some of these key concepts back in the 1990s, as outlined below:

- Decentralization: "No permission is needed from a central authority to post anything on the web, there is no central controlling node, and so no single point of failure…and no 'kill switch'! This also implies freedom from indiscriminate censorship and surveillance."
- Bottom-up Design: "Instead of code being written and controlled by a small group of experts, it was developed in full view of everyone, encouraging maximum participation and experimentation."

The major contribution of Berners-Lee was the discussion on the concept of what he referred to as the Sematic Web. Computers have no reliable way to process the semantics of language, i.e., figure out the actual context in which a word or phrase is used. According to Kuck (2004), Berners-Lee's vision for the Semantic Web was to bring structure to the meaningful content of web pages and enable software that would carry out sophisticated tasks for users. However, within the limitations of Web 2.0, it was very expensive and monumentally difficult to convert human language—with all its subtle nuances and variations—into a format that can be readily understood by computers. Now, Web 2.0 has already evolved substantially over the past two decades and Web 3.0 has moved well beyond the original concept of the Semantic Web as conceptualized by Berners-Lee in 2001.

In Fig. 2, the comparison between the three versions of web highlights the essential enhancements in the web services that entailed ease to the individuals and the economy (Sachs, 2021). **Web 1.0** During the early days or mid-90s, recall the AOL account, the individuals had an ability to look in a curated walled garden at a set of content that was not interactive but was presented the READ only content on AOL. **Web 2.0** enabled to write and edit the content in addition to the read only content and the blogosphere became a big thing. People remember this from the early 2000. Interesting to note that the feature of centralization of the internet allowed a small number of companies like Facebook, Google, Amazon, and Apple to monetise the usage of web services.

However, the advent of **Web 3.0** shifted the organizational structure from central to decentral which also brought the opportunity for owning the network through DAOs which has unleashed the world of possibilities for establishing the financial entities independent of incumbent authorities (JP Morgan, 2022). For example, owning the crypto assets represent ownership stake in the underlying network whereby, so called, layer-1 tokens are earned by the validating node as reward for providing the ledger maintenance services required by the ledger running on Distributed Ledger Technology (DLT), such ledger maintenance services to the network running on web 1.0 and 2.0 have been provided by Google or any other centralized cloud storage service provider.

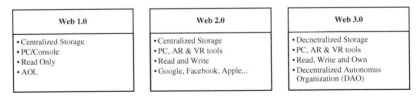

Fig. 2 Comparison between Web 1.0, 2.0 and 3.0 (*Source* Author's Own)

Table 1 Salient features of Web 3.0

Feature	Detail
Decentralization	The organization structure is decentralized and generally governed through DAO by the users owning native tokens. Decisions are based on users' consensus
Peer to Peer Networks	Networks allow the participants to interact directly without a trusted intermediary. Web 3.0 applications run on blockchains like Ethereum without a governing body
Artificial Intelligence (AI) and Machine Learning (ML)	Web 3.0 enable computers to deploy AI and ML and perform the acts of human intelligence through Semantic Web concepts and natural language processing techniques
Connectivity and Ubiquity	Web 3.0 make information and content more connected and ubiquitous, accessed by multiple applications and with an increasing number of everyday devices connected to the web an example being the Internet of things

Source Author's Own

Thus, web 3.0 (Table 1) required the regulators to reconsider the entire ecosystem of finance and economy for ensuring the entire roles of the regulator ranging from stability of economy to client protection, to integrity of the market (Table 1).

4 Technologies Supporting Financial Regtech

The review of the literature proved that there is a perfect integration between FinTech and RegTech in deploying the technologies. Table 2 is based on an extensive study from existing available resources (Das, 2019; Podder et al., 2018; Rabbani et al., 2020) done in both the fields of FinTech and RegTech. Across all the papers, the listed below technologies were consistently referred to and discussed in both FinTech and RegTech related papers. Thus, we conclude that the ecosystems of both the FinTech and RegTech are mostly served by the same technologies.

The empirical evidence in the papers and the latest news confirms that FinTech penetration is increasing and promising, therefore, RegTech is

Table 2 Consistent terminologies used in FinTech and RegTech related papers

RegTech	FinTech					
Regulator and or users	Payments & transfers	Lending & financing	Retail banking	Financial management	Insurance	Markets & exchanges
API	Y	Y	Y	Y	Y	Y
Big Data Analysis	Y	Y	Y	Y	Y	Y
Automation	Y	Y	Y	Y	Y	Y
AI	Y	Y	Y	Y	Y	Y
Biometrics	Y	Y	Y	Y	Y	Y
Cryptography	Y	Y	Y	Y	Y	Y
DLT	Y	Y	Y	Y	Y	Y
Smart-Contract	Y	Y	Y	Y	Y	Y

Source Author's own

anticipated to flourish more in the future. Before moving to the question of "what are the opportunities available for Islamic finance in RegTech" let us consider the areas of interest in research and practice.

In an exhaustive review of 10 data bases consisting of high impact journals, the researchers selected 55 research articles produced until December 2019 and 347 RegTech companies. Looking at the mismatch between the coverage of research literature and services offered by RegTech related firms, the researchers found that RegTech is still a very young field and the technological topics addressed until the date of research are limited (Becker et al., 2020). Researchers agree that banks and other FIs are searching for cost efficient and innovative technical solutions because of the overwhelming and constantly changing higher degrees of complex regulation across the world (Becker et al., 2020). The researchers found that compliance management is the most prominent field with 40.60% of RegTech in practice. Compliance management was followed by identity management and control, risk management, regulatory reporting, and transaction monitoring with 23.9, 13.8, 13.5, and 8.1% of RegTech firms, respectively. It is also determined that there were no RegTech firms in the practical filed for fraud detection and financial regulation until the end of 2020.

However, compared to the practical application of RegTech firms, the available scientific literature varies. The most prominent fields found in the literature on RegTech were related to risk management with 21.8%, followed by regulatory reporting and compliance management with 17.9% for both fields. Financial regulation accounted for 16.7% of the literature research, while transaction monitoring accounted for 12.8%, identity control and management accounted for 9%, and fraud detection accounted for 3.8%. The presence of these fields in practice and in the literature shows a broad future ahead, showing the significance of RegTech.

5 Emergence of RegTech and Current Status

The emergence of RegTech happened far later than the emergence of FinTech. RegTech emerged in the middle of the twentieth century, while FinTech's emergence can be traced back to the late-nineteenth century. The RegTech emergence was in the context of the rapid growth of companies, they were in the stage of 'too-big to-fail' after surpassing two important stages known as 'too-small to-care' and 'too-large to-ignore.' The companies and their enormous size in the context of non-regulated FinTech posed the pertinent question of when the regulators should begin to focus on certain industry participants (Arner et al., 2018; Janos et al., 2019). The answer lies in why the evolution of FinTech requires similar development in RegTech. A brief review of the evolution of RegTech would provide clearer and better answers to those questions.

RegTech 1.0 (1967—2008)

This period witnessed growth in terms of scale and scope of financial institutions markets due to mergers and acquisitions, giving rise to global conglomerates such as Travelers Group and Citigroup. Since globalization entailed operational and regulatory challenges, demanding a shift from risk management facilitation until the 1980s to financial engineering and value at risk (VaR) systems to sync with developing IT systems (Janos et al., 2019). By the beginning of the twenty-first century, the quantitative IT framework helped regulators to introduce the Basel II Capital Accord on internal quantitative risk management systems, in addition to regulations for monitoring public securities to detect unusual behavior such as insider trading. The reliance was on ex-post reporting systems, which had several limitations as exposed in the Global Financial Crisis (GFC) (Fig. 3).

Fig. 3 Evolution RegTech (*Source* Author's own based on the references in below text)

RegTech 2.0 (2008—2018)

The version was emerged in response to post-GFC regulatory requirements. Complex regulation has increased compliance costs substantially, while regulatory fines and settlements have increased 45-fold. This version of RegTech was well equipped with efficient data management and market supervision. Artificial Intelligence (AI) and deep learning, and other advancements have paved the way for the digitization and datafication of regulatory compliance and other regulatory processes. The use of big data approaches, the enhancement of cybersecurity, and the facilitation of macroprudential policy are some of the ways in which this version advances RegTech (Janos et al., 2019).

RegTech 3.0 (2018 Onwards)

After reviewing the setbacks of RegTech 2.0, it was resolved that the regulators must take a coordinated approach to financial regulation harmonization and encourage the further development of RegTech. The increased data centricity that was underlying the evolution of both FinTech and RegTech is just the beginning of a major paradigm shift from know your customer (KYC) to know your data (KYD). Sandboxes and virtual environments are used to test and study the effects of innovative processes and technologies in a controlled environment. The Financial Conduct Authority (FCA) of the United Kingdom has pioneered progress in this field (Arner et al., 2018; Janos et al., 2019).

Islamic finance admired the idea of adopting technology based supervision through RegTech and SupTech because they help improve the transparency, uniformity, and standardization of regulatory processes in a way that encourages appropriate interpretation of regulatory requirements at a lower cost and ensures risk-based supervision as asserted in several reports issued by the Islamic bank regulators (IFSB, 2020). Moreover, the implementation of such a solution for regulatory purposes could play a vital role in harmonizing Islamic finance practices across the world.

For the top 50 economies, which account for approximately 92% of global GDP, there is a clear positive link between perceptions of regulatory quality and GDP per capita. A lack of a supportive regulatory environment, on the other hand, restricts an economy's potential to attract investments and economic developments (Podder et al., 2018). In 2015, the Australian Securities and Investments Commission established an innovation hub, and the UK Government mandated that regulators support RegTech (Podder et al., 2018).

The National Bank of Rwanda (NBR) utilizes an electronic data warehouse system to automate and streamline reporting operations, making market monitoring easier and providing insights to help the country improve financial inclusion. However, looking at the mismatch between the coverage of research literature and services offered by RegTech related firms, the researchers found that RegTech is still a very young field and the technological topics addressed until the date of research are limited (Arner et al., 2018; Becker et al., 2020).

6   What Is the Value in Financial RegTech?

Following the Global Financial Crisis in 2008, a steady increase in regulatory change has been observed, and then a doubling of regulatory alerts per day from 2012 through 2015 has been evident. Many analysts predict these trends are yet to peak (Jason et al., 2019). Ex-post audits and analyses have traditionally been used by regulators to avoid future misconduct and manage systemic concerns. To overcome this, RegTech compliance, on the other hand, can be incorporated into the system (Kálmán, 2018; Podder et al., 2018). Moreover, RegTech serves the interests of many stakeholders in the industry, and broadly, they can be identified as follows.

- **The value recognized by the economies**:
  For the top 50 economies, which account for nearly 92% of global GDP, there is a clear positive link between assessments of regulatory quality and GDP per capita. A lack of a supportive regulatory

environment, on the other hand, restricts an economy's potential to attract investments and development (Podder et al., 2018).

- **The value for regulators**:
Regulators are increasingly striving to digitally change their operations in order to minimize compliance costs and operate as drivers for innovation and business growth. Regulators' primary motivations for adopting RegTech include a desire for enhanced confidence and security in digital services, as well as the benefits that result, most notably in terms of new business opportunities and increased efficiencies (Podder et al., 2018).
- **The value for Islamic finance**:
The Islamic finance aims to improve the transparency, consistency, and needs uniformity in the interpretation of regulatory requirements at a lower cost. While the RegTech has the potential to ascertain all the foregoing aims (IFSB, 2020), additionally it may also provide opportunity for a risk-based supervision for Islamic bank regulators to cover the mismatch between the Islamic finance entities and the corresponding conventional counterparts.

In addition to the above listed stakeholders' interests and the demand arising for RegTech therein, it also assists in the alignment of corporate objectives with values and risks. Furthermore, RegTech assists businesses in achieving their set goals while eliminating the risks associated with business processes. So, when regulations are developing very fast and imposing a lot of pressure on practitioners in the field of finance, it would be a great idea to adopt RegTech, which reduces the cost and helps in monitoring the new regulations in real time and assisting in adopting them in a better manner.

7 The Existing Regulatory Structures

The literature review revealed that, to date, there are two broad types of regulatory structures in practice. The 'Rule Based' regulatory system where the businesses are required to follow a set of detailed rules, in a backwards-looking manner, the regulatory compliance reporting is done via 'tick in the box' format. Although the rule based regulatory system provides a good level of transparency; it attracts high compliance cost, and innovation is depressed, and excessive litigation has happened (Becker et al., 2020; Kálmán, 2018; Podder et al., 2018) (Table 3).

Table 3 Functions of two broad types of regulatory structures in practice

Rule based	Principles based
Set of detailed rules	Standards for desired outcomes: Consequences matter
Tick in the box	Dialogue with regulators
Transparency	Scalability with business
High compliance costs	Flexibility and freedom
Innovation depresses	Enforcement and implementation challenges
Excessive litigation	Uncertainty and Unpredictability

Source Authors own; Courtesy (Podder et al., 2018)

On contrary, the 'Principles Based' regulatory system has standards for desired outcomes approach in which consequences matter a lot. It is based on dialogue with regulators rather than the 'tick in the box' format. It synchronizes with the business in terms of scalability and provides a significant level of flexibility and freedom. However, the practical experience shows the principle based regulatory system has challenges in enforcement and implementation. The biggest problem is that there is no standard implementation due to which uncertainty and unpredictability prevail, moreover there is a call to shift the RegTech model from a rule based or principle-based model to an insight-based model, as highlighted by the world government summit in 2018 (Becker et al., 2020; Kálmán, 2018; Podder et al., 2018). In the recent research works on the RegTech, the researchers highlighted the potential for introducing activity-based regulatory structure and entity-based regulatory structures. We see that the best practice shall be flexible to adopt any of the given options based on the level of the maturity of the financial industry and the possibility of adoptability.

8 Opportunities for Islamic Finance in RegTech

Ex-post audits and analyses have traditionally been used by regulators to avoid future misconduct and manage systemic concerns. RegTech, on the other hand, can be used to integrate compliance into the system (Kálmán, 2018; Podder et al., 2018). Regulators are increasingly striving to digitally change their operations to minimize the cost of compliance and become drivers for innovation and corporate growth. The desire for enhanced trust and security in digital services is one of the main reasons regulators embrace RegTech (Podder et al., 2018). As such, regulators of Islamic finance industry can take advantage of the opportunities that arise notably in terms of new business opportunities and enhanced efficiencies in their operation.

One of the functions of RegTech is to enable compliance which is equally required for Shariah compliance. A survey-based study by Hasan Baber in 2019 to ascertain the influence of FinTech applications and crowdfunding on customer retention in Islamic banks in Malaysia and the UAE revealed that FinTech has no relevance to customer retention. However, other variables such as payments, advisory services, compliance, and crowdfunding have an impact on retaining customers in Islamic banks in these two countries (Baber, 2020). Thus, RegTech is directly relevant to the above-mentioned functions in the Islamic finance industry.

In Islamic finance, RegTech and SupTech are focused on improving the openness, uniformity, and standardization of regulatory processes to promote the appropriate interpretation of regulatory requirements at a reduced cost and assure risk-based supervision for Islamic bank regulators (Yateem, 2019). Moreover, RegTech, in its capacity as a tool for regulators, could help harmonize the practice of Islamic finance through placing the requirement of standardized practice across the jurisdictions and assist the Shariah boards. According to Baan (2020), in addition to risk management, regulatory reporting, and other self-regulated ecosystems, RegTech has great potential to provide a solution for Shariah compliance of IFIs with real-time monitoring and tracking of the Shariah compliance status and a mechanism to update on any new regulations for Islamic banks through online platforms (Baan, 2020). A model for managing Shariah compliance using RegTech can be seen in the Malaysian Islamic financial industry.

By considering the use case of Operational Risk Integrated Online Network (ORION), a model for managing Shariah compliance using RegTech in Islamic finance industry can be identified. Looking at the Malaysian Islamic finance market, the ORION is a significant RegTech that facilitates reporting any Shariah non-compliance event, including reporting other operational risk exposures of the IFIs through the online network (ORION, 2021). In the event of detecting any potential non-shariah compliance event by the Qualified Shariah Officer (QSO), the event shall immediately be reported to ORION within one working day and presented to the Shariah committee of the IFI. Then the potential Shariah non-compliance event will be confirmed by the Shariah Committee and shall be reported on the decision to ORION. If the event is confirmed to be an actual Shariah non-compliance event, then the IFI is also obliged to submit a rectification plan approved by the Board of Directors and Shariah Committee within 30 days from the detection of the event (Omar & Hassan, 2019). This RegTech, through the online network system, helps IFIs comply with Shariah principles in a more effective manner where regulators can address such risks promptly and effortlessly.

Furthermore, primary research conducted by (Turki et al.) in 2020, investigating the impact of RegTech on the prevention of money laundering for Islamic banks and conventional banks in Bahrain, revealed that RegTech effectively drives the prevention of money laundering to a highly statistically significant level (Turki et al., 2020). Therefore, it is very clear that RegTech has the potential to address several needs of the IF industry, especially for regulators in updating their services, operations, and approaches in dealing with industry stakeholders. Eventually, RegTech could also be a better solution for either harmonizing or setting off the conflict of opinions among the Shariah scholars at various Shariah supervisory boards. Although diverse regulators' approaches toward Islamic finance across different jurisdictions are imposing a challenge, RegTech through automation can help improve the situation.

9 RegTech Sandbox

The regulatory sandbox enables the regulatory authority to create a special legal environment—ex ante the real legal regulation—for the FinTech firms to test, along with the protection of the users. The regulatory authorities receive the competence to build on the regulatory sandbox and step up to the next stage of so-called smart regulation, and they have the competence to reshape the regulation with the balance of public interest and financial innovation and to give the competence to issue restricted or full licenses, as provided by the law (Kálmán, 2018). Therefore, in the context of ever-growing FinTech penetration, RegTech should also be applied prior to the launch of any innovative FinTech solution in order to ascertain the safety and security of the users. With this process, the efficiency of RegTech will also be proven.

The consideration and usage of RegTech by the Islamic financial players in the market also creates evidence of demand for the RegTech sandbox. The Shariah supervisory practitioner in Bahrain denoted that "as RegTech and SupTech in Islamic finance are aimed at enhancing the transparency, consistency and standardization of regulatory processes in a way that promotes proper interpretation of regulatory standards at a lower cost and ensures risk-based supervision for Islamic banks' regulators" (Yateem, 2019). Similarly, IFSB also asserts that "RegTech is the use of technology by financial institutions to enhance compliance with prudential regulations, while SupTech is the use of technology by regulatory and supervisory authorities to enforce prudential regulation" (IFSB, 2020). The recognition by leading institutions of Islamic finance such as IFSB, the multilateral standard setting body, and the central bank of Bahrain reflects the growing interest of Islamic finance in RegTech.

Similarly, the regulatory involvement in reporting and managing the Shariah non-compliance events of IFIs through the ORION system is also a significant RegTech that can be followed by other jurisdictions with well-established Islamic financial markets. The regulators of the UK promoted the promulgation of the RegTech sandbox. In the region of GCC, one among the regulators of Qatar called QFC, in collaboration with QDB, is under the process of incubating a FinTech hub. The UAE also has a considerable number of experiences related to FinTech. Recently, Oman also announced the launch of a FinTech sandbox. Thus, all the foregoing developments are promising that RegTech will be more prevalent in the short future.

Although the case of ORION is a practical and interesting example, it is based on the prevailing Web 2.0. However, the prevalence of Web 3.0 and blockchain technology have been promising to embed the Shariah compliant RegTech for the products offered in the arena of FinTech as well as the products offered online by the incumbent conventional banks, capital markets, insurance providers, and fund managers. The way forward to establish a RegTech for compliance on the strength of DAO could be in the following manner:

1. Create a DAO of multiple regulatory authorities of the country with the sole purpose of providing shariah compliant RegTech and SupTech solutions in a shariah compliant way.
2. Program the Smart-Contract of the DAO specifically for shariah compliant RegTech and SupTech services.
3. Integrate the DAO with government entities and central banks for deeper penetration.

4. Issue NFT's as proof of ownership/proof of compliance through the DAO for the organizations being audited and upload it on the blockchain. This allows your RegTech protocols to be globally accessed and not duplicate country wise compliance.
5. Create a common protocol for multiple countries wherein the DAO can also allow and represent RegTech and SupTech authorities of the respective country with multiple countries like GCC/Europe/USA.
6. Build an in-house team of developers within the DAO to constantly update the organization on technological advancements which shall allow the RegTech industry to be updated and be in the core of Islamic FinTech and Web 3.0 related advancements.
7. Bridge the gap through DAO between decentralized networks and various government authorities, especially in the poor countries, struggling to create a RegTech framework and ecosystem around a decentralized network.

10 Conclusion

RegTech has been taken into consideration across the globe by all the stakeholders; governments, regulators, corporates, researchers, and academicians. The central bank of Malaysia, Bank Negara Malaysia (BNM) implementation of ORION is a remarkable RegTech in reporting the Shariah incompliant event that take a vital role in IFIs to comply with the Shariah rules and regulations required in the jurisdiction. The demand for innovative ways to cut compliance costs is widely prevalent in the market, and RegTech has the full potential to provide the needed supply. Cost efficiency, trust-building, as well as real-time monitoring and reporting were found to be the most value-added aspects of RegTech. However, tackling challenges and underlying risks in the implementation of RegTech were not discussed extensively until the end of 2020.

Nevertheless, an integrated RegTech model considering society at large is an area of research to be considered in the future. Even though the limited number of quality-research papers are related to RegTech, attention by the researchers in the Islamic finance domain is further less and limited to certain issues of SupTech. Smart-contracts, DLT, AI, and Big Data analysis have huge potential to better implement transparency and restore trust by avoiding the great levels of uncertainty as called for by the principles of Shariah.

RegTech could be a better solution for either harmonizing or setting off the conflict of opinions among the Shariah scholars at various Shariah supervisory boards. Although diverse regulators' approaches toward Islamic finance across different jurisdictions are imposing a challenge, RegTech through automation can help improve the situation.

The elements which are identified as value-added composites of RegTech are focused on the commercial sustainability, however the environmental sustainability and social welfare has not been discussed to a great extent in the literature of RegTech. The standards by IFSB and AAOIFI, alongside the standards of GRI and IOSCO, can be a good reference guide for developing research serving the purpose of proposing an integrated RegTech model for Islamic finance sectors, namely, Islamic banking, Islamic capital market, Islamic insurance, and NBFIs.

References

Arner, D. W., Barberis, J. N., & Buckley, R. P. (2018, October). *FinTech and RegTech in a Nutshell, and the Future in a Sandbox.* SSRN Electronic Journal. https://doi.org/10.2139/ssrn.3088303

Baan, H. (2020). *Shariah compliant regtech beyond selfregulated ecosystems.* Islamic Finance News, My DBA final project. https://www.researchgate.net/publication/353878580_Shariah_compliant_regtech_beyond_selfregulated_ecosystems

Baber, H. (2020). Fintech, crowdfunding and customer retention in Islamic banks. *Vision, 24*(3), 260–268. https://doi.org/10.1177/0972262919869765

Becker, M., Merz, K., & Buchkremer, R. (2020, May). RegTech—The application of modern information technology in regulatory affairs: Areas of interest in research and practice. *Intelligent Systems in Accounting, Finance and Management*, 1–7.

BNM. Operational Risk Integrated Online Network (ORION) Policy Document (2021). https://www.bnm.gov.my/documents/20124/938039/ORION+PD_2021.pdf

Das, S. R. (2019). The future of fintech. *Financial Management, 48*(4), 981–1007. https://doi.org/10.1111/fima.12297

Grand View Research. (2019). *RegTech market size worth $55.28 billion by 2025|CAGR: 52.8%.* Retrieved 15 September 2021, from https://www.grandviewresearch.com/press-release/global-regulatory-technology-market?utm_source=Medium&utm_medium=referral&utm_campaign=Abhijit_July4_ict_Pr&utm_content=Content

IFSB. (2020). *Stability report 2020.*

Janos, B., Douglas, w. A., & Ross, B. P. (2019). *The FinTech book: The financial technology handbook for investors, entrepreneurs and visionaries*. Wiley. https://doi.org/10.22146/jieb.23554

Kálmán, J. (2018). *Ex ante regulation? The legal nature of the regulatory sandboxes or how to regulate before regulation even exists*. SSRN Electronic Journal, January 2019. https://doi.org/10.2139/ssrn.3255850

Kuck, G. (2004). Tim Berners-Lee's Semantic Web. *SA Journal of Information Management, 6*(1). https://doi.org/10.4102/sajim.v6i1.297

Morgan, J. P. (2022). *Opportunities in the metaverse*. https://www.jpmorgan.com/content/dam/jpm/treasury-services/documents/opportunities-in-the-metaverse.pdf

Omar, H., & Hassan, R. (2019). Shariah non-compliance treatment in Malaysian Islamic Banks. *International Journal of Management and Applied Research, 6*(4), 220–233. https://doi.org/10.18646/2056.64.19-016. https://ijmar.org/v6n4/19-016.html

Podder, S., Pisanu, G., Ghosh, B., Roy, P., Kaulgud, V., & Singh, S. K. (2018, February). Regtech for regulators. *World Government Summit*, 1–39. https://www.worldgovernmentsummit.org/api/publications/document?id=5ccf8ac4-e97c-6578-b2f8-ff0000a7ddb

Rabbani, M. R., Khan, S., & Thalassinos, E. I. (2020). FinTech, blockchain and Islamic finance: An extensive literature review. *International Journal of Economics and Business Administration, 8*(2), 65–86. https://doi.org/10.35808/ijeba/444

Sachs, T. G. (2021). *Framing the future of Web 3.0*. The Goldman Sachs Group, Inc.

Turki, M., Hamdan, A., Cummings, R. T., Sarea, A., Karolak, M., & Anasweh, M. (2020). The regulatory technology "RegTech" and money laundering prevention in Islamic and conventional banking industry. *Heliyon, 6*(10), e04949. https://doi.org/10.1016/j.heliyon.2020.e04949

World Bank Group. (2020). *Leveraging Islamic FinTech to improve financial inclusion* (p. 7). World Bank Group. https://openknowledge.worldbank.org/bitstream/handle/10986/34520/Leveraging-Islamic-FinTech-to-Improve-Financial-Inclusion.pdf?sequence=1&isAllowed=y

Yateem, F. (2019). *FinTech, Regtech and Suptech and their implications for regulation and supervision balancing Shariah compliance and technology-driven growth: A banking perspective*.

Index

A
AAOIFI, 269, 348
Abstract, 261
Accelerate, 9, 68, 129, 133, 134, 154, 244, 286, 290, 291, 293, 298, 299
Access to credit, 8, 245, 246, 249, 252, 257, 302
Access to education, 259, 296
Access to finance, 8, 176, 242, 243, 245, 248–250, 273
Access to financial services, 7, 9, 133, 241, 242, 264, 265, 285, 288
Adverse economic, 46, 48
Adverse impact, 4, 54, 65, 97, 99, 181, 297
Adverse selection, 35, 175, 242, 244, 254
Advisory board, 4, 56
Affordable financial products, 8, 241, 260, 262
Affordable financial services, 267
Affordable financing, 178, 299

Affordable housing, 78, 79, 81, 82, 151
Afghanistan, 161–166, 264, 279
Africa, 9, 206, 277, 283, 285–290, 292, 294, 297, 300
African, 129, 161, 207, 210, 283, 284, 288, 291, 293, 295, 297, 299
Agriculture, 96, 97, 186, 187, 284, 291, 298, 300
Agri-tech, 285, 290
Algeria, 163–166, 279
Alinma
    Alinma Bank, 73
    Alinma Enayah Endowment, 74, 76
    Alinma Endowment, 74–76
    Alinma Investment Company, 60, 68, 73, 99
Altruism, 6, 160, 167, 168, 179
Analysis, 2, 4, 5, 11, 17, 60, 61, 67, 70, 108, 110, 113, 124, 236, 254, 262, 267, 270, 275, 300, 316, 322, 347
Artificial

artificial intelligence (AI), 7–9, 115, 116, 125, 127, 178, 243–249, 254–257, 318, 321, 322, 337, 338, 340, 347
Azerbaijan, 163–166, 269, 279

B
Bahrain, 110, 163, 268, 269, 279, 345, 346
Bangladesh, 111, 129, 161–166, 279
Bangladeshi, xxv
BAZNAS, 319, 322
Behavior, 20, 21, 34, 35, 44, 46, 53, 116, 160, 166–168, 189, 242, 247, 339
Biodiversity, 167, 185, 186
Bioenergy, 193
Biogas, 153, 193, 196
Blockchain
  blockchain-based, 131, 268, 275
  blockchain charity, 318
  blockchain sukuk, 131
  blockchain technology, 9, 10, 130, 132, 268, 310, 316, 318, 346
Bosnia, 161, 163–166, 252, 269
Brunei, 129, 163
Burkina Faso, 161, 163–166, 279

C
Cameroon, 161, 163, 279
Capacity, 6, 48, 165, 172, 173, 179, 185, 188, 193, 194, 253, 296, 299, 344
  capacity building, 97, 99
  capacity challenge, 256
Capital management, 250
Capital markets, 5, 6, 84, 130, 131, 148, 155, 156, 160, 165, 168, 293, 299, 346
Capital requirements, 113, 250

Carbon
  carbon emissions, 153, 185, 304
  carbon reduction, 154
  carbon society, 184
  carbon transition, 153
Cash, 29, 47, 88, 169, 172–174, 176, 245, 251, 313
  cash financing, 43, 47–49
  cash *waqf*, 6, 61, 83, 92, 94, 177, 198
Central Bank
  Central Bank of Bahrain, 117, 269, 346
  Central Bank of Iran, 269
  Central Bank of Malaysia, 89, 347
  Central Bank of Nigeria, 269
  Central Bank of Qatar, 270
Charitable
  charitable foundation, 75
  charitable funds, 174
  charitable giving, 175, 179
  charitable organizations, 41
  charitable projects, 77
  Charitable Society, 77
CIMB, 130
Circular economy, 293
Climate
  Climate Action, 6, 65, 185, 198
  climate change, 6, 7, 150, 151, 153, 181–184, 186, 188, 192, 198, 199
  climate finance, 184
Commercial
  commercial banks, 162, 207
  commercial finance, 130, 172, 177, 179, 199
  commercial transactions, 2, 24
Conclusion, 109, 125, 126, 206, 235, 236, 273, 310
Conditions, 4, 27, 31, 35, 42–45, 47, 52, 54, 55, 90, 124, 132, 155, 228, 311

Consequences, 31, 50, 51, 53, 56, 108, 188, 246, 247, 277, 343
Consumer, 21, 31, 45, 49, 89, 116, 134, 178, 179, 257, 260, 270, 278, 297
  consumer-friendly, 97
  consumer protection, 23, 117, 247
Contemporary
  contemporary economic framework, 172
  contemporary Islamic finance, 152
  contemporary scholar, 48
  contemporary Shariah scholars, 62
Contract, 27, 31–35, 42–49, 51–54, 74, 133, 226, 284, 347
Conventional
  conventional banking, 208, 273
  conventional banks, 111, 206–208, 345, 346
  conventional finance, 4, 27, 60, 129, 292
  conventional fintech, 287, 293
  conventional institutions, 42, 46, 54, 205, 206, 209, 214, 216, 223
  conventional MFIs, 7, 206, 209–214, 216–219, 221–224, 226, 235
  conventional microcredit, 219
  conventional microfinance, 7, 206, 209, 217
Convergence, 3–5, 36, 37, 60, 61, 64, 67, 72, 74, 83, 97, 99, 126, 147, 156
Cote d'Ivoire, 164–166
COVID
  COVID-19, 1, 4, 5, 24, 59, 61, 68, 74, 83–85, 88, 91, 92, 97, 99, 107–114, 117, 123–125, 132, 135, 155, 159, 177, 205, 242–244, 252, 259, 260, 283, 284, 293, 297, 304

Credit
  credit risk, 4, 7, 8, 45, 55, 178, 206–208, 210, 211, 218, 219, 221, 223, 224, 226–229, 233–236, 245, 246, 254, 256
  credit scoring, 245–247, 256, 275
  credit screening, 248, 254
  creditworthiness, 8, 172, 242, 244–246, 256
Crowdfunding, 78–83, 99, 129, 131, 133, 175, 178, 344
Crypto, 310
  crypto assets, 336
  cryptocurrency(ies), 133, 271, 296, 310, 318
  crypto zakat, 316–318
Cybersecurity, 116, 267, 297, 299, 340

D
Debt-based, 60, 209, 223, 235, 249
Debt crisis, 208
Decentralization, 335
  decentralized, 131, 316, 337, 347
DeFi, 268
Decision-making, 7, 34, 236, 252, 273
Definition, 3, 17, 21, 26, 27, 32, 114, 126, 213, 265
Demand, 5, 37, 81, 146, 154, 172, 177, 219, 242, 245, 254, 256, 285, 297, 300, 342, 345, 347
Digital
  digital banking, 116
  digital currencies, 52, 132
  digital economy, 9, 108, 132, 284–287, 290, 293, 295–298
  digital ethics, 8, 274
  digital finance, 242, 249, 256, 262, 277
  digital footprint, 246, 256

digital innovations, 126, 285, 290, 293, 298
digitalization, 4, 89, 109, 115, 117, 118, 125, 129, 244, 260, 272
digital revolution, 277, 292
digital solutions, 243, 286, 290, 292, 293, 295, 296, 299
digital technology, 129, 132, 328
digital transformation, 9, 134, 284, 285, 288, 295
Disease, 64, 65, 75, 91, 314
Disruption, 1, 2, 83, 283
Disruptive, 128, 285, 298
Donation, 44, 173, 252, 325, 326

E
Ecological, 15–17, 21, 166
Economic
  economic crisis, 2, 4, 159
  economic development, 6, 63, 68, 95, 97, 188, 219, 262, 270, 295, 341
  economic distress, 5, 108
  economic downturn, 1, 88, 117, 159, 297
  economic growth, 6, 16, 60, 87, 88, 109, 114, 129, 134, 160, 242, 260, 262, 278, 285, 290, 296, 300, 301, 304
  economic impact, 48, 112
  economic measures, 61, 68
  economic opportunities, 7, 112, 242
  economic policies, 188
  economic recovery, 2, 5, 11, 89, 92, 99, 108, 109, 117, 118, 155
  economic stimulus, 88, 91
  economic studies, 4, 9, 48
Ecosystem, 16, 21, 61, 115, 154, 256, 267, 268, 278, 284, 288, 290, 337, 344, 347

Education, 15, 23, 31, 42, 65, 73, 76, 91, 96, 97, 156, 162, 177, 241, 259, 284, 285, 296, 299
Egypt, 155, 161, 163–166, 269, 279
Emerging economies, 68, 108, 153, 182, 244
Emerging markets, 294
Emissions, 153, 182, 185, 193, 194, 196–198, 301, 304
Empirical, 5, 128, 135, 207, 208, 218, 220, 236, 245, 250, 262, 274, 337
Empowerment, 112, 114, 151, 284, 294
Endowment, 60, 68–70, 72–77, 117
Environment, 9, 19, 21, 22, 32, 63, 66, 72, 91, 98, 99, 118, 124, 131, 153, 155, 167, 182, 186, 188, 190, 198, 254, 256, 298, 340, 341, 345
  environmental, 3, 6, 10, 15, 42, 55, 63, 86, 115, 135, 148, 150, 153, 160, 166, 179, 183–185, 188, 189, 195, 265, 292, 334, 348
Equality, 21, 66, 67, 259, 290
Equity, 21, 60, 74, 169–171, 209, 211, 212, 218, 223–225, 227–230, 232, 248, 250, 252, 253, 257, 292, 303
Ethical, 3, 5, 16, 21, 23, 25, 27, 34, 78, 97–99, 118, 128, 147, 155, 182, 267, 292, 295, 327, 328
  ethical business, 98
  ethical finance, 25, 147, 148
Ethics, 8, 20, 26, 63, 78, 274, 292, 297
European, 7, 207, 208, 276

F
Fairness, 33, 46, 57, 60, 147, 246, 247

Faith, 28, 166
  faith-based, 97, 248
Financial crisis, 7, 48, 111, 206, 211, 214, 216, 222, 236, 242, 247, 277
Financial inclusion, 7–9, 11, 37, 66, 117, 192, 241–244, 246, 248, 251, 254–256, 260–265, 270–275, 277–279, 284, 285, 287, 288, 290, 291, 293, 298, 300–303, 341
Financial innovation, 6, 125, 254, 256, 345
Financial stability, 7, 108, 113, 133, 206, 211, 228, 236
Financial sustainability, 2, 3, 75, 76, 175
Financial technology (FinTech), 2, 3, 5, 8, 9, 11, 36, 108, 109, 115, 116, 118, 129, 130, 133, 135, 161, 178, 179, 242, 243, 254–256, 260, 266–268, 271–273, 275, 277, 285–300, 303, 333, 334, 337–340, 344–347
Fourth industrial revolution (4IR), 5, 10, 107, 108, 115, 125–130, 133–135

G

Governance, 5, 6, 19–21, 25, 27, 31, 32, 35, 68, 74, 118, 130, 146, 247, 310, 312, 313
  governance framework, 29, 30, 35, 56, 174, 311
  governance issues, 4, 115, 177, 319
  governance system, 27, 32, 35, 256
Green bond, 145, 146, 152, 154, 184
Green economy, 155, 188, 192
Green finance, 150
Green projects, 7, 117, 151, 153, 184, 198
Green sectors, 184–186, 190, 191
Green sukuk, 6, 7, 84, 150–155, 182–185, 188–192, 198, 199
Guinea-Bissau, 161, 163–166, 279

H

Halal, 131, 172, 293, 298
Health, 2, 9, 15, 21, 42, 65, 73, 75, 76, 82, 97, 109–111, 113, 117, 134, 154, 159, 162, 175, 181, 186, 260, 271, 283–285, 287, 290, 298, 299, 301, 304
Humanitarian, 6, 159, 160, 168, 179

I

Ijarah, 169, 209
Impact investment, 74, 97, 178
Impact measurement, 115, 318

K

Kazakhstan, 161–166, 269, 279
Kenya, 248, 285, 288, 302, 304
Kuwait, 111, 117, 163, 279, 323

L

Lives, 61, 62, 84, 109, 111, 127, 128, 134, 135, 167, 252, 264, 299, 309, 315, 322
Loan, 47–49, 51, 85, 110, 146, 168, 174, 182, 206, 207, 209–213, 215, 218, 220, 221, 223–229, 231, 233–235, 244, 245, 247, 248, 250, 252, 253, 267, 271, 273, 290, 301, 304

M

Malaysia, 4, 68, 83, 84, 88–92, 98, 99, 109–111, 114, 129–131, 149–153, 155, 161–164, 264, 268, 269, 279, 309, 312, 315, 316, 323, 344, 347
Maldives, 163, 165, 166, 279, 311, 313, 315
Mali, 161, 163–166, 279
Maqasid
 maqasid al-shariah, 2–4, 10, 16, 17, 21, 23, 25–28, 35–38, 60–67, 72, 74, 87, 97, 99, 176, 183, 188–192, 198
Maslahah, 99, 183, 188, 189, 328
Microfinance, 7, 131, 151, 176, 205–211, 215, 217–222, 224, 226, 230, 234–236, 245, 252, 253
Microfinance institutions (MFIs), 7, 206–212, 214–231, 233–236
Moral, 21, 31, 34, 35, 62, 167, 168, 218
Morocco, 161, 163–166, 279
Mozambique, 161, 163–166, 279
Mudhārabah, 46, 85, 113, 169, 170
Murābahah, 49
Mushārakah, 46, 113, 170, 171

N

Niger, 161, 163–166, 279
Nigeria, 161–166, 248, 268, 269, 279, 288, 303

O

Obstacle, 8, 16, 134, 193, 242, 263, 319
Open Banking, 8, 260–262, 265–276
Opportunity, 3, 8, 25, 69, 78, 108, 115, 116, 129, 135, 156, 161, 176–179, 183, 192, 243, 260, 266, 274, 275, 284, 285, 288, 290, 291, 293–298, 333, 334, 336, 338, 342, 344
Outbreak, 24, 83, 84, 87, 88, 93, 110

P

Pakistan, 111, 155, 161–165, 248, 252, 270, 279
Pandemic, 1, 2, 4, 5, 7, 9, 61, 68, 74, 83–85, 88, 90, 91, 93, 97, 99, 107–113, 115–117, 123–125, 133, 155, 177, 205, 242–244, 252, 259, 260, 283–285, 293, 304, 313, 314
Policy, 6–9, 36, 38, 86, 109–111, 114, 118, 129, 132, 133, 155, 156, 160, 172, 185, 191, 198, 206, 236, 249, 254, 256, 257, 269, 275, 278, 297, 298, 340
Poverty, 2, 7, 8, 10, 15, 17, 23, 64, 87, 117, 124, 129, 160–162, 168, 172, 181, 192, 210, 241, 244, 245, 249, 250, 252, 259–262, 274, 277, 287, 288, 290, 291, 304, 310, 321, 326, 327
Preservation, 2, 16, 21, 32, 60, 63–65, 74, 183, 189–191, 197
Problem, 9, 65, 110, 162, 220, 242, 243, 245, 249, 252, 286, 288, 290, 294, 343

Q

Qatar, 3, 111, 155, 163, 270, 279, 334, 346
Quran, 21–23, 27, 33, 34, 63, 65, 66, 167, 168, 188, 310, 311, 319

R

Recommendation, 17, 55, 97, 99, 109, 117, 126, 198, 261, 272, 286, 298, 310, 324

Recovery, 2, 5, 11, 89, 91, 92, 99, 108, 109, 114, 117, 118, 133, 155, 284, 292, 298
Regulation, 5, 6, 21, 25, 29, 33, 35, 43, 73, 78, 86, 93, 115, 116, 118, 132, 134, 154, 190, 262, 267–272, 275, 287, 297, 334, 335, 338–340, 342, 344–347
Regulatory Technology (RegTech), 10, 118, 268, 275, 333–335, 337–348
Religion, 2, 21, 60, 63, 64, 96, 125, 182, 189, 191, 209, 309
Renewable energy, 126, 151, 152, 155, 185–187, 191, 193, 196, 197
Responsible investment, 19, 29, 36
Robo, 321, 322
robo-advisor, 131, 178

S
Sadaqah, 114, 117, 294
Saudi Arabia, 4, 73, 74, 109–111, 149, 152, 153, 155, 163, 268, 270, 279
Shariah compliance, 3–5, 10, 16, 17, 30, 36, 37, 97, 118, 132, 134, 177, 344
Shariah governance, 3, 4, 26–28, 35, 37, 115
Shariah principles, 27, 28, 35, 53, 54, 66, 74, 113, 190, 293, 345
Shariah scholars, 10, 16, 29, 60, 62–64, 66
Social development, 16, 42, 73, 153, 155
Social finance, 2, 5, 6, 68, 108, 112, 114, 115, 117, 133, 152, 160, 165, 172, 175, 179, 198, 199, 293, 298

Social responsibility, 19, 41, 43, 54, 55, 73, 160, 167
Socio-economic, 2–4, 8, 9, 11, 15, 16, 21, 28, 91, 94, 113, 133, 152, 160, 162, 168, 177, 179, 250, 256, 257, 283, 286, 290, 294, 298, 299
Strategies, 9, 25, 26, 36, 61, 67, 68, 83, 99, 131, 133, 134, 184, 192, 206, 218, 220, 221, 223, 234, 236, 245, 254, 284, 294
Sudan, 152, 155, 161–166, 223, 264
Sukuk, 4–6, 24, 46, 50, 61, 68, 74, 83–86, 89, 90, 92–94, 96, 99, 112, 113, 117, 131, 133, 148–156, 165, 168–171, 176, 179, 182–184, 188, 198
Sustainable Development Goals (SDGs), 2–6, 9, 10, 15–18, 24–26, 28, 29, 36–38, 59–61, 64, 67, 72, 74, 83, 87, 92, 97, 99, 147, 148, 150, 151, 153, 154, 156, 176, 181–183, 192, 196, 198, 243, 259, 260, 286, 290–294, 300, 318
Sustainable finance, 5, 28, 145, 147, 155
Sustainable investment, 83, 97–99, 148, 198

T
Tawarruq, 43, 47–49, 53

U
Uganda, 161, 163–166, 278, 280, 291, 301
United Arab Emirates (UAE), 26, 109–111, 130, 131, 149, 150, 152, 154, 163, 268, 270, 280, 344, 346

United Kingdom (UK), 131, 265, 271–273, 275, 340, 341, 346
United Nations (UN), 2, 5, 10, 15–18, 26, 64, 129, 146, 153, 259, 260, 286
Uzbekistan, 161, 163–166, 280

V
Value-based, 29, 66, 115, 131

W
Waqf, 4, 6, 8, 60, 68–74, 78, 92–95, 97, 99, 114, 117, 133, 152, 176, 177, 198, 273, 274, 294
Welfare, 2, 10, 11, 20, 21, 23, 24, 36, 72, 88, 172, 174, 175, 323, 348
Well-being, 6, 22, 28, 31, 33, 61–63, 260, 290

Y
Yemen, 161–166, 210, 280

Z
Zakat administration, 172, 309–312, 316, 318, 319, 321, 322, 329
Zakat collection, 309–312, 318, 329
Zakat distribution, 9, 10, 310, 313, 315, 316, 318, 319, 324, 326–329
Zakat fund, 46, 56, 173, 176, 309, 311–313, 316, 319
Zakat management, 129, 309, 310, 316, 318, 319, 321
Zakat payments, 173
Zakat recipients, 9, 10, 312, 316, 319–322, 327